Vietnam's Economic Leap

Hinh T. Dinh · Hoai Trong Nguyen

Vietnam's Economic Leap

Productivity, Innovation, and the Road to High-Income Status

palgrave
macmillan

Hinh T. Dinh
Policy Center for the New South
and Economic Growth
and Transformation
Great Falls, VA, USA

Hoai Trong Nguyen
University of Economics Ho
Chi Minh City
Ho Chi Minh City, Vietnam

ISBN 978-3-032-08903-8 ISBN 978-3-032-08904-5 (eBook)
https://doi.org/10.1007/978-3-032-08904-5

This Palgrave Macmillan imprint is published by the registered company Springer Nature Switzerland AG.
The registered company address is: Gewerbestrasse 11, 6330 Cham, Switzerland

Acknowledgments This book was prepared by Hinh T. Dinh in Great Falls, USA, and Hoai Trong Nguyen in Ho Chi Minh City, Vietnam. Responsibility for individual chapters is indicated at the beginning of each chapter. The content reflects data available through the end of 2024, with the exception of a few recent policy developments from the first four months of 2025.

We are grateful to Palgrave Macmillan Senior Editor Wyndham Hacket Pain, Professor Arkebe Oqubay, and the anonymous external reviewers for their valuable support and comments. We thank Mr. Anand Manimudichozhan, Ms. Sudha Soundarrajan and their production team for their support. Hinh T. Dinh extends his sincere thanks to the Policy Center for the New South in Rabat, Morocco, and its President, Dr. Karim El Aynaoui, for fostering a warm and supportive research environment during the writing of this book. Hoai Trong Nguyen gratefully acknowledges the support of the University of Economics Ho Chi Minh City, Vietnam (UEH) in the preparation of his chapters.

The views expressed in this book are solely those of the authors and do not represent the positions of the supporting institutions.

Competing Interests The authors have no competing interests to declare that are relevant to the content of this manuscript.

Abstract

Vietnam's rapid integration into global value chains (GVCs) has powered its economic rise, transforming the country from a low-income to a lower-middle-income economy within a generation. By combining its abundant and disciplined labor force with foreign capital, Vietnam has become a manufacturing hub for increasingly sophisticated exports, generating employment and reducing poverty. However, its heavy dependence on low-wage, low-value-added GVC activities—mainly in final assembly—has constrained its ability to upgrade technologically and move up the value chain. Unlike South Korea and Taiwan, where joint ventures fostered domestic learning and innovation, Vietnam's export growth has been dominated by foreign firms, leaving domestic enterprises with weak linkages, limited productivity spillovers, and little control over upgrading decisions. Rising wages, low export value-added per capita, and shortages of skilled labor are eroding Vietnam's competitiveness, while infrastructure bottlenecks and carbon-intensive manufacturing further expose structural vulnerabilities.

To break free from these constraints and achieve high-income status by 2045, Vietnam must transition from an investment-driven to a productivity-led growth model that combines smart investment with innovation. This transformation requires building competitive domestic firms with strong technological capabilities, fostering technology absorption and diffusion through deeper foreign–local linkages, and promoting incremental innovation tailored to local needs. Strengthening human capital across five interconnected areas—labor market reforms, education, reverse migration, an aging population, and female labor force participation—will be essential for Vietnam to transition to a high-income status and achieve long-term sustainable growth.

Only by integrating these elements can Vietnam evolve from a low-cost production base into a dynamic, high-value, and innovation-driven economy.

Contents

About the Authors

Hinh T. Dinh is a Senior Fellow at the Policy Center for the New South in Morocco (https://www.policycenter.ma/experts/dinh) and President and CEO of Economic Growth and Transformation, LLC, based in Great Falls, VA, USA (https://www.egatco.com). He previously spent over 35 years at the World Bank Group, where he held senior positions across three areas of the Bank: Operations, Finance, and Research. His final role was Lead Economist in the Office of the Senior Vice President and Chief Economist.

Dr. Dinh has extensive development experience, having worked across Africa, Asia, South America, and the Middle East. He has authored and co-authored numerous books published by the World Bank, Oxford University Press, and the Policy Center for the New South, as well as articles in professional journals on public finance, international finance, and industrialization.

His recent books include *Tales from the Development Frontier* (2013), *Light Manufacturing in Vietnam* (2013), *Jobs, Industrialization, and Globalization* (2017), *Morocco* (2020), and *COVID-19 and Developing Countries* (2022).

Hoai Trong Nguyen is Professor of Economics at the University of Economics Ho Chi Minh City (UEH) (https://sites.google.com/view/nguyentronghoai). From 2011 to 2021, he served as Vice President of UEH, overseeing international relations and academic research. During this time, Professor Nguyen directed the Vietnam–The Netherlands Programme in Development Economics, a joint initiative between UEH and the International Institute of Social Studies at Erasmus University

Rotterdam. He was also a member of the Center for Education Accreditation under the Vietnam National University Ho Chi Minh City (VNU-HCMC) from 2016 to 2020.

Currently, he serves as Editor-in-Chief of the *Journal of Asian Business and Economic Studies* (JABES) (https://www.emeraldgrouppublishing.com/journal/jabes), UEH's official journal published by Emerald Group Publishing. Since 2021, he has also been an advisory member of the *Asia-Pacific Journal of Business Administration* and serves on the advisory board for Ho Chi Minh City.

His current research spans a broad range of topics, including sustainable development, internationalization of education, green growth and behavior, public health, regional development, and smart cities.

List of Figures

List of Tables

CHAPTER 1

Overview: Charting Vietnam's Next Leap—Productivity, Innovation, and the Quest for High-Income Status

Introduction: From Reform to Renaissance

Over the past three and a half decades, Vietnam has experienced one of the most remarkable economic transformations of the modern era. Since launching the Doi Moi reforms in 1986, the country sustained an average annual GDP growth of 6.6% from 1990 to 2023—double the rate of low-income countries and significantly above the 5.0% average for lower-middle-income peers (World Bank, 2024c). This consistent performance lifted Vietnam from a low-income, agrarian society into a middle-income, export-driven industrializing economy within one generation, with per capita GDP reaching 20% of the OECD average by 2020 (OECD, 2023).

The transformation extends far beyond economic indicators. Life expectancy rose to 75 years by 2022, compared to 63 years in low-income countries and 67 years in lower-middle-income countries. Vietnam achieved near-universal primary education and the highest Human Capital Index among lower-middle-income nations, performing on par with the OECD average in mathematics according to PISA rankings (OECD, 2022). Most dramatically, extreme poverty measured at $2.15 per day plummeted from nearly 50% in 1992 to less than 1% by

Contributed by Hinh T. Dinh

H. T. Dinh, H. T. Nguyen, *Vietnam's Economic Leap*,
https://doi.org/10.1007/978-3-032-08904-5_1

2020, representing one of the most rapid poverty reduction achievements in modern history (World Bank, 2024b).

Yet beneath the surface of this impressive growth model lie growing vulnerabilities and unfinished reforms. Vietnam's development trajectory is increasingly constrained by low productivity growth, weak domestic enterprise capabilities, and limited technological upgrading. Export gains have been driven primarily by FDI-led assembly operations with low domestic value added. Despite rising per capita income, productivity remains one of the lowest among regional peers. A large informal sector, rising inequality, and demographic pressures further compound these challenges. More fundamentally, Vietnam now confronts a strategic inflection point: the need to shift from input-led to productivity-driven growth, and from reliance on foreign actors to endogenous capabilities. The transition to high-income status will require deep structural reforms.

The Foundations of Success

Vietnam's initial success stemmed from pragmatic market-oriented reforms, active integration into the global economy, and a "pro-poor growth" strategy that prioritized equitable access to land, labor markets, and education. The pivotal 1993 Land Law exemplified this approach by granting households basic land rights, providing strong incentives for agricultural investment that increased farm income by 60% between 1993 and 1998 (World Bank, 2022). This reform directly empowered the rural poor, who constituted the vast majority of the population, enabling millions to escape extreme poverty through their primary livelihood.

Vietnam's strategic integration into the global economy proved equally transformative. The country's accession to ASEAN in 1995, the U.S.-Vietnam Bilateral Trade Agreement in 2001, and WTO membership in 2007 were watershed moments that catalyzed export-oriented industrialization. These agreements opened new markets and attracted foreign direct investment, fundamentally reshaping Vietnam's economic structure. Today, Vietnam maintains an extensive network of Free Trade Agreements covering 87% of the global economy (World Bank, 2024b), positioning it as one of the most globally integrated economies in Southeast Asia.

This integration drove a profound structural transformation of the labor market. Between 2010 and 2020, the manufacturing and services sectors collectively generated 10.6 million new jobs (World Bank, 2022), offering higher wages and greater stability than traditional agricultural work. The share of households receiving wage income increased from 64 to 70% over this decade, with annual household wage income nearly tripling in nominal terms. Foreign-owned enterprises played a crucial role in this transformation, not only providing employment but also introducing new technologies and management practices that gradually diffused throughout the economy.

The export basket evolved dramatically alongside this structural change, shifting from primarily agricultural and commodity exports in the 1990s to low-tech light manufacturing in the 2000s and increasingly sophisticated high-tech exports in the past decade. This diversification reflected Vietnam's growing integration into global value chains, particularly in textiles, electronics, and semiconductors, where the country became a preferred destination for multinational corporations seeking efficient production bases.

The Productivity Challenge

However, beneath this impressive growth trajectory lies a fundamental constraint that threatens the sustainability of Vietnam's development model. The country's economic expansion has been driven primarily by factor accumulation—adding more capital and labor—rather than productivity improvements that generate higher and sustainable output from existing resources. Factor decomposition analysis in Chap. 2 reveals that Vietnam's total factor productivity (TFP) has been negative or stagnant in most periods except 2010–2019, indicating heavy reliance on capital inputs rather than efficiency gains.

The implications of this productivity gap are profound. Had Vietnam achieved even zero TFP growth—a modest benchmark comparable to other emerging markets—its GDP per capita could have been 30% higher over the past two decades. This represents not just missed opportunities but a warning signal about the diminishing returns that characterize Vietnam's current growth model. As the country approaches upper-middle-income status, the easy gains from moving workers out of agriculture and attracting foreign investment are becoming exhausted.

This productivity challenge manifests most clearly in Vietnam's pattern of structural transformation. While the country has successfully shifted labor from agriculture to industry and services, much of this movement has been toward low-productivity service sectors rather than high-productivity manufacturing. The result is a dual economy where export-oriented manufacturing enclaves operate alongside a large domestic sector characterized by small, informal enterprises with limited technological capabilities and weak connections to global markets.

Vietnam's integration into global value chains, while successful in generating exports and employment, reveals the limitations of the current model. Only 52% of Vietnam's export value was domestically generated in 2020, compared to over 90% in OECD economies. Much of the country's high-tech exports involve assembly operations using imported components, with minimal domestic value addition or technological spillovers to local firms. The services sector, despite its growing importance in employment, contributes less than 10% of gross export value-added—far below ASEAN and OECD averages—indicating weak linkages between domestic services and the export economy.

Perhaps most troubling, the domestic enterprise sector remains fragmented and poorly integrated into global value chains. The percentage of firms linked to global markets declined from 35% in 2009 to just 18% in 2023, suggesting that the benefits of globalization have become increasingly concentrated among foreign-owned enterprises and a small number of domestic exporters. Most Vietnamese firms remain microenterprises serving local markets with limited capacity for innovation, expansion, or technological upgrading.

A Volatile Global Environment

Vietnam's transition to high-income status now occurs against a backdrop of unprecedented global challenges that fundamentally alter the development landscape in which countries must operate. The post-2008 era has witnessed the gradual unraveling of the neoliberal orthodoxy that previously underpinned globalization and policy convergence, replaced by a fragmented, multipolar, and volatile global economy marked by three major constraints that directly affect middle-income countries such as Vietnam (Anyoui & Dinh, 2024).

The first constraint is rising protectionism and economic nationalism that threatens the globalization setting upon which Vietnam's export success has depended. The U.S.-China trade war exemplifies this shift, with tariff rates rising sharply since 2018 and showing little prospect of reversal under renewed U.S. leadership focused on economic competition with China. The European Union is moving in a similar direction, implementing new trade defense mechanisms and strategic autonomy initiatives (European Union, 2024). Simultaneously, countries are increasingly adopting industrial policies designed to strengthen strategic sectors and reduce dependence on foreign suppliers. The U.S. CHIPS and Science Act, which allocates $52.7 billion to semiconductor development, and China's continued strategic planning through initiatives such as Made in China 2025, illustrate a growing preference for national resilience over economic efficiency.

The second constraint involves the narrowing of macroeconomic policy space in developing countries. Successive crises including the 2008 global financial crisis, the COVID-19 pandemic, and commodity price shocks have depleted fiscal reserves and strained public finances. High debt burdens, aging populations, and rising defense expenditures further limit fiscal flexibility. Simultaneously, high global interest rates, exchange-rate volatility, and weakened central bank independence constrain monetary policy options. Developing countries are forced to raise domestic interest rates to prevent capital outflows and currency depreciation, thereby suppressing domestic investment and growth precisely when they need to accelerate productivity improvements.

The third constraint stems from rapid technological change that is disrupting traditional development models. The window for low-skill, labor-intensive export-led industrialization is closing as automation, reshoring, and the growing importance of intangible assets shift the competitive landscape. Manufacturing has become increasingly skill- and capital-intensive, reducing its capacity to absorb large numbers of workers transitioning out of agriculture. As Rodrik and Stiglitz note in their (2024) analysis, structural transformation can no longer rely on expanding manufacturing employment alone but must emphasize productivity growth in labor-intensive services and comprehensive green transitions backed by strong public institutions.

These global shifts require Vietnam to fundamentally reconsider its development strategy. The external environment that enabled the country's initial success—open markets, stable rules, and clear pathways for export-led industrialization—is giving way to a more complex and uncertain landscape that demands greater domestic capabilities and institutional strength.

The Middle-Income Trap: Vietnam's Strategic Inflection Point

The concept of the "middle-income trap," first articulated by Gill and Kharas in their (2007) World Bank analysis, describes the tendency for countries to experience systematic growth slowdowns after reaching middle-income levels. This pattern reflects the diminishing returns from capital investment and factor accumulation that characterize the transition from extensive to intensive growth. The latest World Development Report (World Bank, 2024a) confirms that middle-income countries often grow more slowly than both low- and high-income peers, underscoring the structural nature of this challenge.

Vietnam faces this transition with additional complexities that make the challenge particularly acute. Demographic pressures are mounting as the country approaches the "aged population" phase by 2036, with rising social security costs and a shrinking working-age population. Climate vulnerabilities pose severe economic risks, necessitating substantial investments in energy, agriculture, and infrastructure adaptation that will strain public resources. Despite overall poverty reduction, inequality has begun to rise, with the Gini coefficient increasing after 2014 as consumption among richer households grew faster than among poorer ones (World Bank, 2022). Chronic poverty remains concentrated among ethnic minorities, rural populations, and those dependent on agriculture, creating pockets of vulnerability that could undermine social cohesion.

The COVID-19 pandemic exposed many of these underlying vulnerabilities, disproportionately impacting informal sector workers, women, and households in the bottom income quintile. The uneven continuity of education during lockdowns threatened to widen human capital gaps, particularly for disadvantaged students who lacked access to digital learning resources. These experiences highlighted the inadequacy of existing social safety nets and the urgent need for more inclusive and resilient growth models.

The Path Forward: From Input-Led to Productivity-Driven Growth

To escape the middle-income trap and achieve its ambitious goal of high-income status by 2045, Vietnam must fundamentally transform its growth model from one based on factor accumulation to one driven by productivity improvements. The 2024 World Development Report describes this transition as moving from a "1i" strategy focused solely on investment to a "3i" strategy that combines investment with technology infusion and innovation. This shift requires comprehensive reforms across multiple dimensions of economic policy and institutional development.

The transformation must begin with building dynamic, competitive domestic enterprises capable of integrating into global value chains while developing indigenous technological capabilities. This means moving beyond the current pattern of microenterprises serving local markets toward firms that can compete internationally, innovate continuously, and generate high-value employment. Success will require addressing persistent constraints including skills mismatches, weak financial access, inadequate infrastructure, and limited research and development investment.

Technology infusion represents the second pillar of this new strategy. Vietnam must move from being a passive recipient of foreign technology to an active adapter and modifier of global innovations. This involves strengthening the absorptive capacity of domestic firms, improving linkages between foreign and local enterprises, and building institutions that can facilitate technology transfer and diffusion. The goal is not to replace foreign investment but to ensure that it generates broader spillovers and capabilities within the domestic economy.

Innovation, the third pillar, requires developing endogenous capacities for technological advancement and product development. For a middle-income country like Vietnam, innovation is less about fundamental research and more about adapting technologies to local conditions, improving production processes, and developing market-specific products and services. This approach, successfully employed by Korea and Taiwan during their transitions to high-income status, emphasizes practical problem-solving and incremental improvement over breakthrough discoveries.

Human capital development underlies all three pillars of this strategy. Vietnam must address skills mismatches between education outputs and labor market demands, improve STEM education while maintaining strength in other disciplines, manage the challenges of demographic transition including aging and urbanization, and increase female labor force participation. These reforms require coordination between education and industry, investment in vocational training, and policies that support work-life balance and social mobility.

Institutional strengthening provides the foundation for this transformation. Effective public institutions, transparent policymaking, and strong state-business collaboration are essential to align incentives, mobilize resources, and coordinate complex reforms. Vietnam must build state capacity not just to manage risks but to catalyze innovation, coordinate industrial upgrading, and ensure that growth benefits all segments of society.

What This Book Offers

This book provides a comprehensive analysis and forward-looking roadmap for Vietnam's transition to high-income status, organized around the key challenges and opportunities identified in this overview. The analytical framework draws on international experience while recognizing Vietnam's unique circumstances and constraints.

Part One: Growth Diagnostics and Structural Change (Chaps. 2 and 3). Through detailed quantitative factor and sectoral decomposition analyses, these chapters document the low productivity growth, assess the completeness of structural transformation, and identify specific areas where policy intervention can generate the highest returns. The analysis reveals both the achievements and limitations of Vietnam's current growth model while pointing toward alternative pathways for future development.

Part Two: Trade and Industrial Upgrading (Chaps. 4, 5 and 6). These chapters examine Vietnam's export structure, technological content, and the untapped potential of services in export competitiveness. Using international classification frameworks including Revealed Comparative Advantage and the Lall technology taxonomy, these chapters highlight both the progress Vietnam has made in export diversification and the continuing limitations of its position in global value chains. The analysis includes detailed assessment of strategic import replacement opportunities that could strengthen domestic industrial capabilities.

Part Three: Clearing the Path (Chap. 7). This chapter examines the macroeconomic, microeconomic, and structural constraints facing Vietnam in its transition to high-income status and proposes a development strategy to address them. It emphasizes the need for fiscal prudence, institutional strengthening, and forward-looking planning to sustain macroeconomic stability while enabling structural transformation.

Part Four: Domestic Enterprises and Innovation Policies (Chaps. 8 and 9). These chapters explore how to foster stronger links between FDI and local firms, deepen technological capabilities, and build effective innovation ecosystems. Drawing on extensive international experience, these chapters provide practical guidance for developing indigenous technological capabilities while maintaining the benefits of foreign investment.

Part Five: Human Capital in a Changing Society (Chaps. 10, 11, 13 and 14). These chapters provide detailed policy guidance on human capital development across five interconnected areas: labor market reforms, education and skills development, migration patterns and reverse migration potential, aging population management, and female labor force participation. Each chapter draws on international evidence while proposing specific interventions tailored to Vietnam's circumstances and development stage.

A Critical Moment

Vietnam stands at a historic crossroads where past success provides the confidence but not guidance for the future. The transition to high-income status is achievable but not inevitable. Success requires moving beyond the comfort zone of factor accumulation toward the more challenging realm of productivity-driven growth, building domestic capabilities while maintaining global integration, fostering innovation while ensuring inclusion.

The experience of successful East Asian economies demonstrates that this transition is possible with appropriate policies and institutions. Korea transformed from a war-torn, aid-dependent economy to a global technology leader within four decades. Taiwan evolved from agricultural exporter to semiconductor powerhouse through strategic industrial policy and human capital investment. Singapore leveraged its small size and strategic location to become a global financial and logistics hub. Each followed a unique path shaped by particular circumstances, but all shared common elements: strong institutions, strategic thinking, and unwavering commitment to excellence and equity through human capital development.

Vietnam's path will be uniquely its own, shaped by its political structure, geographic position, institutions, and particular position in regional and global value chains. The country possesses significant advantages including a young and increasingly educated population, strategic geographic location, growing integration into global supply chains, and hard-won experience in managing economic transition. However, realizing these advantages requires confronting persistent challenges including weak productivity growth, limited domestic enterprise capabilities, institutional fragmentation, and rising social and environmental pressures.

The analytical framework and policy recommendations presented in the following chapters address these challenges systematically. The objective is sustainable, inclusive growth that enhances living standards while maintaining economic stability and social cohesion. This requires coordinated policy implementation across multiple domains, supported by effective institutions and adequate resource allocation. The path forward demands bold vision, competent execution, and shared national commitment to excellence and equity that honors Vietnam's remarkable past while embracing an even more promising future.

The Era of National Rise

This book was finalized in 2024, before the formal launch of Vietnam's ambitious "Era of National Rise" reform agenda led by Communist Party General Secretary Tô Lâm (2024). Framed as a new phase in the country's development trajectory, this agenda sets out a bold vision for transforming Vietnam into a high-income nation by 2045 (Lao Động, 2025) through wide-ranging reforms in governance, institutions, infrastructure, technology, and environmental sustainability. Key elements include streamlined public administration, enhanced anti-corruption efforts, expanded investment in science and innovation, and strengthened support for the domestic private sector—particularly through initiatives such as Resolution 68 (NQ-68). With targets such as 8% GDP growth in 2025 and a longer-term goal of sustained double-digit growth, the plan signals Vietnam's most far-reaching development strategy since the Doi Moi reforms. While its ambition is clear and its priorities well-aligned with the country's needs, successful implementation will require careful monitoring, coordination and resilience, especially in the face of emerging external risks such as rising protectionism and growing environmental pressures.

Because this reform initiative was formally announced in early 2025, after the completion of this volume, the book does not incorporate or respond directly to the detailed policies associated with the "Era of National Rise." Nonetheless, there is a strong and encouraging alignment between the government's new reform priorities and the analyses and recommendations set forth in these chapters. The policy thrusts outlined in this book—including the focus on strengthening domestic enterprise capabilities, institutional reform, private sector dynamism, innovation, and deeper global integration—closely align with the priorities now being pursued at the national level. In this regard, the government's reform agenda reinforces the book's conclusions and offers a strong foundation for translating its recommendations into practical policy actions.

References

Aynaoui, K. E., & Dinh, H. T. (2024, December 18). Développer le nouveau Sud après le consensus de Washington. *Le Grand Continent*. https://legrandcontinent.eu/fr/2024/12/18/developper-le-nouveau-sud-apres-le-consensus-de-washington/

Draghi, M. (2024, September). *The future of European competitiveness*. European Union. https://www.europeansources.info/record/thefuture-of-european-competitiveness/

Kharas, H., & Gill, I. (2007). *An East Asian Renaissance: Ideas for economic growth*. World Bank. http://hdl.handle.net/10986/6798

Lao Động. (2025, February 2). *Tầm nhìn 2045: Việt Nam trở thành nước phát triển, thu nhập cao*. https://news.laodong.vn/kinh-doanh/tam-nhin-2045-viet-nam-tro-thanh-nuoc-phat-trien-thu-nhap-cao-1454902.ldo

Tô Lâm (2024, September 23). *General secretary and president Tô Lâm's speech at Columbia University*. https://en.baochinhphu.vn/general-secretary-and-president-to-lams-policy-speech-at-columbia-university-111240925143443835.htm

Organisation for Economic Co-operation and Development. (2022). *Education GPS: Vietnam student performance PISA 2022*. OECD. https://gpseducation.oecd.org/CountryProfile?primaryCountry=VNM&treshold=5&topic=PI

Organisation for Economic Co-operation and Development. (2023). *OECD economic surveys: Viet Nam 2023*. OECD Publishing. https://doi.org/10.1787/8f2a6ecb-en

Rodrik, D., & Stiglitz, J. E. (2024). *A new growth strategy for developing nations*. https://tinyurl.com/ymrg8qom

World Bank. (2022). *From the last mile to the next mile: 2022 Viet Nam poverty and equity assessment*.

World Bank. (2024a). *World development report 2024: The middle-income trap*. World Bank. http://hdl.handle.net/10986/41919

World Bank. (2024b). *Viet Nam 2045: Trading up in a changing world—pathways to a high-income future*. http://hdl.handle.net/10986/42505

World Bank. (2024c). *World Development Indicators*. https://databank.worldbank.org/source/world-development-indicators

PART I

Growth Diagnostics and Structural Change

CHAPTER 2

Past Growth and Structural Transformation

Introduction

In 2024, Vietnam's per capita income, as calculated using the World Bank Atlas method, stood at $4180 in current US dollars.[1] This places Vietnam at the upper end of the lower-middle-income category, which includes countries with per capita incomes ranging from $1146 to $4515. Vietnam is likely to transition into the upper-middle-income category in the coming years, though at its lower end. In the last 35 years, its per capita income growth has followed the trajectory of most East Asian economies (Fig. 2.1).

Growth and Structural Transformation

Modern economic growth theory has traditionally relied on the Solow (1956) single-sector model, which emphasizes factor accumulation and total factor productivity (TFP) growth but does not account for sectoral

[1] Per capita income is measured by Gross National Income (GNI) per capita. In 2024, lower middle-income economies are those with a GNI per capita between $1146 and $4515; upper middle-income economies are those with a GNI per capita between $4516 and $14,005; high-income economies are those with more than a GNI per capita of $14,005. https://datahelpdesk.worldbank.org/knowledgebase/articles/906519

Contributed by Hinh T. Dinh

H. T. Dinh, H. T. Nguyen, *Vietnam's Economic Leap*,
https://doi.org/10.1007/978-3-032-08904-5_2

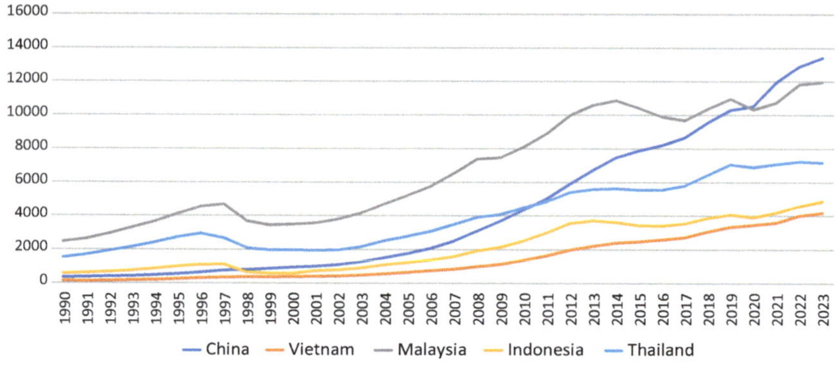

Fig. 2.1 GNI per capita, Atlas method (current US$). Vietnam and comparators. *Source* World Development Indicators; last updated June 28, 2024; accessed September 4, 2024

shifts. Empirical studies have shown that while TFP plays a key role in advanced economies such as the U.S. and Western Europe, factor accumulation has been more significant in the growth of East and Southeast Asian economies. However, beyond a certain point, diminishing marginal returns limit the contribution of factor accumulation, making TFP the key driver of long-term growth. Consequently, policies must focus on innovation, technology adoption, and human capital development. The endogenous growth literature (Romer, 1986, 1990) provides theoretical frameworks and policy insights in this direction, which are widely applied in advanced economies.

A rough measure of productivity—GDP per person employed in 2022–2023 (in constant 2021 PPPs)—shows that Vietnam's productivity is among the lowest compared to its peers (Fig. 2.2).

Economic growth is also driven by structural transformation, a process noted by Kuznets (1966) and Lewis (1954), in which resources shift from low-productivity sectors such as agriculture to high-productivity sectors such as manufacturing and services. More recent multi-sector models (Herrendorf et al., 2014) confirm this pattern in both developed and developing economies. As GDP per capita rises, agriculture's share of employment and output declines, while services expand. Manufacturing follows a "hump-shaped" trajectory—growing initially but declining at later stages of development. The key question is what drives these sectoral

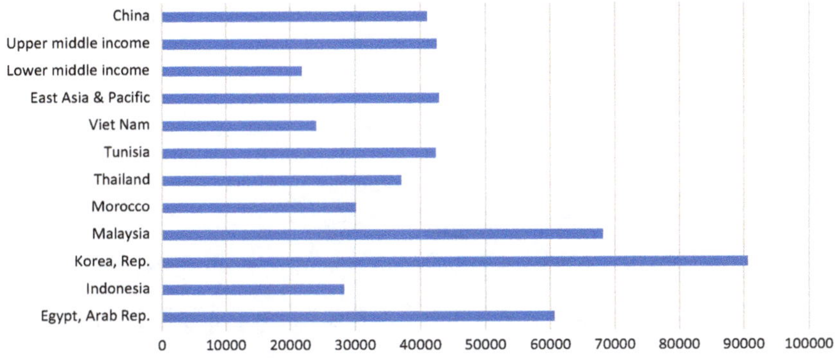

Fig. 2.2 GDP per person employed 2022–2023 (in constant 2021 PPP$). *Source* World Development Indicators; last updated 09/19/2024; accessed October 8, 2024

shifts and how resource allocation across sectors, firms, and regions affects overall productivity and growth.

Recent research (see Gollin & Kaboski, 2023), enabled by micro-level datasets on farms, firms, and households, highlights that low-income economies are not merely smaller versions of high-income ones; they differ structurally. Understanding these differences is critical for explaining development. Growth and structural transformation are deeply interconnected rather than separate phenomena. This book adopts this perspective, emphasizing how sectoral resource allocation affects economic growth.

The left panel of Fig. 2.3 illustrates Vietnam's transformation from a predominantly agrarian economy in 1990 to a semi-modernized one, where industry (including manufacturing, mining, and construction) and services now account for two-thirds of employment. However, while employment shares in industry and services have risen, their contribution to value-added, as shown in the right panel of Fig. 2.3, has not increased proportionally, indicating low efficiency—an issue linked to developments in the manufacturing sector to be discussed later in this Chapter.

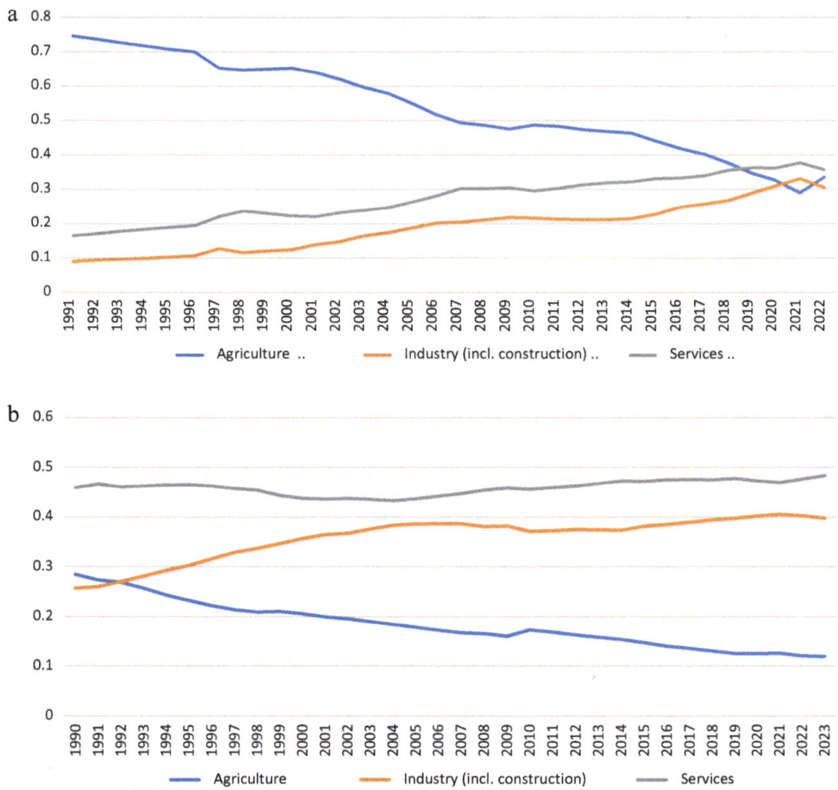

Fig. 2.3 **a** Vietnam employment shares by sector. **b** Vietnam value added shares by sector (in constant LCU). *Source* World Development Indicators; last updated June 28, 2024; accessed September 4, 2024

Analysis of Vietnam's Productivity Growth Using Factor Decomposition

Productivity is the primary driver of sustained economic growth and a key indicator of an economy's long-term health and competitiveness. Unlike short-term growth drivers, such as labor force expansion or capital accumulation, productivity growth—fueled by innovation, improved resource allocation, and technological advancements—has no inherent limits. It enables economies to produce more with the same or fewer inputs, raising living standards, reducing costs, and helping nations break free from diminishing returns. This section examines the evolution of Vietnam's productivity growth using two analytical methods: the factor decomposition approach and the multi-sector decomposition approach.

In a Cobb-Douglas production function, output is linked to factors of production as follows:

$$Y = AK^{\alpha}L^{(1-\alpha)} \tag{2.1}$$

where Y is output (value added), A is the productivity term, or the efficiency with which inputs are used in the production process, K is the capital stock, L is the labor force, and α is the share of capital share of income.

Taking log and differentiating Eq. (2.1) above yields:

$$\hat{Y} = \alpha\hat{K} + (1 - \alpha)\,\hat{L} + \hat{A}$$

where $\hat{Y}$ denotes output growth; $\hat{K}$ and $\hat{L}$ denote growth rates of capital and labor; α and $1\text{-}\alpha$ denote the share of capital and labor in income; and $\hat{A}$ is the growth rate of productivity. This equation shows output growth as a weighted average of capital and labor growth, plus the growth rate of productivity. This last term is commonly referred to as total factor productivity (TFP):

$$\hat{A} = \hat{Y} - \alpha\hat{K} - (1 - \alpha)\hat{L}$$

This economy-wide productivity term, TFP, summarizes everything we do not know about the efficient use of inputs, including technology progress, machinery per worker, institutional arrangements, structural transformation, and so on. The seminal work of Denison (1982), Jorgenson (2005) and Solow (1970), and others showed that this term amounts to almost half of total output growth. Both capital and labor are subject to diminishing returns. Hence, long-lasting change in output depends on the growth of productivity.

In our analysis, we will further differentiate labor quantity and labor quality as well as capital in information and technology (IT) versus capital in non-IT.

A World Bank study by Dieppe (2021) analyzed the evolution of total productivity across global regions. The study found that all emerging market and developing economies (EMDEs) faced productivity declines due to factors such as slowing growth in the working-age population, stagnant educational levels, and reduced expansion of global value chains. Following the 2008 Global Financial Crisis (GFC), productivity growth weakened across all regions, with Latin American countries being the most severely affected.

In this book, the analysis of Vietnamese productivity relies on the Conference Board Total Economy database, an updated dataset tracking global productivity trends. Figure 2.4 presents the contributions of labor (dark blue), labor quality (light blue), non-IT capital (gray), IT capital (yellow), and total factor productivity (TFP) (red), with the green diamond representing GDP growth. The four bars on the left illustrate Vietnam's factor decomposition over four decades, while the bars on the right show the same decomposition for EMDEs.

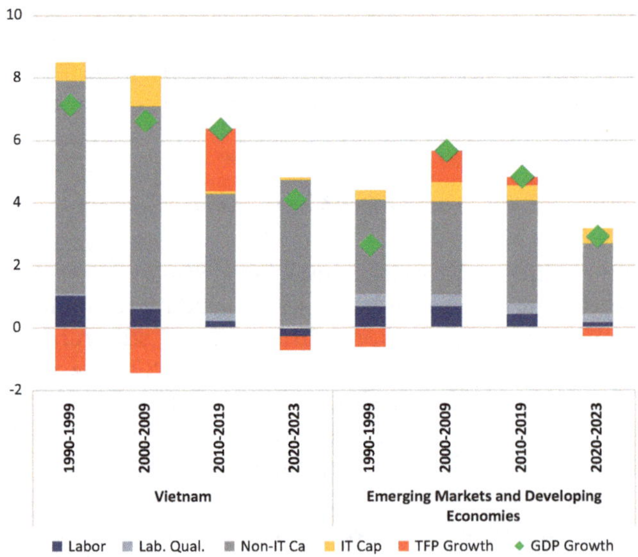

Fig. 2.4 Factors contributing to GDP growth (%). *Source* Author's calculation from The Conference Board Total Economy Database™ (April 2023)

The results are striking. While Vietnam's GDP growth has been exceptional over the last four decades compared to EMDEs, this growth had come mainly from non-IT capital, with other factors play a minor role. Notably, TFP growth, except for the period 2010–2019, was negative throughout. This growth pattern is unsustainable without substantial policy reforms to counteract diminishing returns to capital and shift toward more sustainable growth drivers such as labor quality, IT investment, and TFP growth.

TFP growth is particularly critical. The data suggest that Vietnam's GDP could have grown at least 1.4 percentage points higher per year during the 1990s and 2000s if, at a minimum, TFP growth had been zero—matching the average level of EMDEs (Table 2.1). Over 20 years, this incremental growth would have led to a per capita income level 30% higher than its actual level at the end of the period.

Two key observations emerge: first, labor quality has contributed very little to Vietnam's productivity growth—not just during the pandemic years (2020–2023) but throughout the preceding three decades—compared to other EMDEs. Second, IT investment appears to have slowed in the last decade relative to other EMDEs. Previous studies (e.g., Agenor & Cavuto, 2015) emphasize the crucial role of IT capital, or "advanced infrastructure," in sustaining economic growth.

Figure 2.5 illustrates that this pattern was not observed in Korea, or Taiwan during their respective transitions to high-income status (1960–1989).

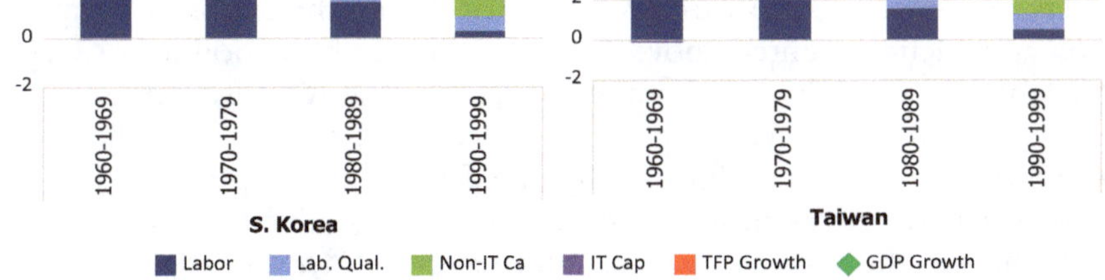

Fig. 2.5 Factor decomposition of South Korea and Taiwan 1990–1999. *Source* Author's calculation from The Conference Board Total Economy Database™ (April 2023)

Table 2.1 Decomposition of GDP growth by factors of production (1990–2023), Vietnam and comparators

	GDP growth	*Labor*	*Labor quality*	*Non-IT cap*	*IT cap*	*TFP growth*
Vietnam						
1990–1999	7.1	1.0	0.1	6.8	0.6	−1.4
2000–2009	6.6	0.6	0.1	6.4	1.0	−1.4
2010–2019	6.4	0.2	0.2	3.8	0.1	2.0
2020–2023	4.1	−0.3	0.1	4.7	0.1	−0.4
Emerging markets and developing economies						
1990–1999	2.7	0.7	0.4	1.9	0.3	−0.6
2000–2009	5.7	0.7	0.4	3.0	0.6	1.0
2010–2019	4.8	0.4	0.3	3.3	0.5	0.3
2020–2023	2.9	0.2	0.3	2.3	0.5	−0.3
South Korea						
1960–1969	8.8	3.3	1.3	4.0	0.0	0.2
1970–1979	9.2	2.3	0.3	4.6	0.3	1.6
1980–1989	7.5	1.5	0.6	2.6	0.5	2.3
1990–1999	6.5	0.3	0.6	2.7	0.8	2.0
Taiwan						
1960–1969	8.7	2.3	0.5	3.1	−0.1	3.0
1970–1979	9.7	2.9	1.1	3.2	0.5	1.9
1980–1989	7.8	1.5	0.9	1.9	0.7	2.8
1990–1999	6.4	0.5	0.8	2.1	1.1	1.9

Source Author's calculation from The Conference Board Total Economy Database™ (April 2023)

Analysis of Vietnam's Productivity Growth Using Sectoral Decomposition

Sectoral decomposition of productivity. While the factor decomposition approach, presented above, identifies which production factor (capital, labor, or TFP) drives output growth, it does not capture inter-sectoral resource shifts, a crucial component of economic growth. Specifically, it overlooks structural transformation—the gains in overall productivity that arise when resources move from low- to high-productivity sectors. To account for this, we employ a multi-sector model that defines labor productivity as the ratio of value-added to employment.

This labor productivity metric has implications beyond data convenience. As noted by Baumol et al. (1989), labor productivity reflects potential consumption and living standards, capturing humanity's efforts to achieve economic output. It serves as a reliable measure of an entity's—whether a firm, industry, or entire economy—ability to reward its workforce.

Assuming an economy with *n* output sectors, one can decompose the overall output growth into three components (McMillan et al., 2014; Timmer et al., 2014) as follows:

$$\Delta Y_t = \sum_{i=1,n} \theta_{i,t-k} \Delta y_{i,t} + \sum_{i=1,n} y_{i,t-k} \Delta \theta_{i,t} + \sum_{i=1,n} \Delta y_{i,t} * \Delta \theta_{i,t} \tag{2.2}$$

The left-hand side of Eq. (2.2) represents the change in economy-wide labor productivity, measured as GDP divided by employment over a given period. The first term on the right hand side (RHS) measures the 'within-sector effect,' which captures changes in sectoral productivity due to capital investment, technological improvements, and other factors—assuming no shift in employment between sectors. For example, in agriculture, improved yields from new seed varieties or enhanced irrigation infrastructure would generate positive within-sector productivity gains, even if the sector's labor share remained unchanged. Conversely, a prolonged war or disaster could reduce agricultural output, leading to a negative effect.

The second term on the RHS, known as the 'static structural change' effect, reflects productivity changes due to shifts in employment across sectors, assuming sectoral productivity remains unchanged. It isolates the direct impact of labor movement on overall productivity. Typically, in growing economies, this term is positive, as job creation in expanding sectors outweighs losses elsewhere.

The third term on the RHS, the 'dynamic structural change' effect, captures the interaction between employment shifts and sectoral productivity changes. This term is positive when an economy undergoes structural transformation—that is, when resources move from low- to high-productivity sectors. It becomes negative if the opposite occurs, such as when workers shift from high-productivity industries to lower-productivity ones.

The sum of the second and third terms constitutes the 'structural transformation effect,' sometimes referred to as the 'between-sector effect' or simply 'structural change' (Diao et al., 2019). In this book, we use the terms 'structural change' and 'structural transformation' interchangeably. However, two key constraints must be considered:

1. Labor movement can only occur if jobs are created in the destination sectors. Without job opportunities in the high-productivity sectors, structural transformation cannot take place.
2. Some high-productivity sectors, such as utilities and resource extraction, are capital-intensive and yet create limited employment, restricting their ability to absorb labor from lower-productivity sectors.

Following the 2008 GFC, productivity gains from structural transformation—resulting from labor reallocation across sectors—slowed worldwide. This decline was particularly pronounced in Latin America and Sub-Saharan Africa (Dieppe, 2021). Meanwhile, within-sector productivity growth also slowed, with East Asia and the Pacific being the only region to maintain within-sector gains during this period.

Analysis of Vietnam Productivity Using the Economic Transformation Database (ETD). Based on ETD data,[2] we conducted a detailed decomposition of Vietnam's productivity growth by sector over a 28-year span, from 1990 to 2018. Figure 2.6 illustrates the decomposition of Vietnamese productivity growth during this period. Except for three years, the within-sector productivity growth was positive, and so was the structural transformation during these three decades.

Figure 2.7 shows the evolution of annual productivity growth for selected Asian countries included in the database, decomposed into within and between effect, the latter is the sum of static and dynamic terms.

The results confirm that between 1990 and 2010, a substantial portion of productivity growth in Vietnam was driven by structural transformation, notably the significant shift of workers from low-productivity agriculture to more productive manufacturing and services sectors.

[2] See De Vries et al. (2021) and https://www.wider.unu.edu/database/etd-economic-transformation-database

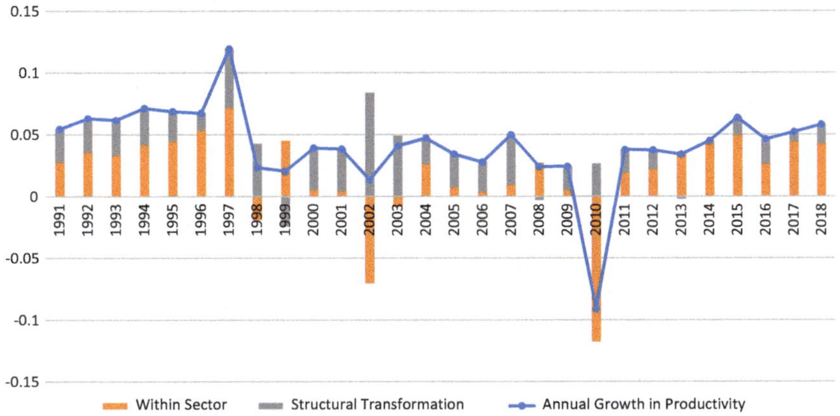

Fig. 2.6 Vietnam sectoral decomposition of annual productivity growth 1990–2018. *Source* Author's calculation from the Economic Transformation Database

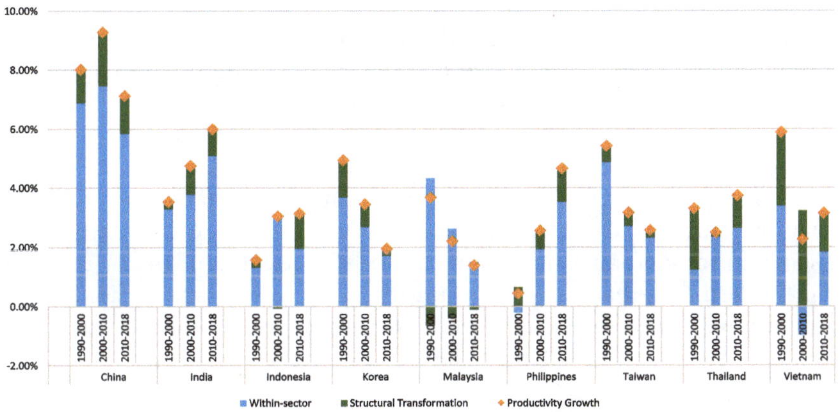

Fig. 2.7 Sectoral decomposition of average annual productivity growth: Vietnam and comparators 1990–2018. *Source* Author's calculations from the Economic Transformation Database

The two approaches above show that, despite low and even negative TFP growth in Vietnam over the past three decades (Table 2.1), the economy's labor productivity recorded respectable annual gains (Fig. 2.6). This discrepancy is largely attributable to capital deepening[3] during the period.

Performance of Vietnam's Manufacturing Sector

At first glance, Vietnam's manufacturing sector appears to be thriving. The left panel of Fig. 2.8 below shows that its share of global manufactured exports nearly quadrupled, rising from less than 0.5% in the 2000s to about 2% a decade later. By 2017, Vietnam had surpassed Malaysia to become ASEAN's largest exporter of manufactured goods. However, as this chapter will demonstrate, this success is somewhat misleading. In terms of value-added—the true driver of economic growth—Vietnam lags behind other East Asian economies (Fig. 2.8, right panel).

Divergence Between Gross Exports and Value-Added

While manufacturing has been the key driver of Vietnam's structural transformation over the past two decades, its contribution to GDP is far less significant than its role in gross exports. This discrepancy arises from Vietnam's integration into global value chains (GVCs), where its role is largely shaped by the skill level of its workforce.

To accurately assess Vietnam's exports, it is essential to consider the trade-in-value-added concept. For instance, in the case of smartphones assembled in Vietnam and exported globally, less than 10% of the final value reflects Vietnamese contributions in terms of labor, capital, and other inputs. The remaining 90% consists of imported components from countries such as South Korea, Japan, and the U.S. Yet, trade statistics

[3] The relationship between labor productivity growth ($\widehat{LP}$) and TFP growth ($\hat{A}$) can be derived analytically from the Cobb-Douglas production function as follows:

$$\widehat{LP} = \hat{A} + \alpha * (\hat{K} - \hat{L})$$

where $\widehat{LP}$ is labor productivity growth, $\hat{A}$ is the growth rate of TFP, $\hat{K}$is the growth rate of capital, $\hat{L}$ is the growth rate of labor, and α is the output elasticity of capital. The expression $\hat{K} - \hat{L}$ captures the growth of the capital-to-labor ratio, or capital deepening. Hence, labor productivity can grow faster than TFP by a fraction of capital deepening.

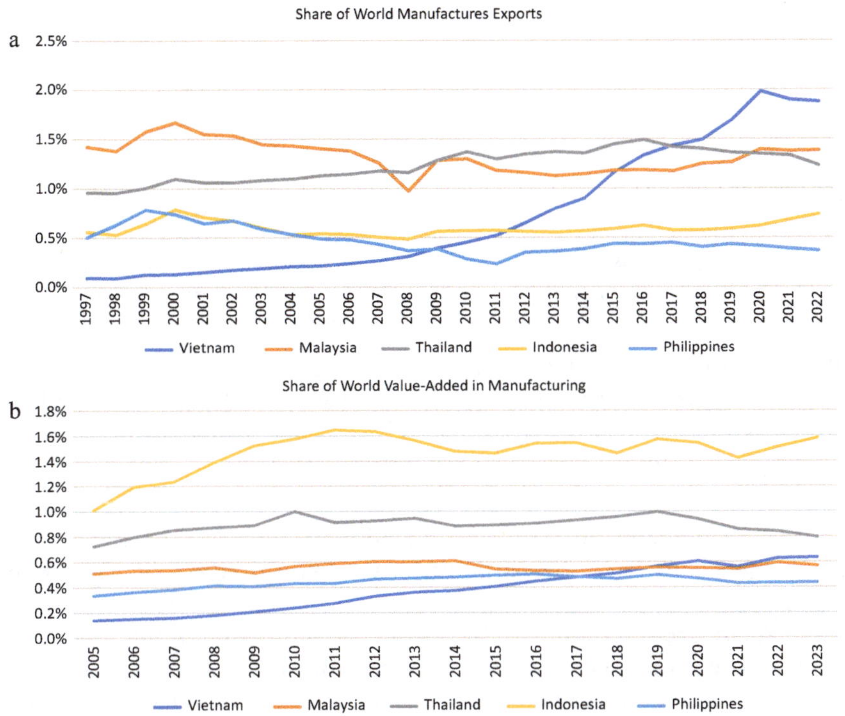

Fig. 2.8 **a** Share of world manufacturing exports. **b** Share of world value-added in manufacturing. *Source* World Development Indicators; last updated June 28, 2024; accessed September 4, 2024

record the full value as Vietnamese exports. In 2020, out of $258 billion in total exports, Vietnam's actual value-added contribution was only $154 billion. In a 2022 study on foreign direct investment (FDI) in Vietnam, Kokko et al. (2023) noted that in 2014, out of 67 first-tier suppliers to Samsung—the largest foreign-invested mobile phone producer in the country—only four were domestic firms, most supplied cardboard packaging for the final products.

This discrepancy underscores the need for a more nuanced understanding of trade balances. More advanced economies generate higher value-added per dollar of exports, with OECD countries averaging 92.6% in 2020, compared to Vietnam's 52% (Fig. 2.9). The left panel of Fig. 2.9

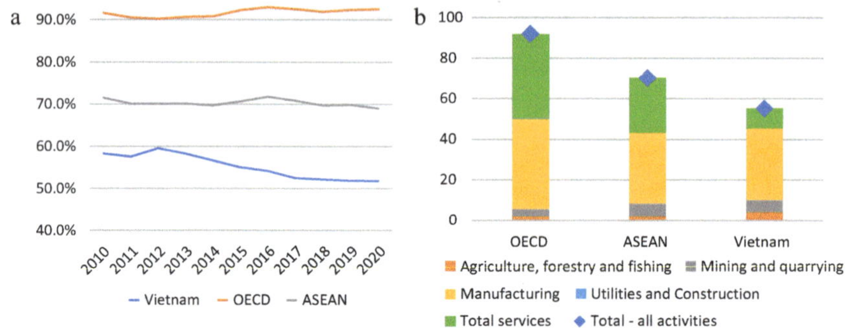

Fig. 2.9 **a** Percentage of domestic value-added in gross exports (2010–2020). **b** Percentage of domestic value added in gross exports by sector, 2010–2020. *Source* (DSD_TIVA_MAINSH@DF_MAINSH) trade in value added (TiVA) 2023 edition: Principal Indicators, shares [cloud replica]

highlights Vietnam's limited value-added generation in GVCs, while the right panel illustrates the particularly weak contribution of its services sector (green bar).

Vietnam's reliance on low-value-added assembly work highlights the urgent need for policies that enhance domestic productivity and industrial capacity. To achieve developed-country status, Vietnam must improve the productivity of its domestic firms and integrate them more deeply into GVCs. The government should facilitate this process through financial and technical support. Simply attracting more foreign direct investment (FDI) will not lead to sustained development if foreign firms continue to use Vietnam solely as a low-cost assembly hub.

Duality in Production

Vietnam's manufacturing sector exhibits a striking duality. On one hand, the country exports increasingly sophisticated products through foreign direct investment (FDI)-led enterprises, where the local workforce remains confined to low-value-added, upstream assembly activities. On the other hand, domestic production is dominated by micro-enterprises—typically employing fewer than three workers—that use outdated technologies to serve local markets. These micro-enterprises account for the majority of employment in the manufacturing sector.

Anh and Perkins (2023) observed that within Vietnam's private sector, a small number of large firms—often referred to as cronies—have been established by owners with close ties to government officials and are primarily engaged in real estate or commercial activities. In contrast, the vast majority of private enterprises are small and medium-sized (SMEs), lack access to land and credit, and remain oriented toward local markets. As a result, very few large private firms have emerged in the manufacturing sector.

This paradox—rapid export growth alongside limited contributions to GDP and employment—has led to persistent underemployment, a large informal sector, and weak trickle-down effects on household well-being. These issues will be examined in greater depth in Chapter 10.

Vietnam's growth has been driven more by capital accumulation than by productivity gains. Total factor productivity (TFP)—which measures the efficiency with which labor and capital are used—has remained weak. Despite some progress in diversifying from natural resource-based exports to modern industrial production, Vietnam's industrialization remains constrained by this underlying structural dualism.

Table 2.2 shows that value-added and employment growth in tradable sectors have lagged behind those in non-tradable sectors. Between 2010 and 2023, value-added in the tradable sector grew by about 5.4% per year, while the non-tradable sector grew by 6.6% annually. This trend existed even before the pandemic, shown in column under 2010–2019. Between 2010 and 2023, the share of the tradable sector in total value-added (GDP) declined from 42 to 39% (Table 2.2). Over the same period, employment in tradable sectors fell by 1.4% annually, while employment in non-tradable sectors grew by 2.6% per year. Consequently, the share of non-tradable sectors in total employment increased from 33 to 44%.

Although manufacturing employment grew by nearly 5% annually, these industries primarily operate within GVCs at the assembly stage. As a result, they experienced high export growth without a corresponding increase in value-added. This happened even before COVID-19 (Column 2010–2019)

Table 2.2 Average annual growth rates of value added and employment in tradable sectors, 2000–2023

Average annual growth rates of value added and employment, 2010–2023			*% of GDP at fc*	
	2010–2023	*2010–2019*	*2010*	*2023*
Value added in 2014 prices	6.1	6.6	100.0	100.0 (%)
Tradable (inc. tourism)	5.4 (%)	5.8 (%)	42.1 (%)	38.9 (%)
Manufacturing	8.7 (%)	9.4 (%)	17.1 (%)	23.0 (%)
Other tradable	2.0 (%)	2.5 (%)	25.0 (%)	15.9 (%)
Non-tradable	6.6 (%)	7.1 (%)	57.9 (%)	61.1 (%)
Employment	0.1 (%)	1.0 (%)	% of employment	
Tradable (inc. tourism)	−1.4 (%)	−0.2 (%)	67.4 (%)	56.3 (%)
Manufacturing	4.9 (%)	5.4 (%)	14.5 (%)	23.3 (%)
Other tradable	−3.9 (%)	−2.1 (%)	53.0 (%)	33.0 (%)
Non-tradable	2.6 (%)	3.2 (%)	32.6 (%)	43.7 (%)

Source Author's calculation from ADB (2024) data. Growth rates are calculated using Ordinary Least Squares method

Conclusion

Economic development fundamentally involves structural transformation—the reallocation of resources from less productive to more productive sectors and activities. Both the Growth Commission Report (2008) and the World Development Report (2013) emphasize that diversification and structural transformation are essential for catching up economically (Commission on Growth and Development, 2008; World Bank, 2012).

The analysis in this chapter indicates that while structural transformation remains an important driver of Vietnam's growth, its pace has slowed over the past decade. Structural transformation played a significant role during the 1990s and 2000s (Fig. 2.6), but its impact has since diminished. A closer look at employment trends reveals that as agriculture and manufacturing shed workers, many moved into service sectors—some of which continue to have productivity levels below the economy's average.

References

Agénor, P. R., & Canuto, O. (2015). Middle-income growth traps. *Research in Economics, 69*(4), 641–660.

Anh, V. T. T., & Perkins, D. H. (2023). Explaining Vietnam's economic growth experience. In B. Ljunggren & D. H. Perkins (Eds.), *Vietnam—Navigating a rapidly changing economy, society, and political order* (142). Harvard University Press.

Baumol, W. J., Blackman, S. A. B., & Wolff, E. N. (1989). *Productivity and American leadership.* MIT Press.

Commission on Growth and Development. (2008). *The growth report: Strategies for sustained growth and inclusive development.* World Bank. https://openknowledge.worldbank.org/handle/10986/6507

De Vries, G., Arfelt, L., Drees, D., Godemann, M., Hamilton, C., Jessen-Thiesen, B., Kaya, A. I., Kruse, H., Mensah, E., & Woltjer, P. (2021). The economic transformation database (ETD): Content, sources, and methods. *Technical Note, WIDER*. https://www.wider.unu.edu/sites/default/files/Publications/Technical-note/PDF/tn2021-2-ETD-content-sources-methods.pdf

Denison, E. F. (1982). *Trends in American economic growth, 1929–1982.* Brookings Institution.

Diao, X., McMillan, M., & Rodrik, D. (2019). The recent growth boom in developing economies: A structural-change perspective. In *The Palgrave handbook of development economics* (pp. 281–334). Palgrave Macmillan.

Dieppe, A. (Ed.). (2021). *Global productivity: Trends, drivers, and policies.* World Bank. http://hdl.handle.net/10986/34015

Gollin, D., & Kaboski, J. P. (2023). New views of structural transformation: Insights from recent literature. *Oxford Development Studies, 51*(4), 339–361. https://doi.org/10.1080/13600818.2023.2280748

Herrendorf, B., Rogerson, R., & Valentinyi, A. (2014). Growth and structural transformation. *Handbook of Economic Growth, 2*, 855–941.

Jorgenson, D. W. (2005). Accounting for growth in the information age In P. Aghion & S. Durlauf (Eds.), *Handbook of economic growth* (Vol. 1, pp. 743–815). Elsevier.

Kokko, A., Nestor, C., & Van, L. H. (2023). FDI in Vietnam: Policies, effects, and linkages to the local economy. In B. Ljunggren & D. H. Perkins (Eds.), *Vietnam—Navigating a rapidly changing economy, society, and political order* (177). Harvard University Press.

Kuznets, S. (1966). *Economic growth and structure.* Yale University Press.

Lewis, W. A. (1954). Economic development with unlimited supplies of labour. *The Manchester School, 22*(2), 139–191.

McMillan, M. S., Rodrik, D., & Verduzco-Gallo, I. (2014). Globalization, structural change and productivity growth, with an update on Africa. *World Development, 63*, 11–32.

Romer, P. M. (1986). Increasing returns and long-run growth. *Journal of Political Economy, 94*(5), 1002–1037.

Romer, P. M. (1990). Endogenous technological change. *Journal of Political Economy, 98*(5, Part 2), S71–S102.

Solow, R. M. (1956). A contribution to the theory of economic growth. *Quarterly Journal of Economics, 70*(1), 65–94.

Solow, R. M. (1970). *Growth theory: An exposition*. Oxford University Press.

Timmer, M. P., de Vries, G. J., & de Vries, K. (2014). *Patterns of structural change in developing countries*. Groningen Growth and Development Centre. GGDC Research Memorandum No. 149.

World Bank. (2012). *World development report 2013: Jobs*. World Bank.

CHAPTER 3

Growth Prospects

Introduction

Over the past thirty years, Vietnam has sustained impressive GDP growth, prompting comparisons with earlier high-growth trajectories in East Asia. To place Vietnam's performance in context, Chap. 2 examined the contributions of various growth drivers—labor, labor quality, capital (both IT and non-IT), and total factor productivity (TFP)—and compared them with those of South Korea and Taiwan during their transformative decades from 1960 to 2000. While Vietnam's experience shares many features with these economies during their ascent to high-income status, a striking difference emerges in the role of TFP. As shown in Figs. 2.4 and 2.5, TFP was a far more powerful engine of growth in Korea and Taiwan than it has been in Vietnam to date, highlighting a crucial gap that may shape the country's long-term prospects.

Opportunity Going Forward

Looking ahead, Vietnam stands at a critical juncture, as its window of opportunity is rapidly closing due to demographic shifts. The demographic dividend that once favored the country is now reversing, placing Vietnam at a crucial decision point. Continuing with past policies, as illustrated in

Contributed by Hinh T. Dinh

H. T. Dinh, H. T. Nguyen, *Vietnam's Economic Leap*,
https://doi.org/10.1007/978-3-032-08904-5_3

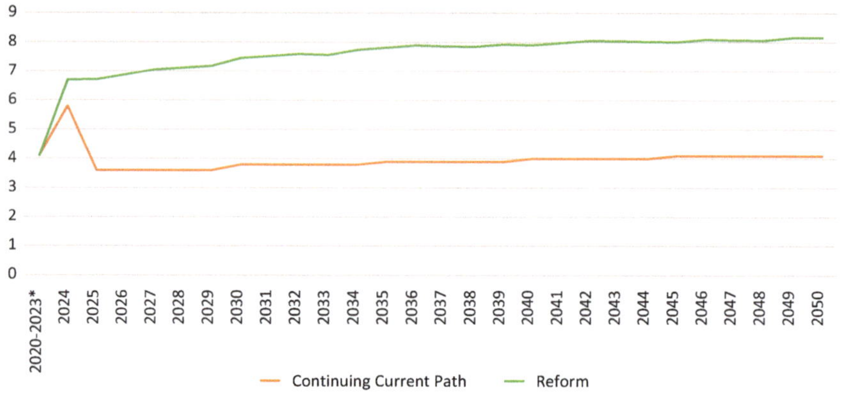

Fig. 3.1 Vietnam GDP annual growth (%), continuing current path versus reform 2024–2050. *Source* Author's calculation based on parameters from Table 3.2 and Annex 1

Fig. 3.1, is likely to result in stagnant per capita income by 2050, keeping Vietnam within the upper-middle-income bracket, much like Argentina and Brazil over the past century. Achieving even this outcome would require a considerable amount of luck, given the increasingly competitive global environment driven by technological advancements in developed nations and the rapid convergence of emerging economies.

Figure 3.1 projects Vietnam's GDP trajectory up to 2050 under two scenarios: a "continuing current path" scenario, where past policies persist and result in per capita income stagnation due to diminishing returns to labor and non-IT capital, and a "reform" scenario, where policies are designed to stimulate domestic industries, absorb higher technological progress, and drive increased productivity growth. Under the reform scenario, Vietnam would achieve upper-middle-income status by 2026 and high-income status by 2047 (Annex 1). Table 3.1 details the parameters underlying each scenario, alongside actual values from the past three decades, based on calculations from the Conference Board Total Economy Database™.

The key distinctions between the "continuing current path" and "reform" scenarios lie in four key areas in Table 3.1: labor (mainly drawing labor from the informal market), labor quality (including education quality and vocational training), IT capital, and TFP growth. Specific policies to achieve these ambitious goals are discussed below

Table 3.1 Average annual parameters underlying Fig. 3.1

		Labor (%)	*Labor quality (%)*	*Non-IT capital (%)*	*IT capital (%)*	*TFP growth (%)*	*GDP growth (%)*
Actual	2000–2009	0.6	0.1	6.4	1.0	−1.4	6.6
Actual	2010–2019	0.2	0.2	3.8	0.1	2.0	6.4
Actual	2020–2023	−0.3	0.1	4.7	0.1	−0.4	4.1
Continuing curr. path	2024–2050	0.2	0.2	3.1	0.3	0.2	4.0
Reform	2024–2050	0.3	0.5	4.3	0.6	2.0	7.7

Source Historical values calculated from The Conference Board Total Economy Database™ (April 2023) and projections based on assumptions.

and in subsequent chapters. Vietnam has a limited time frame to address these challenges before demographic forces take full effect. Notably, the average annual GDP growth rate of 7.7% under the reform scenario appears modest compared to other projections, but to achieve this average, annual GDP growth would need to rise to about 8% beginning in 2042 and be sustained thereafter.

Demographic Window of Opportunity

Vietnam stands on the cusp of a significant demographic window of opportunity that could shape its economic and social landscape over the next 18 years. This "golden" period, during which the working-age population (ages 15–64) is twice as large as the dependent population (under 15 and 65+), offers Vietnam a unique chance to accelerate economic growth. This demographic dividend began at 203% in 2006, peaked at 231% in 2013, and is projected to gradually decline to below 200% by 2039 (United Nations, 2022). This shift is primarily attributed to improvements in healthcare and education, leading to lower mortality and fertility rates.

The economic implications of these demographic changes are significant. With a larger workforce, Vietnam has the potential to boost economic output, increase savings and investment, and accelerate development. However, these trends also present challenges, including declining fertility rates, increasing life expectancy, an aging population, rising old-age dependency ratios, and significant regional disparities.

Fertility Rate. Vietnam's total fertility rate (TFR) has declined dramatically, from over six children per woman in the 1970s to approximately 1.9 in 2022—below the replacement rate of 2.0 (Lee & Mason, 2014). This decline results from policies promoting smaller families, increased education access for women, and improved healthcare. While this trend has contributed to Vietnam's demographic dividend, it also raises concerns about future labor shortages.

Life Expectancy and Aging Population. Life expectancy in Vietnam has significantly improved, rising from around 60 years in the 1960s to over 74 years today. While this reflects advancements in healthcare and living standards, it also means a growing elderly population, which will strain healthcare, pension systems, and social services.

Old-Age Dependency Ratio. Vietnam's old-age dependency ratio, measuring the proportion of elderly dependents per 100 working-age individuals, was 13.3% in 2022 and is projected to rise to 20.1% by 2034

(UN). This increase will pressure public resources, requiring innovative policy solutions to ensure economic sustainability while supporting the aging population.

Regional Disparities. Vietnam's demographic trends vary significantly by region, with urban areas like Ho Chi Minh City and Hanoi experiencing different patterns from rural regions. Urban areas generally have lower fertility rates, higher life expectancy, and different age structures, necessitating region-specific policies for equitable development.

To maximize the demographic opportunity and mitigate challenges, Vietnam must adopt a multi-faceted policy approach, including investment in education, workforce participation incentives, flexible immigration policies, and reforms in healthcare, pension systems, and social services.

Manufacturing Exports

While expanding high-tech, high value-added sectors is essential for Vietnam to achieve high-income status, it is equally important to ensure that a large share of the workforce—including unskilled labor—remains employed during the transition. To this end, Vietnam should redesign its short- and medium-term policies to address two critical objectives simultaneously. First, it must expand labor-intensive manufacturing to absorb the unemployed, particularly among youth. Achieving this will require supportive trade policies, exchange rate reforms, and FDI facilitation, complemented by unconventional strategies such as the development of industrial clusters and export-driven manufacturing growth. This is the path that the country has followed successfully in the past. Second, Vietnam must upgrade its domestic production base and foster innovation to move toward upper-middle-income status. This calls for strengthening traditional exports while prioritizing three dynamic sectors: electronics, automotive products, and aerospace. Given the long gestation period of these initiatives, timely implementation is imperative.

As discussed in later chapters, the most effective strategy for expanding labor-intensive industries while nurturing the growth of new sectors lies in integrating Vietnamese firms into productive clusters and enhancing their access to domestically produced components.

Expanding New Export Products and Improving Existing Ones. Vietnam faces a low risk of premature deindustrialization in labor-intensive manufacturing. Figure 3.2 indicates that Vietnam still has room to expand its

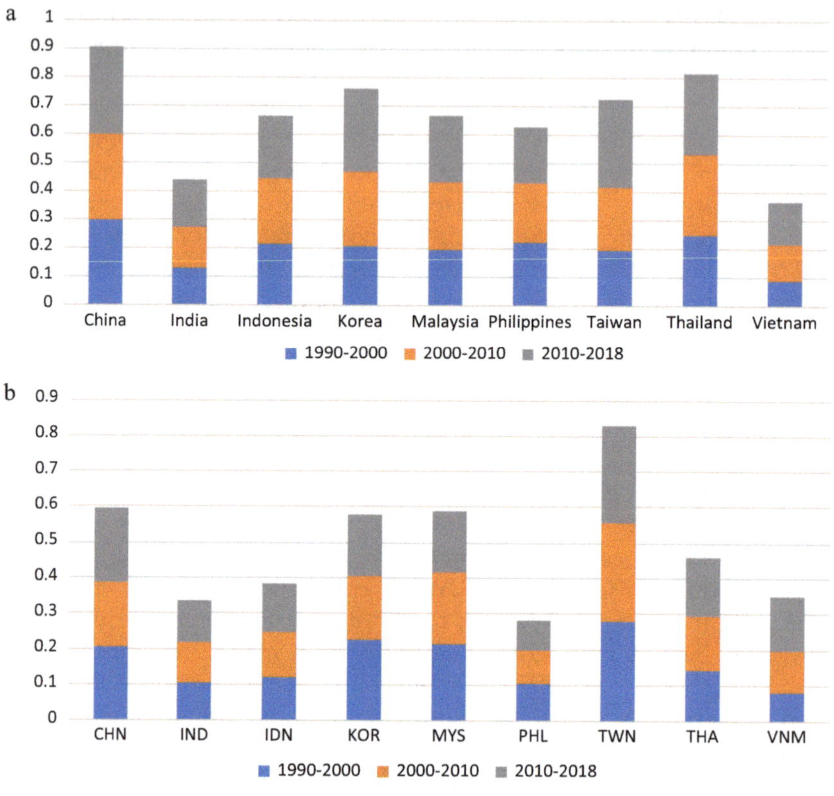

Fig. 3.2 (**a**) Average annual share of manufacturing value-added 1990–2018. (**b**) Average share in manufacturing employment 1990–2018. *Source* Author's calculations from the Economic Transformation Database

manufacturing sector in both employment and value-added terms before reaching a production and export peak similar to South Korea and Taiwan.

A key ingredient of Vietnam's development strategy is the continuing focus on manufacturing. Moving labor from agriculture requires industrial or service job openings. However, non-tradable services have a slow absorption rate. Additionally, if productivity in services is higher than in agriculture but non-tradable services cannot expand without price declines, there is little overall economic gain.

As Baumol and Bowen (1965) noted, as an economy grows, overall productivity may decline because service-sector productivity improvements are harder to achieve than in manufacturing. When sectors compete for resources, service costs rise. If demand for services is price inelastic, their share in national income will increase, even as productivity growth slows. This trend underscores the importance of sustained manufacturing expansion in Vietnam's economic strategy.

In his famous article on cost disease, Baumol (1967) divides the economy into two sectors: the progressive sector, characterized by rising productivity, which leads to its declining share in both income and employment, and the laggard sectors, which require personal interactions, cannot be easily automated, and exhibit low productivity, resulting in rising costs relative to the progressive sector. Despite the drag that laggard sectors impose on the progressive sector, the overall economy can still achieve higher productivity growth—Baumol estimates this at 2% per annum.

A common misconception in economics concerns structural transformation. Many observers claim that in advanced countries, the share of manufacturing rose to about 30% of GDP before declining, while the share of services continued to rise. However, Baumol challenges this notion. He argues that using a quantity-based approach (rather than constant prices) reveals that the manufacturing sector's share would continue to grow even as its share of employment declines.

Dinh (2017) provided empirical evidence on two critical aspects of structural transformation: (i) horizontal diversification (product variety expansion); and (ii) product quality improvement. East Asian economies, for instance, initially pursued development through variety expansion—primarily through imitation—before transitioning to quality improvement, which is more innovation-intensive. The ability to shift from producing simple, low-quality goods to sophisticated, high-quality products is essential for export success and economic development.

A modern industrial sector leverages domestic intermediate goods production rather than depending on imported components—a crucial distinction from Vietnam's current model. Policy interventions should, therefore, focus on stimulating demand for domestically produced intermediate goods, rather than leaving it entirely to market forces, which tend to favor imports.

Trade Integration. Over the past three decades, Viet Nam has vigorously pursued a strategy of comprehensive trade integration, culminating in its accession to the World Trade Organization (WTO) in 2007 and the establishment of an expansive web of trade agreements. Today, Viet Nam is connected to 53 countries through these agreements, encompassing nearly 90% of global GDP, approximately 85% of its own imports, and 70% of its exports. Beyond its WTO commitments, Vietnam is also a party to 19 free trade agreements (FTAs), extending its economic reach across most regions of the world—though notably excluding Africa and the Middle East (World Bank, 2024c).

This deep engagement with global trade has yielded tangible results and should be continued. Tariff barriers have been significantly reduced, with the average applied weighted tariff on manufactured goods falling from 16.6% to just 1.1%, and tariffs on primary goods dropping from 11.2 to 2.7% (World Bank 2024b). Amid increasing global economic fragmentation, Viet Nam's proactive trade policy has established it as a "connector" economy—one that not only facilitates cross-border commerce but also leverages trade for domestic transformation. Firm-level evidence shows a strong association between export intensity and subsequent gains in productivity, employment, and firm revenues (World Bank, 2024a).

Over the past few decades, Viet Nam has reduced its reliance on natural resource exports. However, this diversification has been uneven and has recently shown signs of slowing.

Panel A of Fig. 3.3 illustrates Viet Nam's export diversification index, calculated by the United Nations Conference on Trade and Development (UNCTAD). The index, which ranges from 0 to 1, measures how much a country's export basket deviates from the global average. A lower value indicates greater diversification. Between 1995 and 2012, Viet Nam saw substantial improvement in export diversification, but this progress has stagnated in recent years.

Panel B presents the export concentration index (Herfindahl-Hirschman Index), which measures the degree of product concentration in exports. A lower value indicates greater diversification. Since 2010, Viet Nam has experienced increasing product concentration, suggesting a shift toward fewer export categories.

Data from the World Integrated Trade Solutions (WITS) indicate that Vietnam accounted for about 5% of global textile and clothing exports in 2022, compared to about 34% for China. This suggests that Vietnam still has considerable room to expand in these traditional labor-intensive industries, at least in the short and medium terms.

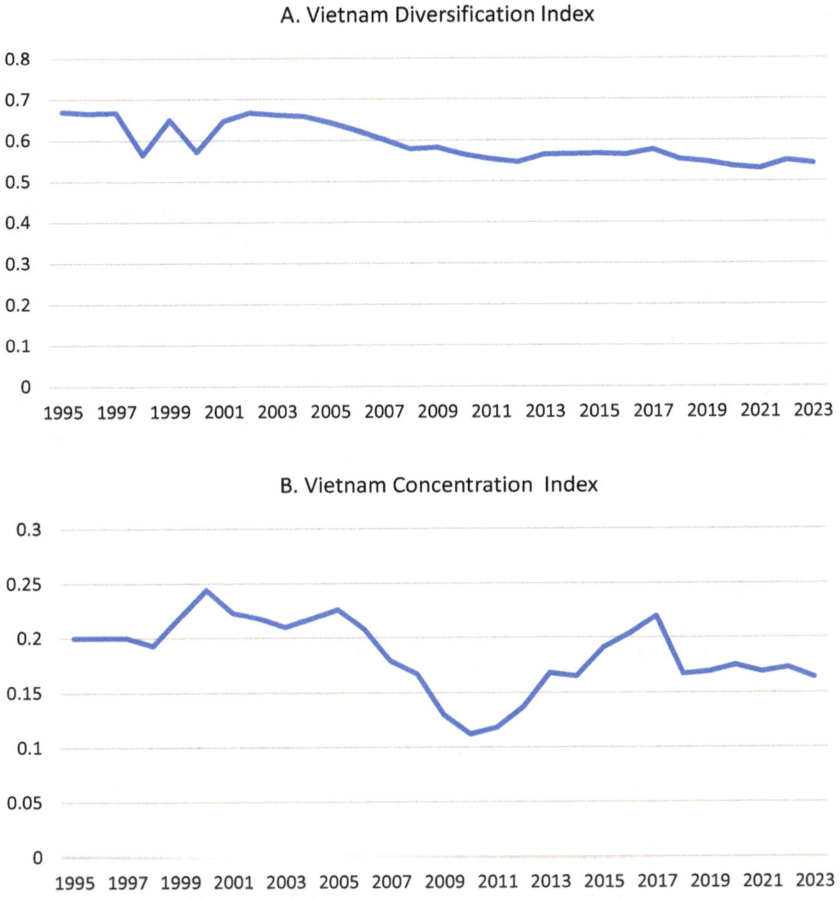

Fig. 3.3 Vietnam's export diversification and concentration indices (%), 1995–2023. *Source* UNCTAD Data Center, accessed February 21, 2025. https://unctadstat.Unctad.Org/datacentre/dataviewer/US.ConcentDiversIndices

Vietnam's Modern Industries

Viet Nam's automotive industry has made notable progress, transitioning from an assembly-based sector to one with growing domestic production capabilities. The emergence of VinFast, the country's first domestic automaker, marks a turning point, with investments in electric vehicles (EVs) and international expansion.

While the industry still relies heavily on imported components, efforts are underway to develop a local supplier base, particularly in metal parts, plastics, and electronics. Government policies—including tax incentives and infrastructure development—have sought to attract foreign investment and promote linkages between multinational car manufacturers and domestic firms. However, challenges remain, including high production costs, limited economies of scale, and competition from established automotive hubs like Thailand and Indonesia. Strengthening supply chain integration and enhancing technological capabilities will be crucial for the industry's long-term sustainability.

Viet Nam's aeronautics sector, though still nascent, has experienced steady growth, driven by increasing demand for air travel and maintenance, repair, and overhaul (MRO) services. Major aerospace firms like Boeing and Airbus have partnered with local companies for component manufacturing. Firms such as Vietnam Airlines Engineering Company (VAECO) and Hanwha Aero Engines have expanded their roles in aircraft maintenance and parts production, embedding Viet Nam into the global aerospace supply chain.

The government has identified aeronautics as a strategic industry, focusing on skill development and infrastructure investment. Although domestic content remains limited, the sector offers potential synergies with Viet Nam's electronics and precision engineering industries, creating opportunities for technological spillovers and increased local value-added in the long run.

Value-Added Concerns in Vietnam's Export Sector

Figure 3.4 illustrates the ratio of domestic value-added to gross exports in Vietnam's manufacturing sector. In 2000, the ratio was 60.2%, but by 2020 it had declined to 48.3%, even as exports rose dramatically from under USD 10 billion to USD 195 billion. In contrast, developed countries tend to exhibit much higher domestic value-added ratios—for instance, 89.3% in OECD countries. The persistently low and even declining ratio in Vietnam is a cause for concern, especially as comparable economies such as China and Malaysia have demonstrated upward trends in domestic value-added contributions to exports.

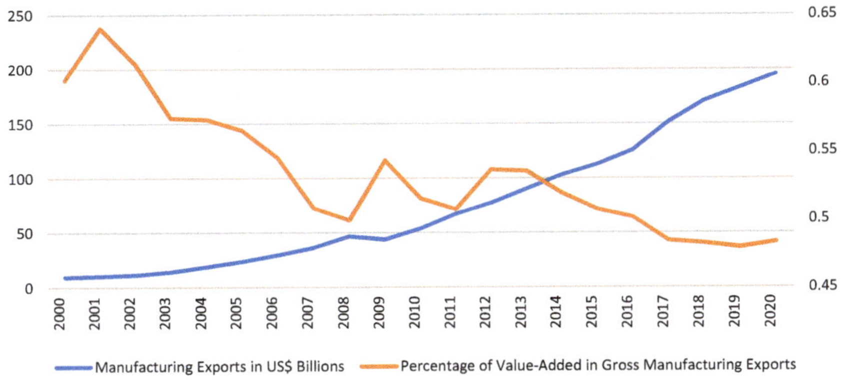

Fig. 3.4 Vietnam manufacturing exports (US$ billions) and ratio of manufacturing value added to gross exports 2000–2020. *Source* Author's calculation from TIVA. https://www.oecd.org/en/topics/sub-issues/trade-in-value-added.html, accessed February 22, 2025

Challenges and Policy Implications

Table 3.2 presents the annual growth rates of Vietnam's exports across various manufacturing subsectors alongside the growth rates of value-added ratios. Most labor-intensive subsectors, such as food products and textiles, recorded strong export growth over the past two decades. However, the value-added-to-gross-export ratio has declined.

This decline suggests that foreign enterprises are increasingly using capital-intensive machinery and imported inputs and Vietnamese labor is used primarily for assembly operations. Domestic enterprises, isolated from foreign-owned firms, largely produce for the domestic market using low technology and relying on informal labor. This duality implies that technology transfer and competitive pressure from foreign firms have yet to penetrate domestic enterprises and the domestic economy.

Although Viet Nam is integrated into global value chains (GVCs), stronger linkages between multinational corporations and local firms could enhance technology transfer and knowledge spillovers, ultimately boosting domestic value-added and long-term economic resilience.

Vietnam should avoid falling into a resource-based growth model. The country's recent rare earth discoveries and its potential integration into the semiconductor supply chain present both significant opportunities and

Table 3.2 Vietnam: annual growth rates of various manufacturing subsectors 2000–2020

	Annual growth in gross exports (%)	*Annual growth in ratio of VA/GX (%)*
Agriculture, forestry and fishing	15.5	−1.0
Manufacturing	17.2	−2.8
Manufacture of food products; beverages and tobacco products	13.2	−3.8
Manufacture of textiles, wearing apparel, leather and related products	16.6	−1.4
Manufacture of wood and of products of wood and cork, except furniture; manufacture of articles of straw and plaiting materials; manufacture of paper and paper products; printing and reproduction of recorded media	14.3	0.6
Manufacture of chemicals and non-metallic mineral products	22.1	3.5
Manufacture of basic pharmaceutical products and pharmaceutical preparations	13.8	4.0
Manufacture of fabricated metal products, except machinery and equipment	8.6	−6.2
Manufacture of computer, electronic and optical products; manufacture of electrical equipment	25.2	5.0
Manufacture of electrical equipment	12.5	−4.9
Manufacture of machinery and equipment n.e.c.	9.5	−4.8
Manufacture of motor vehicles, trailers, semi-trailers and of other transport equipment	23.6	5.7

Source Author's calculation from TIVA. https://www.oecd.org/en/topics/sub-issues/trade-in-value-added.html, accessed February 22, 2025. Annual growth rates are calculated using Ordinary Least Squares method

considerable risks. Rather than focusing on the export of raw materials, Vietnam should prioritize developing higher-value stages of rare earth processing. The experience of many resource-rich countries—where over-reliance on raw material exports has undermined long-term economic growth—serves as a cautionary tale (Dinh & Dinh, 2016).

The economic literature on resource dependence traces its origins to Seers (1964), Furtado (1957), and Mill (1848), with later formalization by Corden

(1984), Corden and Neary (1982), Gelb (1988), and van Wijnbergen (1984). The "resource curse," as articulated by Auty (1994) and analyzed econometrically by Sachs and Warner (1995), demonstrates the negative relationship between resource dependence and long-term growth.

While resource-based economies such as the U.S., Australia, and Canada have succeeded, their growth was driven by domestic technological development and strong institutions. In contrast, many developing countries import technology and expertise, failing to capitalize on resource wealth. Barbier (2005) emphasized that successful resource-based strategies require reinvestment in productive sectors, sound governance, and knowledge spillovers. Few developing nations have met these criteria, explaining their persistent middle-income status.

Vietnam must chart a different course by prioritizing technological development and industrial upgrading. Rather than relying on raw material exports, it should invest in refining, manufacturing, and innovation to capture greater value-added benefits. A well-designed strategy will determine whether Vietnam escapes the middle-income trap or remains constrained by the limitations of a resource-dependent model.

The Political Economy of Reforms

As Vietnam continues its journey toward a more dynamic and market-oriented economy, the government has shown strong commitment to ensuring that this transition remains equitable, inclusive, and in line with the country's long-term development vision. In this process, certain challenges have emerged—many of which are well recognized by the leadership and are being addressed through ongoing and comprehensive reforms.

One such challenge relates to the need for greater transparency and fairness in economic opportunities. Observers, including development partners and policy analysts, have noted that in many instances, personal relationships and informal networks may have played a role in shaping access to key economic resources such as land, credit, licenses, and public procurement. This can potentially limit the growth prospects of smaller and independent enterprises, despite the government's stated goal of fostering broad-based private sector development.

State-owned enterprises (SOEs) have long served as pillars of the Vietnamese economy and continue to play an important role in strategic sectors. However, ensuring that these enterprises operate on a level playing field alongside private firms is essential to realizing the full potential of market competition and encouraging innovation. The government's ongoing SOE reforms and efforts to reduce non-market advantages are important steps toward achieving greater balance and efficiency in the economy.

Land management and real estate development have been vital to rural transformation and poverty alleviation, particularly following newly the 2024 Land Law. At the same time, both domestic and international studies have highlighted the need to further enhance transparency in land allocation and address speculation risks, which can inadvertently contribute to perceptions of inequity or favoritism. Strengthening institutions in this area will help safeguard the integrity of reforms and ensure that land continues to be a powerful driver of inclusive growth.

Vietnam's leaders have clearly recognized these challenges and responded with the "Era of National Rise"—an ambitious and forward-looking reform agenda. Spearheaded by Communist Party General Secretary To Lam, this strategic vision aims to build a modern, transparent, and rules-based economic environment, rooted in integrity and fairness. Through bold institutional reforms, anti-corruption initiatives, and administrative modernization, the government is paving the way for Vietnam to transition from a middle-income to a high-income nation by 2045, while ensuring that all segments of society can share in the country's success.

The Era of National Rise

On September 23, 2024, at Columbia University in the United States, General Secretary To Lam, in his capacity as head of state, declared: "After nearly 80 years of nation-building and nearly 40 years of reform, under the comprehensive leadership of the Communist Party, Vietnam is at the threshold of a historic turning point—a new era: the Era of the Nation's Rise." This represents bold new phase of development driven by digital transformation, institutional reform, infrastructure expansion, green growth and deeper global integration. Mr. To Lam's strategic framework divides modern Vietnamese history into three periods. The first is the era of independence and socialism (1930–1975), followed by the era of reunification and Doi Moi reforms (1975–2025), and the era of national rise (2026–2045). The period from 2025 to 2030 is considered a decisive 'sprint period' that will determine whether Vietnam can lay the critical foundations for its economic future.

Economic Growth Targets and Anti-Middle Income Trap Strategy. The core economic strategy of the government centers on sustained high growth rates to avoid stagnation. Vietnam aims to maintain high and sustainable economic growth until 2045 to escape the middle-income trap, following the examples of Japan, South Korea, and China. Under Prime Minister Pham Minh Chinh's direction, Vietnam's government has set a GDP growth target of at least 8% for 2025, with plans to reach double-digit growth in the following years. Double-digit growth is essential for Vietnam to achieve the goals set by the 13th National Congress of the Communist Party of Vietnam—reaching upper middle-income status by 2030 and advancing towards high-income status by 2045.

Key reform pillars include administrative reforms, science and technology, and private sector development. The centerpiece of Mr. To Lam's vision is streamlining Vietnam's sprawling state apparatus. In a speech on 1 December 2024, he emphasized that Vietnam "can no longer delay" the "institutional revolution" and mandated that the overhaul be completed in the first quarter of 2025. This means merging several ministries, reducing the number of government bodies by 35–40%, and reorganizing 13 party agencies, among other tasks, within four months. Effective July 1, 2025, 63 provincial-level units will be merged into 34 larger entities—28 provinces and 6 centrally governed cities—while eliminating the district tier to create a streamlined two-level local government structure. This consolidation aims to cut bureaucracy, reduce administrative costs, improve public-service efficiency, and bolster regional economic integration

Another key pillar is the focus on science and technology. On January 13, 2025, Vietnam held its first National Conference on Science, Technology, Innovation, and Digital Transformation in over 60 years, attended by nearly one million delegates both in person and online. General Secretary To Lam presented a vision for Vietnam's scientific revolution, advocating for a "Resolution 57" that would act as a catalyst for liberating scientific thought and attracting top global talent, including overseas Vietnamese experts. Vietnam plans to increase budget funding for research and development to 2% of GDP by 2030, aligning with the Politburo's Resolution No.

A key reform pillar is Resolution 68 (NQ-68), which underscores the critical role of Vietnam's domestic private sector in driving productivity, industrial upgrading, job creation, and global integration. The Resolution acknowledges major challenges such as limited Access to Finance, technology, land, skilled labor, and weak institutional support—especially for small and informal firms. NQ-68 proposes appropriate measures to improve access to land, capital, and supply chain finance, and recognizes the need for a high-quality workforce. Overall, NQ-68 is a strategic document aligned with Vietnam's development diagnosis and policy direction and offers comprehensive and direct solutions to core issues.

Challenges and Risks

The "Era of National Rise" represents Vietnam's most ambitious development strategy since the Doi Moi reforms of 1986, combining rapid institutional restructuring with aggressive economic growth targets. Success would position Vietnam as a major economic power in Asia, while failure could result in prolonged middle-income status and missed development opportunities. The compressed timeline and scope of reforms make this a high-stakes gamble for Vietnam's future trajectory.

The ambitious timeline presents significant implementation challenges. The scale and compressed timeline of these reforms, which would affect around 100,000 civil servants, risk causing serious disruptions to government operations. The restructuring of administrative units carries implementation risks from a compressed reform timeline, with concerns that bureaucratic restructuring could disrupt governance and create decision-making paralysis.

Economic Vulnerabilities. Washington's push for reshoring production and the imposition of higher tariffs pose serious risks to Vietnam's export-led growth model. President Trump's "Reciprocal Tariff" policy, announced on April 2, 2025, represents one of the most significant shifts in U.S. trade policy in nearly a century. It establishes a baseline 10% tariff on all imports, supplemented by country-specific tariffs ranging from 10 to 50% for nations deemed to engage in "non-reciprocal trading practices" with the United States. These tariffs are determined based on each country's bilateral trade balance with the U.S. On July 2, 2025, President Trump unveiled a framework agreement under which the U.S. will impose a 20% tariff on most Vietnamese exports and a 40% tariff on goods transshipped through Vietnam, replacing the 46% announced on April 2. In return, Vietnam agreed to provide tariff-free access for

U.S. exports, including large-engine vehicles, signaling a shift toward greater market openness. Compounding these external shocks are domestic environmental vulnerabilities: Vietnam remains highly exposed to climate change and faces escalating urban pollution. In January 2025, Hanoi was ranked the most polluted city in the world, underscoring the intensifying trade-offs between rapid industrialization and environmental sustainability.

Growth versus Political Control. The Communist Party of Vietnam (CPV) has managed to maintain political stability and ideological control even as it increasingly embraces market-based economic reforms. This balancing act is accomplished through strategic planning, strong control over key state-owned enterprises (SOEs), and the integration of Party leadership across both state and government institutions. While the share of SOEs in the economy has declined, they continue to dominate critical sectors such as energy, telecommunications, and finance, with Party members often occupying top leadership positions. Additionally, ideological management remains a priority, with market reforms framed as means to strengthen socialism rather than as ideological deviation. The Party also reinforces its authority through regulatory oversight and anti-corruption campaigns, which, while aimed at improving governance, also serve to maintain political dominance.

However, this system generates an inherent tension between the autonomy and competition necessary for a thriving private sector and the Party's centralized control and ideological coherence. Private firms often operate in an uncertain environment where they may be vulnerable to arbitrary decisions and unequal treatment. The emergence of a wealthy entrepreneurial class can be perceived as contradicting socialist ideals, further exacerbating this tension. Nevertheless, under certain conditions, this friction need not be destructive; instead, it can foster a collaborative relationship that promotes both growth and political stability.

To make this relationship productive, the Party must commit to a consistent and transparent legal framework that ensures fair competition across all sectors—state-owned, private, and foreign. Key reforms include equal access to land, capital, and skilled labor, strong protection of property and contractual rights, and predictable policymaking. These measures would reduce uncertainty and build investor confidence. Complementary to this, a shift in the administrative mindset from control to facilitation is essential. Streamlining bureaucratic procedures, leveraging digital platforms, and combatting corruption would significantly improve the business environment and reduce informal costs borne disproportionately by private firms.

Mutual recognition of shared goals between the Party and the private sector is also crucial. The CPV's acknowledgment of the private sector as a central pillar of the economy must be translated into consistent policy actions that eliminate bias and encourage private sector participation in strategic national initiatives. At the same time, the private sector must fulfill its social responsibilities—not just through philanthropy, but through sustainable business practices that raise labor standards and contribute to community development. This alignment would strengthen the legitimacy of market-oriented growth within the broader socialist framework.

Finally, fostering open communication channels between policymakers and the business community is key to ensuring responsiveness and mutual understanding. Structured dialogue and feedback mechanisms can help fine-tune policies, resolve issues proactively, and align private enterprise with national objectives. Investment in human capital, particularly through skills development and support for research and innovation, will further enable the private sector to contribute meaningfully to economic transformation. Vietnam's continued success under the "Era of National Rise" will depend heavily on its ability to sustain this delicate yet potentially synergistic balance between Party control and private sector dynamism.

Annex 1: Escaping the Middle-Income Trap

This annex explains the assumptions used in this chapter to model a scenario in which Vietnam could escape the middle-income trap within the next 25 years. The calculations presented here are based on data available as of January 25, 2025. If more recent data become available after this date, the calculations will need to be updated accordingly.

We follow the World Bank (WB) methodology for classifying countries based on Gross National Income (GNI) per capita. According to the World Bank's classification for the 2025 fiscal year (July 1, 2024—July 1, 2025), a country is considered upper middle-income if its 2023 per capita GNI falls between $4516 and $14,005.[1] Vietnam's per capita GNI in 2023 was $4110, placing it in the lower middle-income category.

[1] See https://datahelpdesk.worldbank.org/knowledgebase/articles/906519-world-bank-country-and-lending-groups

The World Bank's classification thresholds are set in absolute real terms and updated over time using the Special Drawing Rights (SDR) deflator, which is calculated as a weighted average of the GDP deflators of Japan, the UK, the US, and the Euro Area (Fantom & Serajuddin, 2016; World Bank, 2025). However, for projection purposes, using the SDR deflator presents several challenges, as it requires forecasting the economic trajectories of multiple countries, involving numerous assumptions. Additionally, because GNI per capita and these thresholds are expressed in US dollars, it is unclear whether the SDR deflator is the most appropriate choice for projections. Therefore, following the recommendation of Fantom and Serajuddin (2016), we use the US GDP deflator instead. The projected US GDP deflator for 2024–2029 follows the IMF's World Economic Outlook (International Monetary Fund, 2024) and is shown in the second column of Table 3.3. The thresholds for the upper middle-income category are projected from 2024 onward using this US GDP deflator and are presented in columns 4 and 5 of Table 3.3.

Next, we project Vietnam's GNI per capita. Under the reform scenario outlined in this chapter, the most optimistic GDP growth projections are shown in column 5 of Table 3.3. These projections assume Vietnam successfully implements the necessary reforms discussed in this book and overcomes the middle-income trap. Population growth rates for Vietnam from 2024 to 2050 (column 6) are based on the World Population Prospects 2022, published by the United Nations Population Division (2022) under the Medium Fertility Variant 2022–2100. Vietnam's per capita GNI growth rates (column 7) are derived from columns 5 and 6.[2]

We assume that GDP and GNI grow at the same rate, meaning there are no significant changes in net factor income from abroad, which is the primary difference between GDP and GNI. Additionally, we assume that the exchange rate between the US dollar and the Vietnamese dong remains stable, with no real appreciation or depreciation of the USD/VND over the period.

Based on these assumptions, we calculate Vietnam's projected GNI per capita in US dollars (column 8) and compare it with the upper middle-income range in columns 2 and 3. The results indicate that, under these conditions, Vietnam will reach upper middle-income status by 2026 and high-income status by 2047, roughly in line with official projections.

[2] Using the formula $(1 + G)/(1 + n)$ where G is the growth rate of GDP and n is the growth rate of population.

Table 3.3 Calculation of Vietnam's crossing the high-income threshold

(1)	*(2)*	*(3)*	*(4)*	*(5)*	*(6)*	*(7)*	*(8)*	*(9)*
Year	*US GDP deflator (%)*	*Upper MI lower bound (USD)*	*Upper MI upper bound (USD)*	*VN GDP growth rate (%)*	*VN pop. growth (%)*	*VN GNI per capita growth rate (%)*	*VN GNI per capita (USD)*	*Note*
2023	3.6	4516	14,005				4110	Actual
2024	2.4	4624	14,340	6.7	0.646		4357	Projected
2025	1.8	4708	14,600	6.7	0.609	6.1	4621	"
2026	1.9	4795	14,871	6.9	0.575	6.3	4911	"
2027	1.8	4883	15,144	7.0	0.544	6.5	5228	"
2028	1.8	4973	15,422	7.1	0.513	6.6	5572	"
2029	1.8	5064	15,705	7.2	0.482	6.7	5943	"
2030	1.8	5155	15,987	7.5	0.453	7.0	6357	"
2031	1.8	5248	16,275	7.5	0.422	7.1	6807	"
2032	1.8	5342	16,568	7.6	0.393	7.2	7295	"
2033	1.8	5439	16,866	7.6	0.367	7.2	7818	"
2034	1.8	5537	17,170	7.7	0.340	7.4	8395	"
2035	1.8	5636	17,479	7.8	0.314	7.5	9023	"
2036	1.8	5738	17,794	7.9	0.289	7.6	9706	"
2037	1.8	5841	18,114	7.9	0.267	7.6	10,442	"
2038	1.8	5946	18,440	7.8	0.244	7.6	11,234	"
2039	1.8	6053	18,772	7.9	0.223	7.7	12,097	"
2040	1.8	6162	19,110	7.9	0.203	7.7	13,026	"
2041	1.8	6273	19,454	8.0	0.182	7.8	14,040	"
2042	1.8	6386	19,804	8.1	0.162	7.9	15,148	"

(continued)

Table 3.3 (continued)

(1)	(2)	(3)	(4)	(5)	(6)	(7)	(8)	(9)
Year	*US GDP deflator (%)*	*Upper MI lower bound (USD)*	*Upper MI upper bound (USD)*	*VN GDP growth rate (%)*	*VN pop. growth (%)*	*VN GNI per capita growth rate (%)*	*VN GNI per capita (USD)*	*Note*
2043	1.8	6501	20,160	8.0	0.145	7.9	16,343	"
2044	1.8	6618	20,523	8.0	0.130	7.9	17,632	"
2045	1.8	6737	20,893	8.0	0.115	7.9	19,024	"
2046	1.8	6858	21,269	8.1	0.099	8.0	20,544	"
2047	1.8	6982	21,651	8.1	0.082	8.0	22,186	"
2048	1.8	7107	22,041	8.1	0.066	8.0	23,960	"
2049	1.8	7235	22,438	8.2	0.048	8.1	25,904	"
2050	1.8	7365	22,842	8.2	0.029	8.1	28,011	"

Source Author's calculation based on assumptions listed above

References

Auty, R. M. (1994). Industrial policy reform in six large newly industrializing countries: The resource curse thesis. *World Development*, *22*(1), 11–26.

Barbier, E. B. (2005). *Natural resources and economic development*. Cambridge University Press.

Baumol, W. J. (1967). Macroeconomics of unbalanced growth: The anatomy of urban crisis. *American Economic Review*, *57*(3), 415–426.

Baumol, W. J., & Bowen, W. G. (1965). On the performing arts: The anatomy of their economic problems. *American Economic Review*, *55*(1/2), 495–502.

Corden, W. M. (1984). Booming sector and Dutch disease economics: Survey and consolidation. *Oxford Economic Papers*, *36*(3), 359–380.

Corden, W. M., & Neary, J. P. (1982). Booming sector and deindustrialization in a small open economy. *Economic Journal*, *92*(368), 825–848.

Dinh, H. T. (2017). *Jobs, industrialization, and globalization*. OCP Policy Center. https://www.policycenter.ma/publications/jobs-industrialization-and-globalization

Dinh, H. T., & Dinh, R. (2016). Managing natural resources for growth and prosperity in low-income countries. *OCP Policy Center Policy Paper*, *16*(01).

Fantom, N., & Serajuddin, U. (2016). *The World Bank's classification of countries by income* (World Bank Policy Research Working Paper No. 7528). World Bank.

Furtado, C. (1957). O desenvolvimento econômico e suas ilusões. *O Observador Econômico E Financeiro*, *256*, 32–38.

Gelb, A. H. (1988). *Oil windfalls: Blessing or curse?* Oxford University Press.

International Monetary Fund. (2024). *World economic outlook: Policy pivot, rising threats*.

Lee, R., & Mason, A. (2014). Is low fertility really a problem? Population aging, dependency, and consumption. *Science*, *346*(6206), 229–234.

Mill, J. S. (1848). Principles of political economy with some of their applications. *Social Philosophy*, *1*, 1–329.

Sachs, J. D., & Warner, A. M. (1995). *Natural resource abundance and economic growth* (NBER Working Paper No. 5398). National Bureau of Economic Research.

Seers, D. (1964). The mechanism of an open petroleum economy. *Social and Economic Studies*, *13*(2), 233–242.

United Nations, Department of Economic and Social Affairs, Population Division. (2022). *World population prospects 2022: Summary of results*. United Nations. https://www.un.org/development/desa/pd/content/World-Population-Prospects-2022

van Wijnbergen, S. J. G. (1984). The Dutch disease: A disease after all? *Economic Journal*, *94*(373), 41–55.

World Bank. (2024a). *World Bank East Asia and the pacific economic update, October 2024: Jobs and technology*. World Bank. http://hdl.handle.net/10986/41998

World Bank. (2024b). *World development indicators*. https://databank.worldbank.org/source/world-development-indicators

World Bank. (2024c). *Vietnam 2045: Trading up in a changing world—Pathways to a high-income future*. http://hdl.handle.net/10986/42505

World Bank. (2025). *How does the world bank classify countries?* https://datahelpdesk.worldbank.org/knowledgebase/articles/378834-how-does-the-world-bank-classify-countries

PART II

Trade and Industrial Upgrading

CHAPTER 4

Export Opportunities

Introduction

Over the past decades, Vietnam's export composition in the global market has undergone significant changes (Fig. 4.1). Textiles and electronics have emerged as the leading export sectors, followed by agriculture and machinery. Vehicle exports have remained weak.

In successful developing economies, structural transformation has facilitated growth in value-added sectors while modern industries emerged alongside sustained growth in traditional, labor-intensive sectors. These traditional sectors continued generating substantial employment opportunities for unskilled workers. While the overall share of unskilled workers in production and employment declined, their absolute numbers increased—an important feature of the development process that keeps the labor force employed, as demonstrated in Korea between 1964 and 1981 (Dinh et al., 2021, p. 50).

Vietnam could adopt a similar approach by focusing on expanding labor-intensive industries while simultaneously fostering new industry development through integrating Vietnamese firms into productive clusters and improving access to locally produced components.

Contributed by Hinh T. Dinh

H. T. Dinh, H. T. Nguyen, *Vietnam's Economic Leap*,
https://doi.org/10.1007/978-3-032-08904-5_4

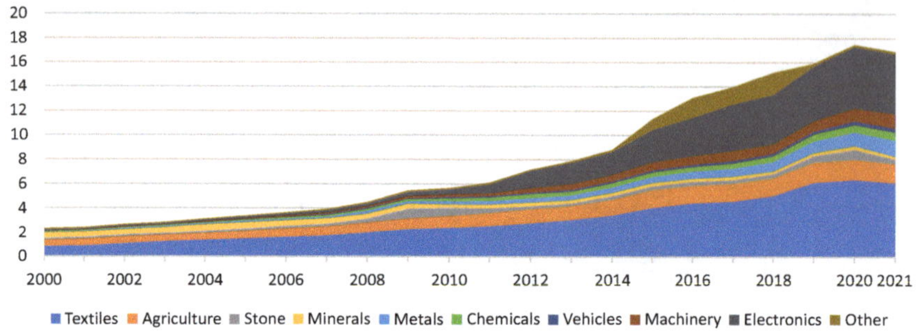

Fig. 4.1 Vietnam's global market share (%), 2000–2021. *Source* Data from the Growth Lab at Harvard University. The Atlas of Economic Complexity. http://www.Atlas.Cid.Harvard.Edu. Accessed January 17 2024

Strategic Priorities for Export Development

Vietnam's traditional labor-intensive industries struggle to compete globally against new, low-wage entrants. However, these industries have a long export history and are well-established in Vietnam. In the short to medium term, given the urgent need to absorb the unemployed workforce, policymakers should prioritize these industries as a means of rapid and large-scale job creation. Addressing public-sector obstacles and market failures that hinder their expansion is essential.

Within these industries, prioritizing products with a high Product Complexity Index (PCI)[1] will yield greater value than focusing on lower PCI subsectors such as agriculture and seafood. While these industries will remain crucial for employment, they are unlikely to generate high enough wages to elevate Vietnam to upper-middle-income status.

[1] According to the Economic Complexity Approach (Hausmann et al., 2014) and the Growth Lab website (https://atlas.cid.harvard.edu/explore), the Product Complexity Index (PCI) ranks products based on the diversity and sophistication of the productive know-how required for their production. PCI is calculated by considering how many other countries can produce a given product and the economic complexity of those countries. The most complex products—those that only a few highly complex economies can produce—include advanced machinery, electronics, and chemicals. In contrast, the least complex products—those that nearly all countries can produce—include raw materials and simple agricultural goods.

A comprehensive list of products with varying PCI levels is presented in the chapter annex. Given the urgency of large-scale job creation, policy-makers should prioritize scaling existing labor-intensive industries where Vietnam has a proven track record. In the short to medium term, a trade-off exists between technological complexity and the ability to absorb low-skilled workers.

Traditional exports ("Classics") account for over two-thirds of Vietnam's total exports, consisting mainly of low-wage, labor-intensive light industries. Given Vietnam's established comparative advantage in these sectors—and until new, high-PCI industries can absorb additional workers—policymakers should proactively preserve their markets by leveraging existing resources and capabilities. This strategy is more efficient and less risky than attempting to build entirely new industries from scratch.

Challenges of Vietnam's Exports

Vietnam has successfully diversified its exports, broadening its product range to accelerate growth and establish new trade partnerships. However, as shown in the previous chapters, its production structure has not significantly benefited from technology-intensive foreign direct investment (FDI).

The Value-Added Challenge. The primary challenge for Vietnam in transitioning to high-income status is not the composition of its exports but rather the value-added content. Most exports are produced by foreign enterprises operating under FDI laws, relying heavily on imported raw materials and intermediate goods while utilizing domestic labor for low-value-added assembly tasks. Domestic enterprises remain isolated from foreign-owned firms, primarily producing for the domestic market with low technology and relying on informal labor. This structural duality has prevented deeper integration of technology and competition into domestic enterprises.

The Need for Diversification. Diversification into new, highly complex products is essential for Vietnam's sustainable income growth. To date, its export expansion has been heavily concentrated in low- and moderate-complexity products, leaving the economy vulnerable to commodity price fluctuations.

Despite these challenges, Vietnam's performance has not been poor. According to the Growth Lab, Vietnam ranked 93rd out of 133 economies in terms of income in 2021, but it stood at 61st in the Economic Complexity Index (ECI)—a much stronger showing. The ECI measures a country's knowledge base through the sophistication of its exported products.

As of 2021, Vietnam had added 41 new products since 2006, which contributed $1486 to income per capita that year. By comparison, China added 20 new products and South Korea 19, with corresponding income per capita contributions of $32 and $680, respectively.

In addition to product diversification, Vietnam also needs to diversify its export markets, which have become increasingly concentrated. In 2021, just three countries—the United States (27%), China (20%), and South Korea (6%)—accounted for over half of Vietnam's total exports. This high degree of market concentration exposes the country to external risks, such as protectionist policies from major trading partners.

The concentration trend is evident in the declining shares of traditional partners: Japan's share in Vietnam's exports declined from 32% in 1995 to 5.6% in 2021. In Europe, Germany and France saw their shares drop from 10% and 5% to 3% and 1%, respectively, over the same period.

Workforce utilization in the era of Industry 4.0. While Vietnam has a young workforce, it must modernize its institutions, legal framework, and regulations to upgrade its technological capacity.

Identification of Export Opportunities

This chapter identifies export opportunities and sectors in which Vietnam could expand production over the next decade, leveraging its comparative advantages to address the challenges outlined above. The analysis draws on a database developed by the Growth Lab at Harvard University, based on COMTRADE merchandise trade data. Trade flows are classified under the 4-digit 1992 Harmonized System (HS) and cover the period 2001–2021 (Growth Lab at Harvard University, accessed June 2024).

Analytical Framework: Revealed Comparative Advantage. For existing products, the concept of revealed comparative advantage (RCA) helps identify industries where increased production could accelerate industrialization. This method is based on a country's trade data and can be calculated using the Balassa index (Balassa, 1965). The Balassa index measures a country's relative advantage or disadvantage in exporting a commodity by comparing its export patterns with those of other countries. RCA is defined as:

$$\mathrm{RCA}_{ij} = \frac{\frac{E_{ij}}{\sum_{k\in n} E_{ik}}}{\frac{\sum_{l\in w} E_{lj}}{\sum_{l\in w}\sum_{k\in n} E_{lk}}}$$

E_{ij} refers to exports of commodity j by country i, w is the set of countries being compared, and n is the set of all commodities. The RCA index measures a country's export performance in a particular commodity relative to its overall export performance, compared to the world's export performance in that commodity relative to total world exports. A country has an RCA in commodity j if the RCA is greater than 1 and a comparative disadvantage in commodity j if the RCA is less than 1.

Alternative Analytical Approach. Another approach that utilizes trade data involves carefully analyzing a country's imports to identify sectors that require only small investments, have limited economies of scale, and could benefit from domestic manufacturing. In this case, imports serve as a proxy for domestic demand, raising the question of whether domestic supply can produce competitive products. This approach is discussed in the next chapter.

Export Classification and Performance Analysis

We divide the period from 2001 to 2021 into three subperiods: 2001–2005, 2005–2015, and 2016–2021. Exports are classified into four groups: **Classics, Emerging Champions, Disappearing Exports,** and **Marginal Exports** (Table 4.1).

- **Classics** are Vietnam's traditional exports, in which the country has maintained a revealed comparative advantage (RCA) since 2001.
- **Emerging Champions** are exports that Vietnam did not have before 2006 but in which it has gained an RCA in recent years.

Table 4.1 Profile of Vietnam's exports, 2001–2021

	RCA ≥ 1	*RCA ≥ 1*	*RCA ≥ 1*	*Average PCI*	*Average PCI*	*Weighted average PCI*	*Weighted average PCI*	*Avegage exports value (mil USD)*	*Average exports value (mil USD)*	*Average exports share (%)*	*Average exports share (%)*
	2001–2005	*2006–2015*	*2016–2021*	*2001–2005*	*2016–2021*	*2001–2005*	*2016–2021*	*2001–2005*	*2016–2021*	*2001–2005*	*2016–2021*
Classics	Yes	Yes	Yes	−1.09	−0.93	−1.26	−0.88	12,641	100,314	58.1	36.5
Emerging champions	No	Yes/No	Yes	0.02	0.02	0.38	0.69	972	123,972	4.3	42.5
Disappearing exports	Yes	Yes/No	No	−0.52	−0.39	−1.78	−0.06	6321	16,806	28.4	6.2
Marginal (greater than $25 million)	No	No	No	0.36	0.31	0.23	0.48	1368	31,621	6.2	10.4
Marginal (less than $25 million)	No	No	No	0.20	0.18	−0.11	0.19	449	2,908	2.2	1.0
Total merchandise exports				0.00	0.02	−1.21	0.02	21,752	275,621	99.2	96.6

Source Author' calculations based on data from Growth Lab at Harvard University, June 2024. *Note* PCI stands for product complexity index

- **Disappearing Exports** refer to products that Vietnam used to export but in which it has since become less competitive.
- **Marginal Exports** are those in which the country has never had an RCA

Classics: The Foundation of Vietnam's Exports

Vietnam had 116 products classified as **Classics**, accounting for about 36% of total exports between 2016 and 2021 (Annex Table 4.2). The composition includes:

- 37 agricultural and wood products
- 2 minerals
- 4 chemical and plastic products
- 55 textiles
- 3 stone and glass products
- 2 metals
- 7 machinery products
- 4 electronics
- 2 transport vehicles

Footwear was the top export in this category during 2016–2021, accounting for approximately 3% of total exports.

Complexity and Performance Trends. Due to Vietnam's reliance on natural resources, the weighted average Product Complexity Index (PDI) for Classics changed slowly over the years, rising from approximately −1.26 in 2001–2005 to −0.88 in 2016–2021. The PCI measures the sophistication of know-how required to produce a product, based on the diversity of countries that manufacture it and the uniqueness of other products they produce. A higher PCI indicates that a product requires more sophisticated knowledge and is produced by fewer countries.

Vietnam's **Classics** exports declined as a share of total exports, dropping from 58% in 2001–2005 to 36% in 2016–2021. These exports are concentrated in agriculture and textiles:

- The 37 agricultural Classics, which accounted for 9% of exports in 2016–2021, saw their share decrease from 20% in 2001–2005

- The top three agricultural products—coffee, cashews and coconuts, and rice—each made up about 1% of total exports
- Textiles and furniture constituted the largest Classics category, representing 22% of exports in 2016–2021, down from 32% in 2001–2005
- The top three products in this category were textile footwear, furniture, and leather footwear

Structural Challenges and Opportunities. **Classics** mainly comprise primary and minimally processed products rather than technologically advanced goods. Between 2016 and 2021, their average PCI was −0.93, and the weighted average PCI was −0.88. Major exports in this category have among the lowest PCIs, including rice (−1.75), coffee (−1.62), textile footwear (−0.59), and sweaters (−1.39). Meanwhile, the share of exports with higher PCIs, such as electric motors and generators (0.86 PCI) or electronic printed circuits (0.93 PCI), hardly increased or even declined.

Vietnam's **Classics** face a structural challenge: exports with large market shares tend to have low PCIs, while those with higher PCIs are losing their market share. This suggests that Vietnam's labor-intensive Classics industries are struggling to compete with new, low-wage entrants in the global market. Given that these are the industries in which Vietnamese firms have extensive export experience, this trend is concerning.

Policy Recommendations for Classics. In the short to medium term, given the need to absorb a large number of young and semi-skilled workers, policymakers should treat **Classics as "low-hanging fruit"**—a potential source of rapid, large-scale job creation. Efforts should focus on removing public sector obstacles and addressing market failures that hinder their expansion.

Among **Classics**, priority should be given to sectors with higher PCIs, such as electronics and motorcycle parts, as they are likely to yield better economic outcomes and offer higher wages than lower PCI sectors like agriculture and seafood. However, even at best, Classics will serve primarily as a source of employment, not as a driver of wage growth significant enough to transition Vietnam to a high-income country.

Emerging Champions: The Growth Engine

Between 2001 and 2021, about 101 products emerged as new exports in which Vietnam gained an RCA—the **Emerging Champions**. Their export value increased more than 127-fold, from an annual average of $972 million (2001–2005) to $123.9 billion (2016–2021), and their share of total exports jumped from 4.3 to 43% (Annex Table 4.3).

Electronics: The Dominant Force. The largest driver of this growth was electronics, whose exports surged from $313 million (1.4% of exports) in 2001–2005 to $96.8 billion (34% of exports) in 2016–2021. Three products dominated this category:

- Transmission apparatus for radio, telephone, and TV ($39 billion annual average, 2016–2021)
- Telephones ($20 billion annual average)
- Electronic integrated circuits ($20 billion annual average)

Together, these three products accounted for 28% of Vietnam's exports in 2016–2021. The average PCI of **Emerging Champions** is 0.02, much higher than that of Classics, and their weighted average PCI was 0.69. The rapid expansion of Emerging Champions bodes well for foreign exchange earnings and job creation in Vietnam.

Policy Recommendations for Emerging Champions. Given their critical importance for Vietnam's economic transformation, **Emerging Champions** should receive the highest policy priority. Policymakers should focus on creating an enabling environment that sustains their growth momentum while addressing structural weaknesses. Key interventions should include strengthening linkages between foreign-invested enterprises and domestic suppliers to increase local content and value addition. This requires targeted programs to upgrade domestic firms' technological capabilities, quality standards, and production capacity to meet international requirements. Additionally, authorities should invest in specialized infrastructure, including industrial parks with advanced telecommunications and logistics capabilities, to support continued expansion in electronics and other high-tech sectors. Skills development programs aligned with Industry 4.0

requirements are essential to ensure Vietnam's workforce can support increasingly sophisticated production processes. Finally, diversifying export markets for these products will reduce concentration risks and enhance resilience against external shocks, particularly given the current heavy reliance on the US, China, and South Korea as primary destinations.

Disappearing Exports: Understanding the Decline

Vietnam had 151 products classified as **Disappearing Exports**, which accounted for $16.8 billion in exports (6% of total) in 2016–2021, a significant decline from their $6.3 billion value (28% of total exports) in 2001–2005 (Annex Table 4.4).

These include vegetables, foodstuffs, wood, minerals, chemicals, plastics, textiles, furniture, metals, machinery, electronics, and transport vehicles. The largest product in this category was computers (2% of exports). Many of these are labor-intensive, and restarting production in these industries may be more feasible than investing in entirely new sectors.

Policy Implications. Authorities should engage with the private sector to assess the reasons behind the decline of these exports and explore policies to reignite their competitiveness. This approach may be more promising than entering completely new sectors.

Marginal Exports: Untapped Potential

Vietnam's **Marginal Exports** include 874 HS 4-digit products, in which it has never had an RCA since 2001. Among them, 204 products had export values exceeding $25 million each (Marginal 1 group). Marginal 1 exports grew from $1.3 billion (6% of exports) in 2001–2005 to $31.6 billion (10.4% of exports) in 2016–2021 (Annex Table 4.5).

While Vietnam has not yet developed a comparative advantage in these products, policymakers should assess their potential for job creation and investigate the factors limiting their expansion.

Potential for Expansion and Scaling Up

Analysis of Production Capacity. Vietnam's **Classics** have relatively low PCIs but are within a feasible production range, suggesting room for policy-driven improvements. The **Emerging Champions** have higher PCIs and significant export growth, while **Marginal Exports** remain underdeveloped.

Most of Vietnam's Classic products have a relatively low PCI range, from an average of −2.31 (natural rubber) in 2016–2021 to 0.93 (electronic printed circuits), with distances between 0.59 and 0.82. This suggests that the country has the capacity to produce these goods. With the right policies, Vietnam could significantly increase the PCI of its Classics products.

Understanding Market Proximity. Emerging Products had a weighted average PCI of 0.69 from 2016 to 2021, ranging from −1.95 (cereal residues) to 1.63 (world glass), with distances between 0.65 (vulcanized rubber) and 0.81 (tar distilled from coal or lignite).

Distance (ranging from 0 to 1) measures how far Vietnam's exports travel for specific products, capturing the country's ability to enter new markets. A shorter distance—indicating a "nearby" product—suggests that entering these markets may be easier because Vietnam has already developed the necessary capacities to produce similar products.

Investigating Marginal Products. Policymakers should investigate why certain products remain in the Marginal category. At one point, despite limited capacities, Vietnam successfully exported a range of Marginal products. This is evident from the country's incumbent exports, which demonstrate that even limited capacities can be leveraged to develop new products.

New Production Opportunities. Based on PCI and distance data in 2021, Harvard University's Growth Lab recommended 50 products as new production opportunities for Vietnam (Annex Table 4.6). Authorities and entrepreneurs should analyze constraints and policy interventions needed to support these industries.

Annex 1: List of Vietnam's Classics, Emerging Champions, Disappearing, and Marginal Exports

See Tables 4.2, 4.3, 4.4, 4.5 and 4.6.

Table 4.2 Vietnam's classics—traditional exports with RCA>= 1 from 2001 to 2021

HS code	*Name*	*PCI 2001–2005*	*PCI 2016–2021*	*Average exports value 2001–2005 (USD mill)*	*Average exports value 2016–2021 (USD mill)*	*Average exports share 2001–2005 (%)*	*Average exports share 2016–2021 (%)*
Vegetable, foodstuffs and wood							
4202	Trunks or cases	−0.68	−0.50	306.37	3257.66	1.43	1.28
901	Coffee	−2.05	−1.62	483.91	2648.49	2.19	1.09
801	Cashew nuts and coconuts	−2.35	−2.25	237.87	2763.53	1.04	1.03
1006	Rice	−1.45	−1.75	785.89	2451.70	3.59	0.92
304	Fish fillets	−1.38	−1.36	229.45	2229.45	0.98	0.85
306	Crustaceans	−1.86	−1.90	957.16	1870.61	4.64	0.70
4401	Fuel wood	−0.58	−0.35	71.99	1821.14	0.32	0.64
1605	Prepared aquatic invertibrates	−1.42	−1.74	225.41	1682.54	1.04	0.61
904	Pepper	−1.65	−1.90	105.59	848.62	0.50	0.35
810	Other fresh fruit	−1.04	−1.55	54.40	935.98	0.28	0.34
1604	Prepared or preserved fish	−1.59	−1.52	57.04	582.01	0.27	0.21
1108	Starches	−0.31	−0.45	45.08	451.54	0.20	0.16
303	Frozen fish, excluding fillets	−1.51	−1.67	60.51	371.68	0.30	0.14
2008	Fruits and nuts, otherwise prepared	−1.08	−1.18	31.19	443.58	0.15	0.14
307	Molluscs	−1.83	−1.76	262.84	318.83	1.29	0.13

(continued)

Table 4.2 (continued)

HS code	*Name*	*PCI 2001–2005*	*PCI 2016–2021*	*Average exports value 2001–2005 (USD mill)*	*Average exports value 2016–2021 (USD mill)*	*Average exports share 2001–2005 (%)*	*Average exports share 2016–2021 (%)*
714	Tubers	−1.99	−2.00	50.43	237.96	0.23	0.10
1902	Pasta	−1.10	−1.16	44.91	238.44	0.21	0.08
4602	Basketwork	−2.05	−1.56	72.89	251.65	0.34	0.08
902	Tea	−1.87	−2.02	68.01	182.47	0.33	0.07
305	Preserved fish	−1.81	−1.52	43.35	194.93	0.23	0.07
4820	Notebooks	−0.98	−0.59	11.93	147.56	0.06	0.05
4203	Leather apparel	−0.94	−0.78	25.83	136.82	0.12	0.05
4421	Other articles of wood	−0.60	−0.37	24.81	138.68	0.12	0.05
906	Cinnamon	−1.37	−1.33	5.94	156.94	0.03	0.05
4419	Wooden kitchenware	−0.90	−0.39	16.49	69.75	0.08	0.03
409	Honey	−0.86	−1.00	14.47	67.28	0.07	0.02
4402	Wood charcoal	−1.42	−1.56	2.35	66.00	0.01	0.02
4201	Saddlery and harnesses	−0.08	0.00	13.64	50.34	0.06	0.01
4420	Wood marquetry, ornaments, etc.	−1.81	−0.84	15.98	41.52	0.08	0.01
909	Anise, fennel, etc.	−1.46	−1.30	6.25	44.60	0.03	0.01
4103	Other raw hides and skins	−1.83	−2.04	4.18	24.77	0.02	0.01
1106	Flour of dried legumes	−1.73	−1.69	0.82	19.56	0.00	0.01
4405	Wood wool or flour	−0.29	−0.01	0.86	16.84	0.00	0.01

(continued)

Table 4.2 (continued)

HS code	*Name*	*PCI 2001–2005*	*PCI 2016–2021*	*Average exports value 2001–2005 (USD mill)*	*Average exports value 2016–2021 (USD mill)*	*Average exports share 2001–2005 (%)*	*Average exports share 2016–2021 (%)*
4601	Products of plaiting materials	−1.77	−1.61	14.54	13.87	0.07	0.01
1401	Vegetable materials used for plaiting	−1.30	−1.21	7.77	10.26	0.04	0.00
1521	Vegetable waxes and beeswax	−1.63	−1.83	0.62	8.18	0.00	0.00
508	Coral and shells	−1.41	−1.40	2.66	3.73	0.01	0.00
Mineral							
2521	Limstone	−0.07	−0.75	4.21	74.86	0.02	0.03
2614	Titanium ore	−0.63	−1.93	23.07	73.96	0.10	0.02
Chemicals and plastics							
3406	Candles	−0.33	0.27	11.42	341.55	0.05	0.10
3805	Turpentines	−0.31	−0.49	0.38	25.94	0.00	0.01
4001	Natural rubber	−2.59	−2.31	270.57	990.48	1.22	0.37
4013	Rubber inner tubes	−0.58	−0.48	10.42	76.63	0.05	0.03
Textiles and furniture							
6404	Textile footwear	−1.21	−0.59	581.50	8877.58	2.74	3.26
9403	Other furniture and parts	0.09	0.40	607.52	6470.21	2.57	2.20
6403	Leather footwear	−1.02	−0.62	1371.79	5607.89	6.19	2.11
6110	Sweaters, pullovers, sweatshirts etc., knit	−1.67	−1.39	336.00	3551.34	1.47	1.29
6402	Other footwear of rubber or plastics	−1.19	−1.24	683.01	3382.46	3.37	1.28

(continued)

Table 4.2 (continued)

HS code	*Name*	*PCI 2001–2005*	*PCI 2016–2021*	*Average exports value 2001–2005 (USD mill)*	*Average exports value 2016–2021 (USD mill)*	*Average exports share 2001–2005 (%)*	*Average exports share 2016–2021 (%)*
9401	Seats	−0.01	0.11	237.33	3533.17	1.04	1.10
6204	Women's suits and pants	−1.26	−1.29	419.99	2814.35	1.79	1.06
6203	Men's suits and pants	−1.45	−1.31	379.17	2528.82	1.74	0.96
6104	Women's suits, knit	−1.76	−1.43	131.77	2492.43	0.57	0.89
5205	Cotton yarn of > 85%	−1.56	−1.75	25.38	2297.23	0.12	0.83
6109	T-shirts, knit	−1.74	−1.47	98.05	1865.68	0.45	0.67
6201	Men's overcoats, not knit	−1.46	−1.18	291.80	1747.84	1.41	0.65
6202	Womens overcoats, not knit	−1.16	−0.92	235.11	1567.80	1.14	0.59
6210	Garments made of textile felts and nonwoven fabric	−1.24	−1.06	68.90	1145.93	0.30	0.42
6211	Activewear	−1.51	−1.16	163.89	939.63	0.82	0.35
6205	Men's shirts	−1.67	−1.31	216.45	889.42	1.00	0.35
6105	Men's shirts, knit	−1.98	−1.53	97.57	803.71	0.42	0.32
6103	Men's suits, knit	−1.86	−1.53	64.04	819.62	0.29	0.28
6307	Other made up articles	−0.86	−1.08	30.48	778.61	0.13	0.27
6212	Brassieres	−1.03	−1.15	83.70	775.12	0.41	0.26
6206	Women's shirts	−1.52	−1.21	45.61	607.36	0.21	0.24
6406	Parts of footwear	−0.26	−0.77	26.51	609.47	0.13	0.23

(continued)

Table 4.2 (continued)

HS code	*Name*	*PCI 2001–2005*	*PCI 2016–2021*	*Average exports value 2001–2005 (USD mill)*	*Average exports value 2016–2021 (USD mill)*	*Average exports share 2001–2005 (%)*	*Average exports share 2016–2021 (%)*
6108	Women's undergarments, knit	−1.31	−1.55	58.17	638.29	0.26	0.22
6107	Men's undergarments, knit	−1.40	−1.52	22.22	548.23	0.11	0.20
6305	Bags for packing goods	−1.63	−1.81	40.14	433.25	0.18	0.15
6114	Other garments, knit	−1.62	−1.38	30.68	409.50	0.13	0.15
6102	Women's overcoats, knit	−1.73	−1.19	61.93	354.64	0.27	0.13
5206	Cotton yarn of < 85%	−1.33	−0.86	15.82	363.54	0.07	0.13
6106	Women's shirts, knit	−1.73	−1.34	63.31	318.27	0.27	0.13
6505	Hats, knit	−1.38	−1.38	63.20	341.76	0.27	0.12
6112	Activewear, knit	−1.21	−0.84	31.51	335.85	0.15	0.12
6101	Men's overcoats, knit	−1.70	−1.30	54.09	280.63	0.23	0.10
5509	Yarn of synthetic staple fibers, not for retail sale	−0.70	−0.45	58.55	263.90	0.27	0.10
6111	Babies' garments, knit	−1.76	−1.70	30.42	287.53	0.14	0.10
6116	Gloves, knit	−1.14	−0.97	10.39	226.89	0.05	0.08
6405	Other footwear	−1.18	−0.72	101.45	191.55	0.46	0.07
5608	Nets	−1.15	−0.84	22.00	132.00	0.10	0.05
6216	Gloves	−1.64	−1.16	17.85	136.20	0.09	0.05

(continued)

Table 4.2 (continued)

HS code	*Name*	*PCI 2001–2005*	*PCI 2016–2021*	*Average exports value 2001–2005 (USD mill)*	*Average exports value 2016–2021 (USD mill)*	*Average exports share 2001–2005 (%)*	*Average exports share 2016–2021 (%)*
6304	Other furnishing articles	−1.13	−1.09	14.40	108.58	0.06	0.04
6306	Tents, tarpaulins, etc.	−0.93	−0.67	21.48	111.80	0.10	0.04
6209	Babies' garments	−1.64	−1.45	21.46	89.52	0.09	0.03
6207	Men's undergarments	−1.81	−1.46	20.37	94.54	0.10	0.03
6506	Other headgear	0.13	0.44	4.23	88.82	0.02	0.03
6208	Women's undergarments	−1.78	−1.41	35.21	82.16	0.17	0.03
6113	Garments knit with impregnated fibers	−1.30	−0.93	8.06	70.64	0.04	0.03
5607	Twine and ropes of baste fibers	−1.01	−0.66	4.41	69.00	0.02	0.02
5004	Silk yarn	−0.94	−0.63	23.99	28.86	0.12	0.01
5901	Stiffened textiles	0.23	−0.43	2.98	30.95	0.01	0.01
5305	Vegetable textile fibers	−1.88	−1.80	7.33	25.89	0.03	0.01
5401	Synthetic sowing thread	−0.27	−0.34	4.35	22.24	0.02	0.01
5604	Rubber textiles	−0.48	0.37	3.52	14.81	0.02	0.01
5609	Articles of yarn, rope etc. not elsewhere clasified	−0.92	−0.56	1.14	14.33	0.01	0.00
6701	Feathers or down	−0.97	−0.54	7.28	12.57	0.04	0.00

(continued)

Table 4.2 (continued)

HS code	*Name*	*PCI 2001–2005*	*PCI 2016–2021*	*Average exports value 2001–2005 (USD mill)*	*Average exports value 2016–2021 (USD mill)*	*Average exports share 2001–2005 (%)*	*Average exports share 2016–2021 (%)*
6504	Hats	−1.49	−1.16	1.84	7.83	0.01	0.00
6213	Handkerchiefs	−1.09	−0.89	7.12	5.84	0.04	0.00
Stone and glass							
6801	Flagstones, of natural stone	−0.66	−0.76	5.34	55.99	0.02	0.02
6913	Ornamental ceramic articles	−0.77	−0.25	76.90	112.25	0.38	0.04
6914	Other ceramic articles	−0.10	0.14	65.34	87.42	0.30	0.03
Metal							
8110	Antimony	−1.35	−0.68	6.35	40.88	0.03	0.01
8215	Cutlery	−0.40	−0.01	27.13	191.19	0.12	0.07
Machinery							
8452	Sewing machines	−0.06	0.43	29.16	561.00	0.15	0.21
9503	Toys	−0.34	0.45	53.90	1281.98	0.26	0.43
9507	Fishing and hunting equipment	−0.56	−0.50	5.87	119.12	0.03	0.04
9601	Worked animal carving material	−1.63	−1.03	1.48	6.49	0.01	0.00
9607	Slide fasteners	−0.25	0.29	7.66	51.92	0.04	0.02
9609	Pencils, crayons, pastels, etc.	−0.44	−0.24	2.09	63.86	0.01	0.03
9613	Cigarette lighters	−0.23	0.13	12.93	31.40	0.06	0.01

(continued)

Table 4.2 (continued)

HS code	*Name*	*PCI 2001–2005*	*PCI 2016–2021*	*Average exports value 2001–2005 (USD mill)*	*Average exports value 2016–2021 (USD mill)*	*Average exports share 2001–2005 (%)*	*Average exports share 2016–2021 (%)*
Electronics							
8501	Electric motors and generators	0.69	0.86	101.71	1312.62	0.46	0.47
8518	Microphones	0.34	0.69	42.77	3571.40	0.19	1.19
8534	Electronic printed circuits	0.56	0.93	131.31	1019.60	0.60	0.35
8544	Insulated electrical wire	−0.50	−0.41	288.39	4574.68	1.29	1.59
Transport vehicles							
8714	Parts of motorcycles or wheelchairs	0.27	0.86	29.41	577.55	0.13	0.20
8804	Parachutes	0.16	0.39	3.63	25.58	0.02	0.01
Total exports—classics				12,641.38	100,313.97	58.12	36.48
Weighted average PCI—classics		−1.26	−0.88				
Average PCI—classics		−1.09	−0.93				

Source Author' calculations based on data from Growth Lab at Harvard University, June 2024

Table 4.3 Vietnam's emerging champions—new exports with RCA > 1 in 2016–2021 but no RCA in most of 2001–2015

HS code	*Name*	*PCI 2001–2005*	*PCI 2016–2021*	*Average exports value 2001–2005 (USD mill)*	*Average exports value 2016–2021 (USD mill)*	*Average exports share 2001–2005 (%)*	*Average exports share 2016–2021 (%)*
Vegetable, foodstuffs and wood							
812	Fruits and nuts, provisionally preserved	−1.09	−1.35	0.48	12.27	0.00	0.00
1504	Fish oils	−0.85	−1.60	0.94	59.26	0.00	0.02
2101	Coffee extracts	−0.51	−0.63	6.00	412.11	0.03	0.16
2301	Flours of fish, for animal feed	−1.57	−1.52	5.64	218.07	0.03	0.08
2302	Cereal residues	−1.82	−1.95	0.49	76.62	0.00	0.02
2308	Vegetable materials for animal feeding	−0.77	−0.91	0.20	25.54	0.00	0.01
4104	Tanned hides of bovines or equines	−1.06	−1.12	14.80	392.37	0.06	0.16
4109	Patent leather	−0.70	−0.60	2.33	10.20	0.01	0.00
4111	Composition leather	−0.36	−0.19	0.72	27.46	0.00	0.01
4302	Other tanned furskins	−0.51	−0.53	2.55	87.39	0.02	0.04
4408	Sheets for veneering for plywood	−0.93	−0.87	6.10	99.56	0.03	0.03
4412	Plywood	−1.34	−0.84	2.34	661.25	0.01	0.20

(continued)

Table 4.3 (continued)

HS code	*Name*	*PCI 2001–2005*	*PCI 2016–2021*	*Average exports value 2001–2005 (USD mill)*	*Average exports value 2016–2021 (USD mill)*	*Average exports share 2001–2005 (%)*	*Average exports share 2016–2021 (%)*
Mineral							
2517	Gravel	−0.34	−0.42	0.74	133.77	0.00	0.05
2518	Dolomite	−0.33	−0.60	0.00	19.06	0.00	0.01
2522	Quicklime	−0.18	−0.53	0.49	56.81	0.00	0.02
2523	Cements	−1.19	−1.30	0.87	1309.30	0.00	0.42
2529	Feldspar	−0.83	−1.22	0.01	70.71	0.00	0.03
2618	Granulated iron or steel slag	0.70	0.17	0.07	16.46	0.00	0.00
2706	Tar distilled from coal, lignite etc.	0.30	0.36	0.00	21.17	0.00	0.01
Chemicals and plastics							
2804	Silicon and rare gases	−0.01	0.05	0.58	262.57	0.00	0.09
2805	Rare-earth metals	0.13	−0.57	0.06	133.46	0.00	0.05
2809	Phosphoric acid etc.	−0.47	−0.44	1.51	81.05	0.01	0.03
2818	Aluminum oxide	−0.60	−0.89	1.32	405.00	0.01	0.14
2823	Titanium oxides	0.91	0.90	0.06	14.86	0.00	0.01
2825	Metal base oxides, n.e.c.	0.03	−0.37	1.74	113.92	0.01	0.04
3505	Dextrins and other modified starches	0.76	0.55	6.91	74.53	0.03	0.02
3806	Rosin and resin acids	0.14	−0.10	1.57	65.77	0.01	0.02
3809	Finishing agents	1.02	0.51	1.46	168.99	0.01	0.06
3923	Packing lids	−0.15	−0.20	65.20	1057.15	0.29	0.38

(continued)

Table 4.3 (continued)

HS code	*Name*	*PCI 2001–2005*	*PCI 2016–2021*	*Average exports value 2001–2005 (USD mill)*	*Average exports value 2016–2021 (USD mill)*	*Average exports share 2001–2005 (%)*	*Average exports share 2016–2021 (%)*
4002	Synthetic rubber	1.13	0.90	4.81	1314.07	0.02	0.44
4012	Used pneumatic tires of rubber	−0.01	0.42	3.04	46.73	0.01	0.02
4015	Vulcanized rubber articles of apparel	−0.96	−0.42	4.73	232.18	0.02	0.06
Textiles and furniture							
5002	Raw silk	−1.61	−0.92	1.32	41.78	0.01	0.01
5003	Silk waste	−1.27	−1.02	0.63	3.23	0.00	0.00
5202	Cotton waste	−1.68	−1.93	0.44	23.29	0.00	0.01
5402	Synthetic filament yarn	0.37	0.28	20.24	774.72	0.10	0.26
5503	Synthetic staple fibers	0.19	0.39	2.86	150.43	0.01	0.05
5505	Waste of man-made fibers	−0.06	−0.24	0.39	3.86	0.00	0.00
5510	Yarn of artificial staple fibers, not for retail sale	−0.38	−0.16	2.87	79.53	0.01	0.04
5802	Terry cloth	−0.71	−1.04	0.61	8.03	0.00	0.00
5807	Labels and badges of textiles	−0.59	−0.43	0.91	22.77	0.00	0.01
5808	Braids in piece	−0.55	−0.52	1.43	10.52	0.01	0.00
5902	Tire cord fabric	0.01	0.66	0.34	460.12	0.00	0.16
6001	Pile fabrics, knit	−0.70	0.04	5.96	99.56	0.03	0.03

(continued)

Table 4.3 (continued)

HS code	*Name*	*PCI 2001–2005*	*PCI 2016–2021*	*Average exports value 2001–2005 (USD mill)*	*Average exports value 2016–2021 (USD mill)*	*Average exports share 2001–2005 (%)*	*Average exports share 2016–2021 (%)*
6002	Other knitted fabrics	−0.65	−0.36	9.69	903.10	0.04	0.31
6303	Curtains	−0.82	−0.36	14.33	113.98	0.06	0.04
6401	Waterproof footwear	−1.11	−0.95	16.29	27.22	0.07	0.01
6507	Headbands	−0.40	−0.26	0.69	17.19	0.00	0.01
6603	Parts of umbrellas or walking sticks	0.04	0.36	0.44	5.83	0.00	0.00
9406	Prefabricated buildings	0.26	0.07	4.15	183.29	0.02	0.07
Stone and glass							
6810	Articles of cement, of concrete or of artificial stone	0.45	0.46	6.92	328.23	0.03	0.10
6814	Mica articles	0.67	0.97	1.44	6.48	0.01	0.00
6910	Ceramic sinks, washbasins, and similar sanitary fixtures	−0.53	−0.45	9.69	190.80	0.04	0.07
7006	Worked glass	0.82	1.63	0.32	185.22	0.00	0.07
7020	Other articles of glass	1.16	1.05	0.77	456.79	0.00	0.18
7117	Imitation jewelry	−0.10	0.09	2.18	139.82	0.01	0.06
Metal							
7209	Flat-rolled iron, width > 600 mm, cold-rolled, not clad	0.04	0.10	1.35	351.77	0.01	0.13

(continued)

Table 4.3 (continued)

HS code	*Name*	*PCI 2001–2005*	*PCI 2016–2021*	*Average exports value 2001–2005 (USD mill)*	*Average exports value 2016–2021 (USD mill)*	*Average exports share 2001–2005 (%)*	*Average exports share 2016–2021 (%)*
7210	Flat rolled iron, width > 600 mm, clad	−0.08	0.04	17.17	1381.61	0.06	0.36
7212	Flat-rolled iron, width < 600 mm, clad	0.79	0.67	0.24	233.51	0.00	0.09
7213	Hot rolled bars of iron	−0.10	−0.04	13.77	372.85	0.05	0.10
7217	Wire of iron or nonalloy steel	−0.25	−0.26	4.26	128.46	0.02	0.04
7229	Wire of other alloy steel	1.07	1.24	0.22	66.42	0.00	0.02
7306	Other tubes, pipes and hollow profiles of iron or steel	0.07	−0.35	19.37	552.62	0.09	0.21
7312	Wire of iron or steel, not insulated	0.35	0.08	0.42	323.36	0.00	0.11
7324	Sanitary ware and parts of iron or steel	0.48	0.40	1.27	56.25	0.00	0.02
7411	Copper tubes and pipes	0.81	0.53	0.52	566.19	0.00	0.19
7413	Copper wire, uninsulated	0.07	0.01	0.21	33.25	0.00	0.01
7801	Lead refined unwrought	−0.36	−1.39	1.63	104.44	0.01	0.05
8106	Bismuth	−0.35	0.23	0.00	7.92	0.00	0.00

(continued)

Table 4.3 (continued)

HS code	*Name*	*PCI 2001–2005*	*PCI 2016–2021*	*Average exports value 2001–2005 (USD mill)*	*Average exports value 2016–2021 (USD mill)*	*Average exports share 2001–2005 (%)*	*Average exports share 2016–2021 (%)*
8201	Handtools for gardening	−0.18	0.13	0.42	46.78	0.00	0.01
8212	Razors	0.43	−0.14	0.21	187.74	0.00	0.06
8214	Other cutlery	0.37	0.21	0.48	18.45	0.00	0.01
8311	Wire etc. used for welding	0.59	0.67	0.30	79.22	0.00	0.03
Machinery							
8402	Steam boilers	0.59	0.42	1.89	116.71	0.01	0.04
8443	Printers and copiers	1.71	1.24	2.80	1105.18	0.02	0.41
8450	Household- or laundry-type washing machines	0.59	0.44	6.98	609.74	0.03	0.22
8470	Cash registers, calculators, etc.	0.57	0.38	0.59	359.93	0.00	0.14
8473	Parts and accessories for office machines	0.82	1.31	259.10	5928.84	1.17	1.64
9002	Lenses and other optical elements	0.34	1.33	15.18	408.15	0.06	0.15
9006	Photographic cameras	0.52	0.30	13.02	459.40	0.07	0.18
9009	Electrostatic photo-copyers	0.79	0.52	5.77	32.08	0.02	0.01
9028	Gas, liquid or electricity meters	0.62	0.24	1.45	193.31	0.01	0.07

(continued)

Table 4.3 (continued)

HS code	*Name*	*PCI 2001–2005*	*PCI 2016–2021*	*Average exports value 2001–2005 (USD mill)*	*Average exports value 2016–2021 (USD mill)*	*Average exports share 2001–2005 (%)*	*Average exports share 2016–2021 (%)*
9506	Sports equipment	0.31	0.52	18.62	552.38	0.08	0.18
9602	Worked vegetable or mineral carving material	−0.52	0.00	0.43	38.16	0.00	0.01
9611	Hand-operated stamps	1.02	0.99	0.03	7.17	0.00	0.00
Electronics							
8504	Electrical transformers	0.32	0.76	64.07	1839.6	0.28	0.57
8507	Batteries	0.55	0.86	19.00	1317.6	0.09	0.46
8517	Telephones	0.89	0.83	20.01	20,023.5	0.10	6.90
8520	Magnetic tape recorders	0.75	0.55	0.10	93.8	0.00	0.02
8521	Video recording apparatus	0.42	0.76	11.42	2,219.7	0.04	0.78
8522	Parts and accessories for video or sound equipment	0.27	0.90	15.19	28.8	0.07	0.01
8525	Transmission apparatus for radio, telephone and TV	1.06	0.61	22.85	39,092.3	0.09	13.82
8527	Reception apparatus for radio broadcasting	0.21	0.49	0.66	308.6	0.00	0.13

(continued)

Table 4.3 (continued)

HS code	*Name*	*PCI 2001–2005*	*PCI 2016–2021*	*Average exports value 2001–2005 (USD mill)*	*Average exports value 2016–2021 (USD mill)*	*Average exports share 2001–2005 (%)*	*Average exports share 2016–2021 (%)*
8528	Monitors and projectors	0.41	0.19	52.69	2819.4	0.25%	0.91
8529	Parts of radios, telephones, and T.V.s	0.74	0.63	32.16	6581.6	0.15	2.09
8541	Semiconductor devices	0.50	0.97	8.27	2722.1	0.04	0.91
8542	Electronic integrated circuits	0.90	1.26	65.85	19,610.8	0.27	6.88
8548	Waste and scrap of batteries	0.78	0.95	0.67	149.0	0.00	0.06
Transport vehicles							
8711	Motorcycles	0.59	0.56	27.70	738.79	0.11	0.25
8713	Wheelchairs	1.20	0.72	0.83	28.47	0.00	0.01
8904	Tugs and pusher craft	−0.44	−0.88	0.58	161.10	0.00	0.07
Total exports—emerging				972.4	123,972.4	4.29	42.5
Weighted average PCI		0.33	0.69				
Average PCI		0.02	0.02				

Source Author' calculations based on data from Growth Lab at Harvard University, June 2024

Table 4.4 Vietnam's disappearing products—exports with RCA > 1 in 2001–2005 but RCA < 1 in recent periods

HS code	*Name*	*PCI 2001–2005*	*PCI 2016–2021*	*Average exports value 2001–2005 (USD mill)*	*Average exports value 2016–2021 (USD mill)*	*Average exports share 2001–2005 (%)*	*Average exports share 2016–2021 (%)*
Vegetable, foodstuffs and wood							
106	Other live animals	−1.79	−1.28	8.78	16.99	0.04	0.01
208	Other meat	−0.34	−0.16	3.48	10.75	0.02	0.00
301	Live Fish	−1.28	−1.14	6.86	16.26	0.03	0.01
302	Fish, excluding fillets	−1.51	−1.32	55.57	15.43	0.27	0.01
402	Milk, concentrated	−0.71	−0.76	91.34	69.54	0.51	0.03
410	Edible animal products, n. e.c.	−0.58	−0.40	4.39	7.47	0.02	0.00
501	Human hair, unworked	−0.71	−1.39	0.10	0.28	0.00	0.00
505	Feathers and down	−0.20	0.35	8.18	35.57	0.04	0.01
511	Animal products n.e.c.	−1.08	−0.92	3.28	37.45	0.02	0.01
711	Vegetables, provisionally preserved	−1.16	−1.24	8.44	11.26	0.04	0.00
712	Vegetables, dried	−1.16	−1.27	6.81	53.06	0.03	0.02
807	Melons and papayas	−1.40	−1.64	5.30	38.21	0.02	0.02
811	Fruits and nuts, frozen	−0.62	−0.53	6.89	94.84	0.03	0.03
813	Fruits, dried	−1.33	−0.98	11.77	19.12	0.08	0.01
908	Nutmeg	−1.73	−1.68	0.48	13.22	0.00	0.00
910	Spices	−1.43	−1.61	2.74	30.19	0.01	0.01
1101	Wheat or meslin flour	−1.34	−1.38	2.49	63.55	0.01	0.02

(continued)

Table 4.4 (continued)

HS code	*Name*	*PCI 2001–2005*	*PCI 2016–2021*	*Average exports value 2001–2005 (USD mill)*	*Average exports value 2016–2021 (USD mill)*	*Average exports share 2001–2005 (%)*	*Average exports share 2016–2021 (%)*
1202	Peanuts	−1.96	−2.33	31.75	40.85	0.17	0.01
1203	Copra	−2.40	−1.86	9.26	1.76	0.04	0.00
1211	Plants used in perfumery, pharmacy or insecticide	−1.91	−1.87	6.12	30.63	0.03	0.01
1213	Cereal straw and husks	−0.49	−0.12	0.00	3.69	0.00	0.00
1301	Lac	−1.93	−2.56	2.21	2.63	0.01	0.00
1402	Vegetable materials used as stuffing	−1.29	1.03	0.69	0.00	0.00	0.00
1404	Vegetable products n.e.c.	−1.94	−1.73	1.02	13.66	0.00	0.01
1603	Extracts and juices of meat or fish	−0.41	−0.10	0.60	3.34	0.00	0.00
1704	Confectionery sugar	−0.65	−0.61	8.19	103.64	0.04	0.04
1903	Tapioca	−1.30	−1.40	2.48	1.57	0.01	0.00
2001	Pickled fruits and vegetables	−0.91	−0.88	4.62	24.66	0.02	0.01
2003	Mushrooms, prepared or preserved	−0.42	0.14	4.16	5.57	0.02	0.00
2102	Yeasts	−0.52	−0.54	5.78	18.37	0.03	0.01
2402	Cigars and cigarettes	−0.71	−0.80	75.11	171.55	0.32	0.07
4107	Bovine leather further prepared	−1.06	−1.00	1.77	13.66	0.01	0.01
4304	Artificial fur	−0.23	−0.24	0.25	0.72	0.00	0.00
4403	Wood in the rough	−1.51	−1.76	6.34	32.55	0.03	0.02

(continued)

Table 4.4 (continued)

HS code	*Name*	*PCI 2001–2005*	*PCI 2016–2021*	*Average exports value 2001–2005 (USD mill)*	*Average exports value 2016–2021 (USD mill)*	*Average exports share 2001–2005 (%)*	*Average exports share 2016–2021 (%)*
4404	Strips and other pieces of wood	−0.87	−0.33	3.09	1.80	0.01	0.00
4409	Wood shaped along its edges	−1.00	−0.93	12.05	42.47	0.05	0.01
4413	Densified wood	−1.17	−0.51	0.26	7.18	0.00	0.00
4414	Wooden frames	−0.44	−0.15	1.84	13.14	0.01	0.01
4417	Wooden tools	−0.74	−0.31	1.17	6.94	0.01	0.00
4803	Tissue	−0.25	−0.45	6.14	56.84	0.02	0.02
4805	Other uncoated paper and paperboard	0.56	0.32	7.94	261.63	0.04	0.08
4823	Other paper cut to size	0.49	0.39	16.01	93.40	0.07	0.03
4908	Transfers (decalcomanias)	1.25	0.66	0.09	13.75	0.00	0.00
Mineral							
2505	Natural sands	−0.43	−0.85	10.77	31.91	0.05	0.01
2506	Quartz	−0.56	−1.02	1.69	3.54	0.01	0.00
2510	Natural calcium phosphates	−1.14	−1.37	0.00	16.72	0.00	0.01
2511	Natural barium sulfate	−1.23	−1.40	5.55	12.50	0.03	0.00
2514	Slate	−0.42	−0.35	0.47	0.04	0.00	0.00
2515	Marble	−1.28	−1.41	2.13	31.71	0.01	0.01
2530	Mineral substances n.e.c.	−0.97	−1.25	1.12	35.11	0.00	0.01
2610	Chromium ore	−1.94	−2.54	7.20	0.02	0.03	0.00
2611	Tungsten ore	−1.59	−1.87	1.29	2.23	0.01	0.00

(continued)

Table 4.4 (continued)

HS code	*Name*	*PCI 2001–2005*	*PCI 2016–2021*	*Average exports value 2001–2005 (USD mill)*	*Average exports value 2016–2021 (USD mill)*	*Average exports share 2001–2005 (%)*	*Average exports share 2016–2021 (%)*
2615	Zirconium ore	−2.06	−2.52	6.67	14.10	0.03	0.00
2617	Other ores	−1.64	−2.54	9.94	1.58	0.05	0.00
2621	Other slag and ash	0.27	0.12	0.09	8.36	0.00	0.00
2701	Coal	−0.89	−1.55	320.29	230.59	1.33	0.09
2709	Petroleum oils, crude	−2.43	−2.57	4342.93	2173.81	19.53	0.91
Chemicals and plastics							
2841	Salts of oxometallic acids	0.08	−0.15	0.48	61.79	0.00	0.02
2846	Compounds of rare-earth metals	0.62	0.79	0.00	14.47	0.00	0.00
2922	Oxygen-function amino-compounds	0.79	0.68	56.90	87.84	0.28	0.03
3101	Animal or vegetable fertilizers	−0.68	−0.70	0.17	9.06	0.00	0.00
3105	Mixed fertilizers	−0.59	−0.91	12.59	160.13	0.06	0.06
3306	Dental hygiene products	−0.64	0.12	9.35	35.66	0.04	0.01
3401	Soap	−1.36	−1.09	18.60	25.23	0.10	0.01
3704	Photographic film, not developed	0.27	0.78	0.03	0.40	0.00	0.00
3802	Activated carbon	−0.41	−0.33	2.89	27.98	0.01	0.01
3915	Plastic waste	0.13	−0.69	1.89	46.10	0.01	0.02
3924	Plastic household articles	−0.61	−0.55	16.01	240.89	0.07	0.08
3926	Other articles of plastic	0.94	0.78	54.03	1067.00	0.24	0.36
4003	Reclaimed rubber	−0.54	0.02	0.06	3.94	0.00	0.00

(continued)

Table 4.4 (continued)

HS code	*Name*	*PCI 2001–2005*	*PCI 2016–2021*	*Average exports value 2001–2005 (USD mill)*	*Average exports value 2016–2021 (USD mill)*	*Average exports share 2001–2005 (%)*	*Average exports share 2016–2021 (%)*
4004	Scrap of rubber	−0.27	−0.18	10.73	1.05	0.06	0.00
4005	Compounded rubber	1.21	1.01	43.20	22.10	0.17	0.01
4017	Hard rubber	−0.26	−0.10	1.24	1.94	0.00	0.00
Textiles and furniture							
5001	Silkworm cocoons	−1.17	−0.88	0.09	0.00	0.00	0.00
5006	Silk yarn, for retail sale	−0.02	0.18	1.43	0.27	0.01	0.00
5007	Woven silk fabrics	−0.39	0.44	6.11	14.87	0.03	0.01
5203	Cotton, carded or combed	−1.91	−1.49	1.18	6.36	0.01	0.00
5207	Cotton yarn for retail sale	−1.36	−0.53	1.22	11.91	0.01	0.00
5303	Textile bast fibers	−2.48	−2.23	0.44	0.55	0.00	0.00
5308	Yarn of other vegetable textile fibers	−1.45	−0.85	2.23	0.79	0.01	0.00
5310	Woven fabrics of jute or of other textile bast fibers	−2.12	−2.11	0.46	0.43	0.00	0.00
5311	Woven fabrics of vegetable textile fibers	−1.20	−0.73	0.31	4.25	0.00	0.00
5407	Woven fabrics of synthetic filament yarn	−0.41	−0.42	51.09	315.99	0.23	0.11
5508	Synthetic staple fibers sewing thread	−1.08	−0.90	3.08	7.91	0.01	0.00
5511	Yarn of synthetic staple fibers, for retail sale	−0.66	−0.75	0.34	6.87	0.00	0.00

(continued)

Table 4.4 (continued)

HS code	*Name*	*PCI 2001–2005*	*PCI 2016–2021*	*Average exports value 2001–2005 (USD mill)*	*Average exports value 2016–2021 (USD mill)*	*Average exports share 2001–2005 (%)*	*Average exports share 2016–2021 (%)*
5514	Woven fabrics of < 85% synthetic staple fibers weighing > 170 g/m^2	−0.73	−0.61	6.43	20.07	0.04	0.01
5515	Other woven fabrics of synthetic staple fibers	−0.57	−0.33	8.79	33.72	0.05	0.01
5803	Gauze	−0.47	−0.08	0.17	1.20	0.00	0.00
5806	Narrow woven fabrics	−0.05	−0.02	5.68	62.95	0.02	0.02
5811	Quilted textile products	0.08	0.17	0.47	2.07	0.00	0.00
6215	Ties, bow ties and cravats	−0.85	−0.35	9.89	5.58	0.04	0.00
6217	Other clothing accesories	−0.50	−0.59	7.65	27.17	0.04	0.01
6302	House linen	−1.16	−1.26	78.53	275.52	0.37	0.10
6310	Used or new rags textile scraps	−1.05	−0.97	0.29	9.32	0.00	0.00
6501	Hat forms	−0.65	−0.70	2.05	0.20	0.01	0.00
6502	Hat shapes	−1.57	−1.05	0.38	0.28	0.00	0.00
6503	Felt hats	−0.74	0.85	0.51	0.01	0.00	0.00
9404	Mattresses and bedding	−0.23	−0.52	29.86	350.23	0.14	0.12
Stone and glass							
6802	Worked building stone	−0.74	−0.98	17.11	114.43	0.08	0.04
6803	Worked slate	0.24	−0.44	0.32	3.72	0.00	0.00
6901	Bricks, blocks, and other ceramic goods	−0.61	−0.67	0.60	0.33	0.00	0.00
6904	Ceramic building bricks	−0.40	−0.33	2.05	5.65	0.01	0.00

(continued)

Table 4.4 (continued)

HS code	*Name*	*PCI 2001–2005*	*PCI 2016–2021*	*Average exports value 2001–2005 (USD mill)*	*Average exports value 2016–2021 (USD mill)*	*Average exports share 2001–2005 (%)*	*Average exports share 2016–2021 (%)*
6907	Unglazed ceramic flags and pavers	−0.19	−0.54	11.91	125.57	0.04	0.04
6908	Glazed ceramic flags and pavers	−0.49	−0.94	7.81	35.69	0.03	0.02
6912	Ceramic household articles	−0.62	0.15	12.10	15.18	0.06	0.01
7003	Glass, cast or rolled	0.12	1.37	2.37	4.80	0.01	0.00
7005	Float glass	0.60	0.10	2.31	112.76	0.01	0.05
7113	Jewelry of precious metal	−0.57	−0.05	59.14	236.69	0.27	0.08
7114	Goldsmith and silversmith wares	−0.47	−0.19	1.12	687.20	0.01	0.27
Metal							
7202	Ferroalloys	−0.49	−0.98	0.25	129.44	0.00	0.05
7223	Wire of stainless steel	1.39	1.27	2.83	29.03	0.01	0.01
7308	Structures and their parts, of iron or steel	0.36	0.43	26.71	582.93	0.11	0.20
7313	Barbed wire of iron or steel	−0.98	−1.05	0.43	0.71	0.00	0.00
7316	Anchors of iron or steel	−0.07	−0.09	0.75	3.20	0.00	0.00
7318	Screws and similar articles of iron or steel	1.60	1.59	26.99	444.73	0.11	0.16
7319	Articles for sewing of iron or steel	0.63	0.98	0.59	1.78	0.00	0.00

(continued)

Table 4.4 (continued)

HS code	*Name*	*PCI 2001–2005*	*PCI 2016–2021*	*Average exports value 2001–2005 (USD mill)*	*Average exports value 2016–2021 (USD mill)*	*Average exports share 2001–2005 (%)*	*Average exports share 2016–2021 (%)*
7323	Household articles of iron or steel	−0.74	−0.31	17.77	119.64	0.08	0.04
7401	Copper mattes	−1.53	−1.13	0.08	9.31	0.00	0.01
7614	Aluminum wire, not insulated	−0.50	−0.64	0.60	6.75	0.00	0.00
7615	Household articles of aluminum	−0.51	−0.47	10.39	71.32	0.04	0.02
7803	Lead bars, rods, profiles and wire	−0.36	1.48	0.27	0.00	0.00	0.00
7805	Lead tubes, pipes and fittings	−0.13	3.91	0.05	0.00	0.00	0.00
7907	Other articles of zinc	0.36	0.57	6.39	11.02	0.03	0.00
8001	Unwrought tin	−1.08	−0.31	11.51	11.30	0.05	0.01
8003	Tin bars and wire	−0.13	0.77	9.50	2.94	0.04	0.00
8007	Other articles of tin	−0.55	0.14	1.98	4.93	0.01	0.00
8111	Manganese	0.45	0.07	0.01	0.60	0.00	0.00
8113	Cermets	1.39	2.04	0.37	5.71	0.00	0.00
8211	Knife sets	0.30	0.79	4.81	34.86	0.02	0.01
8304	Paper trays and similar office equipment, of base metal	−0.15	0.21	0.93	1.43	0.00	0.00
8306	Ornaments, statuettes, etc. of metal	−0.54	−0.45	14.98	10.56	0.07	0.00

(continued)

Table 4.4 (continued)

HS code	*Name*	*PCI 2001–2005*	*PCI 2016–2021*	*Average exports value 2001–2005 (USD mill)*	*Average exports value 2016–2021 (USD mill)*	*Average exports share 2001–2005 (%)*	*Average exports share 2016–2021 (%)*
8307	Flexible tubing of base metal	0.66	0.71	3.25	19.05	0.01	0.01
Machinery							
8437	Machinery for processing grain	−0.27	0.14	2.72	20.19	0.01	0.01
8471	Computers	1.02	1.07	153.37	5317.47	0.59	2.03
9033	Other parts for machines and appliances	1.08	1.09	0.54	34.89	0.00	0.01
9104	Instrument panel clocks for vehicles	0.97	0.86	0.01	2.24	0.00	0.00
9111	Watch cases and parts	0.60	0.54	0.18	9.73	0.00	0.00
9113	Watch straps	−0.04	−0.11	9.16	20.19	0.04	0.01
9603	Brooms and mops	−0.26	−0.11	10.14	163.77	0.05	0.06
9606	Buttons	−0.72	−0.23	6.90	19.51	0.03	0.01
9612	Typewriter ribbons and ink pads	0.78	1.13	2.97	9.84	0.01	0.00
9616	Scent sprays	0.27	0.67	3.16	18.24	0.01	0.01
9618	Mannequins	0.14	0.01	6.17	1.94	0.03	0.00
Electronics							
8502	Electric generating sets and rotary converters	0.66	0.36	15.22	221.14	0.06	0.05
8509	Electromechanical domestic appliances	1.01	0.92	0.78	318.81	0.00	0.09

(continued)

Table 4.4 (continued)

HS code	*Name*	*PCI 2001–2005*	*PCI 2016–2021*	*Average exports value 2001–2005 (USD mill)*	*Average exports value 2016–2021 (USD mill)*	*Average exports share 2001–2005 (%)*	*Average exports share 2016–2021 (%)*
8537	Electrical boards	0.82	0.74	90.17	601.75	0.43	0.19
8540	Thermionic, cold cathode or photocathode tubes	0.76	0.64	50.55	1.61	0.23	0.00
Transport vehicles							
8712	Bicycles	−0.45	0.13	117.49	65.96	0.53	0.02
8801	Gliders, hang gliders	0.01	0.35	0.12	1.19	0.00	0.00
8902	Fishing vessels	−0.86	−0.80	0.03	23.59	0.00	0.01
8906	Other vessels	0.16	−0.22	0.11	85.17	0.00	0.04
Total exports—disappearing				6320.90	16,806	28.4	6.2
Weighted average PCI		−1.78	−0.06				
Average PCI		−0.52	−0.39				

Source Author' calculations based on data from Growth Lab at Harvard University, June 2024

Table 4.5 Selected Vietnam's Marginal Products—exports with no RCA during the whole period (average exports > $25 million during 2016–2021)

HS code	*Name*	*PCI 2001–2005*	*PCI 2016–2021*	*Average exports value 2001–2005 (USD mill)*	*Average exports value 2016–2021 (USD mill)*	*Average exports share 2001–2005 (%)*	*Average exports share 2016–2021 (%)*
Vegetable, foodstuffs and wood							
203	Pork	0.83	0.86	29.42	55.10	0.14	0.02
603	Cut flowers	−1.75	−1.49	4.68	44.49	0.02	0.02
709	Other vegetables	−1.24	−1.33	4.83	77.51	0.02	0.03
710	Frozen vegetables	−1.03	−0.70	7.09	41.47	0.03	0.01
713	Legumes, dried	−1.90	−1.96	1.52	37.95	0.01	0.02
802	Other nuts	−1.34	−1.66	4.65	62.73	0.02	0.02
803	Bananas and plantains	−1.73	−1.88	2.64	107.54	0.01	0.03
804	Avocados, pineapples, mangos, etc.	−1.78	−1.86	3.35	100.82	0.02	0.04
805	Citrus fruit	−0.98	−1.33	0.33	67.52	0.00	0.03
1005	Corn	−1.39	−1.03	4.22	51.66	0.02	0.02
1302	Vegetable saps and extracts	−0.81	−1.21	4.75	54.99	0.02	0.02
1507	Soybean oil	−0.70	−1.00	0.24	36.74	0.00	0.01
1511	Palm oil	−2.10	−2.20	13.55	35.34	0.07	0.01
1513	Coconut and palm kernel oil	−1.94	−1.83	3.52	27.83	0.02	0.01

(continued)

Table 4.5 (continued)

HS code	*Name*	*PCI 2001–2005*	*PCI 2016–2021*	*Average exports value 2001–2005 (USD mill)*	*Average exports value 2016–2021 (USD mill)*	*Average exports share 2001–2005 (%)*	*Average exports share 2016–2021 (%)*
1518	Animal or vegetable fats and oils, processed	0.42	0.00	0.64	28.32	0.00	0.01
1702	Other sugars	0.04	−0.08	0.17	35.11	0.00	0.01
1901	Malt extract	−0.02	0.02	8.54	176.43	0.05	0.07
1905	Bakery products	−0.27	−0.32	24.07	206.68	0.11	0.07
2004	Other vegetables, frozen	0.47	−0.09	3.02	28.45	0.01	0.01
2005	Other vegetables, prepared or preserved	−0.94	−0.85	4.93	38.19	0.02	0.01
2009	Fruit juices	−0.75	−0.90	6.84	125.17	0.03	0.04
2103	Sauces and seasonings	−0.24	−0.55	12.37	76.98	0.06	0.03
2106	Food preparations n.e.c.	−0.20	0.02	3.88	215.29	0.02	0.07
2202	Waters, flavored or sweetened	−0.57	−0.46	6.00	114.36	0.03	0.04
2203	Beer	−0.55	−0.34	1.56	65.80	0.01	0.02
2208	Spirits < 80% alcohol	−0.48	−0.50	5.77	41.66	0.03	0.02
2304	Solid soybean residues	−0.87	−1.03	0.13	49.48	0.00	0.01
2309	Animal feed	−0.33	−0.35	5.65	321.18	0.03	0.11
2403	Other manufactured tobacco	−0.48	−0.70	3.27	27.43	0.02	0.01
4407	Wood sawn lengthwise	−1.38	−1.26	10.28	122.11	0.05	0.06
4411	Fiberboard of wood	0.18	−0.01	1.72	51.69	0.01	0.02
4418	Wood carpentry for construction	−0.28	0.08	11.99	181.06	0.06	0.06

(continued)

Table 4.5 (continued)

HS code	*Name*	*PCI 2001–2005*	*PCI 2016–2021*	*Average exports value 2001–2005 (USD mill)*	*Average exports value 2016–2021 (USD mill)*	*Average exports share 2001–2005 (%)*	*Average exports share 2016–2021 (%)*
4804	Uncoated kraft paper and paperboard	0.48	0.05	1.64	73.14	0.01	0.02
4811	Cellulose wadding, coated	1.39	0.48	3.43	46.50	0.01	0.01
4813	Cigarette paper	0.45	0.11	0.64	25.07	0.00	0.01
4818	Toilet paper	0.17	0.04	7.65	143.42	0.03	0.05
4819	Cardboard packing containers	−0.27	−0.49	15.07	294.66	0.07	0.10
4821	Paper labels	0.16	0.01	0.94	52.50	0.00	0.02
4911	Other printed matter	0.96	0.57	2.21	26.25	0.01	0.01
Mineral							
2601	Iron ores and concentrates	−0.72	−1.75	19.56	70.81	0.08	0.03
2613	Molybdenum ore	−0.18	−0.56	0.15	28.25	0.00	0.01
2707	Oils etc. from high temperature coal tar	−0.70	0.02	0.18	27.02	0.00	0.01
2710	Petroleum oils, refined	−1.17	−0.71	164.58	784.26	0.75	0.30
2711	Petroleum gases	−1.59	−1.96	0.48	195.06	0.00	0.07
2716	Electrical energy	−0.32	−0.56	0.82	104.06	0.01	0.04
Chemicals and plastics							
2835	Phosphates	0.06	0.02	1.68	28.15	0.01	0.01
2836	Carbonates	−0.10	−0.46	1.68	59.42	0.01	0.02
2849	Carbides	0.46	0.21	0.51	25.78	0.00	0.01

(continued)

Table 4.5 (continued)

HS code	*Name*	*PCI 2001–2005*	*PCI 2016–2021*	*Average exports value 2001–2005 (USD mill)*	*Average exports value 2016–2021 (USD mill)*	*Average exports share 2001–2005 (%)*	*Average exports share 2016–2021 (%)*
2902	Cyclic hydrocarbons	0.30	0.66	1.33	283.78	0.01	0.08
2932	Heterocyclic compounds with oxygen hetero-atom (s) only	1.03	0.84	7.40	36.34	0.03	0.02
3004	Medicaments, packaged	0.87	0.76	9.92	139.00	0.05	0.05
3102	Nitrogenous fertilizers	−0.80	−1.26	6.99	114.09	0.03	0.03
3104	Potassic fertilizers	0.00	−0.73	1.64	25.71	0.01	0.01
3206	Other coloring matter	1.17	0.62	0.70	48.90	0.00	0.02
3208	Paints and varnishes, nonaqueous	0.57	0.43	3.87	33.70	0.02	0.01
3304	Make-up preparations	0.17	0.52	4.92	71.37	0.02	0.03
3305	Hair products	−0.02	0.15	7.83	50.18	0.04	0.02
3307	Toiletries	0.50	0.17	11.83	121.43	0.05	0.05
3402	Cleaning products	0.18	0.05	24.81	234.02	0.11	0.08
3506	Glues and adhesives	1.11	1.22	5.12	64.84	0.03	0.02
3808	Insecticides, rodenticides, fungicides, etc.	−0.11	0.06	9.87	146.84	0.04	0.05
3818	Chemical elements for electronics	1.43	2.16	0.01	71.83	0.00	0.01
3823	Industrial monocarboxylic fatty acids	1.48	−0.04	7.53	302.66	0.03	0.10

(continued)

Table 4.5 (continued)

HS code	*Name*	*PCI 2001–2005*	*PCI 2016–2021*	*Average exports value 2001–2005 (USD mill)*	*Average exports value 2016–2021 (USD mill)*	*Average exports share 2001–2005 (%)*	*Average exports share 2016–2021 (%)*
3901	Polymers of ethylene	0.18	0.20	2.59	154.31	0.01	0.05
3902	Polymers of propylene	0.43	0.32	1.28	305.41	0.01	0.09
3903	Polymers of styrene	0.91	0.83	3.06	87.29	0.01	0.03
3904	Polymers of vinyl chloride	0.42	0.66	8.36	90.28	0.04	0.03
3907	Polyacetals	0.92	0.96	14.05	345.54	0.05	0.08
3908	Polyamides	1.60	1.76	1.28	79.24	0.01	0.03
3909	Amino-resins	1.07	1.27	0.77	28.29	0.00	0.01
3917	Plastic tubes and fittings	0.19	−0.09	8.87	109.04	0.04	0.04
3918	Plastic floor coverings	1.02	0.78	4.29	194.93	0.02	0.02
3919	Self-adhesive plastic sheets	1.70	1.18	3.66	124.51	0.02	0.04
3920	Other plates of plastics, noncellular and not reinforced	0.95	0.43	17.87	310.85	0.08	0.11
3921	Other plastic plates, sheets etc.	0.86	0.64	9.31	218.06	0.04	0.07
3925	Plastic builders' ware	0.71	0.26	3.55	119.22	0.01	0.04
4009	Vulcanized rubber tubes	0.94	0.88	2.03	39.31	0.01	0.01
4010	Conveyor belts of vulcanized rubber	0.75	0.86	1.62	27.42	0.01	0.01
4011	New pneumatic tires of rubber	0.12	0.35	20.82	1088.65	0.10	0.35

(continued)

Table 4.5 (continued)

HS code	*Name*	*PCI 2001–2005*	*PCI 2016–2021*	*Average exports value 2001–2005 (USD mill)*	*Average exports value 2016–2021 (USD mill)*	*Average exports share 2001–2005 (%)*	*Average exports share 2016–2021 (%)*
4016	Other articles of vulcanized rubber	0.99	0.81	24.58	340.39	0.11	0.12
Textiles and furniture							
5208	Woven fabrics of cotton of > 85% weighing < 200 g/m^2	−1.18	−1.24	3.82	54.97	0.02	0.02
5209	Woven fabrics of cotton of < 85% weighing > 200 g/m^2	−1.31	−1.32	7.23	88.17	0.04	0.03
5211	Woven fabrics of cotton of < 85% weighing > 200 g/m^2	−0.67	−0.58	3.91	28.95	0.02	0.01
5601	Wadding of textile materials	−0.19	−0.08	0.95	28.78	0.00	0.01
5603	Nonwoven textiles	1.28	1.06	2.77	92.75	0.01	0.03
5703	Carpets, tufted	0.03	0.22	5.78	120.79	0.03	0.03
5903	Textile fabrics impregnated with plastics	0.58	1.18	5.02	95.45	0.02	0.03
6115	Socks, stockings, etc., knit	−0.71	−0.84	7.99	186.39	0.04	0.06
6117	Other clothing accesories, knit	−1.24	−1.15	6.42	36.13	0.03	0.01
6301	Blankets	−1.29	−0.96	3.52	37.81	0.02	0.01

(continued)

Table 4.5 (continued)

HS code	*Name*	*PCI 2001–2005*	*PCI 2016–2021*	*Average exports value 2001–2005 (USD mill)*	*Average exports value 2016–2021 (USD mill)*	*Average exports share 2001–2005 (%)*	*Average exports share 2016–2021 (%)*
6704	Wigs	−1.57	−2.18	1.18	43.86	0.01	0.02
9402	Medical, dental or veterinary furniture	1.21	0.85	0.95	41.38	0.01	0.01
9405	Lamps	0.72	0.69	13.97	272.85	0.06	0.07
Stone and glass							
7007	Safety glass	0.71	0.82	0.99	70.57	0.00	0.02
7009	Glass mirrors	1.14	1.17	4.50	57.22	0.02	0.02
7102	Diamonds	−1.34	−1.27	26.77	165.81	0.13	0.05
7112	Scrap of precious metal	−0.64	−0.51	0.89	341.75	0.00	0.13
7116	Articles of precious stones	−0.70	−0.54	0.69	28.90	0.00	0.01
Metal							
7204	Ferrous waste and scrap	−0.62	−0.55	3.36	64.84	0.01	0.03
7207	Semifinished products of iron or nonalloy steel	−0.66	−0.73	0.89	905.74	0.01	0.19
7208	Flat-rolled iron, width > 600 mm, hot-rolled, not clad	0.39	0.53	5.03	400.80	0.02	0.08
7214	Other bars of iron, not further worked than forged	−1.05	−1.11	12.39	246.83	0.05	0.07
7216	Angles of iron or nonalloy steel	−0.02	−0.31	6.65	149.71	0.03	0.06

(continued)

Table 4.5 (continued)

HS code	*Name*	*PCI 2001–2005*	*PCI 2016–2021*	*Average exports value 2001–2005 (USD mill)*	*Average exports value 2016–2021 (USD mill)*	*Average exports share 2001–2005 (%)*	*Average exports share 2016–2021 (%)*
7219	Flat-rolled products of stainless steel of a width > 600 mm	1.12	1.17	2.33	178.47	0.01	0.06
7225	Flat-rolled products of other alloy steel, width > 600 mm	1.52	1.55	1.52	119.40	0.01	0.04
7227	Bars of other alloy steel	1.19	0.69	0.12	26.58	0.00	0.00
7304	Tubes, seamless, of iron or steel	0.76	0.18	10.38	28.06	0.05	0.01
7305	Other tubes and pipes, diameter > 406.4 mm, of iron or steel	0.35	0.47	2.57	43.58	0.01	0.01
7307	Tube or pipe fittings of iron or steel	0.86	1.18	17.64	128.65	0.08	0.04
7309	Tanks etc. > 300 l, iron or steel	0.06	0.03	1.12	29.97	0.01	0.01
7314	Cloth of iron or steel wire	0.12	0.03	2.02	45.78	0.01	0.01
7321	Stoves and similar non-electric appliances of iron or steel	0.03	0.16	9.36	87.75	0.04	0.03
7325	Other cast articles of iron or steel	0.41	0.37	2.89	37.10	0.01	0.01

(continued)

Table 4.5 (continued)

HS code	*Name*	*PCI 2001–2005*	*PCI 2016–2021*	*Average exports value 2001–2005 (USD mill)*	*Average exports value 2016–2021 (USD mill)*	*Average exports share 2001–2005 (%)*	*Average exports share 2016–2021 (%)*
7326	Other articles of iron or steel	0.83	0.91	23.52	345.36	0.10	0.12
7403	Refined copper and copper alloys	−1.48	−1.35	0.10	46.05	0.00	0.01
7404	Copper waste and scrap	−0.81	−0.98	0.18	56.87	0.00	0.02
7408	Copper wire	−0.18	−0.36	2.10	260.68	0.01	0.08
7412	Copper tube or pipe fittings	1.00	0.90	1.55	33.66	0.01	0.01
7601	Unwrought aluminum	−0.62	−0.98	2.59	337.40	0.01	0.10
7602	Waste or scrap, aluminium	−0.65	−0.84	0.49	57.56	0.00	0.02
7604	Aluminum bars	0.07	−0.06	5.15	165.87	0.03	0.05
7608	Aluminum tubes and pipes	0.77	0.35	0.44	27.94	0.00	0.01
7610	Aluminum structures (bridges, towers etc)	0.35	0.36	2.77	196.54	0.01	0.07
7612	Aluminum containers, <300 l	0.43	0.17	1.86	66.88	0.01	0.02
7616	Other articles of aluminum	0.92	0.74	6.20	138.73	0.03	0.04
8205	Hand tools n.e.c.	0.98	0.79	1.85	32.36	0.01	0.01
8207	Interchangeable tools for hand tools	1.37	1.60	8.43	87.44	0.04	0.03

(continued)

Table 4.5 (continued)

HS code	*Name*	*PCI 2001–2005*	*PCI 2016–2021*	*Average exports value 2001–2005 (USD mill)*	*Average exports value 2016–2021 (USD mill)*	*Average exports share 2001–2005 (%)*	*Average exports share 2016–2021 (%)*
8208	Knives and blades for machines	1.31	1.50	3.58	36.99	0.02	0.01
8301	Padlocks and locks	0.76	0.81	0.58	90.64	0.00	0.02
8302	Base metal mountings, fittings and similar articles	1.01	0.83	5.84	217.12	0.03	0.06
8308	Clasps, buckles etc. of metal	0.62	0.74	0.80	27.81	0.00	0.01
8309	Stoppers, caps and lids of metal	0.38	0.16	2.87	33.12	0.01	0.01
Machinery							
8407	Spark-ignition reciprocating internal combustion piston engines	1.34	1.04	5.64	62.41	0.02	0.02
8409	Parts suitable for use with spark-ignition engines	1.11	1.03	8.33	157.64	0.03	0.06
8411	Gas turbines	0.80	0.78	4.05	257.70	0.02	0.08
8412	Other engines and motors	1.11	1.00	7.22	32.55	0.02	0.01
8413	Pumps for liquids	1.46	1.34	6.08	160.55	0.03	0.05

(continued)

Table 4.5 (continued)

HS code	*Name*	*PCI 2001–2005*	*PCI 2016–2021*	*Average exports value 2001–2005 (USD mill)*	*Average exports value 2016–2021 (USD mill)*	*Average exports share 2001–2005 (%)*	*Average exports share 2016–2021 (%)*
8414	Pumps, compressors, fans, etc.	1.05	1.25	55.80	464.88	0.27	0.14
8415	Air conditioners	0.45	0.69	1.77	38.44	0.01	0.01
8418	Refrigerators, freezers	0.25	0.64	3.24	248.01	0.02	0.08
8419	Equipment for temperature change of materials	1.32	1.33	2.86	57.73	0.01	0.02
8421	Centrifuges	1.52	1.07	5.38	129.85	0.02	0.04
8424	Sprays and powder dispersers	1.12	1.12	3.17	145.46	0.01	0.03
8426	Ships' derricks; cranes	0.42	0.02	0.46	36.35	0.00	0.02
8427	Fork-lift trucks	1.55	1.43	0.11	39.80	0.00	0.01
8428	Other lifting machinery	1.55	1.05	2.32	35.68	0.01	0.01
8431	Parts for use with hoists and excavation machinery	0.96	0.79	8.20	123.06	0.04	0.04
8433	Harvesting or agricultural machinery	1.10	0.88	0.76	94.07	0.00	0.02
8441	Other machinery for making paper	1.30	1.00	0.42	26.27	0.00	0.01
8448	Auxiliary machinery for use with knitting and textile machines	1.01	1.49	6.60	49.76	0.03	0.02

(continued)

Table 4.5 (continued)

HS code	*Name*	*PCI 2001–2005*	*PCI 2016–2021*	*Average exports value 2001–2005 (USD mill)*	*Average exports value 2016–2021 (USD mill)*	*Average exports share 2001–2005 (%)*	*Average exports share 2016–2021 (%)*
8462	Machine tools for molding and forging metals	0.79	1.48	1.09	26.80	0.00	0.01
8466	Parts and accessories for metal working machines	1.51	1.62	4.96	51.56	0.02	0.02
8467	Tools for hand working, pneumatic, hydraulic motors	1.69	1.40	1.16	63.58	0.00	0.01
8472	Other office machines	1.20	0.81	0.47	40.31	0.00	0.01
8477	Machinery for working rubber or plastics	1.48	1.66	1.99	27.59	0.01	0.01
8479	Machines n.e.c.	2.11	2.01	15.04	491.75	0.07	0.16
8480	Molding boxes for metal foundry	1.33	1.40	8.81	90.63	0.04	0.03
8481	Appliances for thermostatically controlled valves	1.53	1.63	47.07	809.30	0.21	0.30
8482	Ball or roller bearings	0.94	1.28	1.59	163.03	0.01	0.05
8483	Transmission shafts	1.54	1.38	7.09	173.95	0.03	0.06
8485	Machinery parts, not containing electrical features, n.e.c.	1.70	1.28	1.88	45.69	0.01	0.02
9001	Optical fibers	0.91	1.03	4.11	230.29	0.02	0.08

(continued)

Table 4.5 (continued)

HS code	*Name*	*PCI 2001–2005*	*PCI 2016–2021*	*Average exports value 2001–2005 (USD mill)*	*Average exports value 2016–2021 (USD mill)*	*Average exports share 2001–2005 (%)*	*Average exports share 2016–2021 (%)*
9004	Glasses	0.69	0.66	0.34	68.80	0.00	0.04
9010	Apparatus and equipment for photographic laboratories, n.e.c.	1.07	2.10	0.63	30.76	0.00	0.01
9013	Liquid crystal devices	0.91	1.19	4.47	1521.74	0.02	0.65
9018	Medical instruments	0.97	0.82	22.30	911.62	0.10	0.32
9021	Orthopedic appliances	1.05	1.05	2.09	514.46	0.01	0.17
9023	Instruments designed for demonstrational purposes	0.95	0.59	0.34	30.38	0.00	0.01
9025	Thermometers, hydrometers etc.	1.08	0.96	0.70	49.05	0.00	0.01
9026	Instruments for measuring properties of liquids or gases	1.53	1.39	1.30	112.11	0.01	0.04
9027	Instruments for physical or chemical analysis	1.80	1.79	0.74	113.81	0.00	0.04
9029	Meters	1.15	1.18	0.18	65.72	0.00	0.02
9030	Instruments for measuring electricity	1.14	1.30	1.36	50.79	0.01	0.02
9031	Measuring instruments	1.42	1.67	5.32	219.33	0.03	0.07

(continued)

Table 4.5 (continued)

HS code	*Name*	*PCI 2001–2005*	*PCI 2016–2021*	*Average exports value 2001–2005 (USD mill)*	*Average exports value 2016–2021 (USD mill)*	*Average exports share 2001–2005 (%)*	*Average exports share 2016–2021 (%)*
9032	Automatic regulating instruments	1.47	1.31	11.21	89.96	0.05	0.03
9102	Watches	−0.01	0.38	1.24	41.97	0.00	0.01
9504	Games	1.30	0.88	1.53	431.10	0.01	0.11
9505	Christmas and other festivity articles	−0.84	−0.32	10.63	40.99	0.05	0.01
9608	Pens	0.63	0.53	6.95	59.16	0.03	0.02
Electronics							
8503	Parts for use with electric generators	0.91	0.74	11.01	100.40	0.05	0.04
8505	Electromagnets	0.51	1.39	7.28	133.97	0.03	0.04
8506	Primary cells and primary batteries	−0.01	0.52	2.50	41.66	0.01	0.01
8508	Vacuum cleaners	1.35	1.21	0.32	342.56	0.00	0.04
8511	Electrical ignition equipment	0.66	0.69	3.68	38.41	0.02	0.01
8512	Electrical lighting equipment used for motor vehicles	1.73	1.11	1.86	213.12	0.01	0.07
8516	Electric heaters	0.51	0.65	10.30	354.35	0.05	0.12
8519	Sound reproducing apparatus	0.25	0.66	0.31	32.34	0.00	0.01
8523	Sound storage media	0.86	1.50	0.56	138.62	0.00	0.05

(continued)

Table 4.5 (continued)

HS code	*Name*	*PCI 2001–2005*	*PCI 2016–2021*	*Average exports value 2001–2005 (USD mill)*	*Average exports value 2016–2021 (USD mill)*	*Average exports share 2001–2005 (%)*	*Average exports share 2016–2021 (%)*
8526	Radar	1.16	1.17	0.67	206.52	0.00	0.07
8531	Electric sound or visual signaling apparatus	0.51	0.83	1.27	347.23	0.01	0.09
8532	Electrical capacitors	0.84	1.10	21.98	49.48	0.11	0.02
8533	Electrical resistors	0.75	0.90	6.04	58.99	0.02	0.02
8535	Electrical apparatus for > 1 kV	0.74	0.56	3.51	33.67	0.02	0.01
8536	Electrical apparatus for < 1 kV	0.81	0.66	31.60	1003.93	0.14	0.34
8538	Parts for electrical apparatus	1.34	1.00	6.15	308.90	0.02	0.11
8543	Electrical machines with individual functions n.e.c.	0.99	1.52	5.07	366.50	0.02	0.11
8547	Insulating fittings for electrical machines	1.25	1.08	3.09	57.02	0.01	0.02
Transport vehicles							
8703	Cars	1.31	1.04	17.98	72.78	0.07	0.01
8708	Parts of motor vehicles	1.61	1.25	32.49	1349.78	0.13	0.48
8716	Trailers and semi-trailers	0.68	0.69	5.77	84.58	0.03	0.03
8802	Other aircraft and spacecraft	0.36	0.32	0.69	40.96	0.00	0.02
8803	Parts of other aircraft	0.28	0.63	2.22	300.84	0.01	0.11

(continued)

Table 4.5 (continued)

HS code	*Name*	*PCI 2001–2005*	*PCI 2016–2021*	*Average exports value 2001–2005 (USD mill)*	*Average exports value 2016–2021 (USD mill)*	*Average exports share 2001–2005 (%)*	*Average exports share 2016–2021 (%)*
8901	Cargo ships and similar vessels	−0.30	−0.58	5.87	446.10	0.02	0.16
8905	Special function vessels, n.e.c.	−0.62	−1.13	1.93	127.70	0.01	0.05
Other							
Total exports—marginal 1				1.368	31,621	6.2	10.4
Weighted average PCI		0.23	0.48				
Average PCI		0.36	0.31				

Source Author' calculations based on data from Growth Lab at Harvard University, June 2024

Table 4.6 List of products recommended by the Growth Lab in 2024

Product name	*Global size (USD)*	*Global growth 5 years (%)*
Inorganic compounds, liquid or compressed air (2851 HS92)	$2.76B	↑215.9
Other salts of acids (2842 HS92)	$3.51B	↑583.5
Ball or roller bearings (8482 HS92)	$35.1B	↑28.9
Electrical machines with individual functions n.e.c. (8543 HS92)	$66.0B	↑76.5
Pumps, compressors, fans, etc. (8414 HS92)	$84.0B	↑29.5
Grindstones (6804 HS92)	$5.59B	↑35.9
Liquid crystal devices (9013 HS92)	$60.9B	↓9.5
Electrical capacitors (8532 HS92)	$39.3B	↑88.1
Primary cells and primary batteries (8506 HS92)	$9.09B	↑29.1
Auxiliary parts for use with boilers (8404 HS92)	$1.51B	↓25.2
Textile fabrics impregnated with plastics (5903 HS92)	$12.9B	↑12.8
Copper foil<0.15 mm thick (7410 HS92)	$9.64B	↑87.7
Transmission belts or belting, of textile material (5910 HS92)	$686M	↑31.1
Diazo-, azo-, or azoxy-compounds (2927 HS92)	$720M	↑44.4
Scissors (8213 HS92)	$996M	↑48.1
Padlocks and locks (8301 HS92)	$14.2B	↑19
Other articles of iron or steel (7326 HS92)	$61.3B	↑49.3
Parts for use with electric generators (8503 HS92)	$22.4B	↑47.3
Clasps, buckles etc. of metal (8308 HS92)	$4.18B	↑49
Meters (9029 HS92)	$8.23B	↑6.5
Electrical resistors (8533 HS92)	$15.0B	↑71.9
Parts and accessories for video or sound equipment (8522 HS92)	$1.94B	↓22.2
Tin bars and wire (8003 HS92)	$681M	↑59.9
Glasses (9004 HS92)	$10.5B	↑14.7
Electrical boards (8537 HS92)	$73.3B	↑35
Lamps (9405 HS92)	$63.7B	↑35.1
Other articles of aluminum (7616 HS92)	$20.3B	↑33.7
Safes (8303 HS92)	$1.42B	↑30.4
Other clock or watch parts (9114 HS92)	$1.69B	↓3.4
Watch cases and parts (9111 HS92)	$1.14B	↓1.5
Air conditioners (8415 HS92)	$55.4B	↑38.8
Electrical apparatus for < 1k volts (8536 HS92)	$116B	↑36.8
Electric heaters (8516 HS92)	$68.2B	↑67.5
Refrigerators, freezers (8418 HS92)	$60.3B	↑51.3
Carbon paper (4809 HS92)	$880M	↓13.1

(continued)

Table 4.6 (continued)

Product name	*Global size (USD)*	*Global growth 5 years (%)*
Articles for sewing of iron or steel (7319 HS92)	$343M	↑23.1
Structures and their parts, of iron or steel (7308 HS92)	$57.5B	↑32.9
Sheet piling of iron or steel (7301 HS92)	$2.16B	↑19.6
Artificial staple fibers, not processed for spinning (5504 HS92)	$3.37B	↑33.2
Frames for spectacles, goggles (9003 HS92)	$6.58B	↑26.1
Children's books (4903 HS92)	$1.68B	↑75.5
Household articles of iron or steel (7323 HS92)	$17.8B	↑74.9
Cigarette lighters (9613 HS92)	$2.08B	↑25.1
Vulcanized rubber thread and cord (4007 HS92)	$821M	↑73.6
Hard rubber (4017 HS92)	$274M	↓8.7
Stoves and similar non-electric appliances of iron or steel (7321 HS92)	$15.8B	↑75.9
Bicycles (8712 HS92)	$11.8B	↑47.1
Glass paving blocks or other molded products (7016 HS92)	$1.13B	↑4.1
Buttons (9606 HS92)	$1.77B	↑14.2
Watch straps (9113 HS92)	$2.00B	↑20.6

Source Data from the Growth Lab at Harvard University. The Atlas of Economic Complexity. http://www.atlas.cid.harvard.edu. Accessed January 17 2024

References

Balassa, B. (1965). Trade liberalization and "revealed" comparative advantage. *Manchester School of Economic and Social Studies*, *33*(2), 92–123.

Dinh, H. T. with contributions from Chandra, V., Pinto-Moreira, E., & Arbouch, M. (2021). *Morocco: Accelerating growth and job creation in a rapidly changing and integrated world*. Policy Center for the New South.

Growth Lab at Harvard University. (2024). *International trade data (HS, 92)*. Harvard University, Center for International Development. https://doi.org/10.7910/DVN/T4CHWJ/4RG21Y

Growth Lab at Harvard University. (Various years). *Atlas of economic complexity*. Harvard University, Center for International Development. http://www.atlas.cid.harvard.edu

Hausmann, R., Hidalgo, C. A., Bustos, S., Coscia, M., & Simoes, A. (2014). *The atlas of economic complexity: Mapping paths to prosperity*. MIT Press.

CHAPTER 5

Technological Content of Vietnam's Exports and Potential for Import Replacement

Chapter 4 identified the exports Vietnam has produced over the last two decades and classified them according to their comparative advantage. This chapter examines two key aspects of Vietnam's international trade in detail: (i) the technological content of Vietnam's exports based on the Lall classification system; and (ii) the potential for import replacement.

Technological Content of Vietnam's Exports According to the Lall System

In recent decades, Vietnam has undergone a remarkable transformation in its export structure. To understand this transformation in a meaningful way, it is essential to move beyond broad categories of trade data and examine the technological content of Vietnam's exports. One of the most insightful tools for this purpose is the classification system developed by Sanjaya Lall (2000). By organizing exports according to their level of technological sophistication, the Lall system offers a structured and policy-relevant framework to assess how far Vietnam has progressed toward higher-value-added and more knowledge-intensive production.

Contributed by Hinh T. Dinh

H. T. Dinh, H. T. Nguyen, *Vietnam's Economic Leap*,
https://doi.org/10.1007/978-3-032-08904-5_5

Before delving into Vietnam's performance, it is useful to first describe the structure of the Lall classification and reflect on both its analytical strengths and inherent limitations.

The Lall system groups traded commodities into five categories. The first is Primary Products (PP), which comprise raw materials, agricultural goods, and other unprocessed commodities. These are followed by Resource-Based Manufactures (RB), which involve simple processing of natural resources—for example, processed food, basic chemicals, and simple manufactured goods. Low-Technology Manufactures (LT) refer to products made with mature, well-diffused technologies that are often labor-intensive; typical examples include textiles, footwear, basic metal products, and simple machinery. A step above are the Medium-Technology Manufactures (MT), encompassing goods that require more complex production processes and moderate R&D intensity, such as automotive components, industrial machinery, and certain types of electronics. At the top of the ladder are High-Technology Manufactures (HT)—products based on advanced, rapidly changing technologies with high R&D requirements, including precision instruments, advanced electronics, and aerospace equipment.

One of the principal strengths of the Lall system is its clear focus on technological sophistication. This orientation allows researchers and policymakers to assess not only the structure of a country's exports but also its underlying industrial and innovation capabilities. Moreover, the system's hierarchical structure—ranging from primary to high-technology products—makes it particularly well-suited for tracking patterns of industrial upgrading over time. Importantly, it aligns with international trade classifications, such as the Harmonized System (HS), which enhances its practical usability across existing trade datasets. For developing countries, the classification provides a valuable lens for identifying opportunities for technological upgrading, evaluating the impact of industrial policies, and benchmarking performance against peer economies.

Nonetheless, the system is not without its weaknesses. It is static in nature, meaning it does not automatically evolve with changes in technology or the global economy. This limitation is especially problematic for fast-moving industries such as electronics and biotechnology, where product categories can quickly become outdated. Furthermore, the system tends to use broad product groupings, which can obscure important nuances within a given sector. For instance, the HT category encompasses a wide range of products with vastly different technological requirements and economic significance. Another shortcoming is the system's emphasis on final goods, which may downplay the importance of economies that specialize in intermediate production (typically advanced economies) or participate at specific nodes of global value chains. Lastly, subjectivity in classification—whereby assigning a product to a specific category may depend on interpretative judgment—can lead to inconsistencies across different studies.

In addition to its technological typology, the Lall classification is closely correlated with patterns of labor and capital intensity. Although the system is not explicitly designed to capture input factors, general trends are discernible. In developing countries, Primary Products tend to be labor-intensive (such as in agriculture), whereas in developed economies they are often capital-intensive (e.g., mining or energy extraction). Resource-Based Manufactures typically require greater capital investment due to the need for processing equipment and infrastructure. Low-Technology Manufactures are overwhelmingly labor-intensive—this is particularly evident in Vietnam's dominant exports of garments and footwear. Medium-Technology Manufactures are more capital intensive than LT goods but less so than HT products, requiring investment in specialized machinery and moderate R&D. Finally, High-Technology Manufactures are the most capital-intensive of all, due to the advanced production techniques, automation, and continuous R&D expenditures they entail. However, it is important to note that labor and capital intensities can vary significantly within each category and change over time due to automation, skill development, and shifts in global value chains.

Lall Classification of Vietnam's Exports

Classics

Applying this analytical framework to Vietnam's export data yields a rich and multifaceted picture of the country's structural transformation. The classification of Vietnam's 116 "Classics" export products—defined and identified in Chap. 4 as those that have remained consistently present in the export basket—shows a clear dominance of Low-Technology Manufactures, which account for approximately 25% of total exports (Annex Table 5.1). This is consistent with Vietnam's comparative advantage in labor-intensive industries such as apparel and footwear. In contrast, Medium—and High-Technology Manufactures each contribute a modest 2% to total Classics (Annex Table 5.1), reflecting the country's limited penetration into more advanced sectors. Primary Products and Resource-Based Manufactures, when combined, make up around 8% of exports. Although the inclusion of certain HT products, such as electronic printed circuits, signals an entry into higher-tech manufacturing, most of these goods are assembled using imported components and therefore generate limited domestic value added.

The policy implications of this structure are significant. First, Vietnam must pursue export diversification to reduce its vulnerability to shocks in labor-intensive and low-margin sectors. Second, there is an urgent need to move up the value chain, even within existing RB and LT industries, by increasing domestic processing and technology content. Third, building the human capital base is essential to support skill-intensive manufacturing, particularly in MT and HT sectors. Fourth, technology transfer from foreign direct investment (FDI) and global firms must be more effectively leveraged to strengthen local industrial capabilities. Lastly, a dual strategy is needed: maintaining competitiveness in traditional sectors while simultaneously investing in higher-value-added industries.

Emerging Champions

Vietnam's performance in **Emerging Champions**—defined and identified in Chap. 4 as those that have recently gained prominence—presents a more dynamic, albeit concentrated, picture. These products are listed in Annex Table 5.2. Here, High-Technology Manufactures account for a striking 29% of total, suggesting rapid progress toward technological upgrading. However, this entire 29% is attributable to just four product lines: telephones, transmission apparatus, semiconductor devices, and integrated circuits (Annex Table 5.2). As discussed in Chaps. 2 and 8, the contribution of these products to the domestic value added is small. This narrow base of high-tech exports reveals a high level of concentration and continued dependence on imported components, particularly from multinational corporations operating in export-processing zones. Meanwhile, Medium—and Low-Technology products contribute 8% and 3% respectively, while Primary and Resource-Based products remain marginal at 0.43% and 2.3%. These figures point to the need for policies that not only foster technological deepening but also broaden the base of high-tech production to include more product lines and greater domestic content.

Disappearing Exports

The analysis of **Disappearing Exports**—those no longer present in Vietnam's trade profile—further illuminates shifting trends. Annex Table 5.3 shows that one-third of these products were in the High-Technology category, accounting for about 2% of total exports. A notable example is computers (HS8471), whose decline may reflect rising competition from East Asian countries, changes in global demand, or rapid technological obsolescence. In addition, Low-Technology and Primary Products accounted for 1.8% and 1.2% of disappearing exports, respectively. These shifts suggest that maintaining export shares in both traditional and high-tech sectors requires constant adaptation, innovation, and strategic investment.

Marginal Exports 1

Finally, the group of **Marginal Exports**—defined as goods exported by Vietnam without a revealed comparative advantage (RCA)—shows a diverse composition (Annex Table 5.4). Here we focus on Marginal Exports 1—the group with individual export values exceeding US$25 million. According to the Lall classification, Medium-Technology products account for 3.6% of total exports, followed by Low-Technology (3.1%), Resource-Based (1.9%), and High-Technology (1.4%) goods. The distribution of these products across all categories suggests that marginal export status is influenced more by market conditions and demand dynamics than by inherent technological sophistication. Still, identifying the technological structure of marginal exports can help policymakers anticipate which sectors may offer future growth opportunities or risk fading into irrelevance.

In conclusion, classifying Vietnam's exports using the Lall system provides a valuable baseline for assessing the country's movement up the technological ladder. While progress has been made—particularly in select high-tech segments—the overall structure remains skewed toward low-technology, labor-intensive products with limited value addition. The policy challenge now is to accelerate technological upgrading, deepen integration into global value chains, and build the domestic capabilities necessary for sustained economic transformation. Only by addressing these challenges directly can Vietnam secure a more diversified, resilient, and innovation-driven export future.

Import Replacement Potential

The remainder of this chapter examines Vietnam's imports that could potentially be produced domestically and exported competitively. The focus is on labor-intensive industries that require skilled workers, have limited economies of scale, and demand relatively small investments. With a population of approximately 100 million, Vietnam's imports provide a stable source of demand, which can reassure domestic producers. Import replacement can also serve as a buffer during periods when exports are negatively impacted by protectionist measures abroad.

Before identifying specific products and subsectors suitable for import replacement, it is important to clarify the rationale behind this approach. The strategy proposed in this book is not the import substitution industrialization (ISI) model of the 1970s and 1980s, which aimed to protect and expand domestic industries through tariffs, import quotas, and subsidized government loans. The ISI approach sought to replace all imports through industrial policies that favored domestic production, often using barriers such as tariffs, overvalued currencies that facilitated the import of raw materials, and restrictions on foreign direct investment (FDI). However, this strategy contradicted the principle of comparative advantage and led to severe economic problems in many developing countries, including balance-of-payments crises and external debt burdens.

As a result of these failures, developing countries shifted their economic strategies in the late 1980s and 1990s toward the "Washington Consensus," which advocated for market-driven policies with minimal government intervention. However, this approach also had significant shortcomings. In the wake of the 2008–09 financial crisis, many mainstream economists have reassessed its effectiveness (see the summary in Dinh, 2017). The emerging consensus is that while markets are efficient, they need to be complemented by pragmatic government policies that support private sector growth.

In the context of globalization and global value chains (GVCs), Vietnam faces significant challenges in upgrading its manufacturing capabilities—for example, transitioning from original equipment manufacturing (OEM) to original design manufacturing (ODM) and, ultimately, to original brand manufacturing (OBM). Three key factors hinder this progression:

1. Dependence on foreign firms: The decision to upgrade is largely in the hands of leading multinational corporations rather than Vietnam itself.
2. High entry costs: GVCs are highly efficient, making it expensive for developing countries to break into these networks.

3. Profit-driven supply chain decisions: The decision to produce components in a particular country is based on corporate profit maximization rather than national development goals, such as fostering backward and forward linkages within the domestic economy.

As a result, a developing country can remain stagnant for years, trapped in the "middle-income trap," even while following a market-based, export-oriented development strategy. In such cases, government intervention is necessary to address market failures and to apply first-mover advantages, thereby preventing the economy from settling into a low-growth equilibrium.

To avoid repeating the mistakes of past import substitution policies, the import replacement measures must be **clear, transparent, time-bound, and well-targeted.** This requires **defining selection criteria for import replacement ex ante**. Some of these criteria include:

- How should domestic product quality be measured against imports to justify policy support?
- How can Vietnam ensure that its selected industries have a comparative advantage? (One method is through Balassa's Revealed Comparative Advantage; see Chap. 4.)
- What indicators, such as the Product Complexity Index or the Economic Complexity Index, can assess Vietnam's potential production capabilities?
- What policy instruments—such as pricing mechanisms, tax incentives, tariffs, or financial support—should be used to support domestic industries, and how can their duration and scope be limited?

This chapter identifies products and subsectors in which Vietnam has both a comparative advantage and the necessary skilled workforce to support domestic production. Chapters 7–10 will discuss the policy instruments available to facilitate this transition.

Structure of Imports

According to the Growth Lab, Vietnam's import structure changed significantly between 1995 and 2021. The share of service imports declined from a peak of 20% in 1997–98 to below 10% in 2021, while electronics and machinery became dominant import categories.

- In 1995: The largest import was petroleum products (9.1%), followed by cigars and cigarettes (4.8%), motorcycles (3.4%), cars (2.9%), and medicaments (2.2%).
- In 2001: Petroleum products remained the top import, followed by motorcycles (2.4%), while cigar and cigarette imports declined to below 1%.
- In 2021: The largest import was electronic integrated circuits (12.3%), followed by telephones (5.8%), knitted products (1.8%), petroleum products (1.3%), and electronic printed circuits.

Potential Products for Import Replacement

Identifying a strategic list of products for import replacement in Vietnam requires a methodical and data-driven approach. Starting from a broad base of 1239 imported products during the 2016–2021 period, the analysis first narrows this pool by selecting only those items with an average annual import value exceeding $600 million. This filtering step yields a shortlist of 92 high-impact products whose replacement could meaningfully reduce Vietnam's reliance on foreign inputs. Subsequent steps draw on the economic complexity approach pioneered by Hausmann and Hidalgo (2011), which warrants some explanation.

The economic complexity approach offers a powerful framework for understanding a country's development trajectory by analyzing the diversity and sophistication of its productive capabilities. This approach emphasizes that economic prosperity is closely linked to the complexity of the goods a country can manufacture, which in turn reflects the amount of embedded productive knowledge in its economy. Using decades of global export data, Hausmann and Hidalgo demonstrate that countries producing a diverse array of complex products tend to experience faster and more sustained income growth. Economic complexity is thus not merely a symptom of prosperity, but also a driver of it—enabling countries to climb the development ladder through the accumulation and coordination of tacit knowledge across individuals and institutions.

Three core concepts underpin this analytical framework. **Distance** measures how closely a new product aligns with a country's existing capabilities; a shorter distance implies higher feasibility for local production. **Complexity of Goods** (COG) refers to the inherent sophistication of products, indicating the breadth and depth of knowledge required for their manufacture. Finally, the **Product Complexity Index** (PCI) ranks products by evaluating both the diversity of countries that export them and the ubiquity of other products these countries produce. High PCI values are associated with goods that are made by only a few highly complex economies—such as advanced machinery and electronics—while low PCI values correspond to simpler products, like raw materials, that are widely produced. Together, these metrics help assess both the challenges and strategic value of potential diversification paths.

We use these three criteria to help reduce the short list of Vietnamese potential import replacement products further. These metrics are evaluated in the context of Vietnam's current production capabilities, with products ranked by percentile to determine how closely they align with what the country already produces. For instance, the average Distance score for HS category 8415—air conditioners—was 0.7856 over the 2016–2021 period. This figure places the product in the 34th percentile, indicating that Vietnam's existing manufacturing capability is better suited to produce air conditioners than at least a third of all other products in the economy. Such metrics suggest that, given the right policy and investment environment, domestic production of air conditioners could become viable.

The strategic recommendation emerging from this analysis is clear: over the next five years, Vietnam should prioritize developing the capacity to manufacture products that fall within the 85th percentile or higher in both Distance and PCI. This more stringent filter yields a refined list of 68 products with high potential for import substitution. These products, listed in Annex Table 5.5, span eight broad industrial categories: vegetables, foodstuffs, and wood; chemicals and plastics; textiles and furniture; metals; minerals; machinery; electronics; and transport vehicles. Together, they represent not just a theoretical opportunity, but also a concrete agenda for review by private enterprises. Should businesses judge certain items on this list to be commercially viable, it becomes imperative for policymakers to engage proactively, identify the specific binding constraints hindering local production, and design supportive policies to overcome them.

An essential consideration in this policy effort is whether Vietnam possesses a comparative advantage in producing these goods. To investigate this issue, we classify each product based on Balassa's Revealed Comparative Advantage (RCA) index, grouping them into four distinct categories: Classics, Champions, Disappearing, and Marginals 1 and 2. These categories were already explained in detail in Chap. 4 and are only summarized here. "Classics" refer to goods that Vietnam has consistently exported over the past two decades, representing stable areas of competitiveness. "Champions" are emerging sectors in which the country is building competitive strength. "Disappearing" industries are those in decline, while "Marginals 1 and 2" denote sectors in which Vietnam currently lacks a comparative advantage. Due to the lack of space, the results are not presented here, but it is important to note that nearly half of the electronics products in the 68-product shortlist fall under the Classics category, underscoring Vietnam's solid and sustained export performance in this field. In stark contrast, most chemical products are found in the Marginals 1 category, highlighting a significant competitive gap in that industry.

The analysis deepens further with Annex 5.6, which evaluates the technological sophistication of these potential import replacement products using Lall's classification system. This categorization sheds light on the broader industrial implications of domestic substitution. In terms of product count, the largest share—37%—falls under medium-tech manufacturing, whereas high-tech manufacturing leads in value terms. Interestingly, most of the products within these two technologically intensive groups are either Classics or Marginals 1. This duality reveals both promise and challenge: it suggests that while Vietnam is already excelling in some segments, other areas remain underdeveloped but could be strategically cultivated for future industrial expansion.

In sum, this systematic identification of products for import replacement offers Vietnam a well-defined roadmap to bolster domestic production capabilities. By aligning policy support with areas of demonstrated and emerging competitiveness, Vietnam can reduce import dependence, foster domestic value creation, and strategically upgrade its industrial base. The findings and classifications presented here are intended as a starting point for constructive dialogue between the private and public sectors—encouraging firms to explore emerging opportunities and the government to support their realization through targeted reforms and investments in enabling infrastructure—with the aim of developing a more refined set of policy recommendations, rather than serving as a final conclusion.

Annex 1: Exports Classified by Technological Content

See Tables 5.1, 5.2, 5.3 and 5.4.

Table 5.1 Lall classification of classics

List of classics	*Average export value 2016–2021 (mil USD)*	*Average export share 2016–2021 (%)*
Primary Products (PP)		
901: Coffee	2648	1.1
801: Cashew nuts & coconuts	2764	1.0
1006: Rice	2452	0.9
304: Fish fillets	2229	0.9
306: Crustaceans	1871	0.7
810: Other fresh fruit	936	0.34
303: Frozen fish, excluding fillets	372	0.14
307: Mollusks	319	0.13
714: Tubers	238	0.1
902: Tea	182	0.07
906: Cinnamon	157	0.05
409: Honey	67	0.02
909: Anise, fennel, etc.	45	0.01
4103: Other raw hides and skins	25	0.01
1401: Vegetable materials used for plaiting	10	0.00
508: Coral and shells	4	0.00
2521: Limestone	75	0.03
2614: Titanium ore	74	0.02
4001: Natural rubber	990	0.4
Subtotal	15,458	5.9
Resource Based Manufactures (RB)		
904: Pepper	849	0.35
4401: Fuel wood	1821	0.6
1605: Prepared aquatic invertebrates	1683	0.61
1604: Prepared or preserved fish	582	0.21
1108: Starches	452	0.16
2008: Fruits and nuts, otherwise prepared	444	0.14
4402: Wood charcoal	66	0.02
1106: Flour of dried legumes	20	0.01
4405: Wood wool or flour	17	0.01
1521: Vegetable waxes and beeswax	8	0.00

(continued)

Table 5.1 (continued)

List of classics	*Average export value 2016–2021 (mil USD)*	*Average export share 2016–2021 (%)*
3805: Turpentines	26	0.01
Subtotal	5966	2.1
Low Technology Manufactures (LT)		
4202: Trunks or cases	3258	1.28
1902: Pasta	238	0.08
4602: Basketwork	252	0.08
305: Preserved fish	195	0.07
4820: Notebooks	148	0.05
4203: Leather apparel	137	0.05
4421: Other articles of wood	139	0.05
4419: Wooden kitchenware	70	0.03
4201: Saddlery and harnesses	50	0.01
4420: Wood marquetry, ornaments, etc.	42	0.01
4601: Products of plaiting materials	14	0.01
3406: Candles	342	0.10
4013: Rubber inner tubes	77	0.03
6404: Textile footwear	8878	3.26
9403: Other furniture and parts	6470	2.20
6403: Leather footwear	5608	2.11
6110: Sweaters, pullovers, sweatshirts etc., knit	3551	1.29
6402: Other footwear of rubber or plastics	3382	1.28
9401: Seats	3533	1.10
6204: Women's suits and pants	2814	1.06
6203: Men's suits and pants	2529	0.96
6104: Women's suits, knit	2492	0.89
5205: Cotton yarn of > 85	2297	0.83
6109: T-shirts, knit	1866	0.67
6201: Men's overcoats, not knit	1748	0.65
6202: Women's overcoats, not knit	1568	0.59
6210: Garments made of textile felts and nonwoven fabric	1146	0.42
6211: Activewear	940	0.35
6205: Men's shirts	889	0.35
6105: Men's shirts, knit	804	0.32
6103: Men's suits, knit	820	0.28
6307: Other made-up articles	779	0.27
6212: Brassieres	775	0.26
6206: Women's shirts	607	0.24

(continued)

Table 5.1 (continued)

List of classics	*Average export value 2016–2021 (mil USD)*	*Average export share 2016–2021 (%)*
6406: Parts of footwear	609	0.23
6108: Women's undergarments, knit	638	0.22
6107: Men's undergarments, knit	548	0.20
6305: Bags for packing goods	433	0.15
6114: Other garments, knit	410	0.15
6102: Women's overcoats, knit	355	0.13
5206: Cotton yarn of < 85	364	0.13
6106: Women's shirts, knit	318	0.13
6505: Hats, knit	342	0.12
6112: Activewear, knit	336	0.12
6101: Men's overcoats, knit	281	0.10
5509: Yarn of synthetic staple fibers, not for retail sale	264	0.10
6111: Babies' garments, knit	288	0.10
6116: Gloves, knit	227	0.08
6405: Other footwear	192	0.07
5608: Nets	132	0.05
6216: Gloves	136	0.05
6304: Other furnishing articles	109	0.04
6306: Tents, tarpaulins, etc.	112	0.04
6209: Babies' garments	90	0.03
6207: Men's undergarments	95	0.03
6506: Other headgear	89	0.03
6208: Women's undergarments	82	0.03
6113: Garments knit with impregnated fibers	71	0.03
5607: Twine and ropes of baste fibers	69	0.02
5004: Silk yarn	29	0.01
5901: Stiffened textiles	31	0.01
5305: Vegetable textile fibers	26	0.01
5401: Synthetic sowing thread	22	0.01
5604: Rubber textiles	15	0.01
5609: Articles of yarn, rope etc. not elsewhere classified	14	0.00
6701: Feathers or down	13	0.00
6504: Hats	8	0.00
6213: Handkerchiefs	6	0.00
6801: Flagstones, of natural stone	56	0.02
6913: Ornamental ceramic articles	112	0.04
6914: Other ceramic articles	87	0.03

(continued)

Table 5.1 (continued)

List of classics	*Average export value 2016–2021 (mil USD)*	*Average export share 2016–2021 (%)*
8110: Antimony	41	0.01
8215: Cutlery	191	0.07
9503: Toys	1282	0.43
9507: Fishing and hunting equipment	119	0.04
9601: Worked animal carving material	6	0.00
9607: Slide fasteners	52	0.02
9609: Pencils, crayons, pastels, etc.	64	0.03
9613: Cigarette lighters	31	0.01
Subtotal	67,248	24.4
Medium Technology Manufactures (MT)		
8452: Sewing machines	561	0.21
8501: Electric motors and generators	1313	0.47
8518: Microphones	3571	1.19
8714: Parts of motorcycles or wheelchairs	578	0.20
8804: Parachutes	26	0.01
Subtotal	6048	2.1
High Technology Manufactures (HT)		
8534: Electronic printed circuits	1020	0.35
8544: Insulated electrical wire	4575	1.59
Subtotal	5594	1.9
Total	100,314	36.5

Source Author' calculations based on data from Growth Lab at Harvard University, June 2024

Table 5.2 Lall Classification of Emerging Products 2016–2021

Emerging products	*Average export value 2016–2021 (mil USD)*	*Average export share 2016–2021 (%)*
Primary Products (PP)		
812: Fruits and nuts, provisionally preserved	12	0.00
1504: Fish oils	59	0.02
2302: Cereal residues	77	0.02
2308: Vegetable materials for animal feeding	26	0.01
2517: Gravel	134	0.05

(continued)

Table 5.2 (continued)

Emerging products	*Average export value 2016–2021 (mil USD)*	*Average export share 2016–2021 (%)*
2518: Dolomite	19	0.01
2522: Quicklime	57	0.02
2529: Feldspar	71	0.03
2804: Silicon & rare gases	263	0.09
2805: Rare-earth metals	133	0.05
5002: Raw silk	42	0.01
5003: Silk waste	3	0.00
5202: Cotton waste	23	0.01
5503: Synthetic staple fibers	150	0.05
5505: Waste of man-made fibers	4	0.00
7801: Lead refined unwrought	104	0.05
8106: Bismuth	8	0.00
Resource Based Manufactures (RB)		
2101: Coffee extracts	412	0.16
2301: Flours of fish, for animal feed	218	0.08
4104: Tanned hides of bovines or equines	392	0.16
4109: Patent leather	10	0.00
4111: Composition leather	27	0.01
4302: Other tanned furskins	87	0.04
4408: Sheets for veneering for plywood	100	0.03
4412: Plywood	661	0.20
2523: Cements	1309	0.42
2618: Granulated iron or steel slag	16	0.00
2706: Tar distilled from coal, lignite etc.	21	0.01
2809: Phosphoric acid etc.	81	0.03
2818: Aluminum oxide	405	0.14
2823: Titanium oxides	15	0.01
2825: Metal base oxides, n.e.c.	114	0.04
3505: Dextrins and other modified starches	75	0.02
3806: Rosin and resin acids	66	0.02
3809: Finishing agents	169	0.06
4002: Synthetic rubber	1314	0.44
4012: Used pneumatic tires of rubber	47	0.02
6810: Articles of cement, of concrete or of artificial stone	328	0.10
6814: Mica articles	6	0.00
6910: Ceramic sinks, washbasins, and similar sanitary fixtures	191	0.07
7006: Worked glass	185	0.07
7020: Other articles of glass	457	0.18

(continued)

Table 5.2 (continued)

Emerging products	*Average export value 2016–2021 (mil USD)*	*Average export share 2016–2021 (%)*
Low Technology Manufactures (LT)		
3923: Packing lids	1057	0.38
4015: Vulcanized rubber articles of apparel	232	0.06
5402: Synthetic filament yarn	775	0.26
5510: Yarn of artificial staple fibers, not for retail sale	80	0.04
5802: Terry cloth	8	0.00
5807: Labels and badges of textiles	23	0.01
5808: Braids in piece	11	0.00
5902: Tire cord fabric	460	0.16
6001: Pile fabrics, knit	100	0.03
6002: Other knitted fabrics	903	0.31
6303: Curtains	114	0.04
6401: Waterproof footwear	27	0.01
6507: Headbands	17	0.01
6603: Parts of umbrellas or walking sticks	6	0.00
9406: Prefabricated buildings	183	0.07
7117: Imitation jewelry	140	0.06
7209: Flat-rolled iron, width > 600 mm, cold-rolled, not clad	352	0.13
7210: Flat rolled iron, width > 600 mm, clad	1382	0.36
7212: Flat-rolled iron, width < 600 mm, clad	234	0.09
7213: Hot rolled bars of iron	373	0.10
7217: Wire of iron or nonalloy steel	128	0.04
7229: Wire of other alloy steel	66	0.02
7306: Other tubes, pipes and hollow profiles of iron or steel	553	0.21
7312: Wire of iron or steel, not insulated	323	0.11
7324: Sanitary ware and parts of iron or steel	56	0.02
7411: Copper tubes and pipes	566	0.19
7413: Copper wire, uninsulated	33	0.01
8201: Handtools for gardening	47	0.01
8212: Razors	188	0.06
8214: Other cutlery	18	0.01
8311: Wire etc. used for welding	79	0.03
9506: Sports equipment	552	0.18

(continued)

Table 5.2 (continued)

Emerging products	*Average export value 2016–2021 (mil USD)*	*Average export share 2016–2021 (%)*
9602: Worked vegetable or mineral carving material	38	0.01
9611: Hand-operated stamps	7	0.00
Medium Technology Manufactures (MT)		
8402: Steam boilers	117	0.04
8443: Printers and copiers	1105	0.41
8450: Household—or laundry-type washing machines	610	0.22
8470: Cash registers, calculators, etc.	360	0.14
8473: Parts and accessories for office machines	5929	1.64
9002: Lenses and other optical elements	408	0.15
9006: Photographic cameras	459	0.18
9009: Electrostatic photo-copyers	32	0.01
9028: Gas, liquid or electricity meters	193	0.07
8504: Electrical transformers	1840	0.57
8507: Batteries	1318	0.46
8520: Magnetic tape recorders	94	0.02
8521: Video recording apparatus	2220	0.78
8522: Parts and accessories for video or sound equipment	29	0.01
8527: Reception apparatus for radio broadcasting	309	0.13
8528: Monitors and projectors	2819	0.91
8529: Parts of radios, telephones, and T.V.s	6582	2.09
8548: Waste and scrap of batteries	149	0.06
8711: Motorcycles	739	0.25
8713: Wheelchairs	28	0.01
8904: Tugs and pusher craft	161	0.07
High Technology Manufactures (HT)		
8517: Telephones	20,023	6.90
8525: Transmission apparatus for radio, telephone and TV	39,092	13.82
8541: Semiconductor devices	2722	0.91
8542: Electronic integrated circuits	19,611	6.88
Total	123,972	50.7

Source Author' calculations based on data from Growth Lab at Harvard University, June 2024

Table 5.3 Technological content of Disappearing Products

List of Disappearing Products	*Average export value 2016–2021 (mil USD)*	*Average export share 2016–2021 (%)*
Primary Products (PP)		
106: Other live animals	16.99	0.01
208: Other meat	10.75	0.00
301: Live Fish	16.26	0.01
302: Fish, excluding fillets	15.43	0.01
410: Edible animal products, n.e.c.	7.47	0.00
501: Human hair, unworked	0.28	0.00
505: Feathers and down	35.57	0.01
511: Animal products n.e.c.	37.45	0.01
711: Vegetables, provisionally preserved	11.26	0.00
712: Vegetables, dried	53.06	0.02
807: Melons and papayas	38.21	0.02
811: Fruits and nuts, frozen	94.84	0.03
813: Fruits, dried	19.12	0.01
908: Nutmeg	13.22	0.00
910: Spices	30.19	0.01
1202: Peanuts	40.85	0.01
1203: Copra	1.76	0.00
1211: Plants used in perfumery, pharmacy or insecticide	30.63	0.01
1213: Cereal straw and husks	3.69	0.00
1301: Lac	2.63	0.00
1402: Vegetable materials used as stuffing	–	0.00
1404: Vegetable products n.e.c.	13.66	0.01
2505: Natural sands	31.91	0.01
2506: Quartz	3.54	0.00
2510: Natural calcium phosphates	16.72	0.01
2511: Natural barium sulfate	12.50	0.00
2514: Slate	0.04	0.00
2515: Marble	31.71	0.01
2530: Mineral substances n.e.c.	35.11	0.01
2610: Chromium ore	0.02	0.00
2611: Tungsten ore	2.23	0.00
2615: Zirconium ore	14.10	0.00
2617: Other ores	1.58	0.00
2621: Other slag and ash	8.36	0.00
2701: Coal	230.59	0.09
2709: Petroleum oils, crude	2173.81	0.91

(continued)

Table 5.3 (continued)

List of Disappearing Products	*Average export value 2016–2021 (mil USD)*	*Average export share 2016–2021 (%)*
5203: Cotton, carded or combed	6.4	0.00
5303: Textile bast fibers	0.5	0.00
5001: Silkworm cocoons	0.00	0.00
8001: Unwrought tin	11.30	0.01
8111: Manganese	0.60	0.00
Subtotal	3074	1.2
Resource Based Manufactures (RB)		
402: Milk, concentrated	69.54	0.03
1101: Wheat or meslin flour	63.55	0.02
1603: Extracts and juices of meat or fish	3.34	0.00
1704: Confectionery sugar	103.64	0.04
1903: Tapioca	1.57	0.00
2001: Pickled fruits and vegetables	24.66	0.01
2003: Mushrooms, prepared or preserved	5.57	0.00
2102: Yeasts	18.37	0.01
2402: Cigars and cigarettes	171.55	0.07
2841: Salts of oxo metallic acids	61.79	0.02
2846: Compounds of rare-earth metals	14.47	0.00
2922: Oxygen-function amino-compounds	87.84	0.03
3101: Animal or vegetable fertilizers	9.06	0.00
3105: Mixed fertilizers	160.13	0.06
3306: Dental hygiene products	35.66	0.01
3401: Soap	25.23	0.01
3802: Activated carbon	27.98	0.01
3915: Plastic waste	46.10	0.02
4003: Reclaimed rubber	3.94	0.00
4004: Scrap of rubber	1.05	0.00
4005: Compounded rubber	22.10	0.01
4017: Hard rubber	1.94	0.00
4107: Bovine leather further prepared	13.66	0.01
4304: Artificial fur	0.72	0.00
4403: Wood in the rough	32.55	0.02
4404: Strips and other pieces of wood	1.80	0.00
4409: Wood shaped along its edges	42.47	0.01
4413: Densified wood	7.18	0.00
4803: Tissue	56.84	0.02

(continued)

Table 5.3 (continued)

List of Disappearing Products	*Average export value 2016–2021 (mil USD)*	*Average export share 2016–2021 (%)*
4805: Other uncoated paper and paperboard	261.63	0.08
4823: Other paper cut to size	93.40	0.03
6802: Worked building stone	114.43	0.04
6803: Worked slate	3.72	0.00
6901: Bricks, blocks, and other ceramic goods	0.33	0.00
6904: Ceramic building bricks	5.65	0.00
6907: Unglazed ceramic flags and pavers	125.57	0.04
6908: Glazed ceramic flags and pavers	35.69	0.02
6912: Ceramic household articles	15.18	0.01
7003: Glass, cast or rolled	4.80	0.00
7005: Float glass	112.76	0.05
7202: Ferroalloys	129.44	0.05
7401: Copper mattes	9.31	0.01
Subtotal	2026.21	0.76
Low Technology Manufactures (LT)		
3924: Plastic household articles	240.89	0.08
3926: Other articles of plastic	1067.00	0.36
4414: Wooden frames	13.14	0.01
4417: Wooden tools	6.94	0.00
4908: Transfers (decalcomanias)	13.75	0.00
5006: Silk yarn, for retail sale	0.27	0.00
5007: Woven silk fabrics	14.87	0.01
5207: Cotton yarn for retail sale	11.91	0.00
5308: Yarn of other vegetable textile fibers	0.79	0.00
5310: Woven fabrics of jute or of other textile bast fibers	0.43	0.00
5311: Woven fabrics of vegetable textile fibers	4.25	0.00
5407: Woven fabrics of synthetic filament yarn	315.99	0.11
5508: Synthetic staple fibers sewing thread	7.91	0.00
5511: Yarn of synthetic staple fibers, for retail sale	6.87	0.00
5514: Woven fabrics of < 85% synthetic staple fibers weighing > 170 g/m2	20.07	0.01

(continued)

Table 5.3 (continued)

List of Disappearing Products	*Average export value 2016–2021 (mil USD)*	*Average export share 2016–2021 (%)*
5515: Other woven fabrics of synthetic staple fibers	33.72	0.01
5803: Gauze	1.20	0.00
5806: Narrow woven fabrics	62.95	0.02
5811: Quilted textile products	2.07	0.00
6215: Ties, bow ties and cravats	5.58	0.00
6217: Other clothing accessories	27.17	0.01
6302: House linen	275.52	0.10
6310: Used or new rags textile scraps	9.32	0.00
6501: Hat forms	0.20	0.00
6502: Hat shapes	0.28	0.00
6503: Felt hats	0.01	0.00
7113: Jewelry of precious metal	236.69	0.08
7114: Goldsmith and silversmith wares	687.20	0.27
7223: Wire of stainless steel	29.03	0.01
7308: Structures and their parts, of iron or steel	582.93	0.20
7313: Barbed wire of iron or steel	0.71	0.00
7316: Anchors of iron or steel	3.20	0.00
7318: Screws and similar articles of iron or steel	444.73	0.16
7319: Articles for sewing of iron or steel	1.78	0.00
7323: Household articles of iron or steel	119.64	0.04
7614: Aluminum wire, not insulated	6.75	0.00
7615: Household articles of aluminum	71.32	0.02
7803: Lead bars, rods, profiles and wire	–	0.00
7805: Lead tubes, pipes and fittings	–	0.00
7907: Other articles of zinc	11.02	0.00
8003: Tin bars and wire	2.94	0.00
8007: Other articles of tin	4.93	0.00
8113: Cermets	5.71	0.00
8211: Knife sets	34.86	0.01
8304: Paper trays and similar office equipment, of base metal	1.43	0.00
8306: Ornaments, statuettes, etc. of metal	10.56	0.00
8307: Flexible tubing of base metal	19.05	0.01
9404: Mattresses and bedding	350.23	0.12
9603: Brooms and mops	163.77	0.06

(continued)

Table 5.3 (continued)

List of Disappearing Products	*Average export value 2016–2021 (mil USD)*	*Average export share 2016–2021 (%)*
9606: Buttons	19.51	0.01
9612: Typewriter ribbons and ink pads	9.84	0.00
9616: Scent sprays	18.24	0.01
9618: Mannequins	1.94	0.00
Subtotal	4981.10	1.78
Medium Technology Manufactures (MT)		
3704: Photographic film, not developed	0.40	0.00
8437: Machinery for processing grain	20.19	0.01
8502: Electric generating sets and rotary converters	221.14	0.05
8509: Electromechanical domestic appliances	318.81	0.09
8537: Electrical boards	601.75	0.19
8712: Bicycles	65.96	0.02
8801: Gliders, hang gliders	1.19	0.00
8902: Fishing vessels	23.59	0.01
8906: Other vessels	85.17	0.04
9033: Other parts for machines and appliances	34.89	0.01
9104: Instrument panel clocks for vehicles	2.24	0.00
9111: Watch cases and parts	9.73	0.00
9113: Watch straps	20.19	0.01
Subtotal	1405.25	0.43
High Technology Manufactures (HT)		
8471: Computers	5317.47	2.03
8540: Thermionic, cold cathode or photocathode tubes	1.61	0.00
Subtotal	5319.08	2.03
Total	16,806	6.2

Source Author' calculations based on data from Growth Lab at Harvard University, June 2024

Table 5.4 Technological content of Marginal 1 Products

List of Marginal Products 1	*Average export value 2016–2021 (mil USD)*	*Average export share 2016–2021 (%)*
Primary Products (PP)		
203: Pork	55.10	0.02
603: Cut flowers	44.49	0.02
709: Other vegetables	77.51	0.03
710: Frozen vegetables	41.47	0.01
713: Legumes, dried	37.95	0.02
802: Other nuts	62.73	0.02
803: Bananas and plantains	107.54	0.03
804: Avocados, pineapples, mangos, etc.	100.82	0.04
805: Citrus fruit	67.52	0.03
1005: Corn	51.66	0.02
1302: Vegetable saps and extracts	54.99	0.02
2601: Iron ores and concentrates	70.81	0.03
2613: Molybdenum ore	28.25	0.01
2711: Petroleum gases	195.06	0.07
2716: Electrical energy	104.06	0.04
7102: Diamonds	165.81	0.05
Subtotal	1265.76	0.46
Resource Based Manufactures (RB)		
1507: Soybean oil	36.74	0.01
1511: Palm oil	35.34	0.01
1513: Coconut & palm kernel oil	27.83	0.01
1518: Animal or vegetable fats and oils, processed	28.32	0.01
1702: Other sugars	35.11	0.01
1901: Malt extract	176.43	0.07
1905: Bakery products	206.68	0.07
2004: Other vegetables, frozen	28.45	0.01
2005: Other vegetables, prepared or preserved	38.19	0.01
2009: Fruit juices	125.17	0.04
2103: Sauces and seasonings	76.98	0.03
2106: Food preparations n.e.c.	215.29	0.07
2202: Waters, flavored or sweetened	114.36	0.04
2203: Beer	65.80	0.02
2208: Spirits < 80% alcohol	41.66	0.02
2304: Solid soybean residues	49.48	0.01
2309: Animal feed	321.18	0.11
2403: Other manufactured tobacco	27.43	0.01

(continued)

Table 5.4 (continued)

List of Marginal Products 1	*Average export value 2016–2021 (mil USD)*	*Average export share 2016–2021 (%)*
2707: Oils etc. from high temperature coal tar	27.02	0.01
2710: Petroleum oils, refined	784.26	0.30
2835: Phosphates	28.15	0.01
2836: Carbonates	59.42	0.02
2849: Carbides	25.78	0.01
2902: Cyclic hydrocarbons	283.78	0.08
2932: Heterocyclic compounds with oxygen hetero-atom(s) only	36.34	0.02
3102: Nitrogenous fertilizers	114.09	0.03
3104: Potassic fertilizers	25.71	0.01
3206: Other coloring matter	48.90	0.02
3208: Paints and varnishes, nonaqueous	33.70	0.01
3304: Make-up preparations	71.37	0.03
3305: Hair products	50.18	0.02
3307: Toiletries	121.43	0.05
3402: Cleaning products	234.02	0.08
3506: Glues and adhesives	64.84	0.02
3808: Insecticides, rodenticides, fungicides, etc.	146.84	0.05
3818: Chemical elements for electronics	71.83	0.01
3823: Industrial monocarboxylic fatty acids	302.66	0.10
4407: Wood sawn lengthwise	122.11	0.06
4411: Fiberboard of wood	51.69	0.02
4418: Wood carpentry for construction	181.06	0.06
4804: Uncoated kraft paper and paperboard	73.14	0.02
4811: Cellulose wadding, coated	46.50	0.01
4813: Cigarette paper	25.07	0.01
4818: Toilet paper	143.42	0.05
4819: Cardboard packing containers	294.66	0.10
4821: Paper labels	52.50	0.02
4911: Other printed matter	26.25	0.01
7007: Safety glass	70.57	0.02
7009: Glass mirrors	57.22	0.02
7204: Ferrous waste and scrap	64.84	0.03
7404: Copper waste and scrap	56.87	0.02
7602: Waste or scrap, aluminium	57.56	0.02
8480: Molding boxes for metal foundry	90.63	0.03

(continued)

Table 5.4 (continued)

List of Marginal Products 1	*Average export value 2016–2021 (mil USD)*	*Average export share 2016–2021 (%)*
Subtotal	5595	1.95
Low Technology Manufactures (LT)		
3901: Polymers of ethylene	154.31	0.05
3902: Polymers of propylene	305.41	0.09
3903: Polymers of styrene	87.29	0.03
3904: Polymers of vinyl chloride	90.28	0.03
3907: Polyacetals	345.54	0.08
3908: Polyamides	79.24	0.03
3909: Amino-resins	28.29	0.01
3917: Plastic tubes and fittings	109.04	0.04
3918: Plastic floor coverings	194.93	0.02
3919: Self-adhesive plastic sheets	124.51	0.04
3920: Other plates of plastics, noncellular and not reinforced	310.85	0.11
3921: Other plastic plates, sheets etc.	218.06	0.07
3925: Plastic builders' ware	119.22	0.04
4009: Vulcanized rubber tubes	39.31	0.01
4010: Conveyor belts of vulcanized rubber	27.42	0.01
4011: New pneumatic tires of rubber	1088.65	0.35
4016: Other articles of vulcanized rubber	340.39	0.12
5208: Woven fabrics of cotton of > 85% weighing < 200 g/m^2	54.97	0.02
5209: Woven fabrics of cotton of < 85% weighing > 200 g/m^2	88.17	0.03
5211: Woven fabrics of cotton of < 85% weighing > 200 g/m^2	28.95	0.01
5601: Wadding of textile materials	28.78	0.01
5603: Nonwoven textiles	92.75	0.03
5703: Carpets, tufted	120.79	0.03
5903: Textile fabrics impregnated with plastics	95.45	0.03
6115: Socks, stockings, etc., knit	186.39	0.06
6117: Other clothing accessories, knit	36.13	0.01
6301: Blankets	37.81	0.01
6704: Wigs	43.86	0.02
7112: Scrap of precious metal	341.75	0.13
7116: Articles of precious stones	28.90	0.01

(continued)

Table 5.4 (continued)

List of Marginal Products 1	*Average export value 2016–2021 (mil USD)*	*Average export share 2016–2021 (%)*
7207: Semifinished products of iron or nonalloy steel	905.74	0.19
7208: Flat-rolled iron, width > 600 mm, hot-rolled, not clad	400.80	0.08
7214: Other bars of iron, not further worked than forged	246.83	0.07
7216: Angles of iron or nonalloy steel	149.71	0.06
7219: Flat-rolled products of stainless steel of a width > 600 mm	178.47	0.06
7225: Flat-rolled products of other alloy steel, width > 600 mm	119.40	0.04
7227: Bars of other alloy steel	26.58	0.00
7304: Tubes, seamless, of iron or steel	28.06	0.01
7305: Other tubes and pipes, diameter > 406.4 mm, of iron or steel	43.58	0.01
7307: Tube or pipe fittings of iron or steel	128.65	0.04
7309: Tanks etc. > 300 liters, iron or steel	29.97	0.01
7314: Cloth of iron or steel wire	45.78	0.01
7321: Stoves and similar non-electric appliances of iron or steel	87.75	0.03
7325: Other cast articles of iron or steel	37.10	0.01
7326: Other articles of iron or steel	345.36	0.12
7403: Refined copper and copper alloys	46.05	0.01
7408: Copper wire	260.68	0.08
7412: Copper tube or pipe fittings	33.66	0.01
7601: Unwrought aluminum	337.40	0.10
7604: Aluminum bars	165.87	0.05
7608: Aluminum tubes and pipes	27.94	0.01
7610: Aluminum structures (bridges, towers etc)	196.54	0.07
7612: Aluminum containers, < 300 liters	66.88	0.02
7616: Other articles of aluminum	138.73	0.04
8205: Hand tools n.e.c.	32.36	0.01
8207: Interchangeable tools for hand tools	87.44	0.03
8208: Knives and blades for machines	36.99	0.01
8301: Padlocks and locks	90.64	0.02

(continued)

Table 5.4 (continued)

List of Marginal Products 1	*Average export value 2016–2021 (mil USD)*	*Average export share 2016–2021 (%)*
8302: Base metal mountings, fittings and similar articles	217.12	0.06
8308: Clasps, buckles etc. of metal	27.81	0.01
8309: Stoppers, caps and lids of metal	33.12	0.01
9004: Glasses	68.80	0.04
9102: Watches	41.97	0.01
9402: Medical, dental or veterinary furniture	41.38	0.01
9405: Lamps	272.85	0.07
9504: Games	431.10	0.11
9505: Christmas and other festivity articles	40.99	0.01
9608: Pens	59.16	0.02
Subtotal	10,377	3.12
Medium Technology Manufactures (MT)		
3004: Medicaments, packaged	139.00	0.05
8407: Spark-ignition reciprocating internal combustion piston engines	62.41	0.02
8409: Parts suitable for use with spark-ignition engines	157.64	0.06
8411: Gas turbines	257.70	0.08
8412: Other engines and motors	32.55	0.01
8413: Pumps for liquids	160.55	0.05
8414: Pumps, compressors, fans, etc.	464.88	0.14
8415: Air conditioners	38.44	0.01
8418: Refrigerators, freezers	248.01	0.08
8419: Equipment for temperature change of materials	57.73	0.02
8421: Centrifuges	129.85	0.04
8424: Sprays and powder dispersers	145.46	0.03
8426: Ships' derricks; cranes	36.35	0.02
8427: Fork-lift trucks	39.80	0.01
8428: Other lifting machinery	35.68	0.01
8431: Parts for use with hoists and excavation machinery	123.06	0.04
8433: Harvesting or agricultural machinery	94.07	0.02
8441: Other machinery for making paper	26.27	0.01

(continued)

Table 5.4 (continued)

List of Marginal Products 1	*Average export value 2016–2021 (mil USD)*	*Average export share 2016–2021 (%)*
8448: Auxiliary machinery for use with knitting and textile machines	49.76	0.02
8462: Machine tools for molding and forging metals	26.80	0.01
8466: Parts and accessories for metal working machines	51.56	0.02
8467: Tools for hand working, pneumatic, hydraulic motors	63.58	0.01
8472: Other office machines	40.31	0.01
8477: Machinery for working rubber or plastics	27.59	0.01
8479: Machines n.e.c.	491.75	0.16
8481: Appliances for thermostatically controlled valves	809.30	0.30
8482: Ball or roller bearings	163.03	0.05
8483: Transmission shafts	173.95	0.06
8485: Machinery parts, not containing electrical features, n.e.c.	45.69	0.02
8503: Parts for use with electric generators	100.40	0.04
8505: Electromagnets	133.97	0.04
8506: Primary cells and primary batteries	41.66	0.01
8508: Vacuum cleaners	342.56	0.04
8511: Electrical ignition equipment	38.41	0.01
8512: Electrical lighting equipment used for motor vehicles	213.12	0.07
8516: Electric heaters	354.35	0.12
8519: Sound reproducing apparatus	32.34	0.01
8523: Sound storage media	138.62	0.05
8526: Radar	206.52	0.07
8531: Electric sound or visual signaling apparatus	347.23	0.09
8532: Electrical capacitors	49.48	0.02
8533: Electrical resistors	58.99	0.02
8535: Electrical apparatus for > 1k volts	33.67	0.01
8536: Electrical apparatus for < 1k volts	1003.93	0.34
8538: Parts for electrical apparatus	308.90	0.11
8543: Electrical machines with individual functions n.e.c.	366.50	0.11

(continued)

Table 5.4 (continued)

List of Marginal Products 1	*Average export value 2016–2021 (mil USD)*	*Average export share 2016–2021 (%)*
8547: Insulating fittings for electrical machines	57.02	0.02
8703: Cars	72.78	0.01
8708: Parts of motor vehicles	1349.78	0.48
8716: Trailers and semi-trailers	84.58	0.03
8901: Cargo ships and similar vessels	446.10	0.16
8905: Special function vessels, n.e.c.	127.70	0.05
9010: Apparatus and equipment for photographic laboratories, n.e.c.	30.76	0.01
9023: Instruments designed for demonstrational purposes	30.38	0.01
9025: Thermometers, hydrometers etc.	49.05	0.01
9026: Instruments for measuring properties of liquids or gases	112.11	0.04
9027: Instruments for physical or chemical analysis	113.81	0.04
9029: Meters	65.72	0.02
9030: Instruments for measuring electricity	50.79	0.02
9031: Measuring instruments	219.33	0.07
9032: Automatic regulating instruments	89.96	0.03
Subtotal	10,863	3.6
High Technology Manufactures (HT)		
9001: Optical fibers	230.29	0.08
9013: Liquid crystal devices	1521.74	0.65
9018: Medical instruments	911.62	0.32
9021: Orthopedic appliances	514.46	0.17
8802: Other aircraft and spacecraft	40.96	0.02
8803: Parts of other aircraft	300.84	0.11
Subtotal	3520	1.35
Total	31,621	10.4

Source Author' calculations based on data from Growth Lab at Harvard University, June 2024

Annex 2: Import Replacement

See Tables 5.5 and 5.6.

Table 5.5 List of products with potential for import replacement in the next five years

HS4	*Product name*	*Average PCI*	*Average 2016–2021*	*Average M 2016–2021*	*Average distance*	*Average X share 2016–2021 (%)*	*Average M share 2016–2021 (%)*	*Per. Dist. (%)*	*Perc. PCI (%)*	*Classics*	*Emerging*	*Disappearing*	*Marginal 1*	*Marginal 2*
Vegetable, foodstuffs and wood														
2106	Food preparations n.e.c.	0.0215	215290389	661107045	0.81266	0.07	0.25	55.2	46.9				X	
1001	Wheat and meslin	−0.2683	9080002	840424992	0.821368	0.00	0.33	62.6	37.2					X
2202	Waters, flavored or sweetened	−0.4631	114356480	610347365	0.792682	0.04	0.24	37.3	31.7				X	
2208	Spirits < 80% alcohol	−0.4999	41663168	827867941	0.799834	0.02	0.34	43.9	30.7				X	
2402	Cigars and cigarettes	−0.8000	171549723	841787755	0.76407	0.06	0.33	21.2	22.0			X		
2304	Solid soybean residues	−1.0273	49478890	1713277163	0.834361	0.02	0.67	74.0	16.8				X	
1005	Corn	−1.0341	51664497	1833564288	0.802276	0.02	0.70	46.6	16.6				X	
4104	Tanned hides of bovines or equines	−1.1172	392367216	1239656768	0.753653	0.15	0.49	16.7	15.1		X			
202	Beef (frozen)	−1.1462	6021072	1422647803	0.821102	0.00	0.60	62.3	14.6					X
4407	Wood sawn lengthwise	−1.2608	122107127	706245525	0.784812	0.05	0.28	32.9	12.0				X	
712	Vegetables, dried	−1.2664	53063672	643586368	0.739903	0.02	0.27	13.0	11.8			X		
1201	Soya beans	−1.5078	745072	676367600	0.83629	0.00	0.26	75.3	7.7					X

(continued)

Table 5.5 (continued)

HS4	*Product name*	*Average PCI*	*Average 2016–2021*	*Average M 2016–2021*	*Average distance*	*Average X share 2016–2021 (%)*	*Average M share 2016–2021 (%)*	*Per. Dist. (%)*	*Perc. PCI (%)*	*Classics*	*Emerging*	*Disappearing*	*Marginal 1*	*Marginal 2*
303	Frozen fish, excluding fillets	−1.6654	371681408	1059261867	0.729491	0.14	0.44	9.7	5.6	X				
306	Crustaceans	−1.9003	1870610325	1387236368	0.681162	0.68	0.60	2.6	3.3	X				
1511	Palm oil	−2.2024	35344321	601420315	0.734334	0.01	0.23	11.5	1.3				X	
801	Cashew nuts & coconuts	−2.2511	2763531584	1809686187	0.666109	1.00	0.70	0.8	1.1	X				
Chemicals and Plastics														
3907	Polyacetals	0.9634	345535194	1642760832	0.827339	0.11	0.63	68.4	82.7				X	
4002	Synthetic rubber	0.8969	1314065259	633127141	0.787881	0.46	0.24	34.9	80.8		X			
3903	Polymers of styrene	0.8301	87286310	678807579	0.833843	0.03	0.26	73.7	78.1				X	
3926	Other articles of plastic	0.7790	1067001397	1379236832	0.810921	0.37	0.52	53.8	75.4			X		
3004	Medicaments, packaged	0.7603	139003504	1655322901	0.838373	0.05	0.65	77.3	74.5				X	
3921	Other plastic plates, sheets etc.	0.6377	218057781	650655605	0.816727	0.08	0.25	58.6	69.6				X	
3920	Other plates of plastics, noncellular and not reinforced	0.4280	310850072	1404140480	0.8112	0.11	0.53	54.1	62.1				X	
3902	Polymers of propylene	0.3178	305408848	1494788779	0.830653	0.10	0.58	71.1	57.3				X	
3901	Polymers of ethylene	0.1985	154307629	2417019691	0.829801	0.05	0.93	70.2	53.6				X	

(continued)

Table 5.5 (continued)

HS4	*Product name*	*Average PCI*	*Average 2016–2021*	*Average M 2016–2021*	*Average distance*	*Average X share 2016–2021 (%)*	*Average M share 2016–2021 (%)*	*Per. Dist. (%)*	*Perc. PCI (%)*	*Classics*	*Emerging*	*Disappearing*	*Marginal 1*	*Marginal 2*
3808	Insecticides, rodenticides, fungicides, etc.	0.0602	146843889	660467264	0.822357	0.05	0.26	63.5	48.0				X	
Textiles and furniture														
9405	Lamps	0.6852	272852605	827489739	0.798244	0.09	0.32	42.9	71.4				X	
5402	Synthetic filament yarn	0.2756	774717355	935073504	0.739224	0.27	0.36	12.7	56.0		X			
6001	Pile fabrics, knit	0.0399	99555928	714387520	0.745037	0.03	0.28	14.8	47.5		X			
6002	Other knitted fabrics	−0.3599	903099216	5082126933	0.700161	0.31	1.97	5.1	34.7		X			
5407	Woven fabrics of synthetic filament yarn	−0.4184	315990736	2388016533	0.746869	0.11	0.94	15.4	33.3			X		
6406	Parts of footwear	−0.7653	609465813	1095202933	0.7061	0.22	0.42	6.1	22.4	X				
5208	Woven fabrics of cotton of > 85% weighing < 200 g/m2	−1.2439	54970599	629095040	0.759554	0.02	0.25	18.5	12.5				X	
6204	Women's suits and pants	−1.2865	2814348203	958557109	0.689049	1.02	0.39	3.4	11.6	X				
5201	Raw cotton	−2.4102	3540371	2113983851	0.778422	0.00	0.82	29.5	0.7					X
Stone and glass														
Metal														
7326	Other articles of iron or steel	0.9102	345360184	807813072	0.80249	0.12	0.30	46.7	81.4				X	

(continued)

Table 5.5 (continued)

HS4	Product name	Average PCI	Average 2016–2021	Average M 2016–2021	Average distance	Average X share 2016–2021 (%)	Average M share 2016–2021 (%)	Per. Dist. (%)	Perc. PCI (%)	Classics	Emerging	Disappearing	Marginal 1	Marginal 2
7606	Aluminum plates > 0.2 mm	0.6710	14839503	715831515	0.832012	0.01	0.27	72.5	71.0					X
7208	Flat-rolled iron, width > 600 mm, hot-rolled, not clad	0.5293	400798286	2921297195	0.816397	0.12	1.10	58.3	65.9				X	
7210	Flat rolled iron, width > 600 mm, clad	0.0381	1381605920	1044538251	0.77561	0.45	0.42	27.6	47.4		X			
7604	Aluminum bars	–0.0569	165873380	865316869	0.791869	0.06	0.40	36.7	43.3				X	
7204	Ferrous waste and scrap	–0.5492	64842097	1494950357	0.815235	0.02	0.56	57.6	28.6				X	
7601	Unwrought aluminum	–0.9754	337404052	947873152	0.79834	0.11	0.36	43.0	18.2				X	
7403	Refined copper and copper alloys	–1.3476	46051615	1551667168	0.786495	0.01	0.59	33.7	10.1				X	
Minerals														
2710	Petroleum oils, refined	–0.7145	784263323	6133622144	0.807103	0.29	2.47	50.8	23.6				X	
2701	Coal	–1.5476	230594536	2336343275	0.822974	0.08	0.86	64.3	7.0			X		
2601	Iron ores and concentrates	–1.7458	70810399	1056909851	0.832204	0.03	0.36	72.6	4.9				X	
2711	Petroleum gases	–1.9650	195062856	753956603	0.795473	0.07	0.29	39.8	2.3				X	
2709	Petroleum oils, crude	–2.5717	2173809493	1959983368	0.805853	0.84	0.70	49.6	0.0			X		

(continued)

Table 5.5 (continued)

HS4	*Product name*	*Average PCI*	*Average 2016–2021*	*Average M 2016–2021*	*Average distance*	*Average X share 2016–2021 (%)*	*Average M share 2016–2021 (%)*	*Per. Dist. (%)*	*Perc. PCI (%)*	*Classics*	*Emerging*	*Disappearing*	*Marginal 1*	*Marginal 2*
Machinery														
9001	Optical fibers	1.0266	230290352	1011085963	0.812761	0.08	0.38	55.6	84.6				X	
8415	Air conditioners	0.6884	38440120	983354859	0.785644	0.01	0.39	33.5	71.6				X	
Electronics														
8538	Parts for electrical apparatus	0.9961	308898563	634691232	0.823229	0.11	0.24	64.5	83.2				X	
8541	Semiconductor devices	0.9748	2722084885	3603424683	0.693674	0.93	1.36	4.2	82.9		X			
8548	Waste and scrap of batteries	0.9533	148969627	1613381803	0.736054	0.06	0.65	12.0	82.2		X			
8534	Electronic printed circuits	0.9251	1019602869	3016035307	0.689938	0.36	1.15	3.6	81.7	X				
8501	Electric motors and generators	0.8608	1312621344	608658085	0.773473	0.47	0.23	25.7	79.7	X				
8507	Batteries	0.8568	1317587531	2051003776	0.77003	0.46	0.76	24.2	79.3		X			
8517	Telephones	0.8310	20023463936	13396275200	0.6725	6.96	5.08	1.3	78.2		X			
8504	Electrical transformers	0.7640	1839595968	1656647136	0.769522	0.62	0.63	23.9	74.7		X			
8537	Electrical boards	0.7446	601753888	647902453	0.796681	0.20	0.25	40.9	74.0			X		
8503	Parts for use with electric generators	0.7413	100404593	602473232	0.796768	0.04	0.22	40.9	73.8				X	
8518	Microphones	0.6906	3571400512	1316214987	0.720134	1.23	0.51	8.3	71.8	X				

(continued)

Table 5.5 (continued)

HS4	*Product name*	*Average PCI*	*Average 2016–2021*	*Average M 2016–2021*	*Average distance*	*Average X share 2016–2021 (%)*	*Average M share 2016–2021 (%)*	*Per. Dist. (%)*	*Perc. PCI (%)*	*Classics*	*Emerging*	*Disappearing*	*Marginal 1*	*Marginal 2*
8536	Electrical apparatus for < 1k volts	0.6600	1003926379	2480866069	0.80332	0.35	0.95	47.5	70.3				X	
8529	Parts of radios, telephones, and T.V.s	0.6311	6581611605	3518844203	0.703806	2.21	1.31	5.7	69.3		X			
8525	Transmission apparatus for radio, telephone and TV	0.6138	39092325376	2909616448	0.736525	13.80	1.10	12.1	68.9		X			
8502	Electric generating sets and rotary converters	0.3569	221136700	656046213	0.823128	0.07	0.24	64.5	58.7			X		
8528	Monitors and projectors	0.1868	2819361131	769127691	0.723437	0.96	0.29	8.8	53.3		X			
8544	Insulated electrical wire	−0.4079	4574681344	1770714603	0.723866	1.60	0.67	9.0	33.7	X				
Transport vehicles														
8704	Motor vehicles for transporting goods	0.6650	4514121	1192521216	0.839841	0.00	0.49	78.6	70.8					X

Source Author's calculations from Atlas data, accessed in May 2024

Table 5.6 Lall classification of Import Replacement Products

	Industry	*Average PCI*	*Average X 2016–2021*	*Average M 2016–2021*	*Average distance*	*Average X share 2016–2021 (%)*	*Average M share 2016–2021 (%)*	*Per. Dist. (%)*	*Perc. PCI (%)*	*Clas-sics*	*Cham-pions*	*Disapp-earing*	*Margi-nal 1*	*Margi-nal 2*
1. Primary Products (PP):														
202: Beef (frozen)	Vegetable, foodstuffs and wood	-1.1462	6021072	1422647803	0.821102	0.00	0.60	62.3	14.6					x
303: Frozen fish, excluding fillets	Vegetable, foodstuffs and wood	-1.6654	371681408	1059261867	0.729491	0.14	0.44	9.7	5.6	x				
306: Crustaceans	Vegetable, foodstuffs and wood	-1.9003	1870610325	1387236368	0.681162	0.68	0.60	2.6	3.3	x				
712: Vegetables, dried	Vegetable, foodstuffs and wood	-1.2664	53063672	643586368	0.739903	0.02	0.27	13.0	11.8			x		
801: Cashew nuts & coconuts	Vegetable, foodstuffs and wood	-2.2511	2763531584	1809686187	0.666109	1.00	0.70	0.8	1.1	x				
1001: Wheat and meslin	Vegetable, foodstuffs and wood	-0.2683	9080002	840424992	0.821368	0.00	0.33	62.6	37.2					x
1005: Corn	Vegetable, foodstuffs and wood	-1.0341	51664497	1833564288	0.802276	0.02	0.70	46.6	16.6				x	
1201: Soya beans	Vegetable, foodstuffs and wood	-1.5078	745072	676367600	0.83629	0.00	0.26	75.3	7.7					x

(continued)

Table 5.6 (continued)

	Industry	*Average PCI*	*Average X 2016–2021*	*Average M 2016–2021*	*Average distance*	*Average X share 2016–2021 (%)*	*Average M share 2016–2021 (%)*	*Per. Dist. (%)*	*Perc. PCI (%)*	*Clas-sics*	*Cham-pions*	*Disapp-earing*	*Margi-nal 1*	*Margi-nal 2*
1511: Palm oil	Vegetable, foodstuffs and wood	−2.2024	35344821	601420315	0.734334	0.01	0.23	11.5	1.3				x	
2601: Iron ores and concentrates	Mineral	−1.7458	70810399	1056909851	0.832204	0.03	0.36	72.6	4.9				x	
2701: Coal	Mineral	−1.5476	230594536	2336343275	0.822974	0.08	0.86	64.3	7.0			x		
2709: Petroleum oils, crude	Mineral	−2.5717	2173809493	1959983368	0.805853	0.84	0.70	49.6	0.0			x		
5201: Raw cotton	Textiles and furniture	−2.4102	3540371	2113983851	0.778422	0.00	0.82	29.5	0.7					x
				17741416131			6.86							
2. Resource-based Manufactures (RB):														
2106: Food preparations n.e.c.	Vegetable, foodstuffs and wood	0.0215	215290389	661107045	0.81266	0.07	0.25	55.2	46.9				x	
2202: Waters, flavored or sweetened	Vegetable, foodstuffs and wood	−0.4631	114356480	610347365	0.792682	0.04	0.24	37.3	31.7				x	
2208: Spirits < 80% alcohol	Vegetable, foodstuffs and wood	−0.4999	41663168	827867941	0.799834	0.02	0.34	43.9	30.7				x	
2304: Solid soybean residues	Vegetable, foodstuffs and wood	−1.0273	49478890	1713277163	0.834361	0.02	0.67	74.0	16.8				x	

(continued)

Table 5.6 (continued)

	Industry	*Average PCI*	*Average X 2016–2021*	*Average M 2016–2021*	*Average distance*	*Average X share 2016–2021 (%)*	*Average M share 2016–2021 (%)*	*Per. Dist. (%)*	*Perc. PCI (%)*	*Clas-sics*	*Cham-pions*	*Disapp-earing*	*Margi-nal 1*	*Margi-nal 2*
2402: Cigars and cigarettes	Vegetable, foodstuffs and wood	−0.8000	171549723	841787755	0.76407	0.06	0.33	21.2	22.0			x		
2710: Petroleum oils, refined	Mineral	−0.7145	784263323	6133622144	0.807103	0.29	2.47	50.8	23.6				x	
2711: Petroleum gases	Mineral	−1.9650	195062856	753956603	0.795473	0.07	0.29	39.8	2.3				x	
4104: Tanned hides of bovines or equines	Vegetable, foodstuffs and wood	−1.1172	392367216	1239656768	0.753653	0.15	0.49	16.7	15.1		x			
4407: Wood sawn lengthwise	Vegetable, foodstuffs and wood	−1.2608	122107127	706245525	0.784812	0.05	0.28	32.9	12.0				x	
				13487868309			5.37							
3. Low-technology Manufactures (LT):														
3926: Other articles of plastic	Chemicals and Plastics	0.7790	1067001397	1379236832	0.810921	0.37	0.52	53.8	75.4			x		
5208: Woven fabrics of cotton of > 85% weighing < 200 g/m2	Textiles and furniture	−1.2439	54970599	629095040	0.759554	0.02	0.25	18.5	12.5				x	
5407: Woven fabrics of synthetic filament yarn	Textiles and furniture	−0.4184	315990736	2388016533	0.746869	0.11	0.94	15.4	33.3			x		

(continued)

Table 5.6 (continued)

	Industry	*Average PCI*	*Average X 2016–2021*	*Average M 2016–2021*	*Average distance*	*Average X share 2016–2021 (%)*	*Average M share 2016–2021 (%)*	*Per. Dist. (%)*	*Perc. PCI (%)*	*Clas-sics*	*Cham-pions*	*Disapp-earing*	*Margi-nal 1*	*Margi-nal 2*
6001: Pile fabrics, knit	Textiles and furniture	0.0399	99555928	714387520	0.745037	0.03	0.28	14.8	47.5		x			
6002: Other knitted fabrics	Textiles and furniture	−0.3599	903099216	5082126933	0.700161	0.31	1.97	5.1	34.7		x			
6204: Women's suits and pants	Textiles and furniture	−1.2865	2814348203	958557109	0.689049	1.02	0.39	3.4	11.6	x				
6406: Parts of footwear	Textiles and furniture	−0.7653	609465813	1095202933	0.7061	0.22	0.42	6.1	22.4	x				
7326: Other articles of iron or steel	Metal	0.9102	345360184	807813072	0.80249	0.12	0.30	46.7	81.4				x	
9405: Lamps	Textiles and furniture	0.6852	272852605	827489739	0.798244	0.09	0.32	42.9	71.4				x	
				13881925712			5.39							
4. Medium-technology Manufactures (MT):														
3004: Medicaments, packaged	Chemicals and Plastics	0.7603	139003504	1655322901	0.838373	0.05	0.65	77.3	74.5				x	
3808: Insecticides, rodenticides, fungicides, etc.	Chemicals and Plastics	0.0602	146843889	660467264	0.822357	0.05	0.26	63.5	48.0				x	

(continued)

Table 5.6 (continued)

	Industry	*Average PCI*	*Average X 2016–2021*	*Average M 2016–2021*	*Average distance*	*Average X share 2016–2021 (%)*	*Average M share 2016–2021 (%)*	*Per. Dist. (%)*	*Perc. PCI (%)*	*Clas-sics*	*Cham-pions*	*Disapp-earing*	*Margi-nal 1*	*Margi-nal 2*
3901: Polymers of ethylene	Chemicals and Plastics	0.1985	154307629	2417019691	0.829801	0.05	0.93	70.2	53.6				x	
3902: Polymers of propylene	Chemicals and Plastics	0.3178	305408848	1494788779	0.830653	0.10	0.58	71.1	57.3				x	
3903: Polymers of styrene	Chemicals and Plastics	0.8301	87286310	678807579	0.833843	0.03	0.26	73.7	78.1				x	
3907: Polyacetals	Chemicals and Plastics	0.9634	345535194	1642760832	0.827339	0.11	0.63	68.4	82.7				x	
3920: Other plates of plastics, noncellular and not reinforced	Chemicals and Plastics	0.4280	310850072	1404140480	0.8112	0.11	0.53	54.1	62.1				x	
3921: Other plastic plates, sheets etc.	Chemicals and Plastics	0.6377	218057781	650655605	0.816727	0.08	0.25	58.6	69.6				x	
4002: Synthetic rubber	Chemicals and Plastics	0.8969	1314065259	633127141	0.787881	0.46	0.24	34.9	80.8		x			
5402: Synthetic filament yarn	Textiles and furniture	0.2756	774717355	935073504	0.739224	0.27	0.36	12.7	56.0		x			
7204: Ferrous waste and scrap	Metal	−0.5492	64842097	1494950357	0.815235	0.02	0.56	57.6	28.6				x	

(continued)

Table 5.6 (continued)

	Industry	*Average PCI*	*Average X 2016–2021*	*Average M 2016–2021*	*Average distance*	*Average X share 2016–2021 (%)*	*Average M share 2016–2021 (%)*	*Per. Dist. (%)*	*Perc. PCI (%)*	*Clas-sics*	*Cham-pions*	*Disapp-earing*	*Margi-nal 1*	*Margi-nal 2*
7208: Flat-rolled iron, width > 600mm, hot-rolled, not clad	Metal	0.5293	400798286	292197195	0.816397	0.12	1.10	58.3	65.9				x	
7210: Flat rolled iron, width > 600mm, clad	Metal	0.0381	1381605920	1044538251	0.77561	0.45	0.42	27.6	47.4		x			
7403: Refined copper and copper alloys	Metal	−1.3476	46051615	1551667168	0.786495	0.01	0.59	33.7	10.1				x	
7601: Unwrought aluminum	Metal	−0.9754	337404052	947873152	0.79834	0.11	0.36	43.0	18.2				x	
7604: Aluminum bars	Metal	−0.0569	165873380	865316869	0.791869	0.06	0.40	36.7	43.3				x	
7606: Aluminum plates > 0.2 mm	Metal	0.6710	14839603	715831515	0.832012	0.01	0.27	72.5	71.0					x
8415: Air conditioners	Machinery	0.6884	38440120	983354859	0.785644	0.01	0.39	33.5	71.6				x	
8501: Electric motors and generators	Electronics	0.8608	1312621344	608658085	0.773473	0.47	0.23	25.7	79.7	x				
8502: Electric generating sets and rotary converters	Electronics	0.3569	221136700	656046213	0.823128	0.07	0.24	64.5	58.7			x		

(continued)

Table 5.6 (continued)

	Industry	*Average PCI*	*Average X 2016–2021*	*Average M 2016–2021*	*Average distance*	*Average X share 2016–2021 (%)*	*Average M share 2016–2021 (%)*	*Per. Dist. (%)*	*Perc. PCI (%)*	*Clas-sics*	*Cham-pions*	*Disapp-earing*	*Margi-nal 1*	*Margi-nal 2*
8503: Parts for use with electric generators	Electronics	0.7413	100404593	602473232	0.796768	0.04	0.22	40.9	73.8				x	
8504: Electrical transformers	Electronics	0.7640	1839595968	1656647136	0.769522	0.62	0.63	23.9	74.7		x			
8507: Batteries	Electronics	0.8568	1317587531	2051003776	0.77003	0.46	0.76	24.2	79.3		x			
8544: Insulated electrical wire	Electronics	−0.4079	4574681344	1770714603	0.723866	1.60	0.67	9.0	33.7	x				
8704: Motor vehicles for transporting goods	Transport vehicles	0.6650	4514121	1192521216	0.839841	0.00	0.49	78.6	70.8					x
				31235057403			12.02							
5. High-technology Manufactures (HT):														
8517: Telephones	Electronics	0.8310	20023463936	13396275200	0.6725	6.96	5.08	1.3	78.2		x			
8518: Microphones	Electronics	0.6906	3571400512	1316214987	0.720134	1.23	0.51	8.3	71.8	x				
8525: Transmission apparatus for radio, telephone and TV	Electronics	0.6138	39092325376	2909616448	0.736525	13.80	1.10	12.1	68.9		x			
8528: Monitors and projectors	Electronics	0.1868	2819361131	769127691	0.723437	0.96	0.29	8.8	53.3		x			
8529: Parts of radios,	Electronics	0.6311	6581611605	3518844203	0.703806	2.21	1.31	5.7	69.3		x			

(continued)

Table 5.6 (continued)

	Industry	*Average PCI*	*Average X 2016–2021*	*Average M 2016–2021*	*Average distance*	*Average X share 2016–2021 (%)*	*Average M share 2016–2021 (%)*	*Per. Dist. (%)*	*Perc. PCI (%)*	*Clas-sics*	*Cham-pions*	*Disapp-earing*	*Margi-nal 1*	*Margi-nal 2*
telephones, and T.V.s														
8534: Electronic printed circuits	Electronics	0.9251	1019602869	3016035307	0.689938	0.36	1.15	3.6	81.7	x				
8536: Electrical apparatus for < 1k volts	Electronics	0.6600	1003926379	2480866069	0.80332	0.35	0.95	47.5	70.3				x	
8537: Electrical boards	Electronics	0.7446	601753888	647902453	0.796681	0.20	0.25	40.9	74.0			x		
8538: Parts for electrical apparatus	Electronics	0.9961	308898563	634691232	0.823229	0.11	0.24	64.5	83.2				x	
8541: Semiconductor devices	Electronics	0.9748	2722084885	3603424683	0.693674	0.93	1.36	4.2	82.9		x			
8548: Waste and scrap of batteries	Electronics	0.9533	148969627	1613381803	0.736054	0.06	0.65	12.0	82.2		x			
9001: Optical fibers	Machinery	1.0266	230290352	1011085963	0.812761	0.08	0.38	55.6	84.6				x	
			109949442742	34917466037			13.28							

Source Author's calculations from Atlas data, accessed in May 2024

References

Dinh, H. T. (2017). *Jobs, industrialization, and globalization*. OCP Policy Center. https://www.policycenter.ma/publications/jobs-industrialization-and-globalization.

Hausmann, R., & Hidalgo, C. A. (2011). The network structure of economic output. *Journal of Economic Growth, 16*(4), 309–342.

Lall, S. (2000). The technological structure and performance of developing country manufactured exports, 1985–98. *Oxford Development Studies, 28*(3), 337–369.

CHAPTER 6

Developing the Services Sector to Support Exports

Introduction

Vietnam has relied heavily on exports as a crucial source of foreign exchange and economic growth. However, the full potential of these exports cannot be realized without the development of ancillary business services to support them, whether they involve commodities or complex products manufactured within global value chains (GVCs). This chapter analyzes key service sectors that support Vietnam's exports, aiming to strengthen export competitiveness and enhance value addition.

Rapid technological advancements necessitate updating the traditional economic development strategies upon which most developing countries rely. Since the Industrial Revolution in 1862, manufacturing has served as the primary pathway for today's high-income countries to achieve growth and development. However, automation has made manufacturing increasingly capital-intensive, diminishing its role as a primary absorber of surplus labor released from agriculture due to modernization.

Recently, some scholars have advocated for services as an engine of growth for developing countries (Rajan, 2025; Rodrik & Stiglitz, 2024). Rodrik and Stiglitz (2024) argue that traditional manufacturing-led growth is no longer viable because technological advancements have made

---

Contributed by Hinh T. Dinh

H. T. Dinh, H. T. Nguyen, *Vietnam's Economic Leap*,
https://doi.org/10.1007/978-3-032-08904-5_6

manufacturing more skill—and capital-intensive. They contend that a new growth strategy for developing countries should focus not only on the green transition but also on enhancing productivity in labor-intensive, non-traded services. With manufacturing's diminished ability to absorb labor, services are expected to remain the primary labor-absorbing sector. However, because productivity in service sectors is generally low, this services-oriented approach is likely to result in weaker economic growth compared to traditional manufacturing-led strategies.

Definition of the Services Sector

The terms "service sector" and "services sector" are often used interchangeably but convey distinct meanings. In this book, we use the singular form to refer to the sector as a whole or as a unified entity, in contrast to other sectors such as manufacturing or agriculture. The plural form is used to denote the broad spectrum of economic activities that involve the delivery of intangible goods, such as healthcare, education, retail, IT, and finance. The singular form is employed when discussing the sector in general terms or making overarching statements, whereas the plural form emphasizes the diversity within the sector or is used to compare different categories of services.

To identify the services that support international trade in Vietnam, we classify them according to the latest Standard International Trade Classification (SITC, Rev. 4). The SITC consists of 98 divisions, with services spanning divisions 45 through 98. Services categorized between 45 and 82 are specifically geared toward supporting business and are collectively referred to as Total Business Sector Services. The remaining services, classified under divisions 84 through 98, include public administration, education, health, and other personal services. While these latter services may influence exports over the long term, they are unlikely to have a significant impact in the short to medium term. Table 6.1 presents the composition of these services.

A growing, developing country must find jobs for surplus labor released from the agricultural sector, whether in industry or services. However, services pose two key challenges. First, tradable services require high skill levels that are often lacking in lower-middle-income countries. Second, the rate of labor absorption in non-tradable services is lower compared to manufacturing. This is because the influx of marginal workers (from agriculture) into any service sector tends to lower the average productivity of that sector. As Baumol and Bowen (1965) noted,

Table 6.1 Composition of Services According to ISIC Rev. 4

Composition of Services by ISIC Rev.4
Total Business Sector Services (GTN)
Wholesale and retail trade; repair of motor vehicles and motorcycles (G)
Land transport and transport via pipelines (H49)
Water transport (H50)
Air transport (H51)
Warehousing and support activities for transportation (H52)
Postal and courier activities (H53)
Accommodation and food service activities (I)
Publishing, mot. pict., video, tel. prog. Prod.; so. Rec., prog. & broad. (J58T60)
Telecommunications (J61)
Comp. progr., consult., and infor. service activities (J62_63)
Financial and insurance activities (K)
Real estate activities (L)
Professional, scientific and technical activities (M)
Administrative and support service activities (N)
Public admin., educ., health, and other personal services (OTT)
Public administration and defence; compulsory social security (O)
Education (P)
Human health and social work activities (Q)
Arts, entertainment and recreation (R)
Other service activities (S)
Total services (GTT)

Source OECD Trade in Value Added https://www.oecd.org/en/topics/sub-issues/trade-in-value-added.html
Note: Letters in parentheses denote ISIC Rev. 4 Divisions

if the demand for services were income-inelastic and price-elastic, the share of services in national income would decline. However, since this is not the case, the share of services rises while productivity in the sector declines. Timmer (2012) highlighted that the fastest structural transformation occurs when surplus workers move into a sector where productivity remains constant—such as manufacturing—because demand and prices are determined beyond national borders.

We next look at how to link a service subsector to a trade-related economic activity. The conventional classification of activities as either tradable or non-tradable is often inaccurate. For instance, a haircut provided to a local resident is a non-tradable activity, but a haircut given to a tourist is effectively a tradable service. Thus, classifying all barbering activities as non-tradable based solely on national accounts data is misleading.

A more accurate approach is to link economic activities to either the domestic economy or exports using an input-output table. This table establishes structural relationships between a sector's output and the inputs and final demand associated with it. The backward linkage of an industry refers to the inputs required from the economy to produce an additional unit of output. Conversely, when an industry's output increases, it enhances the supply of goods or services to industries that use them as inputs. Forward linkages measure the impact of an increase in an industry's output on those sectors that depend on it for production (downstream industries).

Evolution of Forward and Backward Integration of Vietnamese Exports

Due to the expansion of global value chains, traditional trade measures—such as exports and imports—no longer accurately capture the flow of goods and services within global production networks. To address this, the OECD developed a set of tools known as Trade in Value-Added (TiVA) measures, which rely on inter-country input-output tables. This section utilizes these tools to assess Vietnam's evolution in forward and backward integration within its export sector.

Forward integration in an economic activity is measured by its contribution to domestic value-added in foreign demand. Figure 6.1 illustrates the evolution of Vietnam's forward integration indicator across four sectors: agriculture, mining, manufacturing, and business services. Notably, business services exhibit the lowest level of forward integration among the four sectors.

The extent of backward integration is measured by the foreign value-added content of gross exports. Figure 6.2 illustrates the evolution of this indicator from 2010 to 2020. A concerning trend is that, with the exception of the business services sector, all other sectors show an increase in backward integration since 2012—indicating that Vietnam is becoming more reliant on imported raw materials and intermediate goods for production.

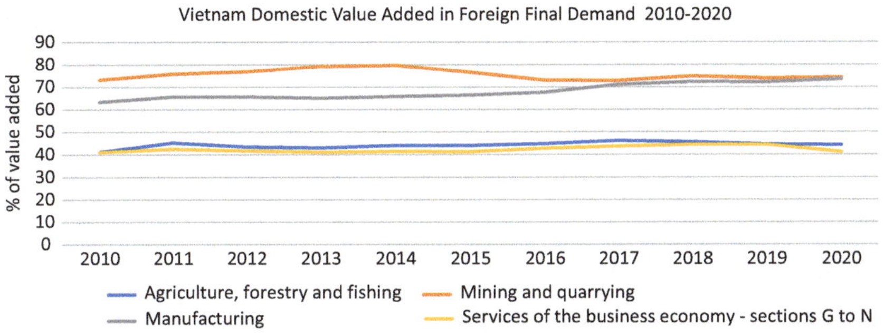

Fig. 6.1 Vietnam Forward integration into Supply Chains. *Source* Author's calculations from OECD-Trade in Value Added (2023). https://data-explorer.Oecd.Org/?pg=0&bp=true&snb=14&tm=TIVA

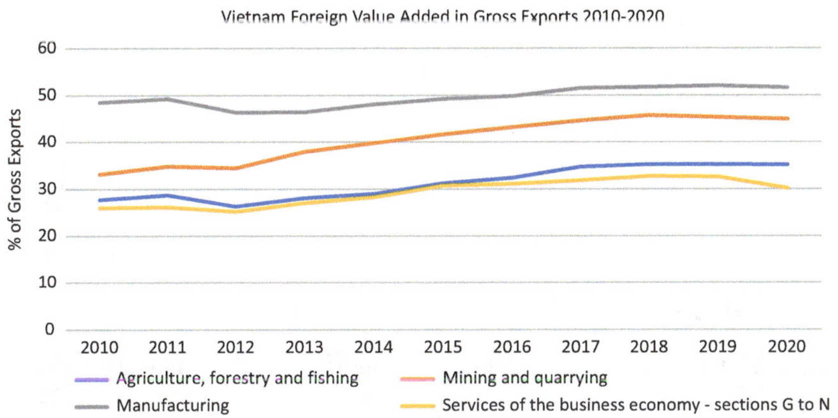

Fig. 6.2 Vietnam Backward Integration into Supply Chains. *Source* Author's calculations from OECD-Trade in Value Added (2023). https://data-explorer.Oecd.Org/?pg=0&bp=true&snb=14&tm=TIVA

For comparison, Fig. 6.3 presents similar data for China and the EU-15, where progress in reducing dependence on imported raw materials and intermediate goods is evident in the manufacturing sector.

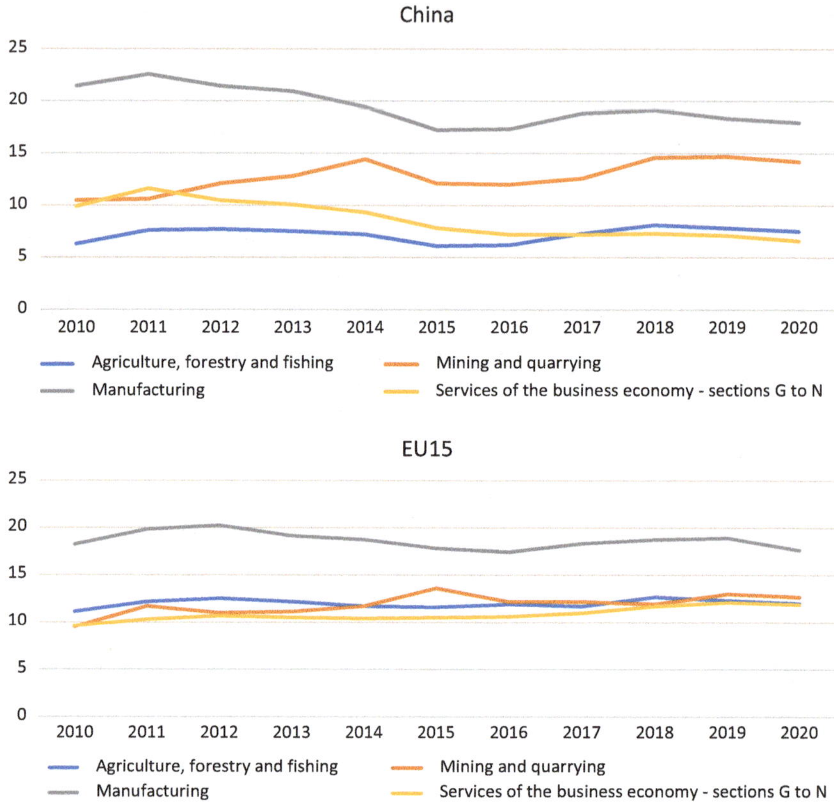

Fig. 6.3 Evolution of Backward Integration into Supply Chains Indicator for China and EU15. *Source* Author's calculations from OECD-Trade in Value Added (2023). https://data-explorer.Oecd.Org/?pg=0&bp=true&snb=14&tm=TIVA

The Services Sector in Vietnam

Table 6.2 shows that the growth rates and shares of value-added and employment in Vietnam's tradable sectors have lagged behind those of non-tradable sectors. From 2010 to 2023, the tradable sector's value-added grew at an annual rate of about 5.4%, compared to 6.6% for the non-tradable sector. This trend was already present before the COVID-19 pandemic, i.e., during 2010–2019, as shown in the Table. As a result, the tradable sector's share of the economy declined from 42% in 2010 to 39% in 2023.

Table 6.2 Vietnam: Average Annual Growth Rates of Value Added and Employment, 2000–2023

Average Annual Growth Rates of Value Added and Employment, 2010–2023			*% of GDP at fc*	
	2010–2023	*2010–2019*	*2010*	*2023*
VALUE ADDED in 2014 prices	6.1%	6.6%	100.0	100.00
Tradable (inc. tourism)	5.4%	5.8%	42.1%	38.9%
Manufacturing	8.7%	9.4%	17.1%	23.0%
Other tradable	2.0%	2.5%	25.0%	15.9%
Non-tradable	6.6%	7.1%	57.9%	61.1%
EMPLOYMENT	0.1%	1.0%	% of employment	
Tradable (inc. tourism)	−1.4%	−0.2%	67.4%	56.3%
Manufacturing	4.9%	5.4%	14.5%	23.3%
Other tradable	−3.9%	−2.1%	53.0%	33.0%
Non-tradable	2.6%	3.2%	32.6%	43.7%

Source Author's calculation from ADB (2024) data. Growth rates are calculated using Ordinary Least Squares method.

Unfortunately, the absence of detailed data at the subsector level limits a comprehensive analysis of the manufacturing sector's performance. However, in countries like Morocco—where such data are available—an in-depth study (El Aynaoui & Dinh, forthcoming 2025) reveals a clear divergence between modern manufacturing industries (such as automotive, aeronautics, and electrical machinery) and traditional sectors (such as textiles, garments, and wood products). While modern exports have gained prominence in Morocco's trade, their domestic value-added share remains lower than that of traditional exports. This suggests that for modern exports to effectively drive future economic growth, they must significantly increase their domestic value-added content.

This growth pattern has significant implications for employment. From 2000 to 2023, employment in tradable sectors in Vietnam declined by 1.4% per year, while employment in non-tradable sectors grew by 2.6% annually (Table 6.2). However, the manufacturing sector experienced robust employment growth of nearly 5% per year.

Non-Tradable Sectors. Table 6.3 provides details on the value-added and employment growth rates of subsectors within the non-tradable

Table 6.3 Average Annual Growth Rates of Value Added and Employment in Non-Tradable Sectors, 2010–2023

	Average Annual Growth Rates		*% of GDP at fc*	
	2010–2023	*2010–2019*	*2000*	*2023*
TOTAL VALUE ADDED (GDP at fc) in 2014 prices	6.1%	6.6%	100.0%	100.0%
Non-tradable	6.6%	7.1%	57.9%	61.1%
Utilities	7.8%	8.4%	8.7%	10.0%
Construction and public works	7.2%	7.6%	6.3%	6.7%
Wholesale and retail trade	7.6%	8.1%	7.4%	9.2%
Transport, warehousing, and communications	7.5%	8.8%	4.7%	5.6%
Information and communication	8.1%	9.1%	4.4%	5.7%
Finance & insurance	7.7%	7.2%	4.5%	5.5%
Real estate	3.1%	3.2%	5.1%	3.5%
Others	5.0%	5.7%	16.8%	14.9%
			% of total employment	
EMPLOYMENT	0.1%	1.0%	100.0%	100.0%
Non-tradable	2.6%	3.2%	32.6%	43.7%
Utilities	2.4%	4.6%	0.6%	0.6%
Construction and public works	4.0%	4.5%	6.3%	9.3%
Wholesale and retail trade	2.2%	2.7%	11.6%	15.1%
Transport, warehousing, and communications	3.0%	3.6%	2.9%	3.9%
Information and communication	0.0%	0.0%	0.6%	0.6%
Finance & insurance	4.7%	5.6%	0.6%	1.0%
Real estate	11.3%	13.6%	0.2%	0.8%
Others	1.6%	2.6%	9.8%	12.5%

Source Author's calculation from ADB (2024) data. Growth rates are calculated using Ordinary Least Squares method

sector. Overall, this sector's annual value-added growth rate (6.6%) exceeded GDP growth (6.1%). The strongest-performing subsectors include information and communication, transport, and wholesale trade. These subsectors also generate more employment than the economy as a whole, though not as much as the manufacturing sector (shown in Table 6.2).

Wholesale and retail trade employ the largest share of the workforce (15% of total employment in 2023, Table 6.3). This subsector's annual employment growth rate exceeds that of the overall economy but remains lower than that of manufacturing. Despite strong value-added growth (approximately 8% per year), employment expansion has been modest. The second-largest employment category is "other services" (13% in 2023), likely comprising various urban delivery services. Construction follows, with a 9% employment share. While these subsectors have demonstrated reasonable value-added growth, employment growth has been less pronounced (Table 6.3).

Challenges in the Service Sector

Services generally contribute less to value-added and employment than agriculture and manufacturing due to several structural and economic constraints. One key limitation is the relatively weak linkages between the service sector and other parts of the economy. As illustrated in Figures 6.1 through 6.3, services have fewer backward and forward connections compared to manufacturing. This limits their multiplier effects on economic growth. In contrast, manufacturing relies extensively on intermediate goods (Agenor & El Aynaoui, 2015), generates significant knowledge spillovers, and tends to drive faster and more sustained economic development.

Another challenge lies in the difficulty of replicating and scaling service production. Unlike manufacturing processes, which can be standardized and expanded efficiently, many services depend on individual labor and hinge on the input of individual workers. As noted by Baumol and Bowen (1965), this labor dependency makes it difficult to achieve economies of scale in the service sector.

Productivity growth in services is also harder to realize. While automation and technological advances have transformed manufacturing and agriculture, many service jobs remain dependent on human interaction and cannot easily benefit from such innovations. The labor-intensive nature of services limits potential productivity gains.

Moreover, services are often non-tradable, meaning that demand is confined largely to the domestic market. As a result, the service sector cannot leverage global demand in the same way manufacturing can, and it does not generate foreign exchange earnings—an important resource for developing economies.

The nature of service sector employment further complicates its contribution to broad-based job creation. There is a pronounced segmentation in the labor market, with some roles—such as physicians or educators—requiring high levels of skill and training, while others—such as sanitation or cleaning services—rely on low-skilled labor. This bifurcation limits the ability of the service sector to provide inclusive employment opportunities across the labor force.

Finally, demand for services tends to be more income-elastic than for manufactured or agricultural goods. This means that growth in the service sector is more strongly tied to rising consumer incomes. In economies where income levels remain modest or unevenly distributed, service sector expansion can be constrained by limited effective demand.

Together, these factors explain why services, while increasingly important, have not yet matched the contributions of manufacturing and agriculture to value-added and employment in many developing countries.

Overall, while the services sector has potential, it must overcome challenges such as limited linkages, scalability constraints, and low productivity to function as an engine of growth. Strategic policy interventions should focus on enhancing the tradability of services, improving skills development, and fostering innovation to maximize the sector's contribution to Vietnam's economic growth.

Technological Change and Trade-Related Services. Rodrik and Stiglitz (2024) recently argued that traditional, manufacturing-led growth is no longer viable due to technological advancements that have made manufacturing more skill—and capital-intensive. They propose that developing countries should adopt a new growth strategy based on both the green transition and productivity improvements in labor-intensive, non-traded services. However, since service-sector productivity is generally low, this shift is likely to result in weaker economic growth compared to manufacturing-led strategies.

To mitigate this challenge, developing countries should focus on:

- Expanding tourism to provide employment for low- and semi-skilled workers in the informal sector.
- Promoting labor-intensive subsectors such as garments and agribusiness (McMillan & Zeufack, 2022).
- Strengthening trade-related services.

Trade-Related Services in Vietnam

Which service subsectors have supported international trade in Vietnam? The International Standard Industrial Classification of All Economic Activities (ISIC) Revision 4 categorizes sections G through N (listed in Table 6.1) as business sector services. The OECD Trade in Value-Added (TiVA) database, using global input-output tables, estimates value-added contributions to gross exports from these activities. Table 6.4 summarizes results for Vietnam and comparator countries, including ASEAN, Morocco (also a lower-middle-income country), and OECD economies.

Table 6.4 Domestic Value Added of Service Activities as Percentage of Gross Exports, Average 2010–2020

	OECD	*Vietnam*	*ASEAN*	*Morocco*
Wholesale and retail trade; repair of motor vehicles and motorcycles (G)	13.1	4.9	10.4	7.2
Land transport and transport via pipelines (H49)	2.0	0.6	1.3	3.5
Water transport (H50)	2.0	0.3	1.9	0.6
Air transport (H51)	2.3	0.4	1.0	2.2
Warehousing and support activities for transportation (H52)	1.1	0.7	0.6	2.9
Postal and courier activities (H53)	0.2	0.1	0.1	0.3
Accommodation and food service activities (I)	2.1	0.9	1.7	5.2
Publishing, mot. pict., video, tel. prog. Prod.; so. Rec., prog. & broad. (J58T60)	1.1	0.1	0.4	0.5
Telecommunications (J61)	0.7	0.2	0.7	1.6
Comp. progr., consult., and infor. service activities (J62_63)	1.6	0.1	1.1	2.4
Financial and insurance activities (K)	5.7	0.3	3.0	0.7
Real estate activities (L)	0.5	0.1	0.5	0.9
Professional, scientific and technical activities (M)	4.0	0.2	1.8	4.3
Administrative and support service activities (N)	2.9	0.4	1.6	2.9
Total Business Sector Services (GTN)	**39.2**	**9.5**	**26.0**	**35.3**

Source Author's calculations from OECD-Trade in Value Added (2023). https://data-explorer.oecd.org/?pg=0&bp=true&snb=14&tm=TIVA, accessed November 17, 2024

Note: The letter inside parentheses refers to Trave-in-Value Added 2023 code. OECD figures refer to OECD15

These data are only available through detailed inter-country input-output tables and are not typically found in national income accounts.

This analysis reveals several important insights into the performance and potential of Vietnam's business sector services. Despite their growing role in the economy, these services currently contribute relatively little to the country's export activities. On average, they account for less than 10% of gross export value-added—far below the levels seen in more advanced or regionally comparable economies. By contrast, business services represent 40% of export value-added in OECD countries, 26% in ASEAN economies, and 35.3% in Morocco. This disparity underscores both the underperformance of Vietnam's service sector in the export domain and the considerable room for improvement.

Encouragingly, there are promising areas within the service sector that could be leveraged for stronger export performance. Wholesale and retail trade, in particular, stands out. Although this subsector currently contributes just 4.9% to Vietnam's export value-added, the figure is still below the ASEAN average of 10.4% and the OECD average of 13.1%, suggesting untapped potential. Moreover, as shown in Table 6.3, wholesale and retail trade is already the country's largest source of employment, indicating a solid foundation on which to build further export-oriented growth.

Beyond trade services, other subsectors also present notable opportunities. Financial and insurance activities, along with computer programming and information services, are especially well-positioned to grow. These high-value, knowledge-based services could significantly enhance Vietnam's export competitiveness if supported through targeted policy measures and strategic investment.

Sectoral Distribution of Domestic Value Added

Figure 6.4 presents the distribution of domestic value-added by major sectors in Vietnam. Over half of export value-added originates from manufacturing, followed by agriculture (13%), wholesale and retail trade (11%), and mining (10%). Other service sectors contribute relatively little to domestic value-added

Table 6.5 compares Vietnam's economic structure with its peers, highlighting Vietnam's weaker position not only relative to OECD countries but also compared to ASEAN and Morocco.

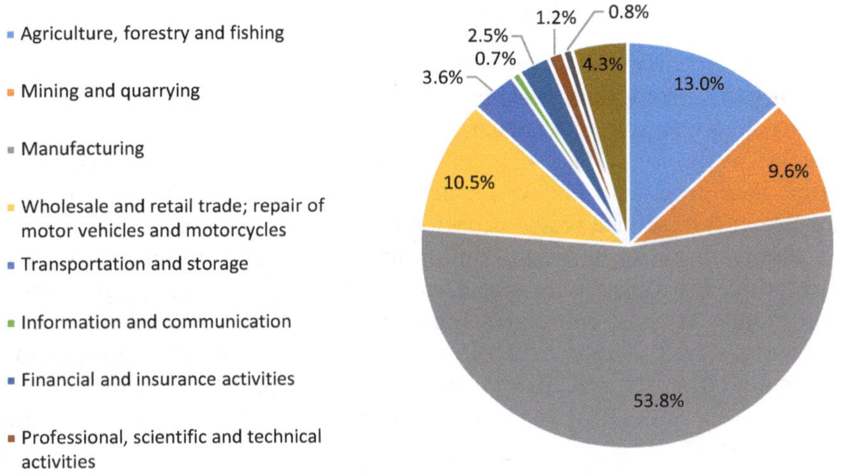

Fig. 6.4 Vietnam Sectoral Distribution of Domestic Value Added in Exports 2020. *Source* Author's calculations from OECD-Trade in Value Added (2023). https://data-explorer.Oecd.Org/?pg=0&bp=true&snb=14&tm=TIVA, accessed January 30, 2025

Table 6.5 A Comparison between Vietnam and Other Countries in Sector Composition of Domestic Value Added in Foreign Final Demand, 2020

Economic activity	*Vietnam*	*Morocco*	*ASEAN*	*EU(15)*
Total—all activities	100.0%	100.0%	100.0%	100.0%
Agriculture, forestry and fishing	13.0%	11.5%	7.5%	1.3%
Mining and quarrying	9.6%	4.7%	8.5%	0.8%
Manufacturing	53.8%	31.0%	35.9%	30.7%
Wholesale and retail trade; repair of motor vehicles and motorcycles	10.5%	11.9%	19.5%	15.7%
Transportation and storage	3.6%	10.0%	6.1%	7.8%
Information and communication	0.7%	4.4%	3.3%	7.4%
Financial and insurance activities	2.5%	5.4%	7.3%	8.3%
Professional, scientific and technical activities	1.2%	7.2%	3.1%	10.2%
Administrative and support service activities	0.8%	5.6%	2.8%	7.0%
Others	4.3%	8.3%	5.9%	10.6%

Source Author's calculations from OECD-Trade in Value Added (2023). https://data-explorer.oecd.org/?pg=0&bp=true&snb=14&tm=TIVA, accessed January 30, 2025

Policy Conclusions

Vietnam can enhance its commodity export performance through targeted policies that strengthen business services. A comprehensive approach is essential, addressing infrastructure gaps, skills deficits, and regulatory barriers within the service value chain. Effective strategies should combine immediate interventions to tackle urgent constraints with long-term investments in service sector capacity and competitiveness.

The relationship between commodity exports and business services is symbiotic. A strong service sector enables more efficient and higher-value commodity exports, while growing export sectors generate demand that supports service sector expansion. By integrating services into export strategies rather than treating them as separate economic activities, policymakers can unlock new sources of value addition and economic diversification.

As global value chains evolve, the distinction between goods and services is becoming increasingly blurred. The competitiveness of developing country exports will depend not only on production costs but also on the quality, availability, and efficiency of supporting services. Forward-looking policies that recognize this reality can help countries transition beyond commodity dependence toward more resilient economic structures.

Vietnam's pursuit of high-income status by 2045 necessitates significant reforms in its service sector. While past economic success has been driven by labor-intensive manufacturing, sustaining long-term growth requires a shift toward higher value-added activities, including a robust and competitive service industry. Achieving this transformation involves addressing existing limitations, leveraging global trade trends, and implementing comprehensive policy reforms.

A dynamic service sector is crucial for economic growth and resilience. Services constitute a substantial portion of Vietnam's economy and are integral to enhancing productivity across industries. As manufacturing becomes more sophisticated, demand increases for complementary services such as research and development, logistics, design, and marketing. A well-developed service industry fosters innovation, attracts foreign investment, and strengthens economic adaptability, positioning Vietnam more competitively in global markets.

Despite its growing importance, Vietnam's service sector continues to face significant hurdles that limit its contribution to the country's economic transformation. One of the primary challenges is its limited role in exports. Business sector services, for example, account for less than 10% of total exports—well below the ASEAN average of 26% and the OECD average of 39.2%, as shown in Table 6.4. This substantial gap underscores the urgency of enhancing the competitiveness of Vietnam's service industries and integrating them more deeply into global value chains.

Regulatory barriers also remain a major impediment. Measures such as data localization requirements, mandates for commercial presence, and complex foreign acquisition approval procedures discourage foreign service providers from entering the Vietnamese market. These restrictions reduce competition, inflate costs, and undermine service efficiency. According to the OECD (2023), Vietnam's regulatory environment imposes significant constraints on competition, which, if left unaddressed, could stifle both growth and innovation in the sector.

Another critical challenge is the continued dominance of state-owned enterprises (SOEs) in key service sectors like energy, finance, and telecommunications. This state-led structure restricts private sector participation and innovation, reducing the dynamism of the service industry. A more vibrant service sector will require a deliberate effort to reduce SOE dominance and encourage greater private sector investment.

Vietnam also struggles with a digital skills gap that hampers its business sector's capacity for digital transformation. The OECD points out that the shortage of skilled workers is a major bottleneck. Bridging this gap will require significant investment in training, technical and vocational education, and broader initiatives to improve digital competencies across the workforce.

To address these challenges and unlock the full potential of the service sector, a set of targeted policy priorities is essential. First, trade liberalization can play a pivotal role by reducing non tariff barriers, liberalizing service trade, and deepening regional integration. This includes easing restrictions on cross-border data flows while safeguarding privacy and cybersecurity, as well as reforming sectors such as telecommunications, finance, and transportation.

Second, strengthening domestic value chain integration is crucial. The World Bank (2024) emphasizes the importance of enhancing linkages between exporting firms and the wider domestic economy. This involves improving the business environment, connecting global firms with local suppliers, and implementing supply chain finance solutions to boost productivity.

Third, skill development remains foundational to the success of the service sector. Participation in global value chains and the adoption of new technologies will depend on increasing both the quantity and quality of skilled labor, particularly at the tertiary education level. Expanding training programs, enabling foreign technical expertise, and aligning local standards with international benchmarks are key steps in this direction.

Finally, as the global economy transitions toward sustainability, Vietnam must seize the opportunity to promote green exports. Transitioning to low-carbon production models is vital not only for maintaining competitiveness but also for meeting environmental goals. The World Bank calls for greater reliance on clean energy, while the OECD highlights the need to implement carbon market mechanisms more rapidly.

Together, these reforms offer a clear roadmap for Vietnam to enhance the performance of its service sector. By addressing structural barriers, improving the regulatory and skills environment, and aligning with global trends in sustainability and trade, Vietnam can position its service sector as a powerful engine for economic growth, resilience, and long-term competitiveness.

References

Agénor, P. R. El Aynaoui. (2015). *Morocco: Growth strategy for 2025 in an evolving international environment*, OCP Policy Center.

Aynaoui, K. E., & Dinh, H. T. (forthcoming 2025). Growth and Structural Transformation in Morocco. In El Aynaoui and A. Oqubay (Ed.), Oxford Handbook of the Moroccan Economy. Oxford University Press.

Baumol, W. J., & Bowen, W. G. (1965). On the performing arts: The anatomy of their economic problems. *American Economic Review*, *55*(1/2), 495–502.

El Aynaoui, K., & Dinh, H. T. (2025). Growth and structural transformation in Morocco. In K. E. Aynaoui & A. Oqubay (Eds.), *Oxford handbook of the moroccan economy.* Oxford University Press.

McMillan, M., & Zeufack, A. (2022). Labor productivity growth and industrialization in Africa. *Journal of Economic Perspectives*, *36*(1), 3–32.

Organisation for Economic Co-operation and Development. (2023). *OECD economic surveys: Viet Nam 2023*. OECD Publishing. https://doi.org/10.1787/8f2a6ecb-en

Rajan, R. G. (2025, January 3). Economic development in a protectionist world. *Project Syndicate*. https://www.project-syndicate.org/commentary/protectionist-world-means-developing-countries-need-services-exports-by-raghuram-g-rajan-2025-01

Rodrik, D., & Stiglitz, J. E. (2024). *A new growth strategy for developing nations*. https://tinyurl.com/ymrg8qom

Timmer, P. (2012). The mathematics of structural transformation. *International Food Policy Research Institute, 2*.

World Bank. (2024). *Viet Nam 2045: Trading up in a changing World—pathways to a high-income future*. http://hdl.handle.net/10986/42505

PART III

Macroeconomic Constraints and Development Strategy

CHAPTER 7

Macroeconomic Constraints and Development Strategy

Introduction

Vietnam has made significant economic strides in recent decades by fully integrating into the global economy. The country has leveraged its abundant and diligent labor force to manufacture increasingly sophisticated products for export as part of global value chains (GVCs). This strategy has resulted in rapid economic growth, decent employment opportunities, and a sharp reduction in poverty. For a nation emerging from a long war, GVC participation provided the fastest route to generating jobs, earning foreign exchange, and transitioning from a low-income to a lower-middle-income economy within one generation.

However, this growth model would have been even more successful if, within a decade, Vietnam had shifted to a development strategy that focused on elevating its workforce beyond low-wage, low-value-added jobs in GVCs. Such a transition would require proactive public policies, as GVCs themselves have little incentive to drive this shift. The private sector in Vietnam was still nascent, and workers had no control over their economic mobility. In contrast, economies like South Korea and Taiwan did not face this issue because foreign direct investment (FDI) in these countries was primarily in the form of joint ventures, compelling domestic companies to learn, innovate, and

Contributed by Hinh T. Dinh

H. T. Dinh, H. T. Nguyen, *Vietnam's Economic Leap*,
https://doi.org/10.1007/978-3-032-08904-5_7

manufacture entire products. Vietnam's reliance on GVCs, however, has resulted in specialization in a single production stage—often final assembly—where decisions about upgrading to other stages remain beyond Vietnam's control and are dictated by multinational corporations.

The failure to move up the value chain has left Vietnam in largely the same position within GVCs as it was 30 years ago, despite the diversification and increased complexity of its exports. The current export model remains reliant on low-skill, labor-intensive, low-value-added activities, leading to many challenges:

- Low export value-added per capita: Vietnam's focus on low-value-added activities results in lower export value-added per capita compared to similar export-led economies like Thailand and Malaysia.
- Overreliance on production roles: A staggering 85% of export sector jobs are in production roles (e.g., craft workers and machine operators). This figure is significantly higher than in peer countries and has not declined, even with the transition to more complex exports such as electronics.
- Rising wages and eroding cost advantage: Between 2010 and 2022, labor costs nearly tripled, surpassing those in the Philippines and Indonesia, while productivity gains remained modest, eroding Vietnam's competitive edge in labor-intensive GVC segments.
- Dual economy structure: Export activity is concentrated within FDI firms, while domestic firms remain largely confined to traditional sectors, leading to minimal productivity spillovers from foreign to local enterprises.
- Weak domestic linkages: Vietnam's domestic firms have fewer GVC connections than firms in comparable economies, limiting technological and productivity transfers.
- Stagnant job growth in domestic demand sectors: While export-related employment has grown rapidly, job growth in sectors tied to domestic demand has stalled, making Vietnam vulnerable to global trade fluctuations.
- Low domestic value contribution in exports: Despite producing high-tech exports, Vietnam's domestic value-added remains low due to heavy reliance on imported components.
- Shortage of high-skilled workers: While Vietnam has achieved successes in basic education, there remains a scarcity of skilled professionals in fields such as engineering, specialized manufacturing, and management.

- Mismatch between skills and labor market demands: A declining wage premium for skilled workers discourages investment in higher education and skill development, despite an overall shortage of skilled labor.
- Emerging infrastructure bottlenecks: The rapid increase in energy demand and freight transport has outpaced GDP growth, placing significant pressure on infrastructure systems.
- Carbon-intensive manufacturing: Vietnam's past industrial expansion relied on a carbon-intensive energy mix, increasing its exposure to risks associated with the global shift toward low-carbon trade.

These constraints underscore the need for Vietnam to transition to a more skill-intensive, integrated, and higher-value-added export model.

Limited Macroeconomic Space

Vietnam's fiscal space has become increasingly constrained due to the impact of recent crises, including the Global Financial Crisis, COVID-19, and commodity price shocks over the past decade. Additionally, competing demands for public spending have intensified due to demographic trends, climate change, high debt burdens, and global interest rates. This complex interplay creates a challenging environment for maintaining economic stability and growth.

Demographic Trends. As discussed in Chap. 3, Vietnam has about two decades to capitalize on its demographic dividend before it dissipates due to declining fertility rates, increasing life expectancy, and an aging population. The country's total fertility rate (TFR) has declined significantly, from over six children per woman in the 1970s to approximately 1.9 in 2022—below the replacement rate of 2.0. Meanwhile, life expectancy has improved from around 60 years in the 1960s to over 74 years today.

The proportion of the population aged 65 and older is expected to increase markedly over the next 20 years, placing additional pressure on healthcare, pension systems, and social services. The old-age dependency ratio, which measures the proportion of elderly dependents per 100 working-age individuals, was 13.3% in 2022 and is projected to rise to 20.1% by 2034 (United Nations, 2022). This increase could strain public resources and the labor force, making it imperative for policymakers to implement innovative solutions that support the aging population while maintaining economic sustainability. These challenges are compounded by the country's limited social safety nets.

Youth unemployment also poses a significant challenge, as governments often need to increase spending on social welfare programs, job training, and education initiatives to enhance economic engagement and prevent social unrest. High youth unemployment reduces tax revenues while increasing public expenditure needs, diverting resources from critical infrastructure and healthcare.

Climate Change. Climate change presents both immediate risks and long-term adaptation challenges for Vietnam. The country faces severe environmental threats, including rising sea levels, desertification, and extreme weather events, all of which can disrupt economic growth and stability. Addressing these issues requires substantial investments in energy systems, agriculture, and urban infrastructure, as well as adaptation measures. Estimates suggest that additional investments equivalent to 2%–4% of GDP per year will be necessary, much of which will rely on external financing.

Global Interest Rates Have Narrowed Monetary Policy Scope. The State Bank of Vietnam's (SBV) ability to use monetary policy for economic stabilization has been significantly constrained by high international interest rates. Many developing nations, including Vietnam, have been compelled to raise domestic interest rates to prevent capital outflows and currency depreciation. However, this also raises borrowing costs, thereby dampening investment and growth. For example, Brazil's central bank raised its benchmark interest rate to 13.75% in 2023 to curb inflation and slow economic expansion. Similarly, Egypt increased rates to control inflation, resulting in reduced investment and higher borrowing costs for businesses and households.

Additionally, capital flows have become more volatile, complicating exchange rate management. Many developing countries, including Vietnam, have seen their foreign exchange reserves decline, making it increasingly difficult to defend their currencies. Pakistan, for instance, saw its reserves drop to less than two months' worth of imports in 2023—falling below the conventional three-month minimum threshold for reserve adequacy—severely constraining its ability to stabilize its currency.

Higher global interest rates exacerbate these issues by increasing the difficulty of maintaining a stable exchange rate under external devaluation pressures. To mitigate these risks, policymakers may need to limit capital flows or adopt more flexible exchange rate policies to preserve domestic monetary policy autonomy. This is particularly crucial as many small and medium-sized enterprises (SMEs) and large firms in Vietnam remain vulnerable following the COVID-19 pandemic. A sharp increase in domestic interest rates in response to global trends could push these enterprises into bankruptcy, further slowing economic growth.

Short—and Medium-Term Macroeconomic Challenges (2025–2030)

Vietnam faces several macroeconomic challenges in the coming years:

- Slowing export demand—The country's major trade partners, including the U.S., EU, China, and Japan, are experiencing economic slowdowns, which could dampen Vietnam's export-driven growth. This slowdown coincides with a negative output gap, increasing the risk of recession.
- Inflationary pressures—Rising import prices, particularly for energy and food, are expected to drive inflation.
- Higher international interest rates—Tightened monetary policies in developed economies could lead to elevated borrowing costs for Vietnam.
- Currency depreciation pressures—The U.S. dollar has appreciated to its highest levels in decades, putting downward pressure on the Vietnamese đồng.

These challenges arise at a time when Vietnam has limited fiscal and monetary policy flexibility due to the lingering effects of past economic shocks—including the Global Financial Crisis, COVID-19, and recent commodity price spikes caused by geopolitical events such as the Russia-Ukraine war. Rising debt and widening fiscal deficits further restrict Vietnam's policy options, with the primary budget deficit reaching 1.6% of GDP in 2024 (IMF, 2024).

At the same time, achieving sustainable, high economic growth is essential for Vietnam to reach high-income status by 2045, as outlined in the government's vision. These competing demands will test the government's administrative and policymaking capabilities.

Policy Conflicts and the Monetary Trilemma. Economic policies aimed at addressing these challenges often generate trade-offs. To combat inflation, some developing countries resort to price controls or quantitative restrictions, but history shows that such measures create distortions and long-term inefficiencies. Alternatively, using a fixed exchange rate as a nominal anchor can stabilize domestic prices but risks speculative attacks and financial crises. Furthermore, maintaining exchange rate stability in an economy with capital mobility limits the central bank's ability to set an independent monetary policy.

These policy dilemmas are encapsulated in the **monetary trilemma** (Mundell, 1963; Fleming, 1962), which states that a country can achieve only two out of three objectives: (1) exchange rate stability, (2) capital mobility, and (3) independent monetary policy. Historically, most economies have struggled to manage this trade-off successfully.[1]

This trilemma is not new. Since the gold standard more than a century ago, countries have had to deal with this trilemma with varying degrees of success. Note that this trilemma does not imply that one policy choice is the best, nor that any one choice can resolve all economic problems, because each policy choice entails a set of advantages and disadvantages, the magnitude of which could vary depending on specific conditions and over time.

Since the 1980s and 1990s, emerging market and developing economies (EMDEs) have increased financial integration and attracted large capital inflows, followed by economic booms. But these countries also experienced crises when these flows suddenly reversed. Consequently, many economies have transitioned to "in-between" exchange rate regimes, such as managed floating, target zones, basket pegs, and crawling pegs, to balance stability and flexibility. Some scholars argue that a fourth dimension—financial stability—should be added to the trilemma, forming a "quadrilemma." Obstfeld and Taylor (2017) suggest that sufficient foreign exchange reserves and sound fiscal and structural policies can serve as additional shock absorbers.

Research also suggests that flexible exchange rates can mitigate external shocks. Di Giovanni and Shambaugh (2008) found that countries with pegged exchange rates and open capital accounts experience significant economic slowdowns when the base country (e.g., the U.S.) raises interest rates, whereas those with floating exchange rates or restricted capital accounts are less affected.

[1] This can be seen intuitively if one focuses on the extreme policy choice of a small economy: a fixed exchange rate or a pure float regime, a complete independent monetary policy or no monetary policy control, and perfect capital mobility or financial autarky. If a country has a fixed exchange rate regime and free capital mobility then it has to give up its independent monetary policy. When a country faces an external shock such as interest rate increases from the base country (the US), the interest rate differential will cause holders of domestic bonds to sell them in search of foreign bonds. This will increase the demand for foreign currency and, due to the fixed exchange rate regime, will require the Central Bank to intervene and force it to reduce the money supply. Hence the country gives up its independent monetary policy.

To shield the domestic economy from external shocks, Vietnam may need to adopt greater exchange rate flexibility or implement selective capital controls to retain monetary policy independence. Ensuring the central bank has the ability to manage domestic interest rates is particularly crucial in the current environment, as many Vietnamese enterprises remain in a fragile state post-pandemic. If the SBV raises interest rates in response to global trends, it could drive businesses into bankruptcy, further hindering economic recovery.

Thus, policymakers must carefully navigate the trade-offs between exchange rate stability, capital mobility, and monetary independence while balancing the urgent need for economic stability and long-term growth.

The trilemma will be exacerbated by debt challenges. Compared to other Asian countries, Vietnam's external debt is relatively high, though not at an alarming level. The primary concern with Vietnam's external debt lies more in its composition than in its magnitude.

First, a significant portion of Vietnam's external debt is held by the private sector and is not guaranteed by the government. The primary creditors for this debt are commercial banks, with a smaller share held by bondholders. As of 2023, private sector external debt amounted to $60.9 billion, compared to $43.9 billion in government debt (World Bank, 2024).

Second, a substantial portion of the total debt stock—$35.1 billion, or one-fourth of the total—is short-term, meaning it must be repaid within a year. This proportion was only one-fifth in 2020, indicating a rapid increase of about 10% annually from 2020 to 2023.

Third, almost half of the external debt stock is subject to variable interest rates, posing additional risks in a volatile financial environment.

Finally, a predominant share of Vietnam's external debt (54%) is denominated in U.S. dollars, which increases debt servicing costs when the dollar appreciates. The rising proportion of debt tied to variable interest rates is a recent phenomenon that warrants close monitoring.

Vietnam's private sector external debt—$60.9 billion at the end of 2023, plus an additional $39 billion in short-term debt due within a year—is particularly concerning. The bulk of this debt ($59.2 billion) is owed to commercial banks, with only $1.7 billion held by bondholders. Principal payments on this debt exceeded $19 billion in 2023. While private sector obligations are theoretically outside the government's purview, large-scale defaults or contract breaches could trigger a financial crisis, impacting the broader economy. The government would likely be compelled to intervene, particularly if the affected businesses are deemed "too big to fail."

The collapse of the Van Thinh Phat Holding Group may be a harbinger of more widespread financial distress, as banks and non-bank institutions continue to grapple with bad loans in the real estate sector and beyond. Without careful oversight, this could lead to significant public losses. The Central Bank must closely monitor these loans and corporate bond issuances to ensure the solvency and credibility of the financial sector.

Vietnam's debt challenges are also significant from a development perspective. Until now, the government has financed its budget deficit through domestic financial repression. This is evident in the size of domestic debt: as of the end of 2023, external debt stood at $141.9 billion (34.3% of GDP), while domestic debt, measured by local currency bonds issued by the government and corporate sector, totaled $141 billion (33% of GDP). Of this, government bonds accounted for $98 billion (23% of GDP).

In total, Vietnam's external and domestic debt amounted to approximately 66% of GDP. The ADB reported that as of end-September 2024, the outstanding local currency bonds amounted to over $140 billion. Government bonds amounted to about $100 billion and include obligations issued by the central government, local governments, and the central bank. The remainder are corporate bonds, which cover both public and private entities, including financial institutions.

Interest rates on outstanding government-issued domestic debt have remained low due to financial repression. However, this has also hindered economic growth by slowing much-needed banking and financial sector reforms.

Debt Sustainability and Investments in Megaprojects

The sustainability of government debt in the medium term depends on the trajectory of GDP growth and international interest rates. Given emerging unfavorable trends in both areas, new borrowing commitments must be carefully scrutinized. In particular, large recent investment projects—spanning aviation, rail, road, urban, and port infrastructure—carry substantial financial and execution risks, making transparent oversight critical moving forward.

The macroeconomic framework for debt sustainability in this book follows the classic model of external and internal balance, which assigns fiscal policy to internal balance and monetary policy to external balance. As Branson (1992) pointed out, the policy implications of this approach align with modern debt sustainability analysis used by Bretton Woods institutions. A basic theoretical framework for Vietnam's current debt sustainability analysis is provided in Dinh (2022, Annex 4A).

This debt sustainability model can help assess the appropriate level of government spending—particularly on large investment projects—to ensure the maintenance of both internal and external balance. Based on assumptions regarding economic growth, inflation, and interest rates, the debt-to-GDP ratio can be estimated as demonstrated in Dinh (2022, Annex 4A):

$$d_t - d_{t-1} = \left[\frac{i_t^f - \pi(1+g) - g + \epsilon\alpha(1+i_t^f)}{(1+g)(1+\pi)}\right] d_{t-1} + pd_t - s_t$$

where dt is the ratio of total debt to the country's GDP in period t,i f is the nominal interest rate in period t,π is the inflation rate (GDP deflator), is the proportion of total debt held by foreign residents in the previous period (hence, a constant in the current period), ε is the exchange rate devaluation, pdt is the ratio of primary deficit to GDP, and st is the ratio of seigniorage to GDP. Note that in addition to seigniorage, additional fiscal resources, such as privatization proceeds, can help improve debt sustainability, whereas quasi-fiscal activities or contingent liabilities can exacerbate debt distress (Dinh, 2022).

Debt Warning Thresholds. What level of debt-to-GDP should serve as a warning signal for Vietnam? Traditional indicators, such as the debt-to-GDP ratio and debt service ratio, do not fully capture debt dynamics. However, a threshold can still be useful for triggering closer debt scrutiny.

For countries classified under the Highly Indebted Poor Countries (HIPC) Initiative, a debt-to-GDP ratio above 63% is considered unsustainable. The HIPC Initiative aimed to bring debt-to-exports ratios down to 150%, which translates into a post-relief debt-to-GDP ratio of 37.5% for low—and middle-income countries. By this benchmark, any debt-to-GDP ratio above 65% could signal potential debt distress.

The two key drivers of Vietnam's public sector debt ratio are:

- The primary budget deficit (net of interest payments), and
- Automatic debt dynamics, which include interest rate effects and GDP growth rate effects.

Medium-Term Fiscal Projections

In the base case scenario (Table 7.1), we adopt the same assumptions as the IMF's latest projections (IMF, 2024), focusing on the primary deficit and automatic debt dynamics. With actual data for 2023 and 2024 and projections for 2025 and beyond, the debt-to-GDP ratio remains below 33% throughout the forecast period. This suggests Vietnam could maintain a sustainable fiscal path if it keeps its primary deficit below 1% of GDP. Including interest payments, the total budget deficit would be around 2% of GDP.

One of the risks associated with rising private sector investment under the "Era of National Rise" is the increased use of government guarantees for borrowing by state-owned enterprises (SOEs) and powerful private sector groups. For instance, some private entities propose to finance major infrastructure projects—such as the North-South rail line—on the condition that the government provides subsidized loans or guarantees. When these contingent liabilities are eventually triggered, hidden fiscal deficits become explicit, obligating the government to cover unanticipated expenditures.

These liabilities need not originate from the Ministry of Finance alone; they may also arise through central bank operations—so-called quasi-fiscal activities. For example, if the central bank guarantees exchange rates or interest rates on loans to commercial banks or other entities, such as SOEs or provincial banks, it may incur significant losses when the exchange rate is later devalued or interest rates are raised, creating a mismatch between its assets and liabilities.

Policies to manage interest rates, exchange rates, the budget, public enterprises, and the financial sector must be coordinated in an integrated manner. Without reform of public enterprises, for example, raising interest rates might improve financial resource allocation but could also reduce the profitability of SOEs. Given soft budget constraints or the lack of central bank independence, this could result in increased budget or quasi-fiscal deficits. Ultimately, how high interest rates can be raised depends on the extent to which the budget can absorb the resulting real-sector losses. The same principle applies in the case of a banking crisis: fiscal reform must go hand-in-hand with reforms in the financial and public enterprise sectors.

The above macroeconomic policies need to be supported by effective microeconomic and structural policies, which should aim at protecting the labor force during global crises and enhancing labor productivity to

Table 7.1 Vietnam Debt Dynamics Base Case

BASE CASE								
Vietnam	*2023*	*2024*	*2025*	*2026*	*2027*	*2028*	*2029*	*2030*
Gross public debt (% of GDP)	34.3%	33.5%	32.5%	31.7%	30.8%	29.8%	28.8%	27.9%
Real GDP growth	5.0%	6.7%	6.3%	6.6%	6.9%	6.8%	7.0%	7.3%
Inflation	1.9%	4.0%	4.0%	3.0%	2.8%	2.7%	2.6%	2.6%
Effective interest rate	0.0%	3.2%	3.3%	3.4%	3.4%	3.4%	3.6%	3.7%
Primary deficit (- = surplus)	1.6%	1.6%	1.2%	1.1%	0.9%	0.8%	0.7%	0.7%
Interest rate/growth differential effect	−2.4%	−2.6%	−2.4%	−2.1%	−2.1%	−1.9%	−1.8%	−1.8%
of which interest rate effect	−0.7%	−0.3%	−0.3%	0.1%	0.1%	0.2%	0.2%	0.3%
of which real GDP growth effect	−1.8%	−2.3%	−2.1%	−2.1%	−2.2%	−2.1%	−2.1%	−2.1%
Exchange rate depreciation effect								
Automatic debt dynamics	−2.3%	−2.4%	−2.2%	−1.9%	−1.9%	−1.8%	−1.7%	−1.7%
Change in debt ratio	**−0.7%**	**−0.8%**	**−1.0%**	−0.8%	−1.0%	−1.0%	−1.0%	−1.0%

Source Author's computation based on methodology presented in Dinh (2022, Annex 4A).

restore pre-COVID growth while laying the foundation for Vietnam's transition to upper-middle-income status.

In the short term, governments can boost domestic demand by targeting non-tradable sectors, particularly those that employ low-skilled workers in the informal economy, such as services and retail trade. One effective measure is the reduction of employers' social contributions, which would lower labor costs and stimulate hiring. For instance, reducing social charges from 34% to 25% of wages could provide immediate relief to employers while encouraging formal employment. Over the medium term, policy efforts should focus on strengthening linkages between domestic firms and foreign-owned enterprises, thereby deepening integration and supporting the expansion of the formal sector.

Technological Change and Economic Transformation

The pace of technological advancement has accelerated markedly in recent years, ushering in what is often called the Fourth Industrial Revolution. Innovations in artificial intelligence, robotics, the Internet of Things, 3D printing, and biotechnology are transforming the global economy as profoundly as the arrival of electricity did in the nineteenth century. These shifts are disrupting established growth models, especially in developing economies.

Traditionally, economic growth in these countries relied heavily on structural transformation—moving labor and resources from low-productivity sectors like agriculture to higher-productivity sectors such as manufacturing. Prior to the 2008 financial crisis, this process accounted for roughly 74% of productivity growth in Africa (Dieppe, 2021). However, several emerging trends are challenging the viability of this model. Technological change has made manufacturing increasingly capital—and skill-intensive, diminishing its capacity to absorb large numbers of low-skilled workers. The COVID-19 pandemic exacerbated existing vulnerabilities, slowing growth and increasing debt burdens. Meanwhile, geopolitical tensions and a growing backlash against hyper-globalization are reshaping global trade dynamics, and climate change continues to disrupt traditional economic sectors, particularly agriculture.

In response to these challenges, Rodrik and Stiglitz (2024) have proposed a new development strategy centered on two foundational pillars. The first is a green transition, involving the transformation of energy systems, investments in sustainable agriculture, and the construction of climate-resilient infrastructure. The second pillar focuses on enhancing productivity in labor-intensive, non-traded services. Recognizing that manufacturing can no longer serve as the primary engine of job creation, they advocate for a strategy that expands employment opportunities in the service sector. This includes encouraging large firms to generate lower-skill jobs in non-tradable services, building public infrastructure to support small enterprises, and promoting technologies that augment, rather than replace, low-skilled labor. They also emphasize the need for policy experimentation—encouraging adaptive approaches where institutions, tools, and objectives evolve in response to real-world conditions.

Despite the promise of the Rodrik-Stiglitz strategy, its successful implementation depends on overcoming three major obstacles. First, many developing countries face institutional weaknesses, particularly within the public sector. Strengthening the capacity of state institutions to effectively partner with the private sector and implement coherent economic strategies is crucial. Second, services-based growth may not deliver the same economic dynamism traditionally associated with manufacturing-led development. To address this, countries should not only enhance tourism and informal services but also promote labor-intensive manufacturing niches, such as garment production and agro-processing, which still hold potential for job creation and value addition.

Finally, while artificial intelligence is poised to reshape global labor markets, its macroeconomic effects are likely to unfold gradually. As Acemoglu (2025) notes, AI-driven gains in total factor productivity are projected to average only 0.7% over the next decade. Moreover, research by Svanberg et al. (2024) underscores that AI adoption remains constrained by both technical and economic barriers, which will likely slow the automation of jobs. This delay offers a window of opportunity—perhaps one to two decades—during which developing countries can still rely on labor-intensive industries before the full impact of AI disruption sets in.

Towards a Viable Development Strategy

To respond effectively to the evolving demands of global integration and national development, Vietnam's policy framework must remain flexible and adaptive, accommodating diverse local realities while providing clear strategic direction. At its core, the country's development approach should rest on three interrelated pillars: building macroeconomic buffers, leveraging technology for productivity, and promoting structural transformation for sustained growth.

Strengthening Macroeconomic Resilience. In today's volatile global environment, Vietnam must bolster its macroeconomic foundations to better withstand external shocks. This requires comprehensive reforms in fiscal, monetary, exchange rate, and macroprudential policy.

On the fiscal front, enhancing the tax system through modernization and base broadening would not only improve revenue collection but also create room for critical investments in infrastructure and human capital. Carefully managing contingent liabilities and public arrears is essential to addressing debt vulnerabilities and ensuring fiscal sustainability.

In terms of monetary policy, adopting a flexible inflation-targeting framework would help strike a balance between price stability, financial health, and economic growth. The development of domestic bond markets in local currency could reduce reliance on foreign-denominated debt, thereby limiting exposure to exchange rate fluctuations. Vietnam could look to India's experience—where the adoption of inflation targeting in 2016 significantly anchored expectations and reduced volatility—as a reference point.

A more flexible exchange rate regime, supported by adequate international reserves, would further help Vietnam absorb external shocks. Instead of defending fixed exchange levels, foreign exchange interventions should aim to moderate excessive short-term volatility. Empirical evidence shows that economies with flexible exchange rates tend to recover more rapidly from external disruptions.

Macroprudential policies must also be strengthened to guard against systemic risks and manage capital flow volatility. These tools must work in tandem with fiscal and monetary policy to ensure financial system stability. South Korea's use of targeted measures—such as limiting foreign exchange derivative positions and imposing levies on non-core foreign liabilities—provides a relevant model for enhancing resilience.

As global economic patterns shift, Vietnam's long-term strategy should prioritize resilience, productivity, and economic transformation. Given the declining role of traditional manufacturing in job creation, a successful path forward will depend on embracing technology, enhancing the service sector, and reinforcing macroeconomic safeguards.

Harnessing Technology to Drive Productivity. Vietnam stands to benefit greatly from adopting advanced technologies, particularly in public sector governance and service delivery. Digital government systems can reduce bureaucracy, improve efficiency, and increase transparency, thereby curbing corruption. Implementing a national digital identity system would promote financial inclusion and improve access to public services. The example of Estonia demonstrates how comprehensive e-governance can significantly strengthen public administration by enabling real-time monitoring of expenditures, enhancing data-driven policy decisions, and improving project implementation.

In the education sector, technology can expand access to quality instruction, especially in underserved rural areas. Digital learning platforms—like India's BYJU'S, which now reaches over 80 million users—offer tailored educational experiences and help close learning gaps through adaptive content.

Emerging technologies such as artificial intelligence (AI) and the Internet of Things (IoT) hold enormous potential to revolutionize research and innovation. These tools allow developing countries to leapfrog traditional barriers by automating tasks, analyzing vast datasets, and enabling remote collaboration. They can transform sectors ranging from agriculture to healthcare by facilitating virtual simulations and streamlining workflows. With the right investments, Vietnam can harness AI and IoT not only to address local development challenges but also to contribute meaningfully to global innovation.

In healthcare, digital tools such as telemedicine and AI-powered analytics offer game-changing opportunities. Telemedicine platforms can bridge the gap between rural patients and urban healthcare providers, while AI can improve disease surveillance, optimize resource allocation, and support health system planning. Rwanda's use of drones to deliver medical supplies to remote communities illustrates how innovation can overcome logistical hurdles in developing contexts.

Similarly, agriculture can benefit immensely from technology. AI-based forecasting systems, along with IoT-enabled sensors, can help farmers monitor soil health and weather patterns in real time, allowing for more precise and sustainable farming practices. Initiatives like Digital Green, which uses community videos to share best practices with farmers in India and Ethiopia, have reached over 1.8 million farmers and demonstrate how digital tools can raise agricultural productivity.

Reinvigorating Growth Through Structural Transformation. Despite the importance of expanding services, relying solely on this sector may be insufficient to absorb the growing number of young workers entering Vietnam's labor force. Services generally offer lower productivity gains than manufacturing, and the demand for non-tradable services typically grows more slowly than demand for manufactured goods. Traditional sectors, therefore, remain critical for employing unskilled and semi-skilled labor, highlighting the importance of supporting their modernization and integration into the broader economy.

Vietnam must pursue a strategy that supports multiple types of enterprises. This includes crafting foreign direct investment (FDI) policies that enhance integration into global value chains, empowering domestic firms to expand within local and regional markets, and promoting digitalization to close the gap between foreign and domestic enterprises. However, one of the major obstacles to industrialization is the increasing capital intensity of manufacturing. As wages rise, foreign investors may favor technologies that reduce labor dependence, thereby undermining job creation goals.

Expanding Employment Opportunities in Key Sectors. To generate employment, Vietnam should tap into sectors with high labor-absorption potential. Tourism is one such industry. As evidenced by Africa's experience—where over 24 million jobs were created in 2023—the tourism sector supports a wide range of activities, including hospitality, food services, cultural preservation, and transportation. Its labor-intensive nature makes it a strong entry point into the workforce, especially for women and youth. Moreover, it creates significant indirect employment across supply chains, amplifying its impact.

Green manufacturing presents another promising avenue, especially in light of Vietnam's renewable energy potential. By transitioning toward sustainable manufacturing practices, the country can simultaneously improve its cost competitiveness and generate jobs aligned with environmental goals.

The pharmaceutical industry also offers dual benefits: it contributes to public health while generating skilled employment. Investment in domestic pharmaceutical production would enhance access to medicines and reduce reliance on imports, while fostering industrial upgrading and technological innovation.

Effective Industrialization

Vietnam's industrialization efforts should be guided by several pragmatic principles. First, the limitations of market-led development must be acknowledged—strategic public intervention remains essential. Second, industrial strategies must be tailored to the country's unique circumstances rather than replicating generic models. Third, policies should remain flexible and grounded in real-world problem-solving, avoiding rigid ideological commitments. Finally, robust partnerships between the public and private sectors are critical to designing and executing effective industrial policies.

Industrial policies can be grouped into two categories: general cross-sectoral strategies and specific policies aimed at boosting manufacturing.

Cross-sectoral strategies should focus on improving the overall business climate through macroeconomic stability and targeted support for labor-intensive sectors. Increasing agricultural productivity—by securing land rights, improving access to markets and finance, optimizing crop selection, and expanding irrigation—can free up labor for higher-productivity activities. Upgrading the informal sector through training, infrastructure, and legal reforms can also facilitate its integration into the formal economy. Easing barriers to labor mobility—by improving transport and housing near industrial zones and simplifying administrative procedures—can further accelerate structural transformation.

In manufacturing, attracting and nurturing FDI is essential. Governments should actively identify and address barriers to investment, while encouraging partnerships between foreign investors and domestic vocational institutions to develop a skilled workforce. Vietnam can draw on East Asia's successful experience, where FDI helped drive job creation, capital inflows, and technology transfer.

Local enterprise development is also critical. Many successful growth strategies in Africa and Asia began small and scaled up strategically, focusing on zones with high potential. Policies should help bridge the divide between small firms and large corporations linked to global value chains. This can be achieved through equitable incentives and the creation of organic industrial clusters—geographically concentrated networks of enterprises working in the same sector. Embracing digital technologies will further enhance both microenterprises and larger firms, enabling greater collaboration and boosting the technological capabilities of the entire industrial ecosystem.

Enhancing Cooperation Among Developing Countries. Closer policy coordination among developing nations could unlock considerable benefits by enhancing bargaining power, sharing knowledge, and building collective capacity. South-South cooperation has already demonstrated its potential through initiatives like the India-Brazil-South Africa (IBSA)

Dialogue Forum, which promotes joint action on global issues and facilitates the exchange of development experiences.

Regional integration efforts, such as the ASEAN Free Trade Area (AFTA) or the Regional Comprehensive Economic Partnership (RCEP), offer additional benefits by creating larger markets and reducing dependence on volatile global trade. Such initiatives can promote the development of regional value chains, boost intra-regional trade, and foster resilience to external shocks.

Joint research and development (R&D) initiatives in areas of common interest—such as tropical agriculture or renewable energy—can accelerate innovation and reduce duplication of efforts. Institutions like CGIAR (formerly the Consultative Group for International Agricultural Research) exemplify how collaborative R&D can address shared development challenges across the Global South.

Finally, the creation of policy learning networks, where policymakers from different countries can share experiences and test ideas through simulations and training programs, will be vital. Programs like the South-South Global Thinkers initiative, supported by the UNDP and UNOSSC, illustrate how structured exchanges can improve policy effectiveness and foster shared progress toward sustainable development.

Summary and Conclusion

In recent years, developing countries have faced a rapidly changing global landscape marked by rising protectionism, shifting global value chains, limited macroeconomic policy space, and rapid technological disruption. The decline of the Washington Consensus has left a void in development strategy, leading many nations to pursue fragmented, uncoordinated policies, which heightens vulnerability and weakens credibility in the face of competing domestic and international pressures.

To navigate this complex environment, there is an urgent need for a new development framework—one that is adaptable to national contexts yet provides clear direction. This book proposes three key pillars: strengthening macroeconomic buffers, leveraging technology to improve productivity, and promoting structural transformation through innovation and long-term investment. Ultimately, developing countries must take ownership of their development paths by crafting policies that reflect their unique needs, investing in education and institutions, and building the resilience needed for sustainable progress.

The next chapter will focus on one of the most critical components of this new development strategy: the growth of domestic private enterprises and their integration into global value chains. These firms are not only central to Vietnam's economic dynamism but are also pivotal to the country's long-term structural transformation.

Vietnam's ability to sustain growth and move beyond middle-income status will depend heavily on the development of its domestic enterprises. These firms are uniquely positioned to absorb labor from the informal sector, especially workers with limited formal training or education. Only through the formalization of these jobs can total factor productivity increase in a meaningful and inclusive way.

Enhancing the capabilities of domestic enterprises—through access to capital, skills development, and technology transfer—is the fastest and most direct route to raising national productivity. Importantly, Vietnam's growth strategy must go beyond boosting export volumes; it must focus on increasing value-added within the domestic economy. Export success, while important, is insufficient on its own unless it translates into higher income and productivity within the country.

Vietnam's comparative advantage lies in its strong presence within global value chains. By leveraging this position, domestic enterprises can gain from the knowledge, marketing channels, and international access already established by multinational firms. When properly supported, these enterprises can deepen their participation in global markets, gradually moving up the value chain and contributing to more resilient and inclusive economic growth.

This central theme—fostering domestic enterprise development and integrating it into global production systems—will guide the analysis in the chapters that follow, offering both strategic insights and practical recommendations for policymakers.

References

Acemoglu, D. (2025). The simple macroeconomics of AI. *Economic Policy, 40*(121), 13–58.

Branson, W. H. (1992). *Macroeconomic policy for trade reform. in trade policy reforms under adjustment programs.* World Bank Operations Evaluation Department, Chapter 3.

Dieppe, A. (Ed.). (2021). *Global productivity: Trends, drivers, and policies.* World Bank. http://hdl.handle.net/10986/34015

Di Giovanni, J., & Shambaugh, J. C. (2008). The impact of foreign interest rates on the economy: The role of the exchange rate regime. *Journal of International Economics, 74*(2), 341–361.

Dinh, H. T. (2022). *COVID-19 & developing countries—The road to recovery.* Policy Center for the New South. https://www.policycenter.ma/publications/covid-19-developing-countries%E2%80%94-road-recovery

Fleming, J. M. (1962). Domestic financial policies under fixed and floating exchange rates. *IMF Staff Papers, 9*(3), 369–379.

International Monetary Fund. (2024). *Vietnam 2024 Article IV consultation* (IMF Country Report No. 2024/306). International Monetary Fund. https://www.imf.org/en/Publications/CR/Issues/2024/09/27/Vietnam-2024-Article-IV-Consultation-Press-Release-Staff-Report-and-Statement-by-the-555679

Mundell, R. A. (1963). Capital mobility and stabilization policy under fixed and flexible exchange rates. *Canadian Journal of Economics and Political Science, 29*(4), 475–485.

Obstfeld, M., & Taylor, A. M. (2017). International monetary relatios: Taking finance seriously. *Journal of Economic Perspectives, 31*(3), 3–28.

Rodrik, D., & Stiglitz, J. E. (2024). *A new growth strategy for developing nations.* https://tinyurl.com/ymrg8qom

Svanberg, M., Li, W., Fleming, M., Goehring, B., & Thompson, N. (2024). Beyond AI exposure: Which tasks are cost-effective to automate with computer vision? *Available at SSRN 4700751.*

United Nations, Department of Economic and Social Affairs, Population Devision. (2022). World population prospects 2022: Summary of Results. United Nations. https://www.un.org/developent/desa/pd/content/World-Population-Prospects-2022

World Bank. (2024). *International debt report 2024.* World Bank. http://hdl.handle.net/10986/42444

PART IV

Domestic Enterprises and Innovation Policies

CHAPTER 8

Integrating Domestic Enterprises into Global Value Chains: The Key to Escaping the Middle-Income Trap

Integrating domestic private enterprises, both formal and informal, into Vietnam's existing global value chains (GVCs) is the most crucial strategy for boosting productivity. This transformation will turn the vast informal labor force into a well-educated, skilled workforce capable of performing high-value-added jobs, earning higher wages, and contributing to tax revenues. It is also the fastest and most sustainable path for Vietnam to achieve a high-income status before the mid-century, while significantly reducing poverty.

As shown in Chap. 3, Vietnam's economic growth has been constrained by slow labor productivity growth (Table 3.3). Instead of shifting from agriculture to more productive manufacturing, a significant portion of the workforce has moved into some low-productivity service sectors. This misallocation highlights the need for policies that channel resources into more productive industries. Historically, economic growth has been driven by increased labor quantity and non-IT capital contributions. With diminishing returns expected from these sources, Vietnam must pivot toward TFP, labor quality, and IT capital as the new growth engines.

Contributed by Hinh T. Dinh

H. T. Dinh, H. T. Nguyen, *Vietnam's Economic Leap*,
https://doi.org/10.1007/978-3-032-08904-5_8

Constraints on the Vietnamese Private Sector

Vietnam's private sector continues to face a range of structural and institutional challenges that constrain its growth and ability to compete globally. Anh and Perkins (2023) noted that domestic enterprises in Vietnam face four fundamental challenges: weak enforcement of private property rights; unequal treatment compared to state-owned enterprises (SOEs); harassment by authorities at both local and central levels; and the absence or poor quality of market-supporting institutions. Most of these issues will take considerable time to address, as they are deeply rooted in the political economy of reform (see Chap. 3), particularly concerning the roles of the State and the Communist Party. In this section, we focus on selected "low-hanging fruit" reforms that can be implemented to yield tangible results in the medium term.

A defining characteristic of the sector is the overwhelming dominance of small-scale and informal enterprises. According to the World Bank (2024), 98% of Vietnamese businesses are household-owned or small informal firms, each employing an average of just three people. These businesses are mostly oriented toward local markets, with only 17% participating in exports. Their contribution to total value added remains modest—only about one-quarter—and their productivity is significantly lower than that of larger firms. For instance, manufacturing firms with fewer than ten employees operate at only 27% of the productivity level of those with 250 or more employees.

A key factor behind this productivity gap is the limited technological and productivity spillovers from foreign direct investment (FDI) firms to domestic firms, stemming from weak linkages between them. Many domestic enterprises still rely on traditional production techniques and lack access to modern machinery and capital equipment. The weak linkages between FDI firms and local suppliers not only hinder the diffusion of advanced technologies but also stifle the productivity catch-up of local enterprises. Vietnamese manufacturing firms also depend less on local inputs than similar firms in other countries, underscoring the supply-side constraints they face. Challenges such as shortages of skilled labor, lack of information about domestic suppliers, and weak managerial capacity all limit the ability of local firms to integrate into production networks. Consequently, FDI firms in Vietnam source only 53% of their inputs domestically—the lowest share among countries in the East Asia and Pacific region (World Bank, 2024).

Another significant constraint is access to finance. Most private firms in Vietnam face difficulties in obtaining the credit they need to expand operations, invest in new technologies, or participate in international trade. Without adequate financing, their ability to improve competitiveness and engage in higher-value activities remains limited.

The shortage of skilled labor presents an equally serious challenge. As wages in Vietnam rise, the traditional comparative advantage of low labor costs is eroding. Unfortunately, wage increases have not been matched by productivity gains. The talent pool for high-skilled occupations—such as engineering, science, and management—is thin, and many employers struggle to find qualified candidates. About one-third of employers report a lack of applicants for open positions, while more than a third cite the limited capacity of their workforce as a key barrier to adopting new technologies.

Compounding these issues is the country's declining participation in Global Value Chains (GVCs) by local firms. In 2023, only 18% of Vietnamese firms had GVC linkages, down sharply from 35% in 2009 (World Bank, 2024). This signals a troubling decline in the integration of domestic firms into the global economy. Most local firms remain focused on non-tradable sectors such as traditional services, construction, or real estate, and they lack the capabilities to become direct participants or suppliers within GVCs. Small firms are particularly disadvantaged, with only 12% involved in GVCs, compared to 62% of large firms. Their lack of scale, skilled labor, and technological readiness undermines their ability to meet the demands of global production networks. As a result, Vietnam lags behind countries like Malaysia, Turkey, and even Cambodia in terms of GVC integration.

Together, these factors paint a picture of a domestic private sector that remains underdeveloped and poorly positioned to drive sustained, broad-based economic growth without significant reforms and targeted support.

A Policy Framework for Integrating Domestic Enterprises Into GVCs

Economic development is an ongoing process of achieving sustained increases in per capita income. This process requires the continuous introduction of new and improved technologies in existing industries and the transformation of labor- and resource-intensive industries into more capital-intensive ones. This technological change is typically represented by Total Factor Productivity (TFP) growth in a neoclassical production function and serves as the foundation of sustained economic growth because both labor and capital will sooner or later run into diminishing returns. TFP growth for Vietnam over the 1990–2023 period was mostly negative, averaging −0.3, except for the 2010–2019 period, where it grew by 2% p.a. (Table 3.1). For comparison, estimates of TFP growth for the United States during the period 1899–1941 ranged from the long-accepted 1.7% (Kendrick, 1961) to 1.3% (Bakker et al., 2019).

Vietnam must balance two critical objectives in its development strategy. First, it needs to create productive jobs for a large, growing, and often low-skilled workforce that cannot immediately transition into high-tech, high-value-added sectors. These jobs should provide a pathway for workers moving out of low-productivity areas such as agriculture and informal urban employment. Second, Vietnam must expand and deepen its high-tech, high-value sectors to advance to a high-income status. The challenge is avoiding a scenario where a large portion of the unskilled workforce remains unemployed or underemployed before advanced sectors can generate sufficient skilled jobs.

To achieve this, Vietnam should adopt short- and medium-term policies addressing two fronts. First, policies must maximize labor force productivity by integrating informal workers into the formal labor market through stronger linkages with existing GVCs. This includes expanding labor-intensive light manufacturing, deepening domestic GVC integration, and encouraging high-quality foreign direct investment (FDI). Equalizing incentives for domestic and FDI companies and diversifying export markets are essential for increasing output and employment in labor-intensive industries.

Second, Vietnam must expand the value-added content of its production and foster innovation to compete with upper-middle-income countries. These long-term strategies require immediate implementation due to their extended gestation period. Policies in this group include firm-level technological adoption, workforce education and training, and research and development initiatives, which will be discussed in subsequent chapters.

Achieving steady 8% annual GDP growth over two decades necessitates comprehensive reforms in policies, institutions, governance, and persistence. Given the existing production structure, this growth must be driven by labor quality improvements, FDI in the IT sector, and TFP growth.

While labor market reforms, particularly in education and vocational training, are addressed in later chapters, the next two sections will address the current Government's program to attract high-tech FDI and policy reforms to enhance TFP, respectively.

Vietnam's Strategic Shift Toward High-Tech FDI

This chapter does not delve into Vietnam's high-tech FDI strategy, as current government efforts are widely seen as effective and well-designed. Over the past two years, Vietnam has moved from a broad-based foreign investment attraction to a more targeted approach, prioritizing high-tech industries such as semiconductors, AI, and advanced electronics.

This strategic shift is anchored in recent regulatory and fiscal reforms. Circular 08/2024 and Decree 10/2024 have streamlined approval processes for high-tech projects, particularly in key zones like Saigon Hi-Tech Park, Hòa Lạc, and Đà Nẵng. These areas now offer competitive advantages, including preferential land use, tax incentives, and simplified customs procedures, attracting global players such as Intel, Samsung, Meta, and Google.

In addition, the Investment Support Fund established under Decree 182/2024 provides generous subsidies—covering up to 50% of R&D-related costs—for firms investing in strategic sectors. These policies are aligned with Vietnam's goal of attracting $30–40 billion in annual FDI by 2025, with an increasing share directed toward high-tech industries.

Broad-based Policy Reforms to Improve TFP Growth

To address the challenges hindering TFP growth, Vietnam must undertake comprehensive reforms, including restructuring of the public sector, strengthening the business environment, integrating multinational enterprises (MNEs) with local firms, and improving workforce skills. These reforms will enhance productivity, attract investment, and ensure sustainable growth toward high-income status by 2045.

Reforming the public sector–where bloated state enterprises and bureaucratic inefficiencies continue to drain resources and stifle private sector dynamism that could otherwise drive innovation and competitiveness are a priority. In this regard, the successful implementation of policy measures under the National Economic Rise initiative, aimed at enabling private capital and entrepreneurship to become primary engines of development, is an essential prerequisite for improving TFP growth. Another priority is regulatory reform. Digitalization can streamline administrative processes, and collaboration between the Administrative Procedure Control Agency (APCA) and ministries can eliminate redundant documentation and improve data sharing. A risk-based approach to licensing and inspections can further simplify compliance.

Connecting MNEs and local firms is another vital step. Investment promotion agencies (IPAs) can strengthen connections between local suppliers and foreign investors through matchmaking, information dissemination, and maintaining supplier databases. The World Bank (2024) recommended organizing "Meet the Buyer" events and supplier forums to help potential suppliers understand quality, cost, and delivery (QCD) standards, as well as technology and skills gaps. Publishing online databases of local suppliers in English can reduce search costs for foreign firms.

To upgrade the absorptive capacity of local firms, Supplier Development Programs (SDPs) are essential. These programs should focus on specific suppliers, sectors, and regions, with explicit targets. SDPs can include consulting services to improve managerial and technical skills, as well as help firms meet labor and environmental standards.

Supply chain finance (SCF) mechanisms between FDI firms and domestic firms can optimize working capital and provide lower-cost financing. These mechanisms can convert receivables and inventories to cash, smoothing transactions between FDI firms and local suppliers. Digital SCF solutions can improve transparency and scale through e-invoicing and platform approaches.

Reducing barriers to services trade in key sectors like telecom, finance, and transportation is also crucial. Addressing restrictive telecom regulations, relaxing foreign exchange rules, eliminating discriminatory regulations against foreign service providers, and reducing barriers in legal services can boost competition and lower costs. Preventing conflicts of interest and ensuring fair treatment of state-owned enterprises (SOEs) and the private sector by establishing independent regulatory authorities is also necessary.

Investing in education and skills development and proactive labor market policies is also critical and given their importance, will be discussed fully in subsequent chapters.

The remainder of this chapter focuses on policies to strengthen linkages between domestic and foreign-invested enterprises, particularly in subsectors where Vietnam holds—or can develop—a comparative advantage.

These subsectors, identified in detail in Chaps. 4 and 5, fall into four product categories for targeted policy attention:

1. **Classics**: long-established, labor-intensive exports (Annex Table 4.2, see also Annex Table 5.1 Lall Classification of Classics);
2. **Emerging Champions**: newer, technologically advanced products (Annex Table 4.3 and Annex Table 5.2);
3. **Marginals 1**: products with high expansion potential (Annex Table 4.5 and Annex Table 5.4);
4. **Import Replacements**: products that match existing capabilities and could substitute imports (Annex Table 5.5 and Annex Table 5.6).

A critical selection criterion for these products is their compatibility with Vietnam's existing production capabilities, measured by the "distance" concept—the closer a product is to current capabilities, the easier diversification becomes.

Raising overall economic productivity requires improving the productivity of both large formal enterprises and micro, small, and informal firms, each of which requires distinct policy measures. While smaller firms must eventually integrate into value chains, large firms play a crucial role in labor-intensive manufacturing by achieving economies of scale. Competitiveness in this sector depends on the ability to fulfill large orders efficiently in terms of cost, quality, and timeliness—an advantage inherently tied to large-scale operations.

A key challenge for manufacturing is whether emerging technologies such as the Internet of Things and Artificial Intelligence will reduce job creation in traditional sectors. Some authors (e.g., Hallward-Driemeier and Nayyar, 2017) questioned manufacturing's role as a growth engine due to technological advances favoring specialized labor. However, they acknowledged that certain sectors, such as garment manufacturing, remain viable for developing countries. While capital-intensive technologies are reducing demand for unskilled workers, Vietnam must address this challenge by both creating jobs for its growing workforce and training workers for new manufacturing technologies. The transition to green manufacturing—supported by solar power—and the growth of the pharmaceutical sector present additional paths for inclusive industrialization.

In the short term, traditional sectors will remain vital for job creation. However, long-term success will depend on building a skilled workforce and facilitating high-tech, high-productivity FDI integration into global value chains—without regulatory bottlenecks.

Firm-Level Reforms to Improve TFP Growth

In addition to these broad-based policy reforms, Vietnam must implement a balanced strategy that supports diverse enterprise types. This entails: (i) incentives to encourage FDI firms to use Vietnamese technical and managerial staff as well as local inputs and services and to integrate more deeply into GVCs; (ii) policies to assist the growth of domestic enterprises; and (iii) policies to establish and strengthen the links between domestic and FDI enterprises.

Incentives for FDI Firms to Use Local Technical and Managerial Staff. Newly established FDIs should be required to transfer technology and expertise by setting annual quantitative targets for replacing foreign nationals in key technical and managerial positions within a feasible period (five to seven years). Progress should be monitored annually and adjusted to accelerate technology transfer. Renewals of existing permits should be conditional on meeting these targets. A dedicated monitoring unit at both central and local government levels (Ministry of Trade and Commerce) should oversee progress and be held accountable for its performance.

Supporting Small and Medium Enterprises (SMEs): Vietnam's economic structure features a dual market: a vast number of micro and SMEs serving the domestic market and a modern, mostly foreign-owned sector of large enterprises focused on exports. The lack of linkages between these sectors results in low productivity among micro and small enterprises, which lack access to modern technology.

Existing industrial policies in Vietnam appear to support the birth, but not the growth of domestic SMEs. The country has not embarked on the explicit objective to foster the growth of small enterprises into middle enterprises, nor encouraged middle enterprises to become large enterprises. Recent advances in the theory of the firm have shown that productivity growth is fastest in middle and large enterprises and that new technology and expertise are more likely to be adopted by organizations of that size. The dearth of large domestic enterprises in Vietnam means that the numerous micro and small enterprises have not been able to benefit from subcontracting through large enterprises, which, likewise, do not draw on the competitive production of smaller enterprises.

To bridge this gap, Vietnam should ensure equal treatment for both direct and indirect exporters. East Asian economies such as Japan and Korea successfully integrated local producers with exporters by providing equal incentives. Policies included realistic exchange rates, free trade, competitive markets, and non-discriminatory domestic taxation. Indirect exporters—those supplying intermediate inputs to manufacturers or final goods to trading companies—benefited from financial support, including pre-shipment working capital loans and post-shipment financing.

Vietnamese policymakers should collaborate with the private sector to address barriers to enterprise growth. Establishing a council with representatives from both sectors could facilitate this cooperation. Encouraging trade associations and linking government officials' promotions to private sector development outcomes could also be effective.

The government should reassess its investment program to balance basic infrastructure with advanced infrastructure, facilitating a transition to skilled labor-intensive activities aligned with national innovation policies. A program similar to STARTUP-Chile could attract talented entrepreneurs, yielding short-term economic benefits.

The Vietnamese government could replicate its successful FDI attraction strategy by extending similar incentives—such as industrial clusters and parks—to domestic enterprises. Industrial clusters, typically composed of SMEs engaged in related activities like garments, woodworking, and metalwork, emerge organically but require active support in developing countries lacking infrastructure and skilled labor. In Vietnam, clustering has proven to reduce entry costs, improve access to inputs and logistics, and promote knowledge spillovers. To be effective, cluster policies must be tailored to Vietnam's specific conditions. Governments should identify and support existing clusters by addressing constraints like land, electricity, and telecom access. Lessons from China suggest that rather than creating clusters artificially, governments should nurture those with growth potential through incentive-compatible policies, such as targeted credit, tax benefits, and subcontracting linkages between small and large firms.

Vietnam's industrial parks have focused mainly on attracting foreign firms, while countries like China and other East Asian economies have developed "plug-and-play" parks to foster **domestic** SMEs. These parks offer low-cost infrastructure, standardized facilities, technical support, and access to finance—enabling local firms to scale up and integrate into global value chains. Such parks help solve critical bottlenecks in light manufacturing and support the growth of industrial clusters by providing shared services, training, and efficient logistics. Vietnam should adopt this model, particularly near major urban centers, allowing organic clusters to emerge and then guiding their transformation into industrial parks. This approach, as demonstrated in China, helps overcome structural barriers and land reform delays while promoting inclusive industrial growth and strengthening the domestic private sector.

Underdeveloped domestic input markets in Vietnam compel firms to rely heavily on imports, driving up production costs. While tariff reductions could improve competitiveness, they risk reducing government revenue and attracting opposition from local producers. China has addressed this by offering tariff exemptions only for inputs that are imported, processed, and re-exported from industrial parks—a model Vietnam could consider. Likewise, access to affordable, serviced land is critical for manufacturing growth. In China, local officials have played a key role in providing such land, helping SMEs launch operations without high setup costs. Vietnam could replicate this approach by expanding industrial parks with accessible land to support domestic manufacturers.

A major constraint facing Vietnamese SMEs is limited access to finance. Unlike Morocco, where banks have established dedicated SME units and tailored products for small firms, Vietnamese banks focus lending on state-owned enterprises. Even in Morocco, however, banks tend to overestimate SME risks and impose excessive collateral requirements, despite guarantees from institutions like the Central Guarantee Fund (CGC). CGC helps lower financing costs, shares risk with banks, and supports viable SMEs lacking collateral. Guarantee rates vary by firm size and sector, covering up to 80% for very small businesses. Vietnam could benefit from a similar mechanism, while also using land within industrial parks as collateral and encouraging local governments to facilitate external financing—an approach successfully used in China to boost SME growth and competitiveness.

Policies to Establish and Strengthen the Links Between Domestic and FDI Enterprises

Current industrial policies in Vietnam support SME formation but not their growth into medium or large enterprises. Unlike Korea and Taiwan, Vietnam has not actively fostered the transition of SMEs into large firms. Since productivity growth is highest in medium and large enterprises, this gap inhibits industrial advancement. Weak subcontracting links between SMEs and larger firms limit domestic technology transfer and productivity gains.

International best practices show that fostering strong SME-LE (Large Enterprise) relationships benefits both parties. Large firms gain flexibility and cost efficiency, while SMEs access markets, technology, and financial resources. Governments can facilitate these linkages through framework contracts, outsourcing agreements, co-development partnerships, and export support mechanisms.

Currently in Vietnam, in seeking to meet their business needs, foreign-invested enterprises and state-owned enterprises avoid relying on small private sector enterprises. The transfer of technology and knowledge between foreign-invested enterprises and domestic enterprises is therefore negligible. Larger enterprises do not depend on inputs produced by their smaller domestic counterparts and instead import raw materials, while domestic firms buy from a variety of sources, including trading companies. In Vietnam, state-owned enterprises, which should play a leading role in key industries (for example, in logistics, machinery and equipment, and chemicals), are unable to provide key inputs to manufacturing enterprises. This fragmentation and lack of interaction are problematic because they limit the ability to source inputs, new technologies, expertise, etc. domestically, preventing the economy from becoming more productive. In addition, time, effort, and foreign exchange could be saved by greater integration among firms, which would also spur other economic benefits.

While governments should avoid forcing the "national content" rules in a medium-sized country such as Vietnam, there are more subtle measures that could enhance the competitiveness of local suppliers and positively influence the nation's attractiveness for lead firms. Among such measures (Cattaneo, Gereffi, Miroudos, and Taglioni, 2013) are tripartite (government, private sector, lead firms) negotiations for production-sharing of value chains; flexible rules for the temporary movement of key personnel, in particular in start-up phases of projects; requirements for new entrants to create explicit supplier development programs; and rewards for existing foreign companies that make an extra effort to help local suppliers, by means of tax deductions or other payments to partially reimburse firms; and expenditures in helping local industries.

Local sourcing could be rewarded and facilitated through a proactive adjustment of local supply to the needs of firms participating in GVCs. Among others, policies to enable the local sourcing of inputs include: i) Assessment and measures to boost the capability of local small and medium enterprises (SMEs) to meet the standards required by lead firms; ii) the removal of unnecessary NTMs; iii) workforce development to match available skills with demand (see below); and iv) building capacity both up- and downstream of the GVC entry point; and v) innovation.

Strengthening Local SMEs–Local LEs Linkages for Greater Competitiveness

Local small and medium-sized enterprises (SMEs) are often more agile and innovative than local large enterprises (LEs), making them better equipped to adapt to demand fluctuations—a key advantage in middle-income countries like Vietnam. In contrast, LEs, with their scale and capital, are better suited to stable environments and standardized production. For LEs to remain competitive amid shifting global conditions, closer collaboration with SMEs is essential—both to enhance productivity and to build more resilient value chains.

A practical example of this synergy is found in cases where LEs outsource non-core activities or inputs to SMEs. This strategy allows large firms to focus on core functions while enabling SMEs to specialize, scale, and upgrade technologically. Renault's plant in Tangiers, Morocco, illustrates the success of this approach: by clustering suppliers around its factory, Renault reduced costs, improved responsiveness, and boosted local value-added content.

Such partnerships take multiple forms, including framework contracts, co-development, outsourcing, and export-oriented collaboration. Framework agreements guarantee local SMEs a stable flow of orders, encouraging them to invest and grow. Co-development brings together the agility and innovation of local SMEs with the technical capacity of LEs. Export partnerships, in turn, allow SMEs to leverage the international experience of LEs, enhancing their market access and competitiveness.

International experience reinforces these strategies. In Germany, Indonesia, and Turkey, SMEs drive job creation and economic growth. East Asian countries, notably Korea and Taiwan, have supported LE-SME integration through coordinated industrial policies, such as equal treatment for foreign and domestic firms, access to low-cost financing, and duty exemptions for exporters. Korea's use of domestic letters of credit, for example, enabled indirect exporters to access incentives usually reserved for direct exporters.

Trading companies have also been instrumental in supporting SMEs by facilitating market access, managing quality control, and lowering transaction costs. In China, such intermediaries played a critical role in helping SMEs overcome infrastructure, land, and financing constraints.

Finally, governments can amplify the spillover effects from global value chains by promoting workforce training aligned with industry needs, encouraging lead firms to invest in supplier development, and facilitating SME compliance with international standards. Trade facilitation efforts—such as streamlined customs, improved logistics, and upgraded infrastructure—further reinforce these links.

In sum, closer SME-LE collaboration is not just desirable but necessary for sustained industrial development. International experience offers Vietnam valuable lessons in how to structure policies that make these partnerships work effectively.

Policy Recommendations

Policy measures to improve Vietnam's competitiveness must address both the challenges faced by small, informal, household firms producing for the domestic market and those encountered by a relatively small number of large, foreign-invested enterprises focused on exports. For small firms, the priority is fostering their growth into larger, more productive enterprises. This requires improvements in labor skills, technology, and the quality and variety of domestically produced goods to better compete with imports. Key policies include reducing the role of state-owned enterprises (SOEs), ensuring equal treatment for direct and indirect exporters, promoting trading companies, encouraging clustering and subcontracting, attracting foreign direct investment (FDI) to upstream activities, using industrial zones to integrate supply chains, promoting Kaizen training, and enhancing global value chain (GVC) spillover effects.

For larger formal enterprises, the main challenge is moving up the value chain by increasing production diversity and quality. Trade facilitation and improved logistics are essential, as is the transfer of skills, technology, and managerial expertise from foreign-invested enterprises to domestic firms. From an international producer's perspective, the origin of raw materials and intermediate goods is irrelevant as long as they meet quality standards, are competitively priced, and are delivered efficiently. It is therefore up to the Vietnamese policymakers and private sector leaders to drive this transformation.

Vietnam's economic growth has largely been fueled by low-cost, low-skilled labor and foreign capital, complemented by increased agricultural productivity. This model has successfully generated employment in labor-intensive, export-oriented sectors. However, as Vietnam moves into a higher per capita income bracket, the growth strategy must evolve to help domestic producers add more value.

While Vietnam has numerous programs supporting SMEs, their effectiveness and focus require reassessment. First, are they achieving their intended impact, and should they be consolidated to target SMEs in priority subsectors identified in Chaps. 2 and 3? Second, what are the primary constraints limiting SME growth, and are existing programs addressing these effectively? To answer these questions, we have developed detailed questionnaires (Annex).

Vietnam's industrial strategy must evolve to deepen SME integration into global markets, increase domestic value addition, and strengthen GVC linkages. Policies should prioritize fostering organic clusters, enhancing SME competitiveness, and leveraging industrial parks to drive long-term growth. By addressing key constraints in finance, trade logistics, and workforce development, Vietnam can accelerate its industrial transformation and sustain economic growth in an increasingly competitive global economy.

References

Anh, V. T. T., & Perkins, D. H. (2023). Explaining Vietnam's economic growth experience. In B. Ljunggren & D. H. Perkins (Eds.), *Vietnam—Navigating a rapidly changing economy, society, and political order* (141). Harvard University Press.

Bakker, G., Crafts, N., & Woltjer, P. (2019). The sources of growth in a technologically progressive economy: The United States, 1899–1941. *The Economic Journal, 129*(622), 2267–2294.

Cattaneo, O., Gereffi, G., Miroudot, S., & Taglioni, D. (2013). *Joining, upgrading and being competitive in global value chains: A strategic framework.* World Bank.

Hallward-Driemeier, M., & Nayyar, G. (2017). *Trouble in the making? The future of manufacturing-led development.* World Bank Publications.

Kendrick, J. W. (1961). *Productivity trends in the United States.* Princeton University Press.

World Bank. (2024). *Viet nam 2045: Trading up in a changing world – pathways to a high-income future.* World Bank. http://hdl.handle.net/10986/42505

CHAPTER 9

Innovation Policies

Introduction

Innovation refers to the use of new ideas in a firm's products, operations, or broader activities that result in greater benefits—whether through increased value added for the firm itself or improvements for consumers and other businesses (Greenhalgh & Rogers 2010). Innovation in developing countries such as Vietnam differs significantly from that in developed countries, necessitating distinct policy frameworks. This difference stems from variations in the nature of innovation, institutional capacity, and the economic context in which innovation occurs. While innovation in developed countries primarily focuses on increasing R&D output, innovation in developing countries emphasizes value-added production and the development of technological capabilities, including technology adoption, adaptation, diffusion, and upgrading. This distinction underscores the need for a tailored approach to innovation policy in developing countries such as Vietnam—one that moves beyond merely adopting policies from developed nations.

Contributed by Hinh T. Dinh

H. T. Dinh, H. T. Nguyen, *Vietnam's Economic Leap*,
https://doi.org/10.1007/978-3-032-08904-5_9

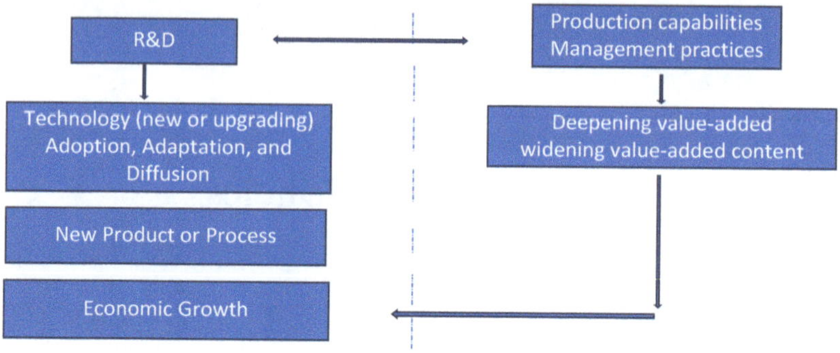

Fig. 9.1 A framework of innovation policies. *Source* Author

Traditional neoclassical economic theory treats innovation and technical progress as "manna from heaven," being exogenous to economic growth.[1] In this chapter we consider them endogenous processes (Aghion & Howitt, 1998) that are "continuously adapted and selected to the broad needs and requirements of society" (Freeman & Soete, 1997).

As shown in Fig. 9.1, this framework differs for advanced and developing countries. The left panel of Fig. 9.1 illustrates how innovation affects economic growth in a developed economy. For a developing economy, there is an additional channel where technology directly affects GDP growth, depicted in the right panel. This additional channel is what Gerschenkron (1962) called the "advantage of backwardness".

Domestic enterprises in developing countries face significant challenges compared to their peers in developed economies due to a lack of resources and facilities, such as soft and hard infrastructure, as well as their geographical distance from sources of innovation and consumer markets, which are often located in developed economies. However, as latecomers, they also have certain advantages. Wong (1999) identified at least four:

[1] In Solow's framework, in the long run, economic growth is determined by population growth and technical progress, both of these are exogenous to the growth process.

- They can benefit from shifts in consumer taste or technology, which make the investments of early market movers obsolete.
- They can learn from the mistakes of pioneers without bearing the costs of trial and error.
- They can observe the market and develop strategies to leverage their own strengths.
- Late-industrializing countries can also have lower labor costs and protected markets that allow their companies to develop without the pressure of full global competition.

The right panel of Fig. 9.1 also represents learning-by-doing, a key channel through which industrialization contributes to economic development. Up to a certain point in the industrialization process, this occurs through knowledge externalities derived from imitation activities and later through innovation activities. This phenomenon caused the Industrial Revolution to spread from the United Kingdom to other countries in Western Europe, the United States, Russia, and Japan (Chandra et al., 2013). Initially, technological knowledge can be acquired through mere imitation of foreign processes, but imitation entails decreasing returns, whereas innovation occurs under constant or increasing returns to scale, at least for a while. The expansion of the manufacturing sector eventually requires a shift from imitation activities to true innovation to achieve sustainable growth (Agénor & Dinh, 2013, 2015).

This transition may require access to highly skilled labor and more sophisticated inputs, such as advanced communication and information technologies. These can be critical in shifting from labor-intensive, light manufacturing activities (which tend to be associated with an imitation regime) to higher-value-added manufacturing (which requires broader and more sophisticated inputs). In this context, after an economy reaches the stage where assembly-type light manufacturing creates jobs, the appropriate development policy should not only emphasize innovation and the knowledge and learning externalities associated with imitation, but it must also increasingly foster local absorption capacity and technological innovation.

Innovation in Developed Countries

Research and development (R&D) is usually seen as a primary means to increase innovation. But does more R&D directly lead to higher productivity? Crepon et al. (1998) provided econometric evidence linking R&D

to productivity at the firm level. Their model relates productivity to innovation output, innovation output to research, and research to its determinants. They find that firm productivity correlates with higher innovation output, which in turn rises with the firm's research effort and with demand-pull and technology-push factors. In turn, the research effort and the probability of engaging in research increase with firm size, market share, and diversification.

In a comprehensive review of policies to promote innovation, Bloom et al. (2019) noted that market forces are unlikely to provide sufficient innovation due to inadequate knowledge spillovers between firms. The authors present a toolkit of five policy interventions they consider most effective: (i) tax incentives for R&D, (ii) free trade, (iii) skilled migration, (iv) training STEM workers, and (v) direct R&D grants.

They noted that subsidies and grants appear to be the most effective way to increase innovation as well as productivity. Reducing the price of R&D by 10% could increase investment in innovation by 10% in the long run. They observed that France, Portugal, and Chile have slashed the cost of R&D spending by more than 30%. Evidence shows that opening trade can spur innovation by increasing competition, allowing new ideas to spread faster, and lowering the cost of innovation by distributing this cost over a larger market. For example, in 2018, freer trade generally increased innovation in South America, Asia, and Europe.

A quick and effective way to increase the supply of researchers in technical fields is to allow more high-skilled immigrants into the country. Bloom et al. cited research showing that increasing the population of immigrant college graduates in the U.S. by one percentage point raised patents per capita by up to 18%. Another way to expand the supply of researchers in the long term is to invest in domestic training. One option is to promote programs that increase the number of students pursuing science, technology, engineering, and math (STEM). Another is to expose more potential inventors from disadvantaged backgrounds to role models and mentoring. Finally, government grants—such as those for university researchers—can be directed toward projects with the highest potential long-term benefits. Research shows that grants to academics, in turn, lead to more patents filed by private firms.

Bloom et al. also identified three policies that could enhance innovation, though the supporting evidence is weaker: (i) providing incentives for university researchers, (ii) engaging in intellectual property reform, and (iii) pursuing mission-oriented projects. "Moonshot" R&D initiatives focused on specific sectors may be necessary to drive innovation in response to challenges such as climate change.

Most of the R&D policies discussed by Bloom et al., as well as those in the broader literature, are more relevant to developed countries than to middle-income economies, where limited public funds restrict subsidies and grants for researchers, and working conditions do not favor the immigration of skilled labor.

Innovation in Developing Countries

Innovation activities in developing countries differ from those in advanced economies in many respects. Slavo Radosevic (2018) noted that these differences stem from the nature of innovation, institutional capacity, trade-offs between accountability and experimentation, and position in global value chains (GVCs).

- **Nature of Innovation:** In middle-income countries (MICs), innovation primarily involves acquiring machinery and production-related knowledge rather than R&D. It also encompasses non-R&D activities, such as acquiring technology and knowledge embodied in machinery and equipment. Innovation policies should therefore broaden their focus beyond R&D to include production capabilities and management practices. Furthermore, Middle-Income countries (MICs) are not only sites for R&D-based innovation but also for various productivity-enhancing activities like engineering improvements, management practices, and incremental innovations. These activities are often more significant for productivity growth in MICs than R&D. Finally, the upstream vs downstream innovation value chain of conventional R&D-driven models maybe less relevant for MICs. Instead, a two-way model recognizing both R&D and production capabilities as drivers of growth would be more appropriate.
- **Institutional Capacity:** Effective innovation policy requires technical, operational, and political capacities, which are often lacking in MICs. These capacities are crucial for designing, implementing, and evaluating policies. Rather than copying best practices from developed regions, it is suggested that MICs should adopt policies that best match their specific institutional capacities.
- **Accountability vs. Experimentation:** Innovation policy requires experimentation to discover effective solutions, but this can conflict

with the need for accountability in public policy. Introducing action learning principles and learning networks can reconcile experimentation with accountability. Learning networks facilitate practical learning among stakeholders, enabling continuous adaptation and improvement of policies.
- **Global Value Chains:** GVCs are crucial for technology transfer and knowledge inflows. GVC integration presents both opportunities and challenges, including the risk of creating dependencies on global markets. Policies should focus on integrating MICs into advanced countries' GVCs to help upgrade their technological capabilities (see Chap. 8).

The implications for middle-income countries such as Vietnam are:

- Innovation policies should go beyond R&D and include production capabilities, design, engineering, and management practices.
- Regular assessments of institutional capacities are necessary to ensure policies are realistic and implementable.
- Policies should incorporate mechanisms for continuous learning and adaptation, such as learning networks.
- Policies should support MICs in integrating into GVCs to enhance their technological capabilities and economic resilience.

The development and refinement of innovation policies tailored to the specific challenges and opportunities in Vietnam are crucial for sustainable economic growth and long-term competitiveness in the global economy.

Technology Adoption, Adaptation, Diffusion, and Upgrading

The successful adoption, adaptation, and diffusion of modern technology and its upgrading are crucial for innovation and economic growth. Technology affects an economy through its diffusion, which varies by product. Factors influencing technology adoption include user benefits, costs, the availability of complementary skills and inputs, customer relationships, and network effects. Policies should focus on reducing adoption costs and increasing benefits to accelerate diffusion.

Demand factors for technology diffusion include worker skill levels and the state of capital goods sectors. Customer commitment and network effects are also significant. On the supply side, technology suppliers play a key role in improving and reducing technology costs. Environmental and institutional factors such as market structure, firm size, and government regulation also influence diffusion, with larger firms more likely to pursue innovation due to their greater appropriability and resource availability.

A product's life cycle consists of three stages: concept, fabrication, and logistics. The fabrication stage typically has the lowest value-added due to the low skill requirements and minimal innovation activities. Vietnam is currently in the fabrication stage for almost all its products, whether traditional or modern. This is also the stage where all low- and middle-income countries find themselves in.

Moving up the value-added scale involves shifting to either an upstream stage—R&D, branding, and design—or a downstream stage—distribution, marketing, and sales/services (Berger et al., 2016). This process, known as upgrading, increases the share of value-added in total output. The World Trade Organization defines this as "climbing up the value ladder (or 'smile curve'), moving away from low-skilled activities characterized by low entry barriers and high competition" (Wood, 2015). Though definitions vary on whether upgrading occurs within the same or different value chains, the outcome remains an increased share of value-added in total output. This does not exclude innovation in the fabrication stage, where process and product innovations can enhance value-added, shifting the curve upward.

Low- and middle-income countries are concentrated in the fabrication stage, with most production and exports based on natural resources, while high-income countries dominate the concept and logistics stages. However, activities and sectors can overlap. Some middle-income countries have penetrated the concept or logistics stages for select products or industries, while some high-income countries still maintain fabrication activities for certain industries.

This concept aligns with the human capital theory of economic growth (Romer, 1989) and the imitative versus innovative stages of economic development (Agénor & Dinh, 2013). It has been widely used in literature analyzing East Asia's rapid transition from middle- to high-income status. It also corresponds to the vertically integrated strategy in development literature. Early in their development, countries typically focus on the final assembly of imported components, a stage known in vertically integrated strategy as the Original Equipment Manufacturer (OEM) phase (Gereffi & Fernandez-Stark, 2011). During this phase, firms and nations gain technical knowledge through reverse engineering and mastering processes and products. Only upon transitioning to the design and branding stages—Own Design Manufacturer (ODM) and Own Brand Manufacturer (OBM)—can they realize higher value-added.

Keun Lee (2013) pointed out that one way for developing countries to escape the middle-income trap is by specializing in short-cycle or emerging technologies or developing upgraded niches within existing industries. One catch-up strategy is entering mature segments of medium- to short-cycle technology sectors (e.g., telephone switches). Once established, countries can pursue a more ambitious leapfrogging strategy into emerging industries, such as cell phone and digital TV development. Because technological leapfrogging involves substantial risks, an active government role is essential in promoting public-private R&D consortia and providing user subsidies for initial market entry.

Radosevic & Yoruk (2016) examined technology upgrading in economies transitioning from middle- to high-income status. They introduced a novel framework and composite index to measure technology upgrading, emphasizing its multidimensionality across different income levels. Their framework includes three key dimensions: the intensity of technology upgrading, the breadth of technology upgrading, and technology and knowledge exchange. To operationalize this framework, they developed a composite indicator based on 35 variables capturing diverse drivers and patterns of technology upgrading. Applying this model to 42 economies, including Vietnam, they identified distinct upgrading trajectories and the presence of a middle-income trap. Vietnam ranked below the lower-middle-income group average in the first two dimensions but above average in technology and knowledge exchange.

Their study finds that middle-income countries lag significantly behind high-income countries in knowledge and technology exchange. Participation in global trade and FDI alone does not ensure technological upgrading unless complemented by strong domestic capabilities. To take a comprehensive approach, the authors recommend policies that: (i) Enhance production and technological capabilities through targeted investments in R&D and innovation infrastructure; (ii) Foster structural changes by promoting organizational diversity and human capital development; and (iii) Strengthen global integration mechanisms to facilitate effective technology and knowledge exchange.

The International Experience

In his study of national innovation systems in Wong et al. (1999) explores how firms in late-industrializing countries build technological capabilities to catch up with more advanced economies. He argues that companies must make critical strategic decisions: whether to focus on designing new products (product capabilities) or improving how efficiently they produce existing ones (process capabilities). These decisions shape how firms compete—not just on cost or quality, but in how they position themselves in the global market.

Wong identifies five broad strategies that latecomer firms can adopt. Some begin by manufacturing products for others (OEMs), then move to designing products (ODMs), and eventually build their own brands (OBMs)—a path known as the *Reverse Value Chain Strategy*. Others take the *Reverse Product Life Cycle Strategy*, starting with outdated or low-end products and gradually improving them to rival global leaders. Some firms become *process specialists*, focusing on perfecting production methods rather than product innovation. A fourth strategy involves *pioneering entirely new products*—a high-risk approach requiring deep R&D investment. Lastly, firms can take the *applications pioneer route*, combining existing technologies in novel ways to serve niche markets.

The success of these strategies depends heavily on the national innovation system—the web of institutions, policies, and partnerships that support innovation. This includes universities, research institutes, government policy, and links to foreign firms. Wong highlights Taiwan as a strong example of how effective coordination between small firms and public research institutes (PRIs) can drive industrial upgrading. In particular, Taiwan's Industrial Technology Research Institute (ITRI) played a crucial role in transferring technology to local firms. By facilitating spin-offs and technology diffusion, ITRI helped Taiwan build a strong presence in sectors like semiconductors and notebook computers. Many of Taiwan's top tech companies—including Taiwan Semiconductor Manufacturing Company (TSMC) and United Microelectronics Corporation (UMC) can trace their roots to ITRI initiatives. A key factor in this success was the return of highly skilled Taiwanese engineers from abroad, who brought back expertise and leadership.

Korea took a different route. Its development was led by large conglomerates, or *chaebols*, which received strong support from the state. These firms accepted low profits to gain market share and scale up quickly, especially in heavy industries like steel, cars, and semiconductors. Korea's approach relied on tight coordination between government and business: state-directed credit, protected domestic markets, and rewards for export performance helped the chaebols grow rapidly. Despite setbacks—most notably the 1997 financial crisis—some chaebols like Samsung and Hyundai emerged with strong global brands and advanced R&D capabilities. However, their focus on large-scale production made them less adaptable in fast-moving industries like software or biotechnology.

In sum, Wong's analysis shows there is no one-size-fits-all strategy. Countries must tailor their approach to their institutional strengths. Taiwan succeeded by fostering networks of innovative SMEs supported by strong public research institutions. Korea, by contrast, relied on centralized planning and powerful conglomerates. Both routes show that strategic choices, supported by the right institutions and policies, are essential for technological advancement and industrial success.

For Vietnam, the creation of a SME-PRI Innovation Network similar to Taiwan's could serve as a catalyst for technological upgrading and industrial diversification. By supporting small and medium-sized enterprises (SMEs)—which make up the backbone of the domestic economy—this entity could help overcome the innovation constraints many Vietnamese firms currently face, such as limited access to finance, weak R&D capabilities, and poor integration into global value chains.

Such an institution would need to be embedded in a broader national innovation strategy. This includes linking universities and research institutes with industry, promoting the return of overseas Vietnamese talent, and encouraging technology transfer from foreign direct investment (FDI) projects to domestic firms. In doing so, Vietnam could create a virtuous cycle in which local firms gradually move up the value chain—from simple manufacturing to more complex, knowledge-intensive activities.

The Taiwanese and Korean experiences show that success depends not only on institutional design but also on sustained state commitment. Vietnam's government must be willing to provide long-term support, foster an enabling policy environment, and ensure that public funding is tied to performance and innovation outcomes. A well-structured SME-PRI innovation network, backed by a capable central institution, could help Vietnam leapfrog in selected sectors such as electronics, green technology, and precision manufacturing.

Ultimately, Vietnam's path will need to reflect its unique economic structure and development goals. But by learning from Taiwan's and Korea's strategic approaches—particularly their early-stage investments in industrial capabilities and coordinated innovation policies—Vietnam can build the foundation for a more competitive, resilient, and innovation-driven economy.

The Government's Role

The government plays a central role in shaping the innovation landscape. Its responsibilities extend beyond passive support to include actively driving sustained economic growth through industrial technology development, crafting a clear strategy to guide this transformation, and ensuring its effective implementation. To do so, the government must rely on strong institutional infrastructure, well-designed incentives, and an open, transparent regulatory environment that welcomes foreign investment.

Lessons from Asia's industrial success stories offer important insights. Countries like Korea and Taiwan aligned their institutional frameworks with industrial needs to adapt imported technologies and promote research and development. Korea established numerous state-backed R&D institutes to serve its heavy and chemical industries, while Taiwan's Industrial Technology Research Institute (ITRI) focused on supporting the laptop sector. A crucial step in these strategies was prioritizing specific sectors and tailoring their technological upgrading. Industrial transformation, however, is never immediate—it often takes decades to fully materialize in the form of a robust, technology-driven economy.

Successful transformation depends on a broad, well-coordinated effort. This includes building up graduate-level education, organizing overseas training for scientists, attracting back expatriate experts, fostering joint research between academia and industry, supporting in-house R&D, and offering financial backing for technological upgrades. Governments must also support the formation of institutions that can bridge gaps between firms, R&D centers, and technical service providers (Fig. 9.2). Such institutions are critical in assisting enterprises to enhance export competitiveness, providing engineering and consulting services, strengthening collaboration between private and public research entities, and supporting high-tech firms with funding and guidance.

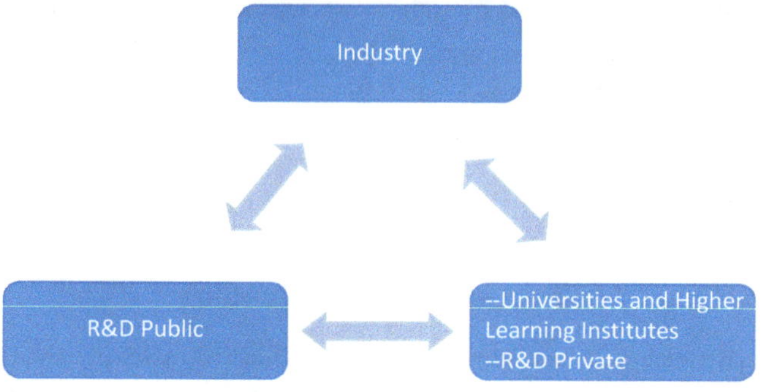

Fig. 9.2 Linkages of R&D to other institutions. *Source* Author

Korea's Technological Development Corporation (KTDC) offers a model of such an institution. KTDC identifies and funds projects ranging from research and development to advanced manufacturing techniques, helping firms absorb new technologies and improve processes. This includes adapting foreign technologies, offering technical training, and supporting commercialization of new products. KTDC also plays an intermediary role in funding high-risk R&D projects, especially those led by industry but executed by research institutes.

Chandra & Kolavalli (2006) analyzes ten countries—including Chile, Malaysia, Taiwan, and India—and highlights the value of such institutional support. They find that acquiring and adapting advanced technologies is often hindered by the "tacit" nature of knowledge, which resides in individuals and organizations and requires sustained investment in managerial and technical capability. Governments can help mitigate the risks firms face in absorbing this kind of knowledge. Despite differences in context, successful countries shared key traits: consistent policy support, embedded institutions, clear goals, and strong political commitment. Support targeted at entire industries—rather than individual firms—tended to be more effective in boosting exports and reducing innovation risks.

Ultimately, government policies must be tailored to industry conditions. Where private firms have strong capabilities, they can lead innovation. But where firms are weak, government-designed institutions must take the lead in fostering technological learning. Taiwan, for example, developed strategies informed by global experts and top industrialists, and successfully encouraged technology transfer through both government research and FDI. Similarly, in Malaysia and Chile, public initiatives played a catalytic role in sectors like electronics and aquaculture.

One of the most important insights from these case studies is the central role of public investment in higher education and research. However, these investments only succeed when aligned with dynamic industries facing competitive pressures. Firms typically adopt new technologies in response to market forces rather than simply because research facilities are available. When public research is closely connected to industry needs—as seen in Taiwan's consortia, Chile's wine sector, and India's work with grape and maize producers—it becomes more market-oriented and impactful.

Beyond research, other public interventions have proven beneficial in specific cases. For example, India and Chile provided regulatory assistance to help exporters meet international health and safety standards. Vietnam could benefit from similar initiatives, such as creating certification bodies to help small and medium-sized enterprises (SMEs) meet export standards. Economies such as Malaysia and Taiwan have also developed industrial parks that foster collaboration among multinational corporations, domestic firms, and public research institutions. Encouraging industry-wide coordination and building platforms for dialogue between government and business are other effective tools.

Policy Recommendations

Vietnam's current innovation framework already includes several institutions and programs dedicated to technology and entrepreneurship. The Ministry of Science and Technology (MOST) leads national policy, while the National Agency for Technology Entrepreneurship and Commercialization Development (NATEC) supports startups. The Vietnam National Innovation Center (NIC), Vietnam Silicon Valley (VSV), and Saigon Innovation Hub (SIHUB) provide funding and mentoring for entrepreneurs. Parks like Hoa Lac Hi-Tech Park serve as industrial centers for tech-driven growth. Universities and corporations, including Vietnam National University, Hanoi University of Science and Technology, FPT Corporation, and Vingroup's VinTech City, have also launched initiatives to promote innovation.

Despite these efforts, challenges persist. Vietnam still underperforms in research spending and university-industry collaboration. To address this, public incentives should shift toward intangible assets such as knowledge, design, and intellectual property, while physical incentives like land and capital should only be expanded where clearly needed. Technology extension policies can further help disseminate innovation, especially among startups. This will require improved use of intangible assets as collateral to unlock finance.

Better coordination between public research institutions and businesses will also be vital. This can be achieved through joint research projects, technology transfer offices at universities, and commercialization support for academic findings. Meanwhile, education and training in STEM fields must align with the needs of industry to build a capable workforce.

To support SMEs, the government could offer assistance in quality control, product design, and marketing, while also providing better access to information on export procedures, regulations, and business partners abroad. Developing specialized clusters in high-potential sectors such as renewable energy, aerospace, and automotive components would help foster collaboration and innovation.

Another priority is strengthening intellectual property protection. Streamlining patent and trademark registration, enhancing enforcement, and raising awareness among entrepreneurs are all essential to fostering innovation. These steps will help Vietnam become more competitive globally and enable sustainable economic growth.

Public-private partnerships (PPPs) present an additional opportunity to drive innovation and growth. By leveraging private sector resources and know-how, PPPs can help address infrastructure gaps, improve logistics, and support SMEs entering global value chains. While PPPs in infrastructure are well established in Vietnam, expanding them to finance innovation and SME growth remains underexplored. A stronger legal framework and clear guidelines for risk sharing, dispute resolution, and returns on investment are needed. Dedicated PPP funds focused on SMEs could unlock new sources of private investment.

Furthermore, PPPs can connect domestic firms with multinational corporations. Programs that encourage MNCs to co-invest in supplier development can help local firms upgrade their capabilities and meet global standards. This would strengthen Vietnam's position in global value chains and diversify its industrial base.

Venture capital (VC) is another essential element of a thriving innovation ecosystem. Traditional bank financing and PPPs are valuable, but VC is particularly important for high-growth startups. Although Vietnam's startup scene is vibrant—especially in fintech, e-commerce, and clean energy—early-stage funding remains scarce.

To fill this gap, the government could establish public-private VC funds, offering seed capital and risk-sharing mechanisms. Tax incentives for VC firms and angel investors would also stimulate private participation. Countries like Singapore and South Korea offer models for how public backing of VC can accelerate technological development. Incubators and accelerators connected to VC funding would further nurture startups with mentorship and access to international markets.

By acting on these recommendations, Vietnam can position itself at the forefront of the global knowledge economy. Stronger innovation policies, robust institutions, better financing mechanisms, and a more collaborative innovation ecosystem will not only create jobs and raise living standards but also ensure long-term competitiveness and national prosperity.

References

Agénor, P. R., & Dinh, H. T. (2013). *Public policy and industrial transformation in the process of development* (World Bank Policy Research Working Paper No. 6405). World Bank.

Agénor, P. R., & Dinh, H. T. (2015). Social capital, product imitation and growth with learning externalities. *Journal of Development Economics, 114*, 41–54.

Aghion, P., & Howitt, P. (1998). *Endogenous growth theory.* MIT press.

Berger, A., Bruhn, D., Bender, A., Friesen, J., Kick, K., Kullmann, F., Roßner, R., & Weyrauch, S. (2016). *Deep preferential trade agreements and upgrading in global value chains: The case of Vietnam* No. 92. Deutsches Institut für Entwicklungspolitik. https://www.idos-research.de/uploads/media/Study_92.pdf

Bloom, N., Van Reenen, J., & Williams, H. (2019). A toolkit of policies to promote innovation. *Journal of Economic Perspectives, 33*(3), 163–184.

Chandra, V., & Kolavalli, S. (2006). Technology, adaptation, and exports: How some countries got it right. In V. Chandra (Ed.), *Technology, Adaptation and Exports (Chapter 1).* World Bank Publications.

Chandra, V., Lin, J. Y. & Wang, Y. (2013). Leading dragon phenomenon: New opportunities for catch-up in low-income countries. *Asian Dvelopment Review, 30*(1), 52–84.

Crépon, B., Duguet, E., & Mairesse, J. (1998). Research, innovation and productivity: An econometric analysis at the firm level. *Economics of innovation and new technology, 7*(2), 115–158.

Freeman, C., & Soete, L. (1997). *The economics of industrial innovation.* MIT Press.

Gereffi, G., & Fernandez-Stark, K. (2011). *Global value chain analysis: A primer.* Center on Globalization, Governance & Competitiveness, Duke University.

Gerschenkron, A. (1962). *Economic backwardness in historical perspective: A book of essays.* Belknap Press of Harvard University Press.

Greenhalgh, C., & Rogers, M. (2010). *Innovation, intellectual property, and economic growth.* Princeton University Press.

Lee, K. (2013). *Schumpeterian analysis of economic catch-up: Knowledge, path-creation, and the middle-income trap.* Cambridge University Press.

Radosevic, S. (2018). *Fostering innovation in less-developed and low institutional capacity regions: Challenges and opportunities.* Background paper for an OECD/EC Workshop on Broadening Innovation Policy.

Radosevic, S., & Yoruk, E. (2016). Why do we need a theory and metrics of technology upgrading? *Asian Journal of Technology Innovation, 24*(sup1), 8–32.

Romer, P. M. (1989). *Human capital and growth: Theory and evidence* (NBER Working Paper No. 3173). National Bureau of Economic Research.

Wong, P. K. (1999). *National innovation systems for rapid technological catch-up: An analytical framework and a comparative analysis of Korea, Taiwan and Singapore.* Paper presented at the DRUID Summer Conference, Rebild.

Wood, A. (2015). World Trade Report 2014 – Trade and Development: Recent Trends and the Role of the WTOWorld Trade Organization 2014. *World Trade Review, 14*(3), 546–548. https://doi.org/10.1017/S1474745615000269

PART V

Human Capital in a Changing Society

CHAPTER 10

Human Capital 1: Labor Market Reforms

Introduction

In Chap. 3, we show that for Vietnam to achieve an annual GDP growth rate close to 8%, both the quantity and quality of labor contribution to growth must increase significantly. Labor market reforms are crucial to achieving this target, particularly through reducing informality and addressing skill mismatches. These reforms will enable Vietnam to adopt advanced production methods and strengthen its position in global markets.

Over the past few decades, Vietnam's labor market has transformed significantly, shifting from a predominantly agrarian economy to one driven increasingly by industry and services. This shift has fueled rapid economic growth, lifting millions out of poverty and modernizing the economy. However, despite these achievements, structural challenges persist, which, if unaddressed, could hinder long-term development. This chapter examines the strengths, weaknesses, and challenges within Vietnam's labor market and outlines policy directions for reform.

Contributed by Hinh T. Dinh

H. T. Dinh, H. T. Nguyen, *Vietnam's Economic Leap*,
https://doi.org/10.1007/978-3-032-08904-5_10

Strengths of Vietnam's Labor Market

A major strength of Vietnam's labor market is its young and growing workforce. With approximately 70% of its 100 million people under the age of 35, the country benefits from a demographic dividend that many economies lack. This youthful population is not only large but also increasingly well-educated, thanks to Vietnam's long-standing emphasis on education and training. As a result, the workforce is both adaptable and prepared to meet the evolving demands of a rapidly changing global economy.

Another strength is Vietnam's high labor force participation rate, which is among the highest in the region. Women's participation is particularly noteworthy, exceeding that of many other Southeast Asian nations. This broad engagement strengthens economic resilience and ensures a steady labor supply for industries and services.

Vietnam's open-door policy towards foreign direct investment (FDI) has also positioned the country as a highly attractive destination for international businesses looking to relocate manufacturing operations. Its strategic location, competitive labor costs, and stable political environment have made it an ideal hub for global supply chains. The influx of FDI has created millions of jobs, boosted economic development, and established a robust manufacturing base that continues to absorb labor.

Structural Weaknesses of Vietnam's Labor Market

Despite these strengths, Vietnam's labor market suffers from deep structural issues, including widespread informal employment, underemployment, and a growing mismatch between workers' skills and market demands. Over half of the workforce is self-employed or informal, with limited access to social protection such as pensions or unemployment insurance. Many workers, especially in rural and family-run businesses, face job instability and insufficient working hours. At the same time, Vietnam's education system struggles to meet labor market needs, with only a small share of workers classified as high-skilled and employers reporting widespread difficulty in hiring qualified staff, especially in advanced manufacturing and technology sectors. The skills gap is worsening, reducing productivity and hindering the country's move up global value chains. In critical sectors like semiconductors, the shortage is especially acute, with only 5000 chip design engineers currently available against a projected demand of 50,000 by 2030, despite government efforts to boost high-tech training. These issues are examined in detail below.

Informality

One of the most persistent issues in Vietnam's labor market is informality. A significant proportion of the workforce operates in the informal sector, where jobs are characterized by low productivity, job instability, and a lack of social protection. Many workers lack social security benefits, employment contracts, and access to training opportunities that could enhance their skills and improve their long-term career prospects. The informal sector, which includes street vendors, small family-run businesses, and unregistered enterprises, remains pervasive due to a combination of regulatory constraints and enforcement limitations. Informal employment often means lower wages, poor working conditions, and minimal job security, making workers vulnerable to economic shocks.

The OECD (2023) reported that in 2019, self-employed workers made up more than half of total employment, a stark contrast to the OECD average of 16%. These workers are typically excluded from public pension programs and unemployment insurance, with social insurance covering only 29% of the labor force in 2020. Consequently, only about one-quarter of employed individuals were covered by the unemployment insurance system in 2018 (World Bank, 2021a).

The high levels of informality can be attributed in part to complex regulatory burdens. Many small businesses find it challenging to navigate administrative procedures and comply with labor regulations, leading them to remain outside the formal system. At the same time, weak enforcement of labor laws allows informal enterprises to operate without adhering to labor standards, exacerbating issues related to job security and wage inequality.

The consequences of informality extend beyond individual workers, as informal employment limits government revenue by reducing tax collection and constrains economic growth by limiting access to credit and investment opportunities. Informality lowers productivity of the economy as a whole because informal businesses often lack access to advanced technology, financial resources, and training programs that could enhance their efficiency and competitiveness. Without these critical inputs, they struggle to grow and contribute meaningfully to economic progress. Additionally, informal employment tends to be associated with lower wages and job instability, contributing to income inequality and social disparities.

Addressing informality will require a comprehensive policy approach that balances incentives for formalization with stricter enforcement measures. Simplifying business registration and reducing bureaucratic barriers can encourage more entrepreneurs to transition into the formal economy. Expanding social security coverage, including innovative insurance schemes tailored for informal workers, can also provide incentives for formal employment. Strengthening enforcement of labor regulations, including more frequent inspections and penalties for non-compliance, is essential, but these measures should be complemented by support mechanisms that help small businesses navigate the transition.

Encouraging financial inclusion can further facilitate formalization. Small businesses often struggle to access credit and financial services, which limits their ability to invest in technology, training, and expansion. Government programs that provide low-interest loans and business development support can play a critical role in helping informal enterprises transition to formality. In parallel, vocational training programs aligned with industry needs can enhance workers' employability, equipping them with skills that increase their chances of securing formal employment.

As discussed in Chap. 8, Vietnamese banks could be encouraged to follow Morocco's example, where banks have created dedicated SME units and developed tailored financial products for small businesses. The establishment of Morocco's Central Guarantee Fund (CGC) has helped reduce financing costs, share lending risks with banks, and support viable SMEs that lack sufficient collateral. Guarantee coverage varies by firm size and sector, reaching up to 80% for very small enterprises.

Encouraging business formalization also requires other measures including tax incentives, legal protections, stakeholder collaboration, and technological advancements. Providing tax incentives alongside simplified tax regimes can ease the transition for small businesses, making compliance more accessible. Ensuring that informal workers and businesses have legal rights and protections is essential, including safeguards against exploitation, unfair working conditions, and access to justice and dispute resolution mechanisms. Collaboration among governments, the private sector, NGOs, and international organizations can further support formalization efforts by leveraging resources, expertise, and networks for greater impact. Additionally, the use of technology, such as digital platforms for business registration, e-government services, and digital identification systems, can streamline formalization processes, bridge information gaps, and enhance access to essential services for the informal sector.

Beyond informality, bridging Vietnam's skills gap is imperative. Strengthening collaboration between educational institutions and industries can help align training programs with labor market demands. Investing in higher education and vocational training for high-tech industries, particularly semiconductors and electronics, will be crucial in ensuring that the country's workforce remains competitive. In addition, policies that make tertiary education more accessible and affordable can incentivize more young people to pursue higher education and specialized skills development.

In summary, addressing informality and bridging the skills gap are essential for Vietnam's long-term economic stability and growth. Labor market reforms that promote formalization, strengthen vocational training, and enhance social protection will be key to ensuring that Vietnam's workforce remains competitive in an increasingly complex global economy. A coordinated effort among government agencies, businesses, and civil society will be necessary to create a more resilient, inclusive, and productive labor market. By implementing targeted policies that support both workers and businesses, Vietnam can build a stronger foundation for sustainable economic development.

Underemployment and Disguised Unemployment in Vietnam

Vietnam's labor market faces persistent challenges in the form of underemployment and disguised unemployment, both of which hinder the country's economic potential. Underemployment, defined as working fewer than 35 hours per week and being willing and ready to work additional hours, occurs when workers do not fully utilize their skills or work fewer hours than they desire. Disguised unemployment refers to individuals who hold jobs that contribute minimally to overall production.

Many workers find themselves in positions that do not fully utilize their skills or provide adequate income. For instance, nearly one in ten women employed in the services sector was classified as an unpaid family worker in 2021 (OECD, 2023). Family-run businesses, while widespread, often fail to provide full-time, stable employment, particularly during economic downturns when reduced working hours become a common adjustment mechanism (World Bank, 2021a). This issue is particularly prevalent in agriculture and family-run businesses, where surplus labor does not translate into higher productivity. Addressing these challenges is essential for sustaining economic growth and improving workers' livelihoods.

One of the main reasons for underemployment and disguised unemployment is the structural transformation of Vietnam's economy. While the country has shifted from agriculture to industry and services over the past few decades, this transition has not been smooth. Many workers possess outdated skills that no longer align with the demands of the modern economy, leaving a large segment of the labor force trapped in low-productivity jobs. Without targeted policies to facilitate a more effective transition, Vietnam risks stagnating in its economic progress by failing to maximize the potential of its workforce.

Another major contributor to underemployment is the widespread mismatch between workers' skills and labor market requirements. Despite high educational attainment, many graduates struggle to find jobs that align with their qualifications. Many individuals accept jobs that do not correspond to their education or training, leading to an inefficient allocation of human capital. This skills mismatch arises from gaps in the education and vocational training system, which often fails to equip graduates with the competencies required by industries. Without significant improvements in workforce development, the misalignment between labor supply and demand will persist, further exacerbating underemployment.

Employers frequently report difficulty in hiring high-skilled workers, particularly in advanced manufacturing and technology-intensive industries. Only 5% of Vietnam's manufacturing workforce is classified as high-skilled, and just 10% of the population holds a bachelor's degree—a lower rate than most regional peers except Indonesia (World Bank, 2024). This skills gap limits productivity growth and hinders Vietnam's ability to move up the global value chain.

Employers increasingly cite the shortage of skilled labor as a key obstacle. One-third of firms report a lack of qualified applicants, and nearly 80% of manufacturing companies face difficulties in hiring skilled workers (World Bank, 2020). More than a third of employers see the limited capacity of their workforce as the principal impediment to technology adoption (World Bank, 2024). Even more concerning is the rising trend: in 2009, 9% of firms identified an inadequately educated workforce as a major constraint, but by 2023, this had risen to 12% of all firms and 20% of exporters. Similarly, the share of tertiary graduates working in high-skill non-manual jobs has fallen in the last 15 years. A declining wage premium, along with the high cost of tertiary education, means that there is less incentive for today's youth (and tomorrow's workers) to invest in higher education and greater skills development.

In the semiconductor industry, the number of available chip design engineers is estimated to be less than half of the projected demand over the next five years. While only 5000 engineers currently work in semiconductor design, demand is expected to reach 50,000 by 2030, including 15,000 chip design engineers. Skills-intensive manufacturing has experienced a rising wage premium for university graduates, reflecting more acute skills shortages in key sectors such as consumer electronics (World Bank, 2024). The Vietnamese government has set ambitious targets to train 30,000 to 50,000 engineers and technicians for high-tech industries, including semiconductors, yet the challenge remains pressing.

Limited job opportunities in certain regions and economic sectors also force many workers into roles that do not fully engage their abilities. Rural areas, in particular, struggle to generate sufficient employment opportunities, compelling workers to accept any available job, regardless of pay or career prospects. In urban centers, rapid industrialization has driven demand for skilled labor, but individuals with inadequate education or training often remain stuck in low-paying informal jobs. The lack of access to stable and well-compensated employment perpetuates economic insecurity for millions of workers.

The prevalence of informal employment (see the previous section) further compounds the problem. Jobs in the informal sector typically involve irregular working hours, low wages, and little to no job security, offering limited opportunities for career advancement. A significant portion of Vietnam's workforce remains in this sector, where employment conditions are precarious and productivity levels are lower than in the formal economy. Reducing informality is crucial to addressing underemployment and ensuring that workers can fully contribute to economic growth.

The consequences of underemployment and disguised unemployment extend beyond individual workers and pose broader economic risks. One immediate impact is reduced productivity. When workers are not fully utilized—either because they are in jobs that do not require their full skill set or because they are engaged in low-value activities—Vietnam's overall economic output declines. This inefficiency weakens the country's competitiveness in global markets and slows economic development.

Underemployment also contributes to lower incomes and widening income inequality. Workers who are unable to find jobs that match their skills and experience often earn less than their potential, reinforcing economic disparities between different regions, particularly between urban and rural areas. Over time, persistent income inequality can lead to social discontent and limit economic mobility.

Beyond economic consequences, prolonged underemployment can have psychological and social repercussions, including discouragement and withdrawal from the labor force. Workers who struggle to find suitable employment may eventually stop searching altogether, reducing overall labor market participation. This creates a cycle in which underemployed individuals fail to acquire the necessary skills for better jobs, leading to long-term economic stagnation.

Underemployment and Informal Employment in Developing Countries: Lessons from International Experience

Vietnam's struggles with underemployment and informality are far from unique. These challenges are endemic to many developing countries, where structural constraints limit the expansion of formal employment and trap large segments of the population in insecure, low-productivity work. This section reviews international experience to shed light on effective strategies for addressing this complex problem.

In many low- and middle-income countries, workers often engage in multiple low-wage, low-productivity jobs not by choice but by necessity. This phenomenon—commonly described as ***precarious underemployment***—is driven by several structural factors: (i) a shortage of formal job opportunities; (ii) stagnant or insufficient wages in primary employment; (iii) weak or non-existent social protection systems; (iv) the dominance of informal sector jobs in the labor market; and (v) limited access to finance for self-employment or enterprise creation. As a result, millions of workers, though technically "employed," remain in poverty or near-poverty conditions.

Addressing underemployment and informality requires an integrated package of labor market and structural reforms. International experience offers several policy pathways:

Expanding Formal Employment Opportunities. Countries that have successfully promoted formal employment often rely on active industrial policies. Bangladesh, for example, created over 4 million jobs in its export-oriented garment sector by combining low labor costs with special economic zones, infrastructure support, and favorable trade agreements (World Bank, 2019). Public employment programs have also proven effective. India's *Mahatma Gandhi National Rural Employment Guarantee Act* (MGNREGA) has provided short-term employment to over 60 million rural households annually, particularly during agricultural off-seasons, thereby reducing seasonal underemployment (ILO, 2018).

Strengthening Social Protection Systems. An adequate safety net is crucial for workers trapped in informal or underpaid jobs. Brazil's *Bolsa Família* conditional cash transfer program significantly reduced extreme poverty while encouraging school attendance and health check-ups, indirectly supporting long-term labor productivity (Soares et al., 2010). South Africa's non-contributory old-age pension system has similarly helped reduce poverty among elderly workers and their households, including those in informal work (Case and Deaton, 1998).

Moreover, setting minimum wages linked to cost-of-living indices has proven useful. Indonesia and the Philippines have used regional minimum wage councils to balance labor market conditions with inflation and productivity trends, helping protect vulnerable workers without deterring job creation (ILO, 2015).

Formalizing Informal Work. Simplifying business registration and reducing the cost of formalization are crucial to transitioning informal enterprises into the formal sector. Rwanda's online business registration platform slashed the time needed to register a business to less than 48 hours, significantly boosting the number of registered small enterprises (World Bank Doing Business, 2020).

In Mexico, the *Monotributo* program—a simplified tax and social security regime for micro-entrepreneurs—offers a promising model. It bundles tax payments with access to social benefits, thus incentivizing informal workers to enter the formal economy (Perry et al., 2007).

Investing in Skills and Human Capital. Skills mismatch is a major constraint in formal employment creation. In response, countries such as Malaysia and Singapore have invested heavily in technical and vocational education and training (TVET), tailored to industry needs and employer feedback. Ghana's *Youth Employment Agency* (YEA) has supported short-term vocational training linked with apprenticeships in construction, ICT, and agribusiness, helping integrate informal youth into formal sectors (African Development Bank, 2018).

Lifelong learning initiatives are also gaining traction. Chile's *ChileValora* program allows workers to have their skills certified regardless of how they were acquired, making informal workers more competitive in the formal labor market (OECD, 2016).

Promoting Entrepreneurship and SME Growth. Supporting self-employment and enterprise development is critical for absorbing under-employed labor. Kenya's *Uwezo Fund* and *Youth Enterprise Development Fund* provide low-interest loans and training for youth and women entrepreneurs. Tunisia's startup act offers tax breaks and regulatory exemptions for new businesses, spurring innovation and job creation in the tech sector (World Bank, 2021b).

In India, the *Micro Units Development and Refinance Agency* (MUDRA) has disbursed billions of dollars in small loans to informal entrepreneurs, helping them scale their businesses and transition toward formalization.

One key approach is to promote structural transformation by facilitating the movement of labor from low-productivity sectors, such as agriculture, into higher-value industries. Investments in infrastructure, technology, and workforce training will be critical in ensuring that workers can transition effectively into more productive roles. Providing access to modern tools and up–to-date knowledge will help workers adapt to the changing demands of the labor market.

The experience of developing countries shows that underemployment and informality are deeply rooted in economic structures but not intractable. A combination of targeted industrial policies, labor market reforms, and inclusive social protection can create a more stable, productive, and equitable labor market. For Vietnam, adapting and sequencing these policy interventions to its specific context will be essential to reducing informality and underemployment over the long term.

Improving labor market information systems will also play a vital role in ensuring that job seekers can access accurate and timely information about employment opportunities. A well-functioning labor market information system will help workers make informed career decisions, reducing skills mismatches by connecting them with employers in need of their expertise. Strengthening job placement services and digital job-matching platforms will help bridge the gap between labor supply and demand.

Facilitating labor mobility is another crucial step. Workers should be able to move freely to regions and sectors where employment opportunities are available. Policies that remove relocation barriers—such as fully eliminating remnants of the 'hộ khẩu' system, promoting affordable housing, and investing in regional infrastructure—will facilitate workers' movement to areas with stronger job markets. Encouraging rural-to-urban migration while ensuring that urban centers can absorb new workers will be key to addressing geographical disparities in employment opportunities.

In the context of Vietnam, other important measures include encouraging domestic SME growth, scaling up vocational training for the digital economy, formalizing informal work through expanded social protections, strengthening wage growth policies aligned with productivity, and developing urban-rural employment strategies through agritech, e-commerce, and decentralized industrial zones.

Underemployment Among Young College Graduates in Vietnam

The issue of underemployment among young college graduates in Vietnam presents a paradox within the country's rapidly growing economy. Despite robust economic expansion and increasing integration into global markets, a significant portion of Vietnam's young, educated workforce remains underutilized. Many graduates find themselves in jobs that do not fully engage their skills or offer adequate compensation.

Several factors contribute to this problem. A major issue is the disconnect between the skills imparted by higher education institutions and the demands of the labor market. Many universities continue to focus on theoretical knowledge rather than practical skills, leaving graduates unprepared for modern workplaces. Curricula often lack emphasis on critical thinking, creativity, and soft skills, which are increasingly valued by employers in a knowledge-driven economy.

The rapid expansion of higher education has also outpaced the job market's ability to absorb new graduates. With educational and job opportunities concentrated in major cities, certain fields and regions now face an oversupply of graduates. At the same time, Vietnam's structural economic transformation has not been accompanied by a proportional increase in high-skilled jobs. As a result, many graduates struggle to find employment that matches their qualifications.

The underemployment of young college graduates has far-reaching implications. On an individual level, it leads to job dissatisfaction, lower income potential, and delayed career progression. On a broader scale, it represents a significant waste of human capital. When a substantial portion of the workforce is not fully utilized, Vietnam operates below its potential productivity level, leading to the negative TFP as discussed in Chap. 2. This inefficiency hampers innovation, reduces competitiveness, and ultimately slows economic growth.

To address this issue, Vietnam must align education with market needs. Universities and vocational institutions should revise their curricula to focus on practical skills, incorporating internships and industry partnerships to provide students with real-world experience. Enhanced career guidance services will also help students make informed decisions about their studies and job prospects.

Encouraging entrepreneurship among young graduates can create new job opportunities and stimulate economic growth. Providing support through incubators, mentorship programs, and access to capital will be essential in fostering a dynamic startup ecosystem. In addition, promoting a culture of lifelong learning will help workers remain competitive by continuously updating their skills in response to labor market changes.

Addressing underemployment and disguised unemployment remains a pressing challenge for Vietnam's labor market. Structural transformation, skills mismatches, limited job opportunities, and high levels of informal employment must be tackled through targeted policies. By investing in workforce development, promoting job creation, improving labor market information, and facilitating labor mobility, Vietnam can unlock the full potential of its labor force and build a more inclusive and resilient economy.

Capitalizing on Global Market Opportunities

To fully capitalize on global market opportunities and sustain long-term economic growth, Vietnam must address key labor market challenges and adapt to rapid changes in the global economy. The country's continued success will depend on its ability to navigate emerging global trends while mitigating potential risks. A proactive approach to labor market reform and economic policy will be essential for strengthening Vietnam's competitiveness in an increasingly complex international landscape.

One of the most significant global shifts shaping Vietnam's economic future is the rising demand in Asia. With a rapidly expanding middle class and increasing consumer spending, the region presents a valuable opportunity for Vietnam to diversify its export markets and strengthen regional trade partnerships. The growing demand for goods and services in neighboring countries provides Vietnam with a chance to reduce its reliance on traditional export destinations such as the United States and Europe. By fostering stronger trade relationships within Asia, Vietnam can position itself as a key regional supplier and benefit from deeper economic integration.

Technological advancements are also reshaping global industries, and Vietnam must ensure that its workforce is prepared for these transformations. The rise of automation, digitalization, and artificial intelligence is changing the nature of work, requiring new skill sets across sectors. While automation poses a challenge to certain low-skilled jobs, it also creates an opportunity for Vietnam to accelerate technological catch-up and improve productivity. Investing in digital infrastructure and workforce training will be critical for building a labor force capable of supporting high-value industries that require advanced technical expertise.

The global transition to a low-carbon economy presents another major opportunity for Vietnam. As countries implement stricter environmental regulations and promote sustainable products, demand for green goods and services is growing. Vietnam has the potential to develop a competitive green manufacturing sector by investing in renewable energy, energy-efficient production, and sustainable supply chains. Embracing clean technology and low-carbon manufacturing will not only help Vietnam fulfill its climate commitments but will also enhance its attractiveness to environmentally conscious investors and consumers. Vietnam could provide incentives for firms to invest in renewable energy, enhance energy efficiency, and adopt sustainable business practices to align with the growing global preference for green production.

The restructuring of global value chains further strengthens Vietnam's position as an investment destination. With companies seeking to diversify production away from a single country, Vietnam has emerged as a key player in global supply chains. However, to fully benefit from this trend, the country must enhance its domestic industrial capabilities and enable local firms to participate more effectively in higher value-added segments of global production networks. Strengthening linkages between foreign investors and local businesses will be crucial for improving technology transfer and increasing domestic firms' contributions to global trade.

To seize these opportunities, Vietnam must take concrete steps to enhance its economic competitiveness. Deepening trade integration is a top priority. Leveraging existing and new trade agreements will allow the country to reduce non-tariff barriers, liberalize trade in services, and strengthen regional economic cooperation. By maintaining an open trade policy and actively engaging in international trade negotiations, Vietnam can reinforce its status as a leading export-driven economy.

Promoting the "servicification" of manufacturing (Chap. 6) is another essential strategy. Integrating services such as logistics, design, and after-sales support into production processes will increase the value-added component of Vietnam's exports. This shift will require policies that encourage service-sector growth, stimulate innovation, and facilitate the integration of digital services into traditional manufacturing industries.

Investing in digital skills development will also be necessary to ensure Vietnam's workforce remains competitive in an increasingly technology-driven world. Expanding access to digital training programs and strengthening the technical and vocational education and training (TVET) system will help workers acquire the skills needed for high-tech industries. The government should prioritize training initiatives in areas such as data analytics, software development, and automation technologies to prepare the workforce for future economic demands.

Strengthening domestic linkages between foreign firms and local enterprises (Chap. 8) will be critical for fostering innovation and increasing productivity. Many multinational companies operating in Vietnam continue to rely on foreign suppliers instead of sourcing inputs from local firms. Encouraging stronger partnerships between foreign investors and domestic businesses will facilitate knowledge transfer, promote technological upgrading, and help Vietnamese companies move up the value chain. As discussed in Chap. 8, the government should introduce policies that support supplier development programs and provide targeted assistance to small and medium-sized enterprises (SMEs) to enhance their competitiveness.

By addressing these challenges and leveraging emerging global opportunities, Vietnam can ensure sustained economic growth and reinforce its position in the global economy. A forward-thinking strategy that prioritizes trade integration, digital transformation, sustainable development, and industrial upgrading will allow Vietnam to navigate the complexities of the modern global economy and secure long-term prosperity.

Beyond economic policies, Vietnam must also strengthen its social protection systems to ensure an inclusive transition. As structural changes reshape the labor market, some workers will face job displacement or struggle to adapt. Expanding unemployment insurance, reskilling programs, and targeted financial assistance will help vulnerable workers reintegrate into the workforce. Ensuring that economic growth benefits all segments of society, including low-income workers, women, and rural laborers, will be critical to fostering a more equitable economy.

The success of these reforms will ultimately hinge on improved governance and stronger policy coordination. Weak governance, bureaucratic inefficiencies, and corruption can undermine labor market initiatives and broader economic reforms. To address these challenges, Vietnam must improve institutional quality, simplify administrative procedures, and ensure greater transparency in policy implementation. Strengthening inter-agency coordination and fostering public-private collaboration will also be essential for effective policymaking. In this context, the successful implementation of the new "Era of National Rise" strategy will be especially critical.

Vietnam stands at a pivotal moment in its economic development. While the country has made remarkable progress, further reforms are needed to sustain growth and ensure long-term prosperity. By addressing labor market inefficiencies, investing in human capital, and embracing global economic shifts, Vietnam can secure a resilient, competitive, and inclusive future for its workforce and society as a whole.

References

African Development Bank. (2018). *Jobs for youth in Africa strategy 2016–2025.* African Development Bank.

Case, A., & Deaton, A. (1998). Large cash transfers to the elderly in South Africa. *The Economic Journal, 108*(450), 1330–1361.

International Labour Organization. (2015). *Minimum wage systems.* International Labour Organization.

International Labour Organization. (2018). *India: Employment and social protection in the informal sector.* International Labour Organization.

Organisation for Economic Co-operation and Development. (2016). *Chile: Enhancing skills for productivity and inclusiveness.* OECD Publishing.

Organisation for Economic Co-operation and Development. (2023). *OECD economic surveys: Viet Nam 2023.* OECD Publishing. https://doi.org/10.1787/8f2a6ecb-en

Perry, G. E., Maloney, W. F., Arias, O. S., Fajnzylber, P., Mason, A. D., & Saavedra-chanduvi, J. (2007). *Informality: Exit and exclusion*. World Bank.

Soares, S. S. D., Ribas, R. P., & Osório, R. G. (2010). Evaluating the impact of Brazil's Bolsa Família: Cash transfer programs in comparative perspective. *Latin American Research Review*, *45*(2), 173–190.

World Bank. (2019). *Bangladesh development update: Tertiary education and job outcomes.* World Bank.

World Bank. (2020). *Doing business 2020: Comparing business regulation in 190 economies.* World Bank.

World Bank. (2020). *Enterprise Surveys: Vietnam 2020 country profile*. World Bank Group. https://www.enterprisesurveys.org

World Bank. (2021a). *The labor market and the covid-19 outbreak in Vietnam: Impacts and lessons learned for social protection*. World Bank. http://hdl.handle.net/10986/35990

World Bank. (2021b). *Tunisia: Startup ecosystem and policy reform report*. World Bank.

World Bank. (2024). *Viet Nam 2045: Trading up in a changing world – pathways to a high-income future*. World Bank. http://hdl.handle.net/10986/42505

CHAPTER 11

Human Capital 2: Pushing the Role of Education

Education, Human Capital and Income

Education is considered a driver of economic growth (Hanushek & Woessmann, 2008) and a crucial element in overcoming the middle-income trap (Jayadevan et al., 2023). Education serves as a bridge between knowledge and practice, establishing a foundation for innovation. It equips individuals with skills to adapt to a changing society, fosters creativity, and contributes to a sustainable society. Countries such as Japan, Taiwan, Hong Kong, and South Korea illustrate the benefits of investing in human capital, as their substantial investments in education, research, and training have propelled them to high-income status (Otsuka et al., 2017).

Human capital, defined by Schultz (1961), Becker (1964), and Benos and Zotou (2014), encompasses knowledge, skills, abilities, and personal attributes acquired through education, training, healthcare, and life experiences. Among these, education is essential for developing human capital and supporting sustainable economic growth (Benos & Zotou, 2014).

New growth theory suggests that economic production depends not only on labor and physical capital but also on education, human capital, and soft infrastructure, like institutions. Investment in education and skill development can significantly improve TFP and drive sustained economic growth

Contributed by Hoai Trong Nguyen

H. T. Dinh, H. T. Nguyen, *Vietnam's Economic Leap*,
https://doi.org/10.1007/978-3-032-08904-5_11

(Kucharčíková, 2011). Schultz (1981) emphasized that human capital investment is fundamental to long-term economic growth, requiring continuous improvement alongside advancements in physical and technological capital.

While the importance of human capital for growth has long been recognized, it wasn't until the late 1980s and early 1990s, with seminal contributions from Lucas (1988), Romer (1990), Stokey (1988), and Mankiw et al. (1992), that it was incorporated into growth models as an independent variable. Mankiw et al. (1992), for example, expanded the Solow growth model by adding human capital, creating a valuable framework for analyzing the impact of education and training policies on growth.

$$Y = A.L^{\alpha}.K^{(1-\alpha-\beta)}.H^{\beta}$$

In this framework, total output (Y) is a function of TFP (A), physical capital (K), labor (L), and human capital (H). Growth can be stimulated by increasing any of these factors; however, physical capital investment alone, without a skilled workforce, is unlikely to achieve sustained growth (Kucharčíková, 2011). Education impacts human capital and TFP through knowledge acquisition, skill development, and learning by doing (Fig. 11.1). As such, education is a key component of human capital, enhancing the effective use of physical capital (Qutb, 2017). Educated workers are better positioned to utilize advanced technologies from developed countries (Sarquis & Arbache, 2002). Additionally, education plays a crucial role in raising labor productivity by equipping workers with modern knowledge and skills (Aghion & Howitt, 2006; Benhabib & Spiegel, 1994; Nelson & Phelps, 1966). Lee (2007) highlights that

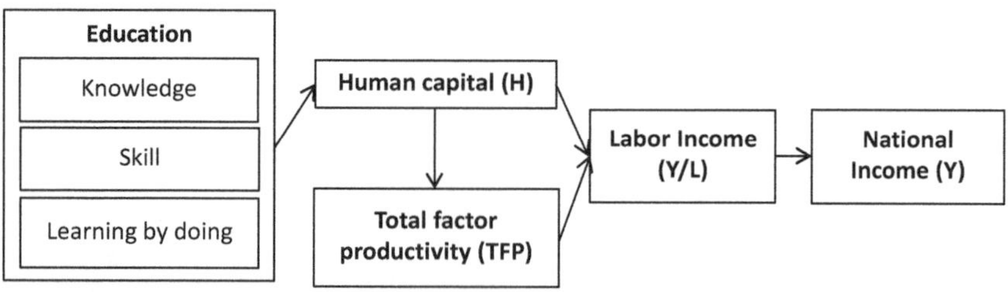

Fig. 11.1 Analytical framework of national income and labor income from education, human capital, and TFP. *Source* Author

a well-trained and experienced workforce is vital for enhancing TFP, noting that learning by doing is an effective way to acquire practical skills and improve work efficiency.

Previous studies have affirmed the critical role of human capital in boosting TFP growth (Schultz, 1961; Becker, 1964; Nelson & Phelps, 1966; Welch, 1970; Mincer, 1974). Cörvers (1994) notes that human capital not only enhances individual productivity but also improves the efficiency of other inputs. Skilled workers are essential for fostering innovation, enabling technology transfer, and improving production efficiency, all of which contribute to TFP growth (Sarquis & Arbache, 2002; Hua, 2005; Wei & Hao, 2011).

In developed countries, education has been instrumental in achieving and maintaining long-term growth. However, in low- and middle-income countries, education's potential remains largely untapped, limiting their progress toward high-income status (Jayadevan et al., 2023). Vietnam is no exception; to become a modern industrialized nation, Vietnam needs a highly skilled workforce, and education is key. Without this, Vietnam risks falling into the middle-income trap.

Challenges to Improving Labor Productivity

Vietnam's education system, while improving, faces significant challenges in producing a workforce capable of supporting a high-income economy through technological advances and innovation. Completion rates, particularly in rural areas and among ethnic minority groups, are low, restricting access to education for many. Teacher shortages, especially in disadvantaged areas, further undermine education quality. Although investments in education in Vietnam have increased, they still fall short of actual needs, as evidenced by a low percentage of schools meeting national standards and insufficient facilities. STEM education, intended to build practical skills, faces challenges such as a lack of qualified teachers and modern laboratories. At the university level, issues including substandard education quality, weak industry-academia linkages, and limited internationalization persist. These obstacles have impeded labor productivity growth, leading to modest and inconsistent increases in real GDP per capita.

Limited Access to Education for Potential Learners

School completion rates in Vietnam, particularly in rural and ethnic minority areas, remain relatively low. This rate is calculated as the percentage of children who are 3–5 years older than the normative age for the final grade of an educational level (primary, lower secondary, or upper secondary) and have completed that grade. For example, if primary education starts at age six and lasts for five years; the completion rate for primary school is measured for children aged 13–15.

In the 2020–2021 academic year, approximately 2 million children aged 5–17 did not complete their education, with the majority in lower and upper secondary levels (Table 11.2). Children from ethnic minority groups, poor households, and remote areas face more challenges accessing quality education. Incomplete rates are significantly higher among these groups (UNICEF, 2022).

Figure 11.2 shows that 44.8% of students not attending school reported "disliking school" or "performing poorly". This issue may stem from education systems that fail to meet students' needs due to factors such as underqualified teachers, inappropriate teaching methodologies, and curricula misaligned with real-world contexts. Consequently, many students lose interest in learning and drop out. Economic hardship is the second-leading cause, with around 30% of out-of-school children coming from families that cannot afford education-related expenses.

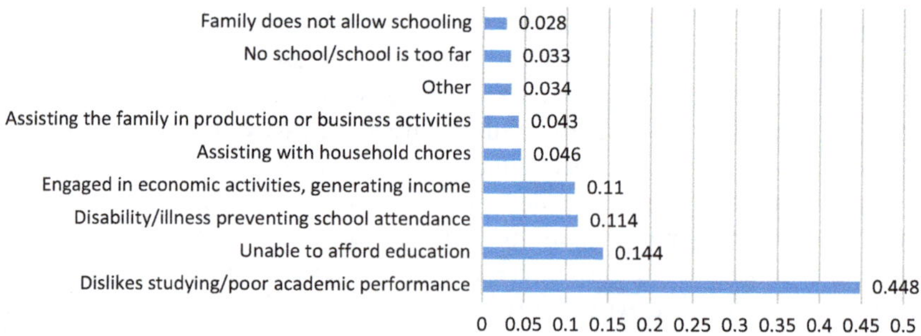

Fig. 11.2 Common reasons for children aged 5–17 not attending school, 2018. *Source* ILO, General Statistics Office of Vietnam, Ministry of Labour, Invalids and Social Affairs (2018). Viet Nam National Child Labour Survey 2018

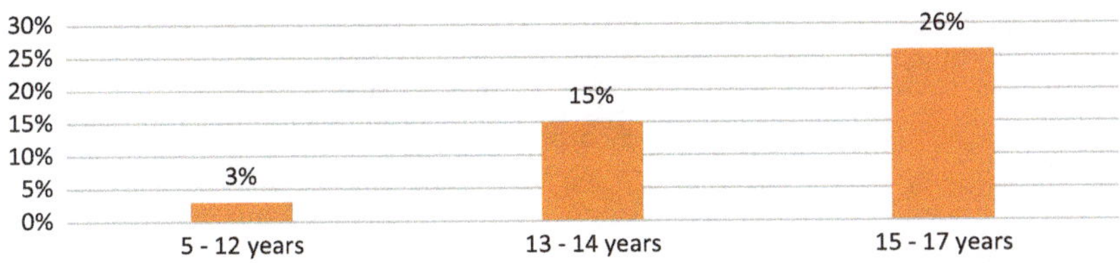

Fig. 11.3 Proportion of children engaged in economic activities by age, 2018. *Source* ILO, General Statistics Office of Vietnam, Ministry of Labour, Invalids and Social Affairs (2018). Viet Nam National Child Labour Survey 2018

In poorer households, particularly in rural areas, children often work to support their families, contributing to high dropout rates. The prevalence of child labor increases markedly with age, as illustrated in Fig. 11.3. Additionally, limited access to schools due to distance, insufficient facilities, complex administrative procedures, and disabilities prevents many children—particularly in remote areas (Fig. 11.4)—from attending school.

The large number of children who do not complete their education (Table 11.1), particularly in rural and minority populations, poses severe societal challenges. The denial of educational opportunities restricts personal growth, hinders community progress, and exacerbates social disparities, perpetuating the cycle of poverty. This reality manifests in increased economic hardship, social instability, and constrained sustainable development for these communities, particularly those of ethnic minorities and the poor.

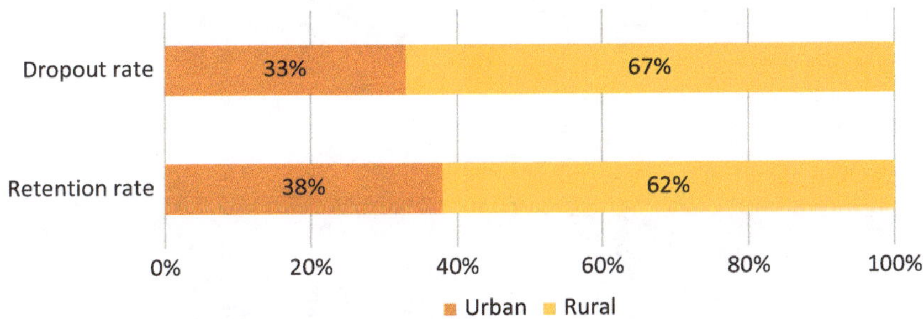

Fig. 11.4 Dropout and retention rates among students in grades 1–12, academic year 2020–2021. *Source* UNICEF (2022), Vietnam Education Summary Report 2022

Table 11.1 Proportion and number of students not completing school, academic year 2020–2021

		Incomplete rate (%)			*Estimated number of students not completing school*		
		Elementary school	*Lower secondary school*	*Upper secondary school*	*Elementary school*	*Lower secondary school*	*Upper secondary school*
Gender	Male	2	16	49	42,200	293,200	859,000
	Female	1	10	35	28,400	214,900	703,400
Area	Urban	2	9	25	20,800	129,200	385,100
	Rural	2	15	53	49,900	378,900	1,177,300
Total		2	13	41	70,600	508,100	1,562,400

Source UNICEF (2022), Vietnam Education Summary Report 2022

Lacking of Teacher Supply

Vietnam faces a critical teacher shortage, with over 100,000 vacancies nationwide (Vietnam Ministry of Education and Training, 2023). The Red River Delta has the largest shortfall, followed by the North Central Coast and the Northern mountainous region. The shortage places significant pressure on education quality and the capacity to meet growing student needs.

Projections of population growth and teacher demand to 2045 indicate that Vietnam will need to recruit more than 400,000 teachers over the next 20 years (Vietnam Ministry of Education and Training, 2023). This requires training and recruiting approximately 40,000 teachers annually, particularly at the preschool and high school levels. However, current teacher training institutions produce only 14,000–17,000 graduates annually (Ministry of Education and Training, 2023), which is insufficient to meet demand. Moreover, recruitment faces obstacles due to relatively low salaries and benefits, challenging working conditions, and inadequate facilities, especially in remote and mountainous areas (Vietnam Institute of Educational Sciences, 2022).

The teacher shortage exacerbates classroom overcrowding and disrupts effective teaching and learning. It also increases educational inequality, particularly in disadvantaged areas. This shortage will persist without prompt solutions, undermining education quality and human resource development.

Low Educational Investment

Vietnam's education budget, particularly for higher education, remains modest compared to regional countries and falls over time in terms of educational expenditure as a percentage of total government expenditure. In 2020, only 0.18% of Vietnam's GDP was spent on higher education, significantly below the 1% regional average (Table 11.2). Moreover, higher education expenditures accounted for just 4.1% of total education spending in 2020, equating to approximately 6.8 million VND per student, compared to averages of 275 million VND, 103.9 million VND, and 62 million VND per student in Singapore, Korea, and Malaysia, respectively. This underinvestment affects training quality and workforce competitiveness.

Although Resolution 37/2004/NQ-QH11 and the Education Law of 2019 (Article 96, Clause 1) set targets for education funding—stipulating that at least 20% of the state budget go to education—the actual

Table 11.2 Budget allocation for higher education

Country	*Higher education expenditure (% GDP)*	*Year*	*Higher education expenditure (% education budget)*	*Year*	*Government funding per student (in millions of VND)*	*Year*
Malaysia	1.13%	2015	21.30%	2018	62.30	2018
Singapore	1.00%	2015	35.28%	2015	274.90	2015
Thailand	0.64%	2013	15.60%	2013	26.00	2013
Korea	0.86%	2016	20.50%	2016	103.90	2016
Vietnam	0.18%	2020	4.10%	2020	6.80	2020

Source Yêm (2023)

allocation ranged from 17.4% to 20.2% between 2011 and 2020, with a decreasing trend in recent years (Fig. 11.5).

Several factors limit Vietnam's educational budget. As a developing country, Vietnam faces competing demands, including poverty reduction, infrastructure, and environmental protection, which restrict education funding. Additionally, the current allocation mechanism lacks transparency, leading to uneven distribution across education levels, regions, and schools (Vietnam Ministry of Education and Training, 2023). Declining foreign direct investment (FDI) and official development assistance (ODA) for education since Vietnam's transition to a lower-middle-income country further constrain resources (Vietnam Institute of Educational Sciences, 2022).

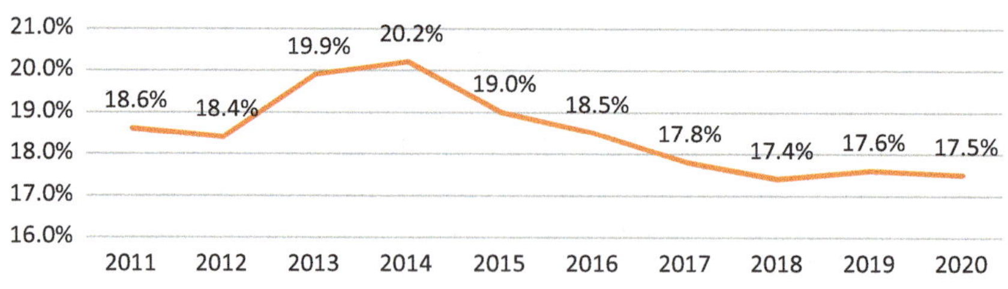

Fig. 11.5 Education expenditure (% total government spending), 2011–2020. *Source* Academy of Finance (2020)

Struggling STEM Training

Vietnam integrated STEM education into its curriculum to equip students with skills needed for the Fourth Industrial Revolution. However, recent national high school graduation exams reveal challenges in STEM education implementation. Despite its importance, the percentage of students achieving high scores in mathematics, physics, chemistry, and English was low in 2023 (Fig. 11.6), highlighting the need for more effective teaching methods.

University enrollment in STEM fields in Vietnam is also low compared to other countries. In 2021, Vietnam had only about 55 STEM students per 10,000 people, trailing behind other regional and global countries. The gap is particularly noticeable in natural sciences and mathematics, where Vietnam's proportion is far below countries like Finland, Korea, and Singapore (Fig. 11.7).

The limitations of STEM education in Vietnam stem from several factors. A shortage of qualified and inspiring educators is a primary challenge, as teachers continue to rely on traditional, theoretical instruction without practical applications. Additionally, limited infrastructure, such as laboratories and equipment, hampers students' learning experiences. Career guidance, societal biases, and psychological barriers further discourage students, particularly females, from pursuing STEM. These issues hinder the development of a skilled workforce crucial for Vietnam's industrialization and modernization.

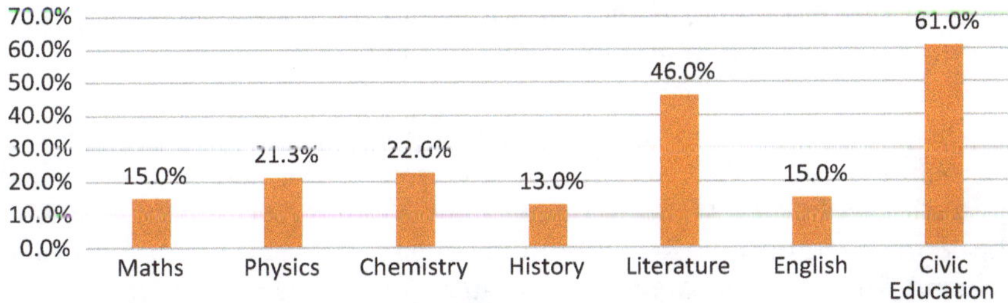

Fig. 11.6 Distribution of scores 8 and above by subject (%), 2023. *Source* Ministry of Education and Training (2023). *Comprehensive report on the planning of higher education and teacher training institution network, 2021–2030, with a vision to 2050*

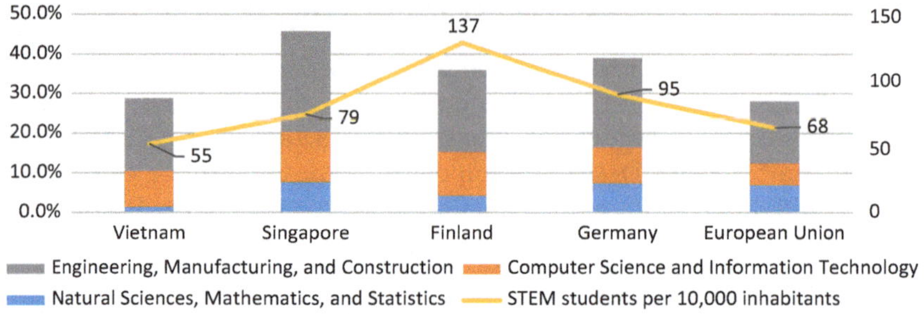

Fig. 11.7 Student distribution by field of study, 2021. *Source* Ministry of Education and Training (2023). *Comprehensive report on the planning of higher education and teacher training institution network, 2021–2030, with a vision to 2050*

Biased Disciplines Toward the Fourth Industrial Revolution

The current structure of academic programs in Vietnamese universities does not sufficiently align with labor market demands. As Vietnam integrates internationally and enters the Fourth Industrial Revolution, the need for a skilled workforce, particularly in technical and technological fields, has become more urgent. However, Vietnamese educational institutions predominantly focus on social sciences. Figure 11.8 illustrates this imbalance, with business and management programs constituting nearly 24% of enrollments, while fields like computer science, information technology, engineering, and natural sciences have significantly lower enrollment rates. This trend is consistent across graduate and doctoral levels, where business and management dominate (27.7%), in contrast to the limited interest in engineering, technology, and basic sciences (Ministry of Education and Training, 2023).

This imbalance in university programs poses significant challenges to Vietnam's sustainable economic development. The shortage of skilled professionals in STEM fields undermines Vietnam's competitiveness in the Fourth Industrial Revolution. The gap between the supply and demand for human resources in high-tech industries restricts innovation and slows economic growth. Additionally, this mismatch leads to social challenges, as many social science graduates struggle to find suitable jobs, while technology firms face a talent shortage.

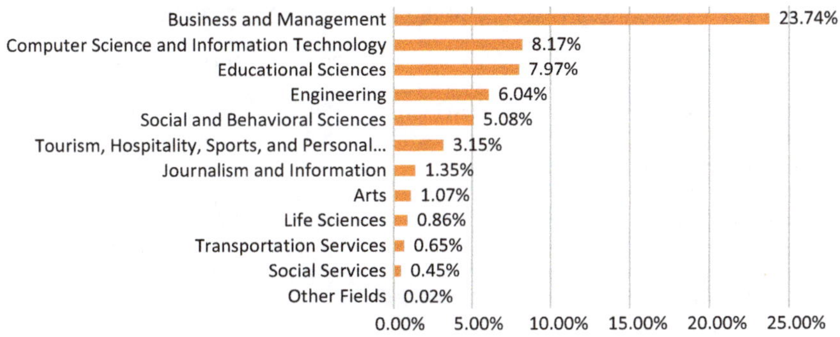

Fig. 11.8 Distribution of students by major, 2023. *Source* Ministry of Education and Training (2023). *Comprehensive report on the planning of higher education and teacher training institution network, 2021–2030, with a vision to 2050*

Risk Factors for Vietnam's Middle-Income Trap

Vietnam's educational deficiencies obstruct sustainable economic development by creating a shortage of highly skilled labor, impeding research commercialization, and slowing innovation. Low labor productivity, compounded by an inadequately skilled workforce, rapid population aging, and limited digital adoption, poses significant risks of trapping Vietnam into middle-income status.

Skilled Workforce: Stagnant and Inefficiency

Despite strides in improving workforce educational attainment, progress has stagnated, with university graduate ratios increasing by only 1.5% between 2017 and 2020 (Table 11.3). Regional and sectoral disparities also persist, with only 11.1% of the national workforce holding a university degree or higher, mainly concentrated in urban areas like Hanoi and Ho Chi Minh City (Table 11.4). This shortage of skilled labor restricts Vietnam's capacity to participate in high-value global supply chain segments, undermining competitiveness and trapping it in middle-income status. Furthermore, uneven educational distribution limits synchronous development across regions and sectors.

Table 11.3 Technical proficiency of the workforce, 2017–2020

	2017	*2018*	*2019*	*2020*
Highest attained technical proficiency level (%)	100	100	100	100
No technical proficiency (%)	78.3	78.0	77.2	76.0
Elementary level (%)	5.4	5.5	3.7	4.7
Intermediate level (%)	3.8	3.8	4.7	4.4
College level (%)	2.9	3.2	3.8	3.8
University degree or higher (%)	9.6	9.7	10.6	11.1

Source GSO (2022), Report on Labor Force Survey 2020

Table 11.4 Proportion of trained workforce, 2020 (%)

	Total	*Elementary level (%)*	*Intermediate level (%)*	*College level (%)*	*University degree or higher (%)*
Nationwide	24.0	4.7	4.4	3.8	11.1
Male	26.9	8.3	4.8	3.3	10.5
Female	20.9	0.7	3.9	4.4	11.8
Urban	39.7	6.1	5.9	5.6	22.1
Rural	16.3	4.0	3.7	2.9	5.7
Region					
Northern Mid-mountains and Highlands	20.5	4.3	5.1	3.5	7.5
Red River Delta	32.6	6.2	6.0	5.2	15.2
Including: Hanoi	44.8	6.6	6.9	6.3	24.9
North Central and Central Coast	22.7	4.5	4.6	4.0	9.5
Central Highlands	16.9	4.0	3.1	2.3	7.4
Southeast	29.5	5.1	3.8	4.5	16.2
Including: Ho Chi Minh City	38.7	4.6	4.0	6.1	23.9
Mekong Delta	14.9	3.4	2.7	2.0	6.8

Source GSO (2022), Report on Labor Force Survey 2020

Higher education quality also remains inadequate, as evidenced by high unemployment rates among university graduates compared to those with vocational training or no formal training (Table 11.5). The lack of alignment between education and market needs contributes to rising graduate

Table 11.5 Unemployment rate by highest educational attainment, 2018–2020 (%)

Educational Attainment	*2018*			*2020*		
	Total	*Male*	*Female*	*Total*	*Male*	*Female*
No formal education	2.4	2.3	2.4	1.6	1.3	1.9
General education	69.9	72.8	67.1	55.3	61.5	50.5
+No primary school completion	6.7	6.9	6.5	5.1	5.2	5.0
+Primary school graduate	17.1	18.2	16.1	14.5	16.1	13.3
+Lower secondary school graduate	24.7	25.6	23.9	19	21.4	17.1
+Upper secondary school graduate	21.4	22.2	20.6	16.7	18.8	15.1
Professional/vocational training	27.7	24.9	30.4	43.0	37.1	47.6
+Elementary level (%)	2.2	4.2	0.3	4.6	9.2	1
+Intermediate level (%)	6.3	5.2	7.4	7.6	4.9	9.7
+College level (%)	6.8	5.0	8.4	10.1	7.2	12.3
+University degree or higher (%)	12.4	10.4	14.3	20.7	15.8	24.6

Source GSO, Report on Labor Force Survey, 2018–2020

unemployment, reduced domestic goods and services quality, decreased national competitiveness, and a waste of educational resources. These challenges widen the development gap between Vietnam and other nations, complicating efforts to escape the middle-income trap.

Ineffectiveness in Research for Labor Productivity Improvement

Vietnamese universities have increased their international scientific publications, reaching 17,625 in 2021, ranking fifth in ASEAN (Vietnam Ministry of Education and Training, 2023). However, research quality remains limited, with low citation indices and modest publication-to-faculty ratios. Patent application rates are low, with only 15.5% coming from higher education institutions compared to 40% from enterprises (Vietnam Ministry of Education and Training, 2023). This reflects the limited ability of educational institutions to convert research into commercially valuable products and services, hampering technology transfer and productivity enhancement.

Vietnamese enterprises' limited research and innovation capacity hampers labor productivity compared to regional peers. For example, approximately 59% of manufacturing workers in 2019 were employed in enterprises with outdated technology, while only around 12% worked in firms using advanced technologies (CSIRO, 2021). This technology gap, especially in agriculture and manufacturing, constrains productivity growth and reduces economic efficiency.

The disparity in innovation capacity among Vietnamese enterprises remains a notable concern. The leading enterprises (top 3%) have maintained a substantial advantage over others, particularly in the service, agriculture, and mining sectors from 2001 to 2019 (CSIRO, 2021). While there are some signs of convergence in certain sectors, the overall pace of technology diffusion remains slow, posing a substantial challenge to enhancing economic efficiency.

Weak FDI-domestic enterprise linkage in Vietnam is hindering domestic productivity growth. While neighboring countries source 90% of inputs domestically, Vietnam's rate is significantly lower at 60% (Vietnam Financial Times, 2023). Additionally, Vietnam has the world's lowest rate of technology transfer from FDI (Vietnam Ministry of Finance, 2018).

The commercialization of research outcomes from higher education institutions remains limited, and the technological innovation capacity of Vietnamese enterprises, especially small and medium-sized enterprises, is generally low. Ineffective linkages between research and production continue to be a critical barrier, hampering improvements in labor productivity.

Slow Labor Productivity Growth

Low labor productivity is a persistent challenge for Vietnam's economy. Despite a large labor force, productivity remains below regional and global averages (Fig. 11.9). Primary reasons include low workforce technical skills and slow digital adoption, compounded by rapid population aging as older workers may be less familiar with or willing to adopt new technologies in their work. Although educational attainment has improved, only about 40% of the workforce has completed high school (Fig. 11.10). Moreover, employers frequently cite a lack of specialized and technical skills among workers (Bodewig et al., 2014; OECD, 2020). Automation risks, especially for workers with only primary education, further exacerbate job insecurity (Frey & Osborne, 2017). Workers with only primary education are 3.1 times more likely to face job loss than those with a university degree (Chang & Huynh, 2016; OECD, 2020).

From 2011 to 2020, Vietnam's labor force structure shifted from agriculture to industry and services, yet this transformation has not

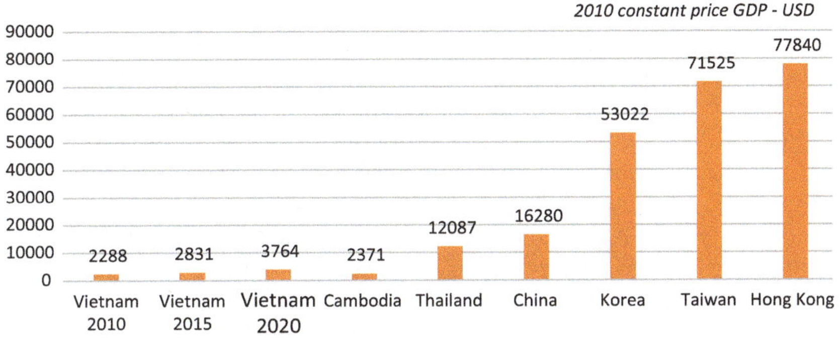

Fig. 11.9 Average labor productivity in Vietnam (2010–2020) and Asian countries (2020). *Source* Vietnam Institute of Educational Sciences (2022), Report on the Analysis of Vietnam's Education Sector 2011–2020

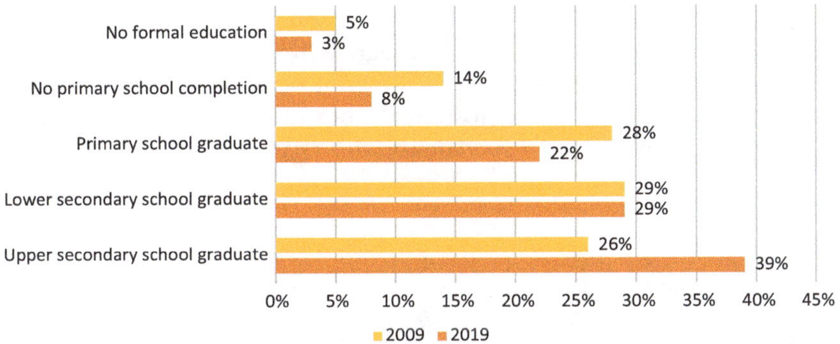

Fig. 11.10 Labor force by educational attainment, 2009–2019 (%). *Source* GSO (2020), Statistical Yearbook 2019

significantly increased productivity. Employment in agriculture, forestry, and fisheries declined from 48.4% in 2011 to 33.1% in 2020, while employment in industry and construction increased from 21.3% to 30.8%, and in services from 30.2% to 36.1% (Fig. 11.11). Many workers leaving agriculture were absorbed into low-productivity sectors in industry and services, limiting value added.

Vietnam has been unable to fully capitalize on scientific and technological advancements due to constraints in labor productivity, which have led to decreased efficiency in production and business operations. This not only results in wasted resources but also impedes the country's economic and social development, posing a significant risk of falling into the middle-income trap. Consequently, upgrading the knowledge and technical skills of the workforce to align with market demands is a pressing need.

To enhance labor productivity and keep pace with the Fourth Industrial Revolution, Vietnam must substantially increase its investment in education and training. A primary focus should be placed on improving workforce quality, particularly through vocational training and retraining. A well-rounded skill set, including both soft skills and advanced technical competencies, is essential for increasing labor productivity and competitiveness. Furthermore, training programs should be tailored to meet the specific needs of enterprises and key industries, facilitating a shift toward a modern labor structure and higher productivity. This approach will enable the transition from a low-skilled workforce to a highly skilled labor pool that meets the demands of the digital economy.

In conclusion, low labor productivity is a critical issue that must be addressed for Vietnam to deeply integrate into the global economy, achieve sustainable development, and avoid the middle-income trap. Improving workforce quality, fostering innovation, and enhancing labor productivity are essential to overcoming this challenge.

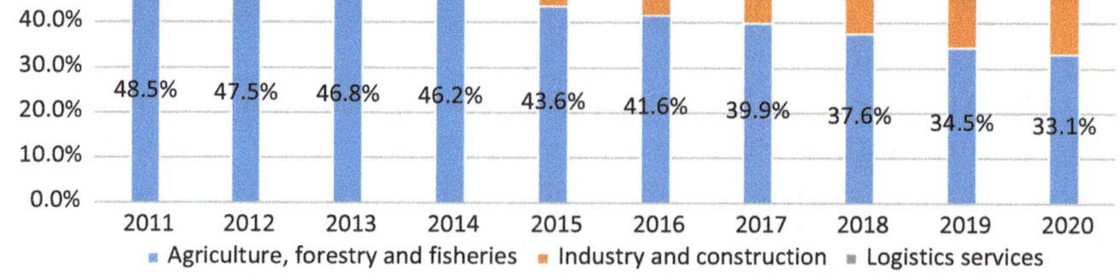

Fig. 11.11 Structure of the labor force aged 15 and over, 2011–2020 (%). *Source* GSO (2023), Report on Vietnam's Labor Productivity 2011–2020: Status and Solutions

International Experience

To escape the middle-income trap and achieve developed country status, Vietnam must prioritize continuous innovation, draw lessons from other countries—particularly East Asian economies—and make substantial investments in education to build a knowledge-based, high-productivity economy.

Figure 11.12 highlights the correlation between educational attainment and the ability to overcome the middle-income trap. For example, in the 1960s, Japan entered a period of rapid economic growth, partly attributed to its superior educational achievements compared to other struggling East Asian economies. Following Japan's success, South Korea and Taiwan made similar strides in education in the 1980s, leading them to become newly industrialized economies with impressive growth rates. Their sustained investment in education and human capital helped propel them into the ranks of the "Asian Dragons."

Overall, during their rapid development phases from the 1960s to the 1990s, East Asian economies such as Japan, Singapore, Hong Kong (China), South Korea, and Taiwan demonstrated the critical role of education in industrialization and modernization. Significant investments in education fostered a high-quality workforce, stimulated innovation, and enhanced productivity, all contributing to the transformation of these nations into leading global economies.

Improving Workforce Skills

Dual Training System in Germany

Germany's dual training system, a unique vocational education and training model, has been highly effective in producing a skilled workforce for the German economy. Currently, around 330 officially recognized dual training programs exist, covering fields from mechanics and electronics to services (Federal Institute for Vocational Education and Training, BIBB, 2017). This model not only provides a high-quality workforce but also helps reduce youth unemployment.

Vocational training is a popular path for German students after lower secondary education. The dual vocational training system has proven successful, with about 52% of the 16–24 age group participating in 2018. Apprentices in this system receive an average monthly stipend of 876 euros (BIBB, 2018), allowing them financial independence and reducing family burdens.

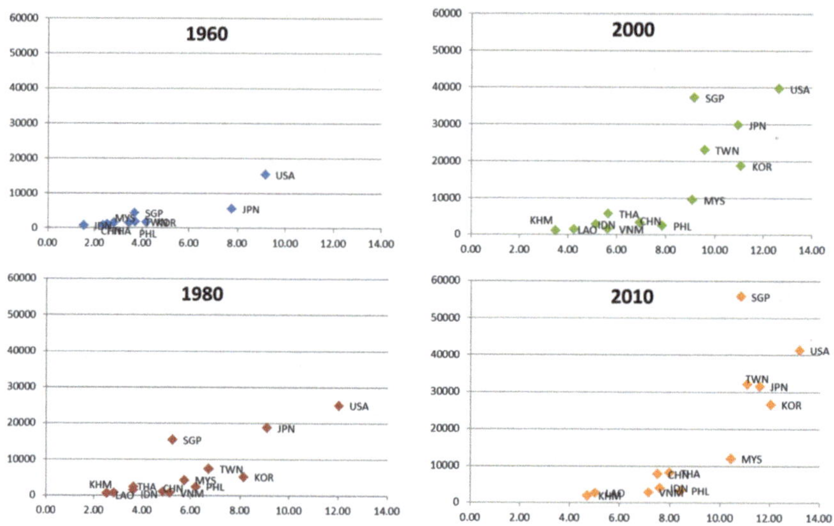

Fig. 11.12 Relationship between real GDP per capita and average years of schooling

A distinctive feature of this model is the close connection between vocational schools and enterprises. Approximately 70% of dual training takes place within companies, where trainees gain real work experience and develop vocational skills, while the remaining time is spent learning theory at vocational schools (Hockenos, 2018). This approach enables them to acquire both specialized knowledge and practical skills that are aligned with labor market demands.

The German Dual System offers valuable insights into Vietnam's vocational education reform. Integrating theory and practice, fostering strong school-enterprise partnerships, and investing in infrastructure and training programs are crucial for an effective vocational education system. Vietnam could benefit from these practices to train a workforce that meets labor market needs and supports economic and social development.

Work-integrated Learning Model in Norway and Japan

Norway's "2+2" Vocational Training Model

Norway pioneered the "2+2" vocational education model, combining two years of classroom learning with two years of practical training in factories or enterprises. Building on this model, Norway has developed various adaptations, including the "1+3" model (one year of study followed by three years of apprenticeship) and the "0+4" model (four years of full-time apprenticeship). This variety offers learners flexibility and accommodates individual preferences, cultivating a workforce well-suited to the evolving labor market.

The Norwegian government also provides financial incentives to enterprises and apprentices to enhance and sustain the quality of vocational training. Companies receive funding to support apprentice training, while apprentices benefit from stipends and opportunities for long-term employment with their training companies. This robust government support, combined with strong partnerships between enterprises and educational institutions, has fostered a vocational training system that integrates theoretical knowledge and practical skills from the outset of education.

Japan's Kosen Model

Japan's Kosen Model was developed to meet the critical demand for highly skilled technical professionals in advanced industries. This approach prioritizes aligning workforce development with industry requirements, emphasizing practical expertise and creativity through hands-on experience and research.

Kosen schools attract talented students from junior high, starting them at age 15 on a five-year technical education track. From the third year onwards, students build a strong foundation of professional knowledge and gain practical experience in modern facilities. This early exposure provides Kosen graduates with a competitive edge over traditional university graduates. After the five-year program, graduates can pursue a two-year postgraduate program (Sensoka) to further specialize.

Beyond technical skills, Kosen students participate in extracurricular activities centered on engineering, such as programming, design, presentations, and, especially, robotics competitions—a tradition since 1988. Language skills are also prioritized, with many students pursuing international certifications like TOEIC and EIKEN.

In summary, Norway's "2+2" model and Japan's Kosen model exemplify successful integration of theory and practice in vocational education. Strong school-business partnerships and government support in these models have created adaptable, high-quality workforces. Vietnam, with its distinct economic and social characteristics, could learn from and adapt these approaches to develop a modern vocational education system that meets its labor market needs and enhances its human resources.

Technology-integrated Education Model

South Korea, once a resource-poor nation, has transformed into an economic powerhouse through strategic vision and substantial investments in education, science, and technology. The nation's phased education policy was carefully designed to align with its evolving developmental needs.

Beyond focusing on enrollment, the South Korean government has continuously sought to enhance the quality of higher education and encouraged students to pursue overseas studies to access advanced technologies. The integrated development of higher education, technical colleges, and vocational schools has produced a high-quality workforce that meets the growing demands of the economy.

Science and technology have been central to South Korea's impressive economic growth. Alongside significant investments in education, the South Korean government established premier research institutions, including the Korea Institute of Science and Technology (KIST) in 1966 and the Korea Advanced Institute of Science and Technology (KAIST) in 1971. These institutions are designed to support both fundamental and applied research, cultivate talent, and facilitate technology transfer to enterprises, thereby strengthening the nation's competitive edge. As a result of these efforts, South Korea has rapidly emerged as a technological leader, achieving remarkable success in fields such as electronics, automobiles, and biotechnology.

Inspired by South Korea's achievements, Vietnam can gain valuable insights into the importance of investing in education and scientific and technological innovation. Elevating workforce educational attainment is not only critical for boosting productivity but also for driving structural economic transformation toward a knowledge-based economy. To realize this vision, the government should implement preferential policies and create favorable conditions for attracting investments in education and scientific research. At the same time, establishing an education and training system closely aligned with labor market demands and the development of modern industries is an urgent priority.

Educational Development Linked to National Economic Stages

Singapore: Aligning Education With Economic Development Phases
Singapore's transformation into one of the world's leading education hubs is remarkable. Once facing high illiteracy rates in 1965, the nation has undergone three phases of educational development. The first phase (1959–1978) focused on establishing a foundational education system from primary to lower secondary levels, expanding school networks, and training teachers. However, the education system at that time had limitations and could not fully meet the needs of a rapidly transitioning economy.

Recognizing the essential role of a highly skilled workforce for sustainable national development, Singapore implemented significant educational reforms between 1979 and 1996. The government shifted from a universal approach to a quality-oriented model, emphasizing vocational skills to prepare a workforce ready for industrialization. The establishment of the Singapore Institute of Technology (SIT) in 1992 exemplifies this vocational focus. With a mission to provide a high-quality workforce, SIT has continuously developed diverse training programs that integrate theory and practice, equipping students with the skills needed for career success. Concurrently, the expansion of university networks significantly increased the supply of scientists, engineers, and skilled professionals, supporting key industries.

Since 1997, Singapore has evolved into a global leader in knowledge-based economies. The nation has prioritized nurturing creativity, research, and innovation through strategic planning. Initiatives such as "Thinking Schools, Learning Nation" and "Teach Less, Learn More" foster a dynamic learning environment that encourages students to be proactive, inquisitive, and independent thinkers. By increasing investments in research and technology and forging strong international partnerships, Singapore's leading universities, including the National University of Singapore and Nanyang Technological University, have achieved impressive global recognition. Singapore has established itself as a premier center for education and innovation in ASEAN and beyond.

Across these three developmental phases, Singapore's education policy has demonstrated flexibility and effectiveness in addressing the economy's evolving needs. From building foundational education to focusing on quality and skilled workforce training, and ultimately transitioning to a knowledge-based economy, Singapore highlights the critical role of education in building a prosperous nation. These valuable lessons can serve as a guide for Vietnam in its education reform and development journey.

Malaysia: Shaping Education Through the New Industrial Master Plan (NIMP) 2030

The NIMP 2030, with its vision to transform Malaysia's manufacturing and manufacturing-related services sectors, plays a crucial role in shaping the nation's educational strategy. This plan identifies the skills and knowledge required for the future workforce, strengthening the connection between education and industry. By outlining key industries and high-level manpower needs, the NIMP 2030 aligns educational curricula with specialized programs that foster innovation. Additionally, the plan promotes the growth of a digital economy, which requires that the education system equips students with essential digital competencies. The NIMP 2030 also emphasizes sustainable development, encouraging the integration of environmental and social issues into the curriculum. Overall, the NIMP 2030 serves as a vital roadmap, guiding Malaysia's education system to meet labor market demands and contribute to national socioeconomic development.

The NIMP 2030's clearly defined objectives and roadmap for developing high-value-added industries—including sectors like Electronics and Electrical (IC design and wafer fabrication), Specialty Chemicals, Aerospace, Pharmaceuticals, and Medical Devices—offer valuable lessons for Vietnam's education reform. The focus on cultivating a high-quality workforce to meet the needs of key industries calls for significant changes in curricula, teaching methodologies, and the infrastructure of universities and colleges.

Building an Efficient Ecosystem to Escape the Middle-Income Trap

Vietnam has made continuous efforts to reform its education system in recent years. Resolution 29-NQ/TW, enacted in 2013, has served as a crucial guiding principle, driving the comprehensive renewal of

Vietnam's education and training over the past decade to meet the demands of industrialization, modernization, and international integration within a socialist-oriented market economy context. This resolution has unified perspectives on the role of education and led to positive changes. The synchronized institutionalization of Resolution 29 through laws, decrees, and guidelines has created a robust legal framework for education reform. The resolution's principles are embedded in critical legislation, such as the Education Law and the Law on Higher Education, shaping a comprehensive legal foundation for education development. Moreover, sub-legal documents have been implemented to establish an effective management system for the education sector.

Notably, the implementation of the 2018 general education program and the promotion of university autonomy have led to significant innovations in teaching and learning methods, enhancing the quality of education. Additionally, increased social engagement in education has created more learning opportunities, contributing to a diverse education system. Resolution 29 has laid a strong foundation for developing Vietnam's education to train high-quality human resources for international integration.

However, challenges remain in Vietnam's education system, including access for learners, ensuring a supply of qualified teachers, and addressing budget constraints to train a workforce aligned with Fourth Industrial Revolution requirements. These limitations impact the economy's total factor productivity, resulting in low per capita income and creating barriers to Vietnam's comprehensive development. Breakthrough solutions and long-term strategies are needed to address these challenges and promote sustainable development.

Easy Access for Potential Learners

Vietnam has enacted specific regulations to facilitate universal access to education. Legal documents, including Decree 81/2021/ND CP, Decree 97/2023/ND–CP, and related circulars, offer a range of solutions, from adjusting tuition fee structures and providing financial support for education to implementing specialized education programs for disadvantaged groups. These measures reaffirm the State's commitment to ensuring free access to education for all citizens and building a learning society.

One key solution to facilitating access to education is the adjustment of tuition fee mechanisms and the provision of financial support for learners. Decrees 81/2021/ND–CP and 97/2023/ND–CP specify tuition fee levels, categories of students eligible for exemptions and reductions, and other forms of financial assistance. This alleviates the financial burden on disadvantaged families, enabling their children to pursue education. Recently, General Secretary of the Communist Party of Vietnam, To Lam, underscored the critical importance of universal education, presenting a vision for providing free education to all students (Vietnamnet, 2024). This initiative reflects a strategic commitment to equitable access to educational opportunities for all citizens. Achieving this objective requires a structured roadmap, initially prioritizing the full waiver of tuition fees from primary to lower secondary levels, with the potential to expand to upper secondary education in subsequent phases.

Beyond tuition policies, the Vietnamese government has implemented specialized education programs to meet the needs of individuals in unique circumstances. Examples include literacy eradication (Circular 33/2021/TT-BGDĐT), Vietnamese language instruction for ethnic minority children before entering Grade 1 (Circular 23/2023/TT-BGDĐT), and the establishment of inclusive education support centers (Circular 20/2022/TT-BGDĐT). These programs illustrate the government's commitment to enhancing educational access.

In summary, Vietnam's legal framework provides comprehensive regulations to promote inclusive access to education. Various solutions—including tuition adjustments, specialized education programs, and expanded learning opportunities—ensure the right to education for all citizens and foster an inclusive learning environment, particularly for disadvantaged groups.

Enhancing Teacher Quality

Improving teacher quality is a central goal of Vietnam's education reform strategy, aimed at building a high-caliber workforce equipped for the demands of Industry 4.0 and global integration. Two key documents, Decision No. 89/QD-TTg and Decree No. 71/2020/ND–CP, provide the legal and strategic foundation for enhancing the qualifications and competencies of teachers across all levels, from preschool to university.

Decision No. 89/QD-TTg, issued by the Prime Minister in 2019, launched the "Project to Enhance the Capacity of Lecturers and Managers at Higher Education Institutions," aligned with comprehensive education reforms from 2019 to 2030. This project focuses on developing a highly qualified teaching staff, with an emphasis on doctoral training and opportunities for lecturers to participate in international research programs and collaborate with countries that have advanced education systems. Additionally, the project aims to strengthen educational management capabilities to improve institutional management, thereby elevating the quality of education and research.

Decree No. 71/2020/ND–CP, effective since 2020, outlines a roadmap for upgrading teacher qualifications from preschool to lower secondary levels. Under this decree, preschool teachers are required to hold at least a college-level teaching certificate, while primary and lower secondary school teachers must possess at least a bachelor's degree in education. The roadmap is divided into two phases: phase 1 (2020–2025) and phase 2 (2026–2030). During phase 1, the targets are for at least 60% of preschool teachers, 50% of primary school teachers, and 60% of lower secondary school teachers to meet the required standards, with support from teacher training institutions to allow teachers to study and work simultaneously. By 2030, all teachers are expected to meet the qualification requirements. The decree also calls for coordination among local governments, educational institutions, and relevant ministries to ensure financial and logistical support for teachers, particularly in disadvantaged areas.

Decision 89/QD-TTg and Decree 71/2020/ND–CP illustrate Vietnam's commitment to improving education quality across all levels. These policies reflect the government's recognition of the crucial role of teachers in enhancing human resources and driving sustainable national development. Timely implementation and close monitoring of these initiatives will be essential for achieving these goals comprehensively and effectively.

Addressing the Teacher Shortage

Addressing the teacher shortage requires coordinated efforts across all levels of government and sectors. A flexible budgeting framework is essential, empowering local governments to adjust teacher quotas based on specific needs. Additionally, granting the education sector greater autonomy in recruitment is necessary to ensure an adequate and well-structured teaching workforce. The rigid reduction of the civil servant quota, as stipulated in Decree 108/2014/ND–CP, has created challenges in maintaining educational quality by mandating a 10% reduction in the civil servant quota from 2015 to 2021. This has led to a teacher shortage in many areas despite growing demand. To address this issue, a mechanism allowing local governments to flexibly recruit contract teachers with comparable compensation to permanent teachers should be implemented.

A flexible and efficient teacher rotation mechanism, combined with incentive policies, is crucial for attracting talented individuals to the education sector. Rotations can range from intra-provincial to inter-provincial and even nationwide transfers to balance teacher resources between localities, especially in disadvantaged areas. Establishing a competitive salary and bonus system tailored to various positions (administrators, teachers, specialists, and researchers) would motivate educators to improve their qualifications and meet the sector's increasing demands.

The salary reform, effective from July 1, 2024, introduces significant changes to the salary structure for Vietnamese teachers. The system has been simplified by abolishing the base salary and salary coefficient, replacing them with a specific salary table. Previously, a teacher's salary was calculated as Base salary x Salary coefficient. According to Resolution 27-NQ/TW, the new salary structure consists of three components: salary, allowances, and bonuses, calculated as follows: Teacher's salary = Salary + Allowances + Bonuses (if any). Resolution 27 establishes two salary tables: one for officials, civil servants, and public employees in leadership roles at all political levels, and another for professional and occupational civil servants and public employees without leadership roles. Salaries will increase by 7% annually to compensate for inflation and ensure a decent living standard for teachers.

Promote STEM Education

Integrating STEM Into the Curriculum

Integrating STEM education into the curriculum is essential for developing a generation in Vietnam that is creative, dynamic, and adaptable. STEM projects, innovation contests, and field trips can effectively ignite students' interest in science, technology, and engineering while equipping them with the skills needed for success in the digital age. Reducing curriculum content at all levels is also necessary to create more room for STEM activities. By adopting Singapore's "Teach Less, Learn More" model, Vietnam's education can shift its focus from extensive theoretical instruction to fostering students' critical thinking and problem-solving abilities. Reducing theoretical workloads allows for more time dedicated to practical activities, research, and exploration. Strengthening collaboration among schools, research institutions, businesses, and social organizations can expand the STEM ecosystem beyond schools, enabling students to apply their knowledge practically and explore their potential.

To comprehensively assess STEM education outcomes, a diverse evaluation system is needed that not only focuses on theoretical knowledge but also assesses students' practical skills, creativity, and teamwork abilities.

Enhancing Educators' Capacity for STEM Education

Improving STEM education quality requires substantial investment in teacher training and development. Diverse and continuous professional development programs should be designed to provide teachers with advanced STEM knowledge, modern pedagogical techniques, integrated teaching strategies, and the skills to foster creativity and problem-solving in students. Bridging gaps in teachers' expertise through interdisciplinary teaching initiatives is a practical approach. Encouraging collaboration among teachers from different subject areas to co-design and deliver STEM curricula helps students grasp the interconnections across STEM fields while offering educators opportunities to refine their expertise and create high-quality STEM lessons.

Investing in modern teaching facilities and equipment is also crucial. Well-equipped laboratories, workshops, and learning tools enable students to engage in hands-on activities, experiments, and explorations, fostering interest and developing practical skills.

Encouraging Enrollment in STEM Fields

To attract more students to STEM fields, effective outreach and communication strategies are essential to convey the importance of these fields and their career opportunities. Providing comprehensive information on STEM programs to students and parents helps them make informed career choices. Financial support, such as scholarships and preferential loans, is also critical in encouraging students to pursue STEM studies.

In addition to outreach and financial incentives, establishing a transitional program for Arts and Science graduates interested in STEM could equip them with the necessary skills for successful career transitions and address workforce demands.

Balance Training Across Sectors

Addressing the imbalance between labor supply and demand calls for coordinated efforts across all levels of government and sectors. Developing a flexible education and training system that adapts to the evolving needs of the labor market is an essential and urgent solution.

Strengthening partnerships between educational institutions and enterprises is essential. Through collaborative activities such as workshops, internships, and joint training programs, educational institutions can stay informed of the latest workforce requirements and adjust their training accordingly. At the same time, enterprises can participate in the training process, ensuring that students are equipped with practical knowledge and skills aligned with market demands.

Building a comprehensive and accurate labor market information system is also crucial. This system should provide detailed information on occupations, workforce demand, job prospects, income, and related support policies, enabling students, parents, and educational institutions to make informed decisions. The Ministry of Labor, Invalids, and Social Affairs, in coordination with the Ministries of Information and Communications and Education and Training, should lead the development and implementation of this system.

Adjusting enrollment quotas to reflect labor market demand is another important solution. Educational institutions should flexibly adjust quotas to avoid a surplus or shortage of workers in certain fields, requiring close collaboration among educational institutions, ministries, and government agencies.

Finally, enhancing career guidance quality helps students make informed career decisions. In addition to providing detailed labor market information, practical experience activities, such as internships and simulated work environments, can help students better understand the demands of different occupations, discover their abilities, and align their career goals accordingly.

In conclusion, balancing labor supply and demand requires cooperation among all stakeholders—from the government and enterprises to educational institutions. A flexible education and training system tailored to labor market needs, stronger partnerships between schools and businesses, a labor market information system, and improved career guidance will contribute to a high-quality workforce that meets national development needs.

Enhance Investment in Education

Increasing investment in education is a critical component of Vietnam's sustainable development strategy. The Politburo's Conclusion No. 91-KL/TW, issued on August 12, 2024, reaffirmed the importance of enhancing education quality in line with Resolution No. 29-NQ/TW, with an emphasis on increased investment. Similarly, Decision No. 2236/QĐ-BGDĐT outlines key tasks and solutions for the 2024–2025 academic year, including prioritizing investments in infrastructure, curriculum innovation, and teaching methods to create a modern educational environment with access to advanced technologies.

The state needs to implement appropriate policies to improve infrastructure and secure financial resources for educational activities. This includes prioritizing the state budget for education to reach at least 20% of the total budget, as stipulated in Resolution 29-NQ/TW. Programs to strengthen school infrastructure and build national-standard schools should be aggressively pursued, aiming for 100% reinforced classrooms by 2030. Special attention should be paid to disadvantaged areas, such as ethnic minority regions and remote areas, to bridge the gaps in educational quality.

To mobilize and efficiently utilize resources, the state should improve investment mechanisms and policies. Moving from a uniform allocation model to demand-driven, task-oriented, or bidding approaches will foster a competitive environment and optimize budget use. This implies educational institutions must demonstrate their ability to utilize these resources most effectively. Creating a supportive environment for private and international investments in education is equally essential.

Expanding international cooperation and attracting foreign investment are also priorities. Decree No. 125/2024/ND–CP provides a favorable legal framework, simplifying procedures and offering incentives for foreign investment in education. As of June 2024, Vietnam had attracted 605 foreign investment projects in the education sector, with a total value of over $4.57 billion. Approximately 430 joint training programs with foreign partners have been implemented across 65 universities, with five foreign-invested universities operating in Vietnam. This underscores the potential of Vietnamese education and its growing appeal to foreign investors.

Finally, increasing financial resources for higher education is essential, with a target to reach 1.5% of GDP by 2030, up from 0.6% in 2020 (GSO, 2021). The state should continue to provide funding for autonomous universities, as practiced in developed countries. Currently, Vietnamese universities rely heavily on tuition fees, accounting for 60–90% of total revenue, compared to much lower proportions in other countries. For instance, in the United States, tuition fees make up only 20% of revenue for public universities, with the state contributing 43%, while in New Zealand, tuition fees account for 28%, and the government provides 42% (National Assembly's Committee on Culture and Education, 2023). Regular budget cuts could pose challenges for Vietnamese universities, potentially affecting the quality of education and research.

Ensure a High-Quality Workforce

To develop a high-quality workforce, Vietnam can learn from the successful models of developed countries, especially East Asian economies. These nations have demonstrated the pivotal role of education in building knowledge-based, high-productivity economies. Substantial investments in education not only elevate the educational level of the workforce but also foster innovation, creativity, and economic competitiveness.

A key solution lies in enhancing the quality of vocational and professional training. Successful models, such as Germany's dual training system, Norway's integrated theoretical and practical training approach, and Japan's Kosen system, have demonstrated their effectiveness in developing a skilled workforce. Strong collaboration between educational institutions and enterprises, coupled with government support and funding, has fostered an environment that prioritizes practical, high-quality training aligned with labor market needs.

Integrating technology into education is another important trend. South Korea has built a high-tech economy by investing heavily in science and technology education. The establishment of leading research institutes and strong partnerships between academia and industry have supported talent development and facilitated technology transfer.

The government also plays a vital role in fostering a high-quality workforce. This includes formulating priority policies for education and training, securing sufficient funding for these activities, and creating a favorable legal environment to support the growth of educational institutions and businesses. By combining these elements, Vietnam can build a workforce that meets the demands of a modern economy and advances sustainable development.

Promoting an Innovation Ecosystem

Fostering innovation within educational institutions and enterprises is fundamental to Vietnam's economic and social development. Decree No. 109/2022/ND–CP provides universities with a specific legal framework for science and technology activities, emphasizing the importance of research capacity and technology application as foundations for training high-quality human resources and promoting creativity and technology transfer. The decree also encourages collaboration between universities and enterprises to develop high-impact scientific and technological products, strengthening the link between research and practice.

Decision No. 569/QĐ-TTg, approving the "Strategy for Science, Technology, and Innovation Development to 2030," aims to make science, technology, and innovation key drivers of economic development. This strategy emphasizes creating a supportive environment for scientific research in both educational and business sectors. Increasing investment in research and development and encouraging enterprise participation in innovation are central to the strategy.

In this context, the government's role is essential. It has proactively established mechanisms to encourage collaboration between educational institutions and enterprises, including financial support policies, tax incentives, and clear regulations on intellectual property rights. These measures promote the development of new products and technologies and enhance Vietnam's competitiveness on the global stage. With a long-term vision and concrete steps, the government's commitment to fostering innovation is setting Vietnam on a path to not only participate but also lead in the future science and technology revolution.

Acknowledgements This chapter was funded by the University of Economics Ho Chi Minh City (UEH), Vietnam. Data collection was conducted by Hieu Minh Ngo of the Vietnam–Netherlands Programme at the UEH.

References

Academy of Finance. (2020). *Research on proposed solutions to improve the efficiency and effectiveness of state budget expenditure for education in Vietnam*. Project code KHGD/16-20.ĐT.023. National Science and Technology Program 2016–2020.

Aghion, P., & Howitt, P. (2006). Appropriate growth policy: A unifying framework. *Journal of the European Economic Association*, *4*(2–3), 269–314.

Becker, G. S. (1964). *Human Capital.* NBER.

Benhabib, J., & Spiegel, M. M. (1994). The role of human capital in economic development evidence from aggregate cross-country data. *Journal of Monetary Economics*, *34*(2), 143–173.

Benos, N., & Zotou, S. (2014). Education and economic growth: A meta-regression analysis. *World Development*, *64*, 669–689.

BIBB. (2017). *Datasheet on dual VET.* https://www.bibb.de/govet/en/54886.php

BIBB. (2018). *Online documentation.* https://kongress2018.bibb.de/en/congress/online-documentation/index.html

Bodewig, C., Badiani-Magnusson, R., Macdonald, K., Newhouse, D., & Rutkowski, J. (2014). *Skilling up Vietnam: Preparing the workforce for a modern market economy.* World Bank Publications.

Chang, J. H., & Huynh, P. (2016). *ASEAN in transformation: The future of jobs at risk of automation.* International Labour Organization.

Circular No. 20/2022/TT-BGDĐT promulgating the Regulation on the organization and operation of the center for inclusive education Development Support Center. (2022).

Circular No. 23/2023/TT-BGDĐT on Vietnamese teaching and learning for pre-first-grade children of ethnic minority groups. (2023).

Circular No. 33/2021/TT-BGDĐT on the Illiteracy Elimination Programme. (2021).

Conclusion No. 91-KL/TW on the continued implementation of Resolution No. 29-NQ/TW. (n.d.).

Cörvers, F. (1994). *Human capital factors at the firm level* (Working Paper 7E). Research Centre for Education and the Labour Market.

CSIRO. (2021). *Report on technological innovation in Vietnam—The contribution of technology to economic growth.* http://dean844.most.gov.vn/doi-moi-cong-nghe-o-viet-nam-dong-gop-cua-cong-nghe-vao-tang-truong-kinh-te.htm

Decision No. 2236/QĐ-BGDĐT on the Plan of key tasks and solutions for the 2024–2025 school year of the Education sector in Vietnam. (2024).

Decision No. 569/QĐ-TTg on Promulgating the Strategy for the development of science, technology, and innovation by 2030. (n.d.).

Decision No. 89/QĐ-TTg of 2019 approving the proposal for enhancing competencies of lecturers and administrators of higher education institutions meeting requirements for radical changes in education and training during the period of 2019–2030. (2019).

Decree No. 108/2014/NĐ-CP on downsizing policies. (2014).

Decree No. 109/2022/NĐ-CP on regulations on scientific and technological activities in higher education institutions. (2022).

Decree No. 125/2024/NĐ-CP on regulatory requirements for educational investment and operation. (2024).

Decree No. 71/2020/NĐ-CP on providing the roadmap for raising qualification standards for teachers of early childhood, primary and lower secondary schools. (2020).

Decree No. 81/2021/NĐ-CP on the mechanism of collection and management of tuition fees for education institutions under the national education system and policies on tuition fee exemption and reduction, support for study costs and service charges in the field of education and training. (2021).

Decree No. 97/2023/NĐ-CP on amending and supplementing a number of articles of Decree No. 81/2021/ND-CP. (2023).

Frey, C. B., & Osborne, M. A. (2017). The future of employment: How susceptible are jobs to computerisation? *Technological Forecasting and Social Change, 114*, 254–280.

General Statistics Office. (2021). *Education and training in Vietnam - Evaluation results from the 2021 Economic Census.*

General Statistics Office. (2022). *Report on labor force survey 2020.* https://www.gso.gov.vn/en/data-and-statistics/2022/02/report-on-labor-force-survey-2020-2/

General Statistics Office. (2023). *Report on Vietnam's Labor Productivity 2011–2020: Status and Solutions.*

Hanushek, E. A., & Woessmann, L. (2008). The roles of cognitive skills in economic development. *Journal of Economic Literature, 46*(3), 607–668.

Hockenos, P. (2018). *How Germany's vocational education and training system works.* Clean Energy Wire. https://www.cleanenergywire.org/factsheets/how-germanys-vocational-education-and-training-system-works

Hua, P. (2005). *How does education at all levels influence productivity growth? Evidence from the Chinese provinces* (CERDI Working Paper No. 200515). CERDI.

ILO, General Statistics Office of Vietnam, Ministry of Labour, Invalids and Social Affairs. (2018). *Viet Nam National Child Labour Survey 2018.*

Jayadevan, C. M., Hoang, N. T., & Yarram, S. R. (2023). Human capital and the middle-income trap revisited. *Applied Economics, 55*(34), 4003–4022.

Kucharčíková, A. (2011). The human capital as the production factor. *Scientific Papers of the University of Pardubice, Series D, Faculty of Economics and Administration, 19*(1), 1–15.

Lee, E. (2007). *The role of education upgrading and experience accumulation in driving labour productivity growth in Hong Kong.* Third Quarter Economic Report.

Lucas Jr, R. E. (1988). On the mechanics of economic development. *Journal of Monetary Economics, 22*(1), 3–42.

Mankiw, N. G., Romer, D., & Weil, D. N. (1992). A contribution to the empirics of economic growth. *The Quarterly Journal of Economics, 107*(2), 407–437.

Mincer, J. A. (1974). Schooling and earnings. In *Schooling, Experience, and Earnings* (pp. 41–63). NBER.
National Assembly's Committee on Culture and Education. (2023). *Proceedings of the 2023 education conference: institutions and policies to improve the quality of higher education.*
Nelson, R. R., & Phelps, E. S. (1966). Investment in humans, technological diffusion, and economic growth. *The American Economic Review*, *56*(1/2), 69–75.
Organisation for Economic Co-operation and Development. (2020). *Analysis of the Vietnam labour force survey 2018.* OECD.
Otsuka, K., Higuchi, Y., & Sonobe, T. (2017). Middle-income traps in East Asia: An inquiry into causes for slowdown in income growth. *China Economic Review*, *46*, S3–S16.
Qutb, R. (2017). How education does at all levels influence total factors productivity growth? *International Research Journal of Finance and Economics*, *159*, 1–15.
Resolution No. 27-NQ/TW on reform of pay policy for public officials and public employees, armed forces' personnel and employees in enterprise. (n.d.).
Resolution No. 29-NQ/TW on "fundamental and comprehensive innovation in education, serving industrialization and modernization in a socialist-oriented market economy during international integration". (n.d.)
Resolution No. 37/2004/NQ-QH11 on education. (2004).
Romer, P. M. (1990). Endogenous technological change. *Journal of Political Economy*, *98*(5, Part 2), S71–S102.
Sarquis, J. B., & Arbache, J. S. (2002). *Human capital, external effects and technical change.* London School of Economics & Universidade de Brasília.
Schultz, T. W. (1961). Investment in human capital. *The American Economic Review*, *51*(1), 1–17.
Schultz, T. W. (1981). *Investing in people: The economics of population quality.* University of California Press.
Stokey, N. L. (1988). Learning by doing and the introduction of new goods. *Journal of Political Economy*, *96*(4), 701–717.
UNICEF. (2022). *Vietnam Education Summary Report 2022.*
Vietnam Financial Times. (2023, December 5). The linkage between FDI enterprises and domestic enterprises remains weak. https://thoibaotaichinhvietnam.vn/lien-ket-giua-doanh-nghiep-fdi-va-doanh-nghiep-trong-nuoc-con-yeu-140874.html
Vietnam Institute of Educational Sciences. (2022). *Vietnam education sector analysis report 2011–2020.* Vietnam National University Press.
Vietnam Ministry of Education and Training. (2023). *Comprehensive report on the planning of higher education and teacher training institution network, 2021–2030, with a vision to 2050.*

Vietnam Ministry of Finance. (2018, March 19). Strengthening linkages between FDI enterprises and domestic enterprises. https://mof.gov.vn/webcenter/portal/btcvn/pages_r/l/tin-bo-tai-chinh?dDocName=UCMTMP120634

Vietnamnet. (2024). *General secretary: The state should take responsibility for school-age children*. https://vietnamnet.vn/en/general-secretary-the-state-should-take-responsibility-for-school-age-children-2348586.html

Wei, Z., & Hao, R. (2011). The role of human capital in China's total factor productivity growth: A cross-province analysis. *The Developing Economies*, *49*(1), 1–35.

Welch, F. (1970). Education in production. *Journal of Political Economy*, *78*(1), 35–59.

Yem, V. V. (2023). *Some investment policies for the development of higher education in Vietnam*. National Assembly Library. http://thuvienso.quochoi.vn/handle/11742/58459

CHAPTER 12

Human Capital 3: Reverse Migration

Introduction

Migration has long been a critical factor shaping economies and societies worldwide, influencing labor markets, urbanization, and demographic trends. As countries face varying challenges, such as population decline in developed nations or economic pressures in developing regions, understanding the complexities of migration becomes essential. The movement of people, whether driven by economic opportunity, education, or better living conditions, has profound implications for public services, social welfare systems, and employment dynamics. However, migration also poses challenges, including labor market integration, urban congestion, and the economic costs of supporting migrant populations. These multifaceted issues call for a deeper exploration of migration patterns and their socio-economic impacts.

A review of previous research is vital to understanding these migration phenomena, as it allows us to build on existing knowledge and identify key factors that influence migration outcomes. By examining empirical studies, we can uncover the diverse experiences of migrants, the effectiveness of policies designed to support them, and the long-term implications for both sending and receiving regions. Such a review not only highlights gaps in

Contributed by Hoai Trong Nguyen

H. T. Dinh, H. T. Nguyen, *Vietnam's Economic Leap*,
https://doi.org/10.1007/978-3-032-08904-5_12

current research but also informs future studies and policymaking, ensuring that strategies to address migration are evidence-based and context-specific. This comprehensive understanding is crucial for developing effective policies that can maximize the benefits of migration while mitigating its challenges.

Empirical Studies on Migration

Mardonov (2024) explored the relationship between increasing urbanization and population decline in developed countries, emphasizing the associated issues and potential solutions. While urbanization, driven by migration from rural areas to cities, often contributes to economic growth and improved living standards, it also brings demographic challenges, such as declining birth rates and an aging population. These new trends can create several difficulties for developed nations, including a shrinking labor force, reduced economic productivity, and increased pressure on social welfare systems. It also affects consumer demand and strains public services, such as healthcare and education, which were originally designed for larger populations.

Li et al. (2024) conducted a study to investigate how urban integration influences migrants' intentions to settle in cities. Using data from the China Migrants Dynamic Survey (2012–2017), the study identifies four key dimensions of urban integration: economic, healthcare, social, and psychological. The findings reveal that psychological integration has the most significant impact on both settlement and residency intentions, followed by social, healthcare, and economic integration. Migrants with higher incomes, better education, non-agricultural household registration, and marital status show stronger intentions to settle. Personal factors, such as household registration, gender, education level, and marital status, significantly moderate the relationship between urban integration and settlement intentions. The research highlights the need for comprehensive urban integration policies to strengthen migrants' willingness to settle, emphasizing the importance of economic support, healthcare services, social participation, and psychological acceptance (Li et al., 2024).

The reviewed studies highlight the diverse impacts of migration on labor markets, urbanization, and demographic trends. Mardonov (2024) explored the link between urbanization and population decline in developed countries, noting the challenges posed by shrinking labor forces and aging populations. Díaz-Sánchez and Correa (2024) examined immigration in Ecuador, revealing the difficulties that recent international and domestic migrants face in accessing formal employment. Li et al. (2024) focused on urban integration in

China, emphasizing the importance of psychological and social integration for migrants' settlement intentions. Awasthi and Mehta (2020) studied out-migration from India's mountainous Uttarakhand region, identifying economic pressures as the key driver of permanent migration, further exacerbated by the COVID-19 pandemic. Collectively, these studies underscore the complex dynamics of migration and the necessity of targeted policies to address both migration challenges and opportunities.

Migration Trends in Vietnam

The labor market in Vietnam, particularly in urban centers like Ho Chi Minh City and others in Southeast Asia, reflects the broader economic challenges and migration trends facing the country. While Ho Chi Minh City, as well as Southeast Asia, have experienced robust economic growth driven by skilled labor, technological advancements, and policies supporting gender equality, regions like the Mekong Delta are grappling with out-migration and limited job opportunities. This disparity underscores a critical issue: the uneven economic development across regions, leading to mass migration from rural areas such as the Mekong Delta to more industrialized cities. The outflow of workers, particularly the youth, not only exacerbates the economic stagnation of less-developed regions but also places a strain on urban centers, contributing to issues like overcrowding and inequality.

Understanding and addressing these migration patterns is essential for promoting balanced economic development across Vietnam. By exploring the factors driving youth migration and the migration of workers from rural areas, particularly from regions like the Mekong Delta, it becomes clear that targeted interventions are needed. Investments in local infrastructure, industry, and education, alongside policies that promote innovation and entrepreneurship, can help create sustainable economic opportunities in underdeveloped areas, thereby reducing the need for migration. This review of labor market trends and migration patterns is crucial for informing policymakers and stakeholders on how to create a more equitable and prosperous future for all regions in Vietnam.

Mass migration from the Mekong Delta to South-East provinces in Vietnam is largely due to limited job opportunities, unattractive economic prospects, and inadequate economic development policies in the region. Addressing this requires several solutions. Prioritizing local economic development by increasing investment in key industries and establishing industrial clusters can encourage businesses to invest in agricultural production and food processing. Additionally, improving infrastructure such as transportation, electricity, and water systems, and enhancing education and healthcare services are crucial. Labor support policies, such as free or low-cost vocational training programs, can encourage young workers to build careers in their hometowns. Strengthening business-farmer connections to create value chains in agricultural production would further boost economic opportunities. Finally, promoting innovation and entrepreneurship in agriculture and technology through loans, tax incentives, and technical assistance can help curb mass migration by creating sustainable job opportunities in the Mekong Delta. To sum up, this perspective aligns with several previous studies, which suggest that combining industrial and agricultural sectors can stimulate sustainable economic growth in rural regions by diversifying job opportunities and reducing the economic reliance on agriculture alone. Expanding into industrial clusters could create a more balanced economic structure, providing a solution to the outmigration problem and promoting long-term regional development.

Reverse Migration: Theoretical and Practical Context

Theoretical Context

The trend of reverse migration from urban to rural areas can be understood through several key theoretical frameworks. Migration systems theory of Faist (1997) emphasizes the interconnectedness of migration regions and the influence of economic, social, and political factors on migration patterns. Push-pull theory of Lee (1966) explains migration by identifying push factors from the origin and pull factors from the destination that drive migration decisions. The human capital theory of Becker (1964) posits that individuals make migration choices based on the economic returns and associated costs of relocation. Granovetter (1973), in his social network theory, highlights the role of social networks in facilitating and sustaining migration processes. Finally, the theory of social change of Ogburn (1922) underscores how large-scale societal shifts, such as technological advancements or pandemics, can impact migration dynamics. Collectively, these theories provide a comprehensive framework for analyzing the drivers and factors influencing the reverse migration trend from urban to rural areas (Becker, 1964; Faist, 1997; Granovetter, 1973; Lee, 1966; Ogburn, 1922).

Faist's migration systems theory (1997) highlights the interaction between migration regions and economic, social, and political factors. According to Faist, migration is not solely driven by economic factors, such as income levels and job opportunities, but also by social networks and political policies. Social factors, including family and friend networks and migrant communities, offer essential support and information. Political factors, such as immigration laws and political stability, also play a crucial role. This theory provides a flexible and comprehensive framework for understanding migration drivers and consequences in the context of globalization.

Push-pull theory of Lee (1966) explains migration through the identification of push factors at the place of origin and pull factors at the destination. Push factors, such as unemployment, conflict, or natural disasters, compel people to leave, while pull factors, such as job opportunities, higher living standards, and safer environments, attract them to migrate. Migration decisions result from weighing and comparing these push and pull factors along with the barriers and opportunities encountered throughout the migration process.

The human capital theory of Becker (1964) suggests that individuals make migration decisions based on the economic benefits and costs associated with the move. Migration, according to Becker, is an investment in human capital. Migrants weigh potential benefits, such as higher income and better job opportunities, against costs like relocation expenses, the loss of social networks, and uncertainties. When the expected benefits outweigh the costs, individuals are more likely to migrate. This theory emphasizes the significance of economic factors in migration decisions, framing migration as an investment in one's future.

In his book "Human Capital: A Theoretical and Empirical Analysis, with Special Reference to Education," Becker (1964) argued that education and training are investments in human capital that increase productivity and income. He examined the relationship between education, skills, and income, showing how investment in human capital drives economic growth and shapes income distribution. Becker's work underscores the vital role of economic factors in decisions related to education and training, viewing them as essential investments in both personal and societal development.

Granovetter (1973) developed social network theory, emphasizing the importance of social relationships in facilitating migration. Granovetter argued that social networks, particularly weak ties, provide information, financial assistance, and emotional support to migrants, helping mitigate the risks and costs associated with migration. This theory demonstrates that migration is not purely an economic decision but a complex social process where social connections play a crucial role.

Among these theories, Faist's (1997) theory of migration systems is considered the most comprehensive, as it integrates economic, social, and political factors, providing a more nuanced understanding of migration processes. While the push-pull theory of Lee (1966) focuses on specific factors driving migration and human capital theory of Becker (1964) frames migration as an economic decision, Faist's approach offers a more holistic explanation of the drivers and consequences of migration in a globalized world.

Reverse migration post-COVID-19 can be explained through these theoretical lenses. Push-pull theory of Lee (1966) suggests that difficult conditions in urban areas, such as high unemployment, expensive living costs, and environmental pollution, push people to leave in search of better opportunities in rural areas. At the same time, rural areas offer pull factors, such as job opportunities in agriculture, a cleaner environment, and lower living costs. The human capital theory of Becker (1964) frames migration from urban to rural areas as an investment decision, where individuals weigh the economic benefits, such as a lower cost of living, against the costs, including relocation expenses and potential loss of social networks. Social network theory of Granovetter (1973) highlights the role of strong social relationships in both urban and rural areas, helping to reduce the risks and costs of migration while enhancing the appeal of rural living. These theories provide valuable insights into the drivers and consequences of reverse migration in the context of globalization and economic development.

Practical Context

During the COVID-19 pandemic, reverse migration became a key topic, with many articles and media outlets discussing a "rural revival" that reflected the "urban exodus" hypothesis. González-Leonardo et al. (2022) documented a 20.5% increase in internal migration to rural areas in Spain during 2020, with a net gain of 88,000 people, far exceeding pre-pandemic levels. Using administrative population registry data, González-Leonardo et al. analyzed the main types of rural areas attracting internal migrants and the demographic characteristics of those migrants. The study found that migration to rural areas near cities and those with a high proportion of second homes increased significantly in 2020, with a wide range of domestic migrants, from young people and families to retirees. Migration patterns remained elevated in 2021, although outmigration returned to pre-pandemic levels. Foreign-born individuals, particularly from Latin America, also contributed to these migration flows.

Khan and Arokkiaraj (2021) explored the challenges of reverse migration in India during the COVID-19 pandemic, focusing on both domestic and international migrant workers. Factors such as unemployment, competitive labor markets, and better livelihood prospects initially drove migration. However, the pandemic and lockdowns led to reverse migration, requiring coordinated government strategies for economic reintegration. Challenges faced by returning migrants included wage theft, unemployment, stigma, discrimination, and mobility difficulties due to poor coordination among different levels of government. At the same time, the Indian government implemented relief measures and long-term reintegration programs.

Hu et al. (2023) examine the emerging trend of reverse migration in both developed and developing countries, with a specific focus on China. The question of whether reverse migrants complement or substitute local labor remains underexplored. In their study, the authors develop a theoretical model to uncover the effects of reverse migration on rural populations. Using a self-collected nationwide household survey dataset, which includes agricultural production and income data from rural China, they investigate how reverse migrants influence rural household incomes, including income growth, relative income, and expected income growth. The results show that reverse migration negatively affects rural household income due to competition and spillover effects between reverse migrants and local villagers. The study also examines the identity of reverse migrants before and after their return to clarify the transmission channels of these effects. The authors suggest that the government should continue to encourage urbanization and promote reverse migrants' engagement in complementary work with local villagers.

Wang et al. (2024) used data from the 2017 China Migrants Dynamic Survey to empirically examine the impact of rural e-commerce development on migrants' intentions to return. They found that the development of rural e-commerce significantly increases migrants' desire to return, particularly in eastern regions, among interprovincial migrants, and among unemployed migrants. These findings offer valuable insights into rural-urban migration patterns and rural development strategies.

Ghani and Morgandi (2023) explored the impact of reverse migration on labor market outcomes, particularly wages, consumption, and worker welfare in South Asia. The pandemic triggered unprecedented changes, leading to significant volatility and the reverse migration of millions of workers over the past two years. This reverse migration could expand the labor force and employment in South Asia. Ghani and Morgandi (2023) found heterogeneous results in labor returns depending on workers' skill levels and industries, with manufacturing and services seeing greater demand increases than agriculture and primary industries.

Rajan and Arcand (2023) focus on reverse migration caused by the COVID-19 pandemic in South and Southeast Asia. Their research compiles primary and secondary data to document the effects of lockdowns and mobility restrictions on migrants, migration flows as borders reopened, and conditions upon their return. The pandemic led to a sharp decline in remittances, widespread unemployment, and severe income losses among migrants. Major challenges included migration logistics, reintegration after returning home, and insufficient government support. The study emphasizes the need for effective reintegration policies to support returning migrants.

Shen et al. (2023) found that in efforts to promote local socioeconomic development in developing countries, attracting younger generations to return to their hometowns for work and entrepreneurship by improving their identification with rural society and focusing on organizational factors has proven highly effective. Shen et al. conducted an empirical study to explore the impact of organizational factors on young returnees' identification with rural societies. Data were collected from 2202 questionnaires across 31 provinces. The results indicate that organizational factors in rural society can enhance returnees' material, relational, and personal adaptability, improving their identification with rural life. Material adaptation, including consumption patterns, employment structures, and social security, forms the external foundation for identification. Personal adaptation, including self-identification, self-efficacy, and personal expectations, provides the intrinsic motivation for returnees to identify with rural society. Social support through blood ties, professional connections, and geographic relationships also strengthens returnees' integration. However, there was insufficient evidence to conclude that group adaptation is a key factor influencing identification.

Farooq and Arif (2023) investigates the negative impacts of the COVID-19 pandemic on the overseas migration of Pakistani workers, focusing on both outbound and return flows. The primary objective is to propose a policy framework for the successful reintegration of returnees into their home communities. The findings reveal that around 2 million overseas Pakistanis were affected by the pandemic: 1.6 million were unable to migrate abroad, and approximately 300,000 to 400,000 were forced to return, primarily from the Middle East. The reintegration measures implemented by the Pakistani government were largely small-scale, and most returnees lacked information about available government support and tracking mechanisms. The proposed reintegration policy framework suggests that potential migrants and their families should be educated about reintegration or resettlement options within their home communities when planning to work abroad. Proper use of remittances, channeled into productive investments, would not only ensure the successful reintegration of returning workers but also promote domestic entrepreneurship, creating more job opportunities. Government support and district-level opportunities are crucial in ensuring the various aspects of reintegration, including economic self-sufficiency, social stability, and the psychosocial well-being of returnees.

Low et al. (2023) examine the impact of the COVID-19 pandemic on preferences for rural migration in Northwest Missouri. The research finds that while the pandemic did not significantly increase the appeal of rural living for those who had previously left the area, it did enhance the attractiveness for self-employed individuals and those with a strong sense of community belonging. Women, parents with children, and older individuals also showed a greater preference for rural living. The study suggests that targeted efforts to attract entrepreneurs, early retirees, and families with children, along with initiatives to strengthen community engagement, could be effective strategies for rural development. These findings offer valuable insights for policymakers seeking to counter population decline in less amenity-rich rural areas.

Saklani et al. (2021) employ both quantitative and qualitative methods to explore the push and pull factors influencing reverse migration and the socio-economic conditions of reverse migrants during the first wave of the COVID-19 pandemic. The findings show that, before the COVID-19 pandemic, push factors such as unemployment and poor agricultural productivity, combined with pull factors like better employment opportunities, drove migration. During the pandemic, fear of COVID-19, job loss, food insecurity, and loneliness were the primary reasons for reverse migration. In terms of socio-economic conditions, most reverse migrants were aged 20–34, predominantly male, married, and had secondary or higher education, with employment in the private sector. Migrants experienced significant income reductions during the pandemic, particularly among lower-income groups. The study highlights the need for comprehensive government strategies to support reverse migrants and address their socio-economic challenges.

The study by Zhou et al. (2024) explores the impact of internal reverse migration on the entrepreneurial activities of rural households in China, utilizing data from the China Household Finance Survey (CHFS). The analysis demonstrates that reverse migration significantly increases the likelihood of rural households engaging in entrepreneurship, with education and household debt levels playing critical roles. Specifically, reverse migration raises the probability of rural households having entrepreneurial intentions by 2.7% and undertaking entrepreneurial activities by 21.3% (Zhou et al., 2024). Education and household debt act as key moderating factors, enhancing the influence of reverse migration on entrepreneurial intentions. The study highlights that facilitating education and financial support for returning migrants can foster a conducive entrepreneurial environment for rural households, thereby promoting rural economic development. Policymakers are encouraged to incentivize rural-to-urban migrants to return and participate in entrepreneurial activities through educational initiatives, access to credit, and other supportive interventions.

In Vietnam, reverse migration from urban to rural areas has not yet become a dominant trend. However, with the strong push from economic policies and investment in rural development, this trend has the potential to grow rapidly, creating new opportunities for sustainable development. Undeniably, rural areas face challenges such as insufficient job creation and underdeveloped agricultural entrepreneurship models. Moreover, many rural residents have abandoned agriculture, leading to a shortage of skilled labor in the sector. Climate change, including salinization and drought in the Mekong Delta, has further exacerbated these challenges, highlighting the need for supportive policies to improve rural infrastructure, create stable employment opportunities, and promote sustainable agricultural entrepreneurship models that enhance climate resilience.

International Experience on Reverse Migration

Lessons from immigration studies offer valuable insights for policy development in Vietnam. These lessons offer Vietnam a framework to develop policies that enhance immigrant participation in the labor force, improve living conditions, and promote sustainable economic development. Regarding reverse migration, several important lessons from international studies can be applied in Vietnam. Drawing from international experiences, particularly from China and Japan, Vietnam can develop a comprehensive policy framework to encourage young people to return to rural areas and engage in entrepreneurial activities, especially as urban areas become increasingly expensive.

The factors discussed below provide a comprehensive understanding of the drivers behind reverse migration, as well as the challenges that must be addressed to support sustainable rural development.

Economic Factors

Living costs and employment opportunities are critical economic factors influencing reverse migration from urban to rural areas. Studies show that the cost of living in urban centers, including housing, food, services, and utilities, is significantly higher than in rural regions, prompting many individuals to migrate back to rural areas to reduce financial burdens (Lee, 1966). At the same time, rural employment prospects are improving due to the expansion of e-commerce and emerging economic sectors, creating favorable conditions for return migration (Wang et al., 2024). Strategic investments in these sectors have the potential to attract more workers to rural areas, contributing to local economic development.

Social Factors

Family reunification and community support are key social drivers of reverse migration. Returning to rural areas to live near family is a common motivation, particularly for the elderly and individuals with young children who require care and support (Lin et al., 2024). Community support, including social relationships and assistance from friends, relatives, and neighbors, also plays a crucial role in helping return migrants stabilize their lives and reintegrate into their communities (Granovetter, 1973). Studies show that individuals with strong social networks in rural areas are more likely to return and remain there (Shen et al., 2023).

Policy Factors

Government policies and rural development initiatives play a critical role in promoting reverse migration. Financial support programs, vocational training, and incentives for rural investment can help return migrants stabilize their lives and seek new employment opportunities (Farooq & Arif, 2023). Policies supporting infrastructure development, education, healthcare, and public services in rural areas are also key factors in improving the quality of life and attracting workers to return (Ogburn, 1922). The effectiveness of these policies must be continuously evaluated and improved to meet the needs of return migrants and promote sustainable rural development.

Psychological Factors

Quality of life and perceptions of safety are psychological factors influencing reverse migration. Many individuals choose to return to rural areas because they perceive a higher quality of life, characterized by a cleaner environment, more spacious living conditions, and less stress compared to urban areas (Li et al., 2024). Perceptions of safety, including personal and family security, are also significant. Studies indicate that safe living environments, social stability, and reduced crime rates are key factors attracting migrants back to rural areas (González-Leonardo et al., 2022).

Environmental Factors

Living conditions and climate change also play significant roles in reverse migration decisions. Rural living conditions, such as mild climates, abundant natural resources, and green spaces, create an ideal environment for many individuals (Hu et al., 2023). However, climate change and natural disasters can negatively impact migration decisions, as rural areas are often more vulnerable to droughts, floods, and extreme weather events (Becker, 1964). Developing strategies to address climate change and protect the environment is essential to creating sustainable living conditions that attract workers back to rural areas. Together, these factors provide a comprehensive understanding of the drivers behind reverse migration from urban to rural areas and the challenges that must be addressed to support sustainable rural development (Becker, 1964; Faist, 1997; Granovetter, 1973; Lee, 1966; Ogburn, 1922).

Policy Implication of Reverse Migration in Vietnam

Current Policy Context in Vietnam

In recent years, Vietnam has experienced a significant rural-to-urban migration. This movement is largely driven by rapid industrialization and the expansion of the service sectors in urban areas, which have created numerous employment opportunities. While this migration has contributed to the economic growth and urbanization of these regions, it has also resulted in serious socio-economic challenges for rural migrants. Many migrants, especially women, are employed in the informal sector, where they face low and unstable incomes. Additionally, the rising cost of living in major cities has led to a troubling phenomenon: many female workers are forced to leave their children behind in rural areas, often under the care of grandparents. This separation has significant social consequences, as the younger generation is deprived of proper care, education, and skill development, leading to a cycle of poverty and limiting their ability to contribute to economic growth.

In response to these issues, there has been a growing trend of reverse migration, with many migrants returning to rural areas in search of more sustainable living conditions. However, rural regions in Vietnam still face substantial challenges, including limited infrastructure and a lack of stable employment opportunities, making it difficult for returnees to improve their quality of life. Recognizing the need for comprehensive solutions, the Vietnamese government has implemented various policies aimed at promoting rural development and supporting reverse migration. Programs such as the National Target Program for New Rural Development and the Financial Assistance and Skills Training Program focus on enhancing rural infrastructure, creating stable job opportunities, and improving access to vocational training. These initiatives are designed to foster local economic development, encourage entrepreneurship, and reduce migration pressures on urban areas, ultimately contributing to balanced and sustainable growth across the country.

Rural-to-urban migration, especially from the Mekong Delta to Ho Chi Minh City and the Southeast provinces in Vietnam, has become widespread. These regions are experiencing rapid growth in the industrial and service sectors, with high urbanization rates contributing to the economic development of Ho Chi Minh City and the Southeast. However, an unintended consequence of this migration is that many rural migrants work in the informal sector, earning low and unstable incomes. The rising cost of services in major urban centers forces many female workers to leave their children in rural areas under the care of grandparents, leading to serious social issues. As a result, the younger generation is deprived of adequate care and education, lacks essential skills, and remains trapped in low-income jobs, unable to contribute to overall economic productivity and income growth.

As the cost of services in cities continues to rise without a corresponding increase in incomes, many migrants are returning to rural areas, where stable employment opportunities remain limited, making it difficult to improve their living conditions. This situation calls for comprehensive policies to address these root causes, including improving rural infrastructure, creating stable job opportunities, and enhancing skills for female workers so they can participate in the formal labor market, earning higher and more sustainable incomes.

Vietnam has implemented several policies to encourage and support reverse migration from urban to rural areas, focusing on local economic development and improving living conditions in rural regions. One notable policy is the National Target Program for New Rural Development (NTP-NRD), also known as "Tam Nông." This program promotes comprehensive rural development, including infrastructure upgrades, improved living conditions, and the creation of employment opportunities for rural residents (IOM Viet Nam, 2021). The government has also pursued the Socio-Economic Development Strategy, which aims to balance development between urban and rural areas. This strategy includes enhancing rural infrastructure, providing financial support for rural economic development projects, and facilitating entrepreneurship in rural areas (World Bank, 2020; UNFPA, 2021).

Another key initiative is the Financial Assistance and Skills Training Program, which helps rural residents improve their skills and access better employment opportunities. The government has also promoted the use of information and communication technology (ICT) to enhance production efficiency and expand agricultural markets, allowing rural workers to work remotely and reduce transportation costs (ADB, 2021; IOM, 2021). These policies not only improve living conditions in rural areas but also create favorable conditions to attract workers back to rural regions, thereby reducing pressure on major urban centers and promoting sustainable socio-economic development in rural areas.

The Rural Start-up and Development Program encourages young people to return to their hometowns to start businesses, fostering rural socio-economic development and alleviating migration pressures on major cities. Below are examples of provinces that have implemented this program, along with evaluations.

In Quang Ninh province, the "One Commune, One Product" (OCOP) program has achieved significant success. The program develops agricultural, non-agricultural, and service products that leverage local advantages. Quang Ninh has supported cooperatives and small and medium-sized enterprises (SMEs) in product development, from production and processing to marketing and distribution. As a result, many high-quality OCOP products have been developed, increasing local incomes, stabilizing livelihoods, and reducing migration to major cities. The "One Commune, One Product" (OCOP) program in Quang Ninh can certainly be scaled up across Vietnam by leveraging its success in developing agricultural, non-agricultural, and service products that capitalize on local advantages. To do so, the government can replicate the model in other provinces, tailoring it to local resources while providing financial incentives, technical assistance, and capacity-building programs to cooperatives and SMEs. Expanding digital platforms and e-commerce will allow OCOP products to reach wider markets, while strengthening supply chain logistics and ensuring product standardization will enhance competitiveness. Additionally, integrating OCOP with rural tourism can create synergies, further boosting local economies and reducing migration pressures. A national branding and marketing campaign, along with geographical indications, will elevate the visibility of OCOP products domestically and internationally, fostering sustainable economic development and job creation across rural regions.

In Dak Lak province, the agricultural start-up program has encouraged and supported young people in agricultural entrepreneurship. The program includes technical training, preferential loans, business consulting, and market access. Many young people in Dak Lak have successfully established effective business models, contributing to local socio-economic development and improving livelihoods.

In Dong Thap province, the agricultural start-up support program has focused on high-tech farming models such as greenhouses and automated irrigation systems. The program has provided technical assistance, high-quality crop and livestock varieties, and organized workshops and start-up conferences to share experiences. Many agricultural start-ups in Dong Thap have succeeded in producing high-quality products and expanding market access.

The Rural Start-up and Development Program has provided substantial benefits to various provinces across Vietnam. Technical support activities, preferential loans, and market connections have created favorable conditions for young people to start businesses and develop enterprises in their hometowns. The positive outcomes from provinces such as Quang Ninh, Dak Lak, and Dong Thap demonstrate the program's effectiveness in increasing income, improving living standards, and reducing migration pressures on large urban areas. The successful implementation of this program reflects the Vietnamese government's commitment to promoting rural socio-economic development and supporting young entrepreneurs.

Beyond Quang Ninh, Dak Lak, and Dong Thap, other provinces have also implemented rural start-up and development initiatives. For instance, Lam Dong province introduced the High-Tech Agricultural Start-up Support Program to encourage advanced technology application in agriculture, boosting productivity and product quality. Bac Giang province's Local Specialty Product Start-up and Development Program focuses on promoting local specialties such as lychees, Van Village traditional wine, and Yen The hill chickens. Key activities include organizing start-up workshops and conferences, offering loan support, and providing product development consulting. These efforts have led to high-quality certifications for local specialties, which are now widely sold in both domestic and international markets (Government News, 2023). Nghe An province's Start-up and Innovation Support Program promotes value-added processed agricultural products, fostering entrepreneurship in the agricultural processing sector.

Overall, this current policy context already includes financial support, capacity building and training, infrastructure and service improvements, tax incentives, market development, and innovation encouragement. The rural start-up fund offers interest-free loans for the first five years and initial investment grants for start-up projects. The entrepreneurship training and mentorship program organizes courses and connects experts with young entrepreneurs. Rural infrastructure and services are being upgraded to facilitate business operations and improve living conditions, while new businesses are eligible for income tax reductions and property tax exemptions during their early stages. In addition, the current policies also supports market access through agricultural fairs and branding for local products. An agricultural innovation center will be established to promote technology use and creativity, with start-up competitions offering financial and technical support. These measures create a favorable environment for young people to return to their hometowns to start businesses, contributing to the sustainable development of rural areas. This also aims to alleviate population and economic pressures on major urban centers while promoting balanced development across regions.

Regions with tailored immigration strategies that align with their development goals could further boost local industries and economies. Flexible immigration policies that offer employment opportunities and support services could attract talent and contribute to regional socio-economic development. Moreover, increasing the participation of women, older workers, and immigrants in the labor force can significantly boost Vietnam's economic growth and development. Therefore, addressing challenges and creating opportunities for these groups is essential for building a sustainable and equitable economy.

Encouraging young people to stay in or migrate from urban to rural areas requires a comprehensive strategy that includes economic, social, and infrastructural elements. First, significant investment in infrastructure such as roads, electricity, water, and internet in rural areas is crucial for improving living and working conditions. This not only enhances the quality of life but also narrows the development gap between urban and rural areas. Additionally, offering tax incentives and financial support to businesses willing to invest in rural areas will create attractive employment opportunities for young people. The development of high-tech agriculture is also key, as it increases productivity and product quality while creating new and appealing business opportunities.

Support for entrepreneurship and skill development is indispensable. Start-up support programs should provide preferential loans, business consulting, and technical assistance for young people wishing to start businesses in rural areas. Furthermore, vocational training programs tailored to market needs and local economic trends are essential to help young people confidently establish and grow their careers in their hometowns. Additionally, the government and relevant organizations need to strengthen communication campaigns to change young people's perceptions about the opportunities and potential in rural areas, fostering a renewed sense of pride and ambition to build prosperous rural communities. If these initiatives are implemented comprehensively and effectively, they will not only encourage young people to stay in rural areas but also attract those who have migrated to cities to return, contributing to sustainable development in Vietnam's rural regions.

Escaping the Middle-Income Trap Through Reverse Migration in Vietnam

In Vietnam, overcoming the middle-income trap and supporting reverse migration requires a comprehensive strategy focused on enhancing rural infrastructure, promoting entrepreneurship, and expanding vocational training programs. As rural-to-urban migration continues to impact the economic and social fabric of both urban and rural regions, it is essential to address the root causes of rural underdevelopment. Investments in transportation, electricity, water supply, and internet connectivity in rural areas can stimulate local business growth and attract investment, while entrepreneurship initiatives and vocational training will empower returning migrants to contribute meaningfully to the local economy. By fostering job creation through modernizing agriculture, developing agro-processing industries, and enhancing digital skills, Vietnam can create sustainable opportunities for returning migrants. Additionally, policies that improve access to finance and social protection programs will ensure the long-term well-being and successful reintegration of returnees, supporting the country's broader goal of sustainable and balanced development.

To overcome the middle-income trap and support reverse migration, it is essential to prioritize investments in rural infrastructure. Upgrading transportation networks, electricity, water supply, and internet connectivity in rural areas will enhance access to markets, employment, and essential services. Improved infrastructure will also facilitate the growth of local businesses, attract investment, and enable returning migrants to reintegrate into the economic and social fabric of rural communities.

Promoting entrepreneurship in rural areas is a critical strategy for job creation and economic development. Government policies should provide financial support, such as low-interest loans and grants, to returning migrants seeking to start businesses. The establishment of business incubators and mentoring programs can further assist in developing sustainable business models. Moreover, modernizing agriculture and promoting agro-processing industries will help create employment opportunities and reduce dependence on urban centers for livelihoods.

Expanding vocational training and skill development programs is essential to align the rural workforce with labor market demands. Training programs focused on modern farming techniques, agribusiness, and rural industries will equip returning migrants with the skills necessary to secure employment or start businesses. Additionally, integrating digital literacy and e-commerce training will empower rural workers to engage in remote work and access broader markets, fostering economic resilience.

Access to finance is a significant barrier for returning migrants seeking to invest in their communities. Policy measures should prioritize improving access to credit through microfinance programs, government-backed loans, and financial literacy initiatives. Encouraging the formation of rural cooperatives and savings groups can also help return migrants pool resources and invest in collective enterprises, fostering community-based economic development.

Social protection programs are critical in supporting the livelihoods of return migrants, especially those affected by economic disruptions such as the COVID-19 pandemic. Policies should ensure the provision of unemployment benefits, health insurance, and pensions tailored to the needs of informal sector workers. These safety nets will prevent return migrants from falling into poverty and give them time to reintegrate into rural labor markets.

Encouraging investment in agriculture and agricultural technology is vital to boosting rural productivity and income. Government policies should incentivize the adoption of advanced farming technologies, such as precision agriculture, irrigation systems, and high-yield crops. Returning migrants can apply these technologies to modernize agricultural practices, while also fostering job creation in agro-processing and export-oriented industries.

Developing green industries and promoting sustainability in rural areas is another essential policy focus. Government initiatives should support the growth of renewable energy, organic farming, and eco-tourism industries to create long-term employment opportunities. Public-private partnerships and international cooperation can facilitate the establishment of green industrial zones, thus enhancing job creation and sustainable development in rural regions.

Leveraging digital technology for rural economic development is key to reversing migration strategies. Policies should encourage the use of digital platforms for e-commerce, teleworking, and online education to create new opportunities for returning migrants. Providing digital literacy training and fostering digital entrepreneurship will enable rural populations to access broader markets and participate in the growing digital economy.

Fostering social integration and community building is crucial for the successful reintegration of returning migrants. Policies should promote community engagement through local governance, cultural events, and social support networks. Psychological counseling and health services are also important in helping return migrants overcome challenges and adapt to their new environments, ultimately strengthening their sense of belonging in rural areas.

Public-private partnerships are essential for the successful implementation of reverse migration policies. Collaboration between government, private enterprises, and non-governmental organizations (NGOs) can facilitate infrastructure development, financial support for rural businesses, and job creation in sustainable industries. International organizations can also provide technical expertise and resources to support comprehensive rural development strategies.

Regional development policies should aim to reduce economic disparities between urban and rural areas by fostering balanced growth across regions. Government efforts should prioritize investments in economically lagging regions, such as the Mekong Delta and Central Highlands, creating employment opportunities for returning migrants and enhancing the overall competitiveness of rural areas.

Finally, ensuring environmental sustainability in rural development is crucial for long-term success. Policies that promote sustainable agricultural practices, conservation, and the responsible use of natural resources will create a conducive environment for returning migrants. Supporting eco-friendly businesses and community initiatives will not only generate employment but also safeguard natural resources, contributing to the long-term prosperity of rural areas.

Conclusion

To ensure the effectiveness and practicality of policies for Vietnam, it is important to clearly define the main goals: creating job opportunities, increasing labor productivity, and raising income, while striving to escape the middle-income trap. Vietnam is at a critical stage of economic development, with numerous opportunities and challenges. Therefore, it is necessary to focus on technological applications, invest in education and vocational training, improve infrastructure, and encourage foreign investment. Specific policies should include local economic development, infrastructure and service improvement, vocational training support, innovation and entrepreneurship promotion, and the advancement of high-tech agriculture. These policies aim to improve living standards, facilitate business and production, and help rural sectors/remote areas achieve a sustainably higher standard of living, and higher income per head, and from there reduce the middle-income trap in Vietnam.

Acknowledgements This chapter was funded by the University of Economics Ho Chi Minh City (UEH), Vietnam. Data collection was conducted by Nhan Thi Thanh Nguyen of the Vietnam-Netherlands Programme at UEH.

References

Asian Development Bank (ADB). (2021). *ADB annual report 2021: Toward a green and inclusive recovery*. Asian Development Bank. https://www.adb.org/sites/default/files/institutional-document/788046/adb-annual-report-2021.pdf

Awasthi, I., & Mehta, B. (2020). Forced out-migration from hill regions and return migration during the pandemic: Evidence from Uttarakhand. *The Indian Journal of Labour Economics, 63*(4), 1107–1124. https://doi.org/10.1007/s41027-020-00291-w

Becker, G. S. (1964). *Human capital: A theoretical and empirical analysis, with special reference to education*. University of Chicago Press.

Díaz-Sánchez, J. P., & Correa, H. (2024). Immigration and formal labor market participation in Ecuador: Empirical insights from a developing nation. *Research in Globalization, 8*, 100198. https://doi.org/10.1016/j.resglo.2024.100198

Faist, T. (1997). The crucial meso-level. In *International migration, immobility and development* (pp. 187–217). Berg Publishers.

Farooq, S., & Arif, G. M. (2023). The facts of return migration in the wake of COVID-19: A policy framework for reintegration of Pakistani workers. *Journal of Ethnic and Migration Studies, 50*(20), 5190–5218. https://doi.org/10.1080/1369183X.2024.2268976

Ghani, S., & Morgandi, N. A. (2023). Return migration and labour market outcomes in South Asia: A CGE exploration. *Journal of Ethnic and Migration Studies, 50*(20), 5153–5168. https://doi.org/10.1080/1369183X.2024.2268965

González-Leonardo, M., Rowe, F., & Fresolone Caparrós, A. (2022). Rural revival? The rise in internal migration to rural areas during the COVID-19 pandemic: Who moved and where? *Journal of Rural Studies, 96*, 332–342. https://doi.org/10.1016/j.jrurstud.2022.11.006

Government News. (2023, March 22). Bac Giang creates the most favorable conditions for tech start-ups. *Government of Vietnam*. https://baochinhphu.vn/bac-giang-tao-dieu-kien-thuan-loi-nhat-cho-cac-start-up-cong-nghe-102230322171640879.htm

Granovetter, M. S. (1973). The strength of weak ties. *American Journal of Sociology*, *78*(6), 1360–1380. https://doi.org/10.1086/225469

Hu, Y., Wang, Y., & Zhang, P. (2023). Anti-urbanization and rural development: Evidence from return migrants in China. *Journal of Rural Studies*, *103*, 103102. https://doi.org/10.1016/j.jrurstud.2023.103102

International Organization for Migration Vietnam. (2021). *IOM Viet Nam COVID-19 Response*. IOM. https://vietnam.iom.int/en/iom-viet-nam-covid-19-response

Khan, A., & Arokkiaraj, H. (2021). Challenges of reverse migration in India: A comparative study of internal and international migrant workers in the post-COVID economy. *Comparative Migration Studies*, *9*(1), 49. https://doi.org/10.1186/s40878-021-00260-2

Lee, E. S. (1966). A theory of migration. *Demography*, *3*(1), 47–57. https://doi.org/10.2307/2060063

Li, C., Zhang, Y., & Tian, L. (2024). The impact of urban integration on the intention of settlement and residence among migrants: The empirical evidence from China. *Heliyon*, *10*(3), e26541. https://doi.org/10.1016/j.heliyon.2024.e26541

Lin, M., Pyyry, N., & Luukkonen, J. (2024). Effects of the Hukou system on the geographies of young people in contemporary urban China. *Children's Geographies*, *22*(6), 985–1001. https://doi.org/10.1080/14733285.2024.2421217

Low, S. A., Rahe, M. L., & Van Leuven, A. J. (2023). Has COVID-19 made rural areas more attractive places to live? Survey evidence from northwest Missouri. *Regional Science Policy and Practice*, *15*(3), 520–541. https://doi.org/10.1111/rsp3.12553

Mardonov, S. S. (2024). Increasing urbanization and population decline in developed countries: Problems and solutions. *Oriental Renaissance: Innovative, Educational, Natural and Social Sciences*, *4*(3), 450–462.

Ogburn, W. F. (1922). *Social change with respect to culture and original nature*. B. W. Huebsch.

Rajan, I. S., & Arcand, J. L. (2023). COVID-19 return migration phenomena: Experiences from South and Southeast Asia. *Journal of Ethnic and Migration Studies*, *50*(20), 5133–5152. https://doi.org/10.1080/1369183X.2024.2268963

Saklani, R. P., Bhatt, B., Purohit, K., Nautiyal, A., & Pokhriyal, G. (2021). Push-pull factors and socio-economic condition of reverse migrants during 1st wave of COVID-19: A grass root survey in Garhwal Himalaya. *Indian Journal of Economics and Development*, *17*(4), 872–879. https://doi.org/10.35716/IJED/21210

Shen, F., Ye, W., Wang, C., & Huang, X. (2023). Effects of organizational factors on identification of young returnees from urban areas with rural societies—A perspective of adaptability. *Social Indicators Research*, *167*(1), 363–390. https://doi.org/10.1007/s11205-023-03120-7

United Nations Population Fund (UNFPA). (2021). *UNFPA annual report 2021*. UNFPA. https://www.unfpa.org/annual-report-2021

Wang, X., Yi, F., & Cai, Y. (2024). The effect of rural e-commerce development on return migration intentions: Evidence from the China migrants dynamic survey. *Applied Economics Letters, 31*(20), 2104–2109. https://doi.org/10.1080/13504851.2023.2211323

World Bank. (2020). *Vibrant Vietnam: Forging the foundation of a high-income economy*. https://hdl.handle.net/10986/33831

Zhou, J., Zhang, X., Korkmaz, A. G., Ding, X., & Yue, P. (2024). Mirroring the urban exodus: The impact of return migration on rural entrepreneurship. *Finance Research Letters, 66*, 105619. https://doi.org/10.1016/j.frl.2024.105619

CHAPTER 13

Human Capital 4: Coping with Aging Population

Introduction

Becker (1992) pointed out that a country's fertility often declines after a period of economic boom. When economies transition from agricultural to urban, industrial, and service-based structures, women gain increased educational and employment opportunities, leading to later marriages and fewer children, and additionally, raising child-rearing costs. These are some of the reasons why middle-income countries often face slow population growth, leading to population aging.

Population aging can contribute to the middle-income trap (MIT) through both supply and demand channels. On the supply side, it reduces the available labor force due to a high dependency ratio, affecting national and per capita income. On the demand side, it also impacts savings and consumption patterns, slowing per capita income growth. Research by Bulman et al. (2017) found that countries successfully escaping the middle-income trap typically had lower older people-to-working-age population ratios. Ha and Lee (2016) emphasized the role of support ratio (ratio of the number of workers to the number of dependents) for MIT, and argued that high economic growth leads to low support rates and thus leads to a middle-income trap.

Contributed by Hoai Trong Nguyen

H. T. Dinh, H. T. Nguyen, *Vietnam's Economic Leap*,
https://doi.org/10.1007/978-3-032-08904-5_13

Vietnam is one of the fastest aging countries in the world, with its total fertility rate (TFR) declining significantly from 4.9 in 1980 to 1.9 in 2022 (World Bank Open Data, n.d.). According to the United Nations Population Fund in Vietnam (UNFPA), by 2036, Vietnam's older population will account for 14.17% of the total population, so that Vietnam will officially become an "aged population" (General Statistics Office, 2021). This puts Vietnam at risk of falling into the middle-income trap due to rapid population aging.

In response to the population aging, many Asian countries have implemented policies to improve the quality of life and create job opportunities for older people. These policies have helped solve the problem of labor supply shortage, reduced the proportion of the dependent population, and created conditions for older individuals to contribute to the overall income of the economy. Vietnam can creatively learn from the lessons of previous Asian countries to come up with appropriate policies to overcome the middle-income trap.

This chapter is organized into 5 sections: Section 1: Overview of population aging in Vietnam; Section 2: Population aging policies in Asian countries; Section 3: Policy recommendations for older people in Vietnam; Section 4: Conclusion.

Trends of Vietnam's Elderly Population

Vietnam's population will officially enter the "aged population" phase in 2036 with the proportion of older people reaching 14.2% of the total population (Fig. 13.1). Vietnam had one of the world's fastest aging rates, averaging 4.4% annually (General Statistics Office, 2021). While Western countries typically took 100 years to transition from "aging" to "aged" phases, and regional leaders Thailand and Japan required 22 and 26 years, respectively, Vietnam will complete this transition in just 20 years.

Age distribution projections show that the number of younger older people (60–74 years) will peak and then decline, while the 75–79 and 80+ age groups will continue growing (Fig. 13.2). The 80+ demographic is expected to expand most dramatically, from 2.1 million in 2029 to 8.8 million in 2069, indicating rapidly increasing care needs.

Gender distribution shows a feminization of the older population, although the sex ratio is expected to decrease over time, particularly among the oldest age groups (Fig. 13.3).

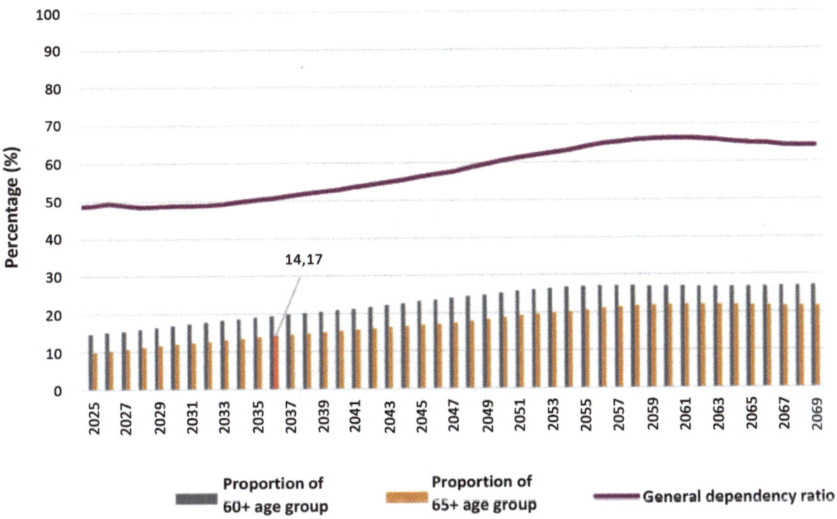

Fig. 13.1 Forecast of proportion of 60+ and 65+ age group, and general dependency ratio. *Source* General Statistics Office of Vietnam (2021)

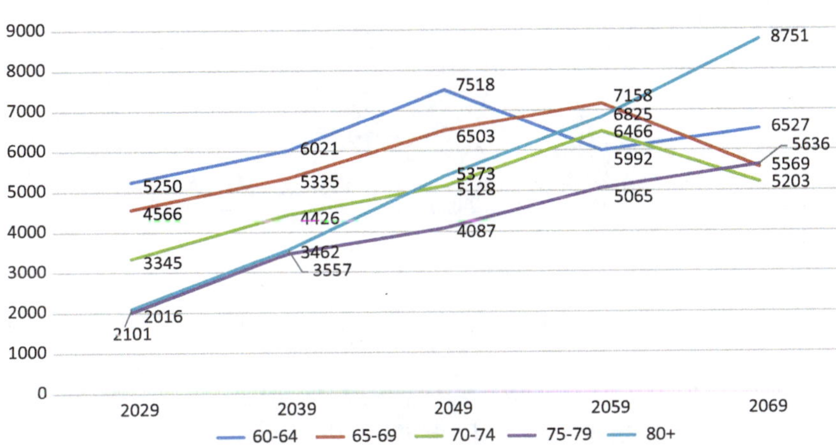

Fig. 13.2 Forecast of Vietnam's older people population by age group, 2029–2069. *Source* General Statistics Office of Vietnam (2021)

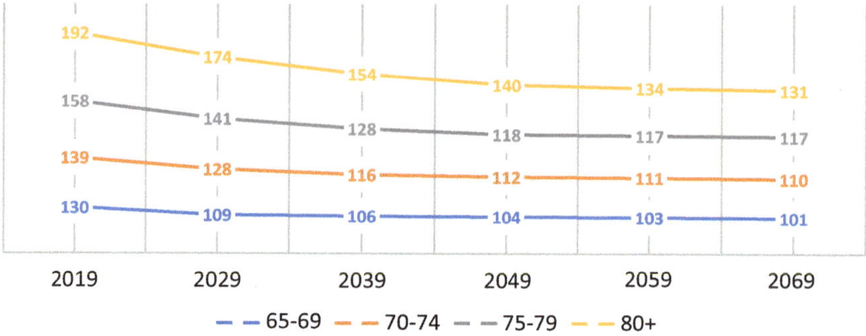

Fig. 13.3 Forecast of sex ratio (%) of the older population by age group, 2019–2069. *Source* General Statistics Office of Vietnam Vietnam (2021)

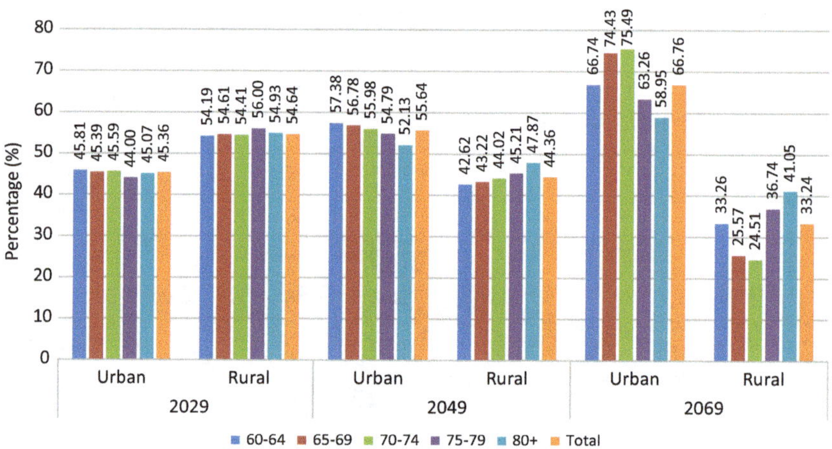

Fig. 13.4 Distribution of older people population by age group and living area, 2029–2069. *Source* General Statistics Office of Vietnam (2021)

In terms of living area, Fig. 13.4 shows that the proportion of people living in rural areas will decrease from 45.4% in 2029 to 33.2% in 2069: corresponding to the proportion of people living in urban areas increasing from 54.6% in 2029 to 66.7% in 2069. In the same general trend, people in all age groups also have a decrease in rural living rates and an increase in urban living rates, which not only puts pressure on the health care system in urban areas but also affects the employed workforce when they are dominated by having to take care of dependents along with them. This trend is inevitable because the urbanization process in Vietnam is forecast to take place strongly in the coming decades.

Analytical Framework of Older People Workforce Participation and MIT

Health status and work capacity are important factors influencing the decision of older people to continue working or retire. Woźniak et al. (2022) found that health status and disability affect employees' motivation to continue working. When comparing participants who continued working with those who voluntarily retired, Tur-Sinai et al. (2022) confirmed the hypothesis that there is a correlation between older people's health and their ability to continue working into retirement. Many other studies have also shown that improvements in health and health care can positively influence their participation in the labor force (Anxo et al., 2019; Ben-Bassat et al., 2021; Gonzales & Nowell, 2017; Sharabi et al., 2020; Zaccagni et al., 2024; Zitikytė, 2019).

Increased life expectancy and pension benefits policies may influence older workers' decisions to continue working. A systematic review of 19 studies by Pilipiec et al. (2021) showed that increasing the retirement age increased labor force participation. Tur-Sinai et al. (2022) suggested that policies to financially support older people when they retire will contribute to reducing the rate of involuntary retirement and increasing the rate of participation of older people.

The skills and work experience of older workers can help them want to continue working and contribute to the economy. A qualitative study conducted by Sewdas et al. (2017) with 18 older people who continued to work showed that skills and knowledge were one of the motivations for them to continue working. Brooke and Taylor (2005) also showed the importance of skills and experience of older people when many companies in the UK and Australia re-employ retired older people because of their abilities. However, suitable employment opportunities and supportive work environments are also important to attract and retain older workers (Brooke & Taylor, 2005; Sewdas et al., 2017; Wattanasaovaluk, 2021).

Ultimately, older people will continue to participate in the workforce when their rights to be respected and their status affirmed are ensured.

Age discrimination can cause older people to leave the workforce (Blackham, 2024; Suberry & Bodner, 2024). Measures to ensure that their rights are respected and to create a positive work environment for older workers can help attract and retain these workers.

In summary, from the above arguments, the factors affecting the decision to continue participating in the labor force of the older people include: (1) health status and working capacity, (2) life expectancy and welfare policies, (3) skills and work experience and (4) the right to respect and affirm the position of the older people. Policies that help improve these factors will create conditions for older people to continue working, contributing to the total national income, reducing the burden of dependence and helping Vietnam overcome the middle-income trap.

The analytical framework of this chapter is presented in Fig. 13.5. Policies to improve the four factors affecting labor force participation for older people are divided into two groups: policies to improve the quality of life for older people and policies to create job opportunities for them.

In the following sub-sections, we will analyze the current status of factors affecting the participation of the older people in the labor force in Vietnam as well as the policies being implemented.

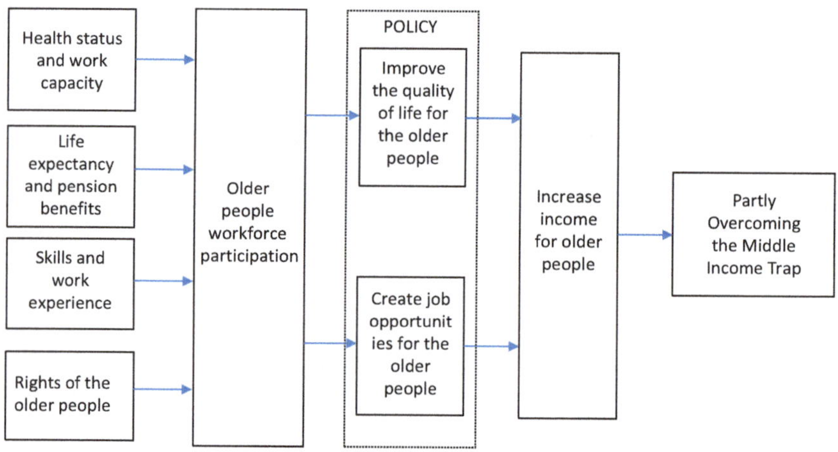

Fig. 13.5 Analyical framework of older people workforce participation and MIT participation

Vietnam's Current Situation

The General Statistics Office of Vietnam (General Statistics Office, 2021) reported that 11.7% of older people have at least one functional disability (difficulties in vision, hearing, mobility, cognition and communicating in a common language). Care patterns show strong family dependence, with 80% of care needs met by family members and minimal community or facility-based care. Nearly 90% of older people prefer home-based care over institutional options (General Statistics Office, 2021). However, Vietnam's trend toward nuclear families suggests a future shift toward external care services in order to make a better chance for young people to go to work effectively rather than taking care of their dependent people at home and hospital when older people get sick.

Despite health challenges, many older people remain capable of working. The 2019 data revealed that 35% of older people were employed for income (Fig. 13.6), although employment patterns showed concerning vulnerabilities. The majority, 60.9%, were self-employed, while 23.8% worked as unpaid family workers, and only 12.9% held wage-earning positions (Fig. 13.7). These statistics indicate particular vulnerability among older people, women, and rural residents, who show significantly lower rates of wage employment than their counterparts (Bui, Bui et al., 2022; General Statistics Office, 2021).

Notably, 3–4% were business owners, creating substantial employment opportunities, while thousands more contributed through scientific research,

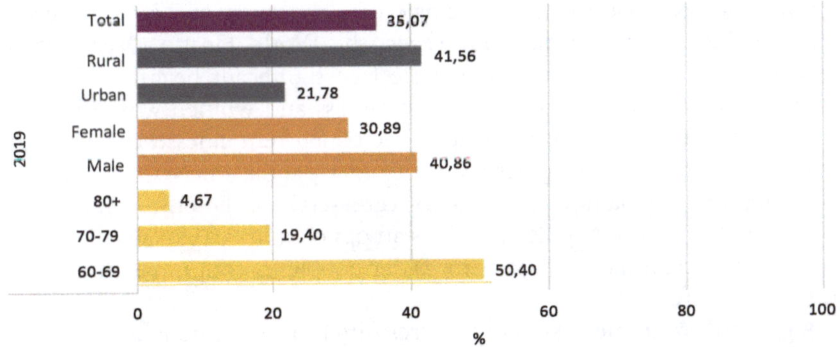

Fig. 13.6 Proportion of working older people in 2019 (%). *Source* General Statistics Office (2021)

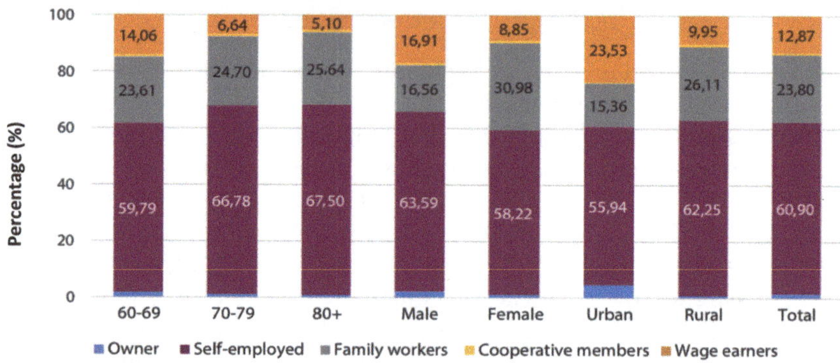

Fig. 13.7 Older people's job position by typical groups in 2019. *Source* General Statistics Office (2021)

teaching, and cultural activities. So, if the government can take advantage of this human resource along with policies to support employment and provide appropriate labor skills training, older people in Vietnam will continue to contribute to the overall income of the entire economy, thereby partially supporting Vietnam to surpass the middle-income trap.

Life Expectancy and Retirement Benefits

Vietnamese life expectancy reached 74.5 years in 2023 (Fig. 13.8), marking a one-year increase from 2022. Gender disparities show that women live 5.3 years longer than men, with female life expectancy at 77.2 years compared to 72.1 years for men. However, the World Health Organization estimates that older Vietnamese people face significant health challenges, with men averaging 8 years living with illness and women with 11 years. Each older person typically manages three concurrent illnesses. The healthcare system currently struggles to meet older people's needs, with insufficient geriatric specialties and primary care services (Duong, 2022). The increasing life expectancy also provides an opportunity to expand the retirement policy, creating conditions for older people to continue participating in the workforce.

Vietnam's retirement system features different retirement ages for men (60 years plus) and women (55 years plus), with annual increases of 3 months for men and 4 months for women since 2021. The system offers

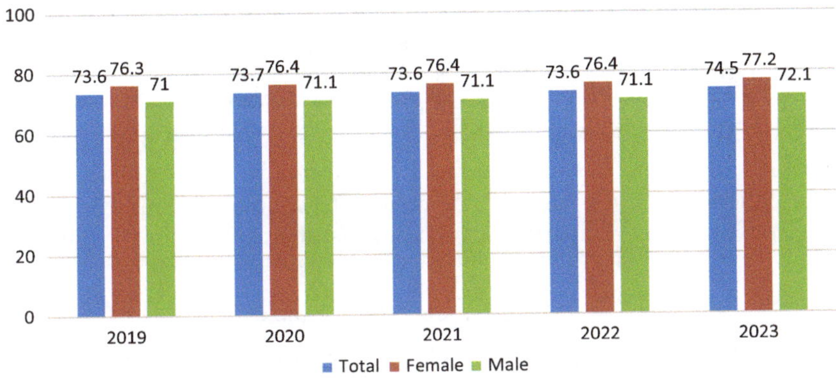

Fig. 13.8 Average life expectancy of Vietnamese people 2019–2023. *Source* General Statistics Office (2021)

maximum pension benefits of 75% of base salary through two insurance schemes: compulsory for organization employees and voluntary for self-employed workers (Vietnam Social Security, 2017). By the first quarter of 2024, pensioners will have an average pension per capita of 5.6 million VND/month, higher than the average income per capita of 5.2 million VND/month (Vietnam Social Security, 2024). For older people who do not have a pension, the state will provide them with a monthly social subsidy. By January 2024, the minimum subsidy had been raised to 500 thousand VND per month and will be applicable to all older people aged 80 and over (Vietnam Social Security, 2024). The Vietnamese government is drafting a law to reduce the age of support to 75 from 2025. However, by 2024, 73% of older people do not have a pension or monthly subsidies, and 23.5% of older people will still belong to poor households (Ha, 2025). Therefore, the retirement benefits still do not cover all older people, and many older people continue to live a difficult life.

Skills and Work Experience

Vietnam has implemented several policies to leverage the skills of older people, including preferential loans without collateral requirements, vocational training fee exemptions, agricultural extension course fee reductions, technology transfer support, product promotion assistance, agricultural risk protection, and priority in land allocation. Despite these initiatives, participation remains limited due to insufficient retraining programs, lack of employer incentives, and absence of distribution employment mechanisms for older workers. Although job centers are available in all provinces and cities, there are no job centers specifically for older people. The lack of information about jobs and specific policies to encourage employment for older people is also a challenge in the process of creating jobs for them.

Rights for the Older People

The 2013 Constitution established the rights of older persons and recognized their status. However, specific policies to protect older persons in the workplace have not yet been enacted. Older individuals face challenges due to inadequate recognition of their achievements and initiatives. These things reduce the motivation of older people to continue dedicating themselves, thereby increasing the social burden. When older people are guaranteed fairness in the workplace, they will be motivated to work and willing to contribute to the total national income, contributing to Vietnam overcoming the middle-income trap.

In Vietnam, there are still prejudices about older people that can lead to discrimination. Tuyet et al. (2022) surveyed the prejudices about older people among 332 residents in Hai Phong province. The results showed that the majority had negative prejudices about older people, such as being sick, having cognitive impairment, needing medical care, being conservative, not interested in sex, and having limited access to modern technology.

The Asian Experience

Based on the analytical framework presented in the previous chapter, this section reviews key population aging policies in Asian countries designed to encourage older people's participation in the labor market. The surveyed countries include Japan, South Korea, China, Singapore, and Thailand. The selected countries share anthropological, cultural, and social characteristics with Vietnam, making their experiences valuable for Vietnam's efforts to cope with rapid population aging and overcome the middle-income trap.

The policies fall into two main categories: those that aim at improving the quality of life and working capacity of older people, and those that focus on creating employment opportunities for older people.

Policies to Improve the Quality of Life for the Older People

Long-term care insurance (LTCI)
As the population ages, the number of people with disabilities requiring long-term care increases, creating a greater burden on healthcare systems and families, who are traditionally the primary caregivers for older people in Asian countries. To address these challenges and share the burden of long-term care, countries have developed Long-Term Care Insurance (LTCI) programs that increase private sector involvement while improving healthcare quality for older people.

Several countries have implemented LTCI through different approaches. Japan introduced LTCI in 2000 after nationwide discussions. South Korea followed suit, passing its LTCI law in 2007 and launching the program in July 2008. China began exploring this approach by piloting LTCI in 15 cities in 2016. Thailand established an LTCI fund in 2015 in cooperation with Japan and began implementing its national system in 2016. Singapore took a slightly different approach, passing mandatory LTCI legislation in September 2019 through its CareShield Life program, which applies to all eligible adults aged 30 and above.

According to WHO, LTCI is an institutional arrangement designed to share nursing costs for people unable to care for themselves due to chronic illness or physical and psychological disabilities. The program aims to provide support services for physical activities and housekeeping, ultimately improving older people's quality of life. It typically serves those aged 65 and older who have experienced difficulty in daily activities for at least six months.

LTCI benefits come in both in-kind and cash forms. The in-kind benefits include comprehensive home care services such as day and night care center services, various types of home visits for care, nursing, cognitive activity promotion, and bathing, as well as short-term institutionalized care and welfare device provision. These services are delivered through several institutional care models: medical institutions partnering with long-term care facilities, dedicated medical facilities within long-term care facilities, expanded medical institutions offering post-acute and long-term care services, and community-based medical service delivery.

The program ensures older people have access to affordable care services from the private sector. Funding comes through a combination of the universal health insurance system and participant premiums. All individuals 40 years and older must contribute LTCI premiums based on their public health insurance premium rating. Eligibility determination involves an in-person assessment using LTCI checklists or Barthel score evaluations.

Developing the Older People Care Industry

Many countries have established comprehensive initiatives to develop the older people care industry, often called the Silver Economy. These initiatives aim to improve health quality, reduce dependence, and enhance labor market participation among older people. Notable examples include China's "New Initiatives on the Development of the Silver Economy to Improve the Welfare of the Older people" (The General Office of the State Council, 2024) and Singapore's "Action Plan for Successful Aging" (Singapore Ministry of Health, 2023).

The development of the older people care industry encompasses several interconnected areas. In terms of home-based care, facilities and service companies are encouraged to provide comprehensive home care while supporting retail and social work agencies in assisting with daily tasks. Healthcare services are being enhanced through improvements to geriatric departments in hospitals and the establishment of research foundations for geriatric studies.

Meal support services have been expanded through the organization of delivery platforms and logistics companies, with many regions providing subsidies for these essential services. Community services have seen significant development through the establishment of Health Care Centers in community areas, renovation of community consumer service centers, and creation of older people-friendly retail spaces.

Cultural and educational services have received substantial attention, with the establishment of national universities for older people, improving accessibility of entertainment and communication media, and creating volunteer programs. Rural areas have not been neglected, with policies focusing on utilizing existing support facilities and expanding care services to these regions.

Transportation and urban planning have been adapted to better serve older people's needs through the creation of "Silver Zones" for traffic safety, implementation of older people-friendly infrastructure, and adjustments to public transportation systems for improved accessibility. Finally, intergenerational support has been promoted through policies encouraging multi-generational living arrangements and the co-location of older people and childcare services, fostering community integration and social support networks.

Policies to Create Job Opportunities for the Older People

Re-employment Policy

Asian countries have implemented various re-employment policies for retired older workers through legislation such as Singapore's Retirement and Re-employment Act (RRA) (Singapore Statutes Online, 2022), Japan's Act on Stabilization of Employment of Older people Persons (Otsuki & Ando, 2020), and the Income security for older persons in the Republic of Korea (Yoon, 2016).

A key feature of these laws requires employers to offer re-employment opportunities to eligible employees who have reached retirement age. When employers are unable to offer positions to eligible older employees, they must either transfer the re-employment obligation to another employer with the employee's consent or provide a one-off Employment Support Payment.

The re-employment contract framework requires terms of at least one year, with annual renewals until the maximum re-employment age. For employers, the process involves identifying eligible employees, initiating discussions six months before retirement age, providing re-employment contracts three months before retirement, and ensuring fair and reasonable terms and conditions. They must also give early notice to ineligible employees to allow time for retirement preparation or alternative employment seeking. Older employees, in turn, are expected to present their job preferences early in the consultation process and maintain flexibility regarding work arrangements and employment terms.

Regarding compensation, older workers' salaries can be adjusted based on reasonable factors such as new responsibilities or tasks, with room for negotiation between employer and employee. When direct re-employment isn't possible, employers may transfer their obligation to another employer, provided both the new employer agrees to take over the existing obligations and the older employee accepts the new offer. If employees decline re-employment offers from new employers, they become eligible for an Employment Support Payment from their current employer, designed as a last resort to help bridge financial gaps while seeking alternative employment.

Employers are encouraged to extend retirement and internal re-employment ages beyond statutory requirements, clearly documenting these provisions in employment documents. They are also empowered to create more age-friendly workplaces through restructuring existing health benefits and offering flexible benefits such as premium payments for older workers.

Employment Stabilization Policy

Employment stabilization for the older people has been addressed through various legislative measures across Asia, including Japan's Act on Stabilization of Employment of Older people Persons (Otsuki & Ando, 2020), the Income security for older persons in the Republic of Korea (Yoon, 2016), and Singapore's Silver Job Program (Singapore Government, 2006).

These policies aim to raise retirement ages and eventually abolish mandatory retirement, implement continuous employment systems until age 70 (including employment at subsidiaries and affiliated companies), extend labor contracts to age 70, and establish systems for continued business engagement beyond 70, including through non-profit organizations and volunteer associations that provide compensation to older people workers.

Implementation is overseen by specialized agencies such as the Korea Labor Force Development Institute for the Aged (KORDI), the Japan Silver Human Resources Center, and Singapore Senior Activity Centre. These organizations help provide suitable employment opportunities through two main channels: social-contribution jobs and market-entry jobs.

Social contribution jobs encompass public services and education, providing opportunities for older people with lower skills but a willingness to work. These positions include roles such as subway conductors, security guards, school librarians, wildfire monitors, and historic site protectors. Education jobs leverage older workers' accumulated knowledge and experience, placing them as tutors, nature guides, or instructors for special needs children and foreign workers.

The market entry category includes labor dispatch positions and self-employment opportunities. Government support for self-employment includes startup assistance, partial coverage of initial costs, and labor expenses. Unlike social contribution jobs with fixed monthly salaries, income from self-employment varies based on business success.

Eligibility typically begins at age 65, though this can be flexible depending on the position. Selection criteria vary by job type, with public service roles prioritizing low-income applicants, education positions favoring those with teaching experience, and self-employment opportunities considering physical capability and business acumen.

Policy Recommendations for Vietnam

In this section, we provide several policy recommendations for older people in Vietnam, in addition to the policies currently being implemented, which are reviewed in Sect. 1. These recommendations are based on policies of Asian countries, which are reviewed in Sect. 2, and are applied appropriately to the situation of the older population in Vietnam. The policy recommendations are divided into two main policy groups: (1) policies to improve the quality of life and working capacity of older people, and (2) policies to create job opportunities for older people. The former will create more chances for not only older people to contribute more to labor market by their working capacity, but also can help the young generation receive better family performance due to less burden in cases of dependent people illness in order to work effectively in the working place without interruption. The latter will directly increase more opportunities for older people to re-enter the labor market to earn their income and partly contribute to increasing income per head in the country.

Improving the Quality of Life and Working Capacity of the Older People

Long-term care insurance (LTCI) policy

Vietnam faces similar challenges to other aging Asian nations, with increasing life expectancy accompanied by rising health disabilities. By 2021, 11.70% of older Vietnamese people had at least one functional disability, and 6.32% faced difficulties with daily living activities. Currently, long-term care in Vietnam primarily occurs at home through family members, suggesting an urgent need for formal home based care service packages.

Understanding the importance of elderly health care, the Vietnamese government has issued national programs "Older People Health Care Program to 2030" (Vietnam Government, 2020) signed by prime minister in 2020. According to this program, LTCI has been oriented to be formed by improving the capacity of hospitals and medical stations, forming day care centers, and nursing homes in appropriate forms, training health workers, etc. According to Vietnam Social Security (Châu, 2025), 3 million older people have had their health records established, nearly 4 million older people have had regular health check-ups, 96% of elderly people have Health Care Insurance, and 32/63 provinces and cities have established 59 private nursing homes for the care of the elderly. However, there are no specific regulations on the formation of the LTCI model in Vietnam. Drawing from the experiences of Japan, South Korea, Singapore, China, and Thailand, Vietnam should consider implementing LTCI through several key steps.

Firstly, comprehensive LTCI legislation should be established, defining eligible participants, budget sources, and covered services. The system should ensure 24-hour availability of care provided by trained and licensed professionals. Funding could combine public tax revenue or mandatory social insurance with participant premiums, similar to Korea's model, which requires premium payments from taxpayers aged 40 and over. In Vietnam, the source of funding for older people care services should mainly be from the universal health insurance fund. LTC fee can be financed as a part of mandatory insurance premiums paid by participants.

The government should implement care subsidies both for facility development and direct support to vulnerable older people populations, particularly those over 80 or living alone. Public-private partnerships could help develop a comprehensive care system encompassing both institutional and home-based services. Before national implementation, pilot programs in major cities could provide valuable implementation experience.

Developing the Older People Care Industry

The older people care industry has received attention from many Asian countries, but in Vietnam, parliamentary discussions have not mentioned this concept much. Initial policies to develop this industry can be found in the "Older People Health Care Program to 2030" (Vietnam Government, 2020) and the "National Action Program on Older people for the 2021–2030 period" (Vietnam Government, 2021) issued by the Prime Minister. Learning from the policies of China and Singapore, Vietnam can improve and introduce specific policies to develop this industry.

Regarding the development of geriatrics, Vietnam established a geriatric hospital in 2016, 50/63 provincial and municipal general hospitals have geriatric departments; more than 900 examination departments have separate rooms for the elderly, over 10,000 inpatient beds prioritize the elderly for both treatment and rehabilitation for the elderly with 1791 medical staff trained in geriatrics and nationwide 3 geriatric training facilities (Châu, 2025). Learning from China, the government should promote the application of information technology in the management of medical examination and treatment, and have a plan to establish a National Research Foundation to facilitate geriatric research.

Regarding transportation and urban planning, Vietnam has policies such as building new or renovating apartment buildings and public works to suit the characteristics and needs of the older people, and when using public transportation, the older people are assisted and arranged with convenient seating (Vietnam Government, 2021). Vietnam can learn from Singapore to establish "Silver Zones" to reduce traffic and increase safety for the older people, create "Green Man Plus" pedestrian walkways with extended travel times, install elevators at specific pedestrian overpasses, wheelchair-friendly buses, and adjust bus routes according to the travel needs of the older people. The government should encourage shopping malls, supermarkets, and other retail stores to open special areas or windows that are convenient for older people.

Vietnam has implemented policies on older people care in cultural, educational, physical education, sports, entertainment, and tourism activities. These policies include: providing information, documents, and instructors for the older people to participate in learning and research, supporting the older people to participate in cultural, recreational, tourism, health care and other physical and sports activities suitable for their health and psychology, reducing ticket prices and service prices for the older people when using some public services (Vietnam Government, 2021). Learning from previous countries, Vietnam can do better by establishing a national university for the older people and promoting open education, and based on this university, building a national public service platform for older people education, and establishing a resource database and teacher database for older people education. The government should improve access to entertainment and media, such as providing large print books and promoting content creation for the older people.

Regarding intergenerational connections, Vietnam is implementing policies to promote the role of the older people, helping them to promote their wisdom, valuable experience, and good qualities for the young generations to follow. In particular, the policy of establishing intergenerational self-help club models has achieved resonance when 7000 clubs have been established, attracting over 170,000 participants (Châu, 2025). We can do better when learning from countries that have policies to encourage the older people to live with or near their married children, promoting intergenerational harmony and co-located older people and child care services.

Finally, the government needs to improve elderly care services in rural areas by utilizing support service facilities (nursing homes) for the extremely poor in rural areas and use commissioned activities and other methods to provide elderly care services.

Creating Job Opportunities

The policy of creating job opportunities for the older people is emphasized in the "National Action Program on the Older people, 2021–2030 period" (Vietnam Government, 2021). The program sets specific goals: In the 2022–2025 period, at least 50% of the older people with the need and ability to work will have jobs; in the 2026–2030 period: at least 70% of the older people with the need and ability to work will have jobs. To achieve this goal, the Ministry of Labor, War Invalids and Social Affairs is developing a draft Law on Employment (amended) to submit to the Government and the Congress for consideration. Therefore, Vietnam currently does not have specific policies to create employment opportunities for older people; current policies mainly provide preferential loan policies for them. Learning from previous lessons from other Asian countries, Vietnam can improve the law on creating employment opportunities for older people.

First of all, policies for creating jobs for the elderly need to be legalized as a separate law, such as the "Japan's Employment Stability Act for the Elderly" or the "Singapore Retirement and Reemployment Act".

Secondly, the government should encourage employers to retain or rehire older workers, specifically those who are in good health, willing to work, and have high work experience and skills to return to work after retirement. These older workers can easily receive continuing vocational training, helping to improve their technical and scientific qualifications and increase their adaptability.

Thirdly, Vietnam needs to have a reasonable allocation mechanism and create job opportunities for the older people. "The Korean Senior Employment Program (KSEP)" is a model for Vietnam to flexibly apply. Under this program, the older people are provided with job opportunities in two main groups: social contribution jobs and market entry jobs.

Fourthly, job introduction centers (job banks) for only older people need to be widely established to introduce jobs suitable to their expertise, as well as jobs related to their activities in the local community where they live. Elderly community clubs should also be established to encourage older people to start small businesses in the community.

Fifthly, the government needs to have policies to create conditions for older people to continue their education. Learning from Singapore, Vietnam can establish a "Silver Academy" and sponsor community organizations to provide learning spaces for the older people.

Finally, there should be a law prohibiting age discrimination in the workplace to create good psychological conditions for older workers.

These policies require coordinated implementation across government departments and society to create a unified framework supporting the workforce participation of older people. Successful implementation could help Vietnam overcome the middle-income trap while ensuring older people citizens can continue contributing meaningfully to society.

Acknowledgements This chapter was funded by the University of Economics Ho Chi Minh City (UEH), Vietnam. Data collection was conducted by Ha Thanh Huu Dang of the Vietnam-Netherlands Programme at UEH.

References

Anxo, D., Ericson, T., & Herbert, A. (2019). Beyond retirement: Who stays at work after the standard age of retirement? *International Journal of Manpower*, *40*(5), 917–938.

Becker, G. S. (1992). A treatise on the family. *Population and Development Review*, *18*(3), 563.

Ben-Bassat, A., Gronau, R., & Zussman, A. (2021). *The Israeli economy, 1995–2017: Light and shadow in a market economy*. Cambridge University Press.

Blackham, A. (2024). Age discrimination and mandatory retirement. In G. Davidov, B. Langille, & G. Lester (Eds.), *The Oxford Handbook of the Law of Work* (p. 605–620). Oxford University Press. https://doi.org/10.1093/oxfordhb/9780192870360.013.46

Brooke, L., & Taylor, P. (2005). Older workers and employment: Managing age relations. *Ageing and Society*, *25*(3), 415–429. https://doi.org/10.1017/S0144686X05003466

Bui, T. H. L., Quang, T., Pham, N. T., Nguyen, T. T., Nguyen, H. N., & Le, T. L. (2022). *Study on promoting employment for the elderly in the context of an aging population in Vietnam*. World Bank.

Bulman, D., Eden, M., & Nguyen, H. (2017). Transitioning from low-income growth to high-income growth: Is there a middle-income trap? *Journal of the Asia Pacific Economy*, *22*(1), 5–28.

Châu, V. D. (2025). Công tác chăm sóc, phát huy vai trò người cao tuổi - Những kiến nghị và giải pháp [Elderly care and role promotion - Recommendations and solutions]. *Tạp chí mặt trận*. https://vnpa.moh.gov.vn/tin-tong-hop/cong-tac-cham-soc-phat-huy-vai-tro-nguoi-cao-tuoi-nhung-kien-nghi-va-giai-phap

Duong, N. T. (2022, October 1). Tuổi thọ người Việt cao nhưng không khỏe mạnh [Vietnamese lifespan is high but not healthy]. *VnEconomy*. https://vneconomy.vn/tuoi-tho-nguoi-viet-cao-nhung-khong-khoe-manh.htm

General Statistics Office. (2021). *Population ageing and older persons in Viet Nam*.

Gonzales, E., & Nowell, W. B. (2017). Social capital and unretirement: Exploring the bonding, bridging, and linking aspects of social relationships. *Research on Aging*, *39*(10), 1100–1117.

Ha, J., & Lee, S.-H. (2016). Demographic dividend and Asia's economic convergence towards the US. *The Journal of the Economics of Ageing*, *8*, 28–41.

Ha, N. (2025, January 23). Khoảng 275.000 người cao tuổi đang tiếp tục tham gia BHXH [About 275,000 elderly people continue to participate in social insurance]. *Tạp chí Bảo hiểm xã hội*. https://tapchibaohiemxahoi.gov.vn/khoang-275000-nguoi-cao-tuoi-dang-tiep-tuc-tham-gia-bhxh-133563.html

Otsuki, K., & Ando, S. (2020). Amendment of the Act on Stabilization of Employment of Elderly Persons. *Labour and Employment Law Bulletin*, *52*, 1–10.

Pilipiec, P., Groot, W., & Pavlova, M. (2021). The effect of an increase of the retirement age on the health, well-being, and labor force participation of older workers: A systematic literature review. *Journal of Population Ageing*, *14*(2), 271–315. https://doi.org/10.1007/s12062-020-09280-9

Sewdas, R., de Wind, A., van der Zwaan, L. G. L., van der Borg, W. E., Steenbeek, R., van der Beek, A. J., & Boot, C. R. L. (2017). Why older workers work beyond the retirement age: A qualitative study. *BMC Public Health.*, *17*(1), 672. https://doi.org/10.1186/s12889-017-4675-z

Sharabi, M., Shdema, I., & Abboud-Armaly, O. (2020). Nonfinancial employment commitment among Muslims and Jews in Israel: Examination of the core–periphery model on majority and minority groups. *Employee Relations: The International Journal*, *43*(1), 227–243.

Singapore Government. (2006). *SILVERJOBS*. https://silverjobs.sg/

Singapore Ministry of Health. (2023). *Action plan for successful ageing*. https://www.moh.gov.sg/others/resources-and-statistics/action-plan-for-successful-ageing

Singapore Statutes Online. (2022). *Retirement and re-employment act 1993*. https://sso.agc.gov.sg/Act/RRA1993

Suberry, A., & Bodner, E. (2024). Psychological well-being and self-aging attitudes moderate the association between subjective age and age discrimination in the workplace. *Behavioral Sciences*, *14*(9), 751.

The General Office of the State Council. (2024). *Opinions on developing a silver economy to improve the well-being of the elderly*. https://www.gov.cn/zhengce/content/202401/content_6926087.htm

Tur-Sinai, A., Shahrabani, S., Lowenstein, A., Katz, R., Halperin, D., & Fogel-Grinvald, H. (2022). What drives older adults to continue working after official retirement age? *Ageing and Society*, *44*(2), 283–309. https://doi.org/10.1017/S0144686X22000915

Tuyet, D. H., & Thai, V. (2022). Định kiến xã hội về người cao tuổi trong bối cảnh già hóa dân số ở Việt Nam [Social prejudice about the elderly in the context of population aging in Vietnam]. *Khoa h?c Xã h?i Vi?t Nam*, *2*(182), 19–28. https://doi.org/10.56794/KHXHVN.2(182).19-28

Vietnam Government. (2020). *Phê duyệt Chương trình Chăm sóc sức khỏe người cao tuổi đến năm 2030* [Approval of the Elderly Health Care Program until 2030]. https://vanban.chinhphu.vn/default.aspx?pageid=27160&docid=201275

Vietnam Government. (2021). *Chương trình hành động quốc gia về người cao tuổi giai đoạn 2021-2030*. National action program on elderly people for the period 2021-2030.

Vietnam Social Security. (2017). *Pension regime*. https://baohiemxahoi.gov.vn/gioithieu/pages/gioi-thieu-chung.aspx?CateID=0&ItemID=8421

Vietnam Social Security. (2024). *The joy of pensioners at the new scheme*. https://baohiemxahoi.gov.vn/tintuc/Pages/linh-vuc-bao-hiem-xa-hoi.aspx?ItemID=23240&CateID=168

Wattanasaovaluk, K. (2021). The economic significance of work experience for elderly employment in Thailand. *Journal of Population and Social Studies*, *29*, 82–99.

World Bank. (n.d.). *World Bank open data*. https://data.worldbank.org/indicator/SP.DYN.TFRT.IN

Woźniak, B., Brzyska, M., Piłat, A., & Tobiasz-Adamczyk, B. (2022). Factors affecting work ability and influencing early retirement decisions of older employees: An attempt to integrate the existing approaches. *International Journal of Occupational Medicine & Environmental Health*, *35*(5), 509–526. https://doi.org/10.13075/ijomeh.1896.01354

Yoon, S. M. (2016). Income security for older persons in the Republic of Korea. *ESCAP Working Paper Series*, 1–56.

Zaccagni, S., Sigsgaard, A. M., Vrangbaek, K., & Noermark, L. P. (2024). Who continues to work after retirement age? *BMC Public Health.*, *24*(1), 692. https://doi.org/10.1186/s12889-024-18161-1

Zitikytė, K. (2019). To work or not to work: Factors affecting bridge employment beyond retirement, case of Lithuania. *Ekonomika*, *98*(2), 33–54.

CHAPTER 14

Human Capital 5: Female Labor Force Participation

Introduction

A review of previous studies on female labor force participation is essential for understanding the diverse factors that influence women's employment patterns across different socio-economic contexts. By analyzing existing literature, one can identify common challenges, such as the effects of social norms, economic transitions, and education levels on women's labor market participation, while also recognizing country-specific variations. Additionally, reviewing prior research enables the evaluation of the effectiveness of existing policies and interventions, helping to uncover gaps in the current knowledge and approaches. This process provides a critical foundation for the development of more targeted, evidence-based policies and strategies that address the unique barriers women face in the labor market, ultimately contributing to sustainable economic development and gender equality.

The Asian Experience

A study by Parida and Bhagavatula (2022) in India suggests that women's participation in the labor market is influenced by both macroeconomic and microeconomic factors. From a macroeconomic perspective, there is

Contributed by Hoai Trong Nguyen

H. T. Dinh, H. T. Nguyen, *Vietnam's Economic Leap*,
https://doi.org/10.1007/978-3-032-08904-5_14

a U-shaped relationship between the female labor force participation rate (FLFPR) and economic growth. Participation tends to decrease as countries transition from low-income to middle-income stages but increases as they become more developed, mainly due to improved education and employment opportunities in the service sector. Microeconomic theories focus on individual and household factors, such as intra-household bargaining and occupational choices. The study uses a theoretical model that maximizes family welfare and employs probit and instrumental variable probit models to analyze survey data from Indian cities. The findings reveal that economic growth alone does not explain India's low FLFPR, pointing to the importance of household income, education, and socioeconomic characteristics. The study calls for targeted policies addressing both demand-side factors (job opportunities) and supply-side factors (education and social norms) to improve women's labor market participation.

Similarly, Kapsos et al. (2014) analyze the participation of women in India's labor market and find that both macroeconomic and microeconomic factors play a role. Their study focuses on the participation of young women in urban areas, particularly those acting as "supplementary family labor" or those discouraged by reservation wages higher than current market wages. Using econometric analysis, the study concludes that even highly educated women face stagnant participation rates because of social norms and limited job opportunities that match their skills. The authors identify key subsectors in manufacturing (textiles, footwear, food, and beverage processing, electronics) and services (information technology, healthcare, education, and financial services) that could help boost female labor force participation. They stress the need for policies that invest in women's education and vocational training, along with initiatives to create a gender-equal work environment and raise social awareness about the role of women in the workforce.

In India, Gupta (2023) focuses on the determinants of female labor force participation (FLFP) using both macroeconomic and microeconomic frameworks. Their study finds that higher household income reduces FLFP due to the income effect, while higher wages encourage participation. Key personal factors, such as education level and marital status, also influence participation. Like previous studies, Gupta (2023) identifies potential sectors for job creation that could improve female employment in urban India.

The COVID-19 pandemic has exacerbated pre-existing challenges for women's employment in India. As Mitra (2021) notes, the government's economic stimulus package primarily supported micro, small, and medium enterprises (MSMEs) without specific provisions for women-owned businesses. The increasing burden of unpaid domestic work and limited market access has made it difficult for women to sustain their businesses during the recession. Mitra calls for targeted financial support and credit access programs for women entrepreneurs.

In Vietnam, post-COVID-19 economic stimulus packages included various support measures to help businesses overcome challenges, such as tax, fee, and charge exemptions and reductions, interest rate subsidies, and extensions on tax and land lease payments. The State Bank of Vietnam implemented credit support programs through preferential loans to help businesses access capital. However, these programs did not specifically address credit access for female-owned small and medium enterprises (SMEs) (UNDP, 2021). Other support measures included direct payments to workers who lost their jobs, assistance for businesses to pay wages and retain employees, and social insurance support policies (World Bank, 2021; UNDP, 2021).

The lack of targeted support for women-owned businesses in the economic stimulus packages presents a critical lesson for Vietnam. To promote women's participation in the labor force and ensure sustainable economic development, it is essential to design financial and credit support policies aimed at women-owned enterprises. This could include special preferential credit programs, enhanced training, and raising awareness about financial and business management for female entrepreneurs. Additionally, fostering collaboration between government agencies and financial institutions to create comprehensive support programs is crucial.

Cameron (2019) found that Indonesia's female labor force participation rate remained stable from 1996 to 2013, despite significant economic changes. The study suggests that women's participation increased, particularly in urban areas, due to shifting social attitudes. However, to achieve the G20 target of 58.5% FLFP by 2025, policies supporting women returning to work after childbirth and providing childcare services will be necessary.

Klasen et al. (2021) examined married women's labor force participation in urban areas across eight low—and middle-income countries, including Vietnam. Overall, the economic, social, and institutional constraints shaping women's labor force participation remain largely country-specific. They found that while education levels and declining fertility rates generally raise participation, rising household income has a negative effect, especially in poorer countries where many women work out of economic necessity.

The COVID-19 pandemic has disproportionately impacted women's employment globally. In India, the labor force shrank by 11.5 million people between December 2019 and December 2020, with 7.5 million of these being women. As Nikore (2021) highlights, stricter mobility restrictions and a rise in unpaid domestic responsibilities have pushed many women out of the workforce. Women, especially those with children under six or from lower-income groups, were more likely to leave the labor market, as childcare disruptions exacerbated pre-existing inequalities (Lim et al., 2023).

The current pandemic-induced recession has affected industries with predominantly female workforces, such as hospitality and retail, more than it has affected male-dominated industries. The situation has worsened due to the closure of schools and childcare centers, forcing many working mothers to exit the labor force to manage household responsibilities (İnce-Yenilmez, 2020). To address these issues, policymakers must implement solutions aimed at redistributing household work and providing affordable childcare services.

The Female Labor Market in Vietnam

An analysis of female labor market trends in Vietnam from 2000 to 2022 shows significant fluctuations. Between 2000 and 2019, the number of women in the labor force grew steadily, from 19 million to more than 26 million (GSO, 2024). This increase reflects improved employment opportunities and evolving gender equality policies. However, the COVID-19 pandemic caused a significant setback, with the number of female workers dropping to 23.5 million by 2021. Preliminary data for 2022 suggests a modest recovery as economic activities resumed. This trend highlights the crucial role of women in Vietnam's labor market and the need for supportive policies and improved working conditions to sustain their contributions to economic development.

Figure 14.1 illustrates the steady growth in the number of female workers in Vietnam from 2000 to 2019, followed by a sharp decline in 2020–2021 due to the pandemic. The recovery in 2022 indicates that Vietnamese women remain key contributors to the labor market, despite the challenges they face.

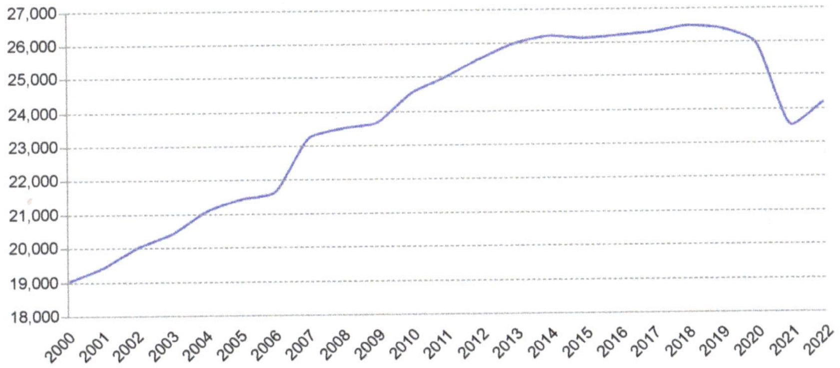

Fig. 14.1 Female Labor Force in Vietnam, 2000–2022. *Source* GSO (2024)

Vietnam has a relatively high female labor force participation rate compared to many countries, supported by cultural norms where both men and women are expected to contribute to household income. Government efforts, including legal protections against gender discrimination and initiatives promoting women's representation in leadership, have also been pivotal.

To sustain and enhance women's labor force participation, targeted policies are essential. Investments in education and vocational training, tax incentives, and financial support for businesses in service sectors like information technology, finance, healthcare, and tourism should be prioritized. Additionally, family-friendly policies such as extended maternity leave, childcare support, and flexible work arrangements are critical. Social awareness campaigns and gender equality awards for businesses will further promote women's participation in the workforce. Inclusive economic growth policies and infrastructure investments will support the broader participation of women in Vietnam's labor market, contributing to sustainable development.

In conclusion, enhancing women's participation in the labor force requires measures such as pay equity, maternity and parental leave policies, and a supportive work environment offering flexible working hours and childcare support. These initiatives will not only tap into a vast pool of talent but also promote economic equality.

Lessons Drawn From Asian Countries

Building on lessons from other nations, Vietnam has introduced several comprehensive policies to foster greater female participation in the labor market. These include the National Strategy on Gender Equality 2021–2030, financial support schemes, training programs, labor law reforms, and initiatives aimed at enhancing skills and promoting entrepreneurship. These policies provide preferential loans, technical assistance, and entrepreneurial training, while also improving digital infrastructure to create better working conditions for women. In response to the COVID-19 pandemic, the government also implemented targeted financial support for pregnant women, new mothers, and female healthcare workers. This approach underscores Vietnam's commitment to reducing gender disparities and fully integrating women into the workforce, thereby contributing to sustainable economic growth.

Research across Asia, particularly in India and Vietnam, indicates that female labor force participation (FLFP) is shaped by a combination of macroeconomic and microeconomic factors. Parida and Bhagavatula (2022) identify a U-shaped relationship between FLFP and economic growth, where participation tends to decline as nations move from low—to middle-income status but rises again as economies further develop due to improved education and employment opportunities, especially in the service sector. Social norms, educational attainment, and household income significantly influence FLFP, with limited job prospects and high reservation wages discouraging women's labor market engagement (Kapsos et al., 2014). The COVID-19 pandemic has further exacerbated these challenges, particularly for women entrepreneurs, as highlighted by Mitra (2021). In Vietnam, post-pandemic recovery measures have largely overlooked the specific needs of female-owned businesses, underscoring the necessity of financial policies that specifically target women entrepreneurs. These studies collectively emphasize the need for comprehensive, targeted interventions, such as affordable childcare, financial assistance, and job creation in high-growth sectors, to improve FLFP and promote inclusive economic growth.

Based on studies from other countries, Vietnam can learn several key lessons to increase women's participation in the labor force:

- Develop service and manufacturing sectors and encourage women to engage in entrepreneurship while providing targeted financial support for women-owned businesses (Parida & Bhagavatula, 2022; Mitra, 2021).

- Tailor education and skills training to meet the labor market's demands, enabling women to access better employment opportunities (Albarico & Galigao, 2024).
- Expand childcare services and implement flexible working policies to help women balance work and family responsibilities (Cameron, 2019; Lim et al., 2023).
- Promote gender equality education and raise awareness, encouraging women to take leadership roles in both the public and private sectors (Klasen et al., 2021).
- Address the impacts of the COVID-19 pandemic by providing financial support, easier credit access for women-owned businesses, and digital skills training to bridge the gender digital divide (Nikore, 2021; İnce-Yenilmez, 2020).

These lessons can guide Vietnam in developing effective policies to increase women's labor force participation, contributing to sustainable and equitable economic growth as well as to be able to avoid partly middle-income trap.

Policy Implications

A comprehensive policy approach to encourage FLFP is a vital component of economic growth, social progress and contributes to overcoming middle income trap, yet women in many countries, including Vietnam, continue to face considerable barriers to full and equitable participation in the labor market. Issues such as insufficient labor protections, persistent gender pay gaps, and a lack of supportive measures for balancing work and family responsibilities disproportionately affect women, particularly those in low-income or informal sectors. Additionally, rising costs in healthcare, education, and childcare often compel women to withdraw from the workforce or delay important life decisions, such as marriage and childbearing. The COVID-19 pandemic has further exacerbated these challenges by widening the digital divide and limiting access to education and job opportunities, particularly for women in rural areas. These barriers not only restrict women's economic potential but also perpetuate broader gender inequalities.

Addressing these challenges is not only a moral imperative but also a strategic necessity for sustainable economic development. Enhancing working conditions, providing financial support, and expanding access to education and skills training are crucial to empowering women to participate fully in the labor market. Implementing policies that promote flexible working arrangements, affordable childcare services, and targeted entrepreneurship support will create a more inclusive and equitable labor environment. These initiatives will not only reduce poverty and narrow the gender gap but also contribute to Vietnam's long-term economic stability. Empowering women in the workforce is essential to unlocking the country's full economic potential and achieving its sustainable development objectives.

Improving Working Conditions and Strengthening the Protection of Female Workers

Improving working conditions and protecting female workers is essential to ensuring their rights in the labor market. This includes enforcing labor laws that guarantee benefits like minimum wage, social insurance, and maternity leave, particularly in the informal sector. Supporting women in transitioning from the informal to the formal sector through training programs and financial assistance is also crucial, enabling them to access more sustainable, higher-income jobs (UNFPA, 2021).

Financial Support and Reducing the Cost of Services

Female workers in Vietnam, particularly in low-income sectors, face numerous challenges as rising healthcare and education costs in major cities limit their opportunities to enhance their skills. This financial pressure often forces women to exit the labor market or delay marriage and childbearing. To alleviate these burdens, subsidies or affordable childcare services should be provided, helping women balance work and parenting. Additionally, reducing educational costs through scholarship programs, tuition reductions, and educational support services for the children of female workers is crucial (UNFPA, 2021; UN Women, 2020).

Skill Development and Career Opportunities

The COVID-19 pandemic has highlighted the digital divide between men and women, particularly in rural areas where many women lack access to digital devices and internet services. This hinders their ability to learn and work online. Expanding investment in digital infrastructure, digital skills training, and vocational programs for women, especially in high-income fields such as information technology, finance, and services, is essential. Offering preferential loans and mentorship programs will encourage women to start businesses and develop entrepreneurial skills, opening new job opportunities and helping them move beyond low-income employment (UN Women, 2020; UNFPA, 2021).

Family Support Policies and Promoting Work-Life Balance

Family support policies, such as extending paid maternity leave and providing high-quality childcare near workplaces, will help women balance their work and family responsibilities. Encouraging businesses to adopt flexible working arrangements, including remote work and flexible hours, will create more favorable conditions for women to maintain employment while managing family obligations (UNFPA, 2021).

Raising Awareness and Shifting Societal Mindsets

Media campaigns that change societal perceptions and raise awareness about the critical role of women in the workforce are essential. These campaigns should encourage women to take on leadership roles in business and social organizations, promoting gender equality and creating a fairer, safer work environment (UN Women, 2020).

The implementation of these policies will enhance women's skills and career opportunities while reducing their financial burdens, contributing to the country's sustainable economic development. Promoting women's participation in the workforce and ensuring they can work in safe, equitable environments is crucial for achieving sustainable development goals and gender equality in Vietnam (UNFPA, 2021; UN Women, 2020).

Overcoming the Middle-Income Trap in Vietnam

To escape the middle-income trap, it is essential to promote equal access to education and skills training for women. Encouraging STEM (Science, Technology, Engineering, and Mathematics) education through scholarships and targeted programs will increase the number of women in high-paying sectors like technology and engineering. Vocational training should focus on industries with high growth potential, such as manufacturing and finance, where women are underrepresented. Lifelong learning opportunities will help women continuously upgrade their skills to meet the demands of a modern economy, particularly in emerging fields like digital technologies and healthcare.

Creating supportive work environments is crucial. Implementing flexible workplace policies, such as remote work and flexible hours, can help women balance family responsibilities while advancing their careers. Strengthening maternity and paternity leave policies will allow women to re-enter the workforce without losing momentum. Safe, inclusive workplaces free from harassment will empower women to succeed, and businesses should establish women's support networks and mentorship programs.

Increasing female representation in leadership and high-value sectors is another key strategy. Leadership development programs and mentorship opportunities should be created to help women advance into management roles, improving diversity in decision-making. Financial and tax incentives should be provided for women to enter high-growth sectors like IT, renewable energy, and finance. Supporting female entrepreneurs in these sectors can drive innovation and close the gender gap.

Encouraging women's entrepreneurship is essential for economic growth. Equal access to finance for female entrepreneurs, including dedicated loan programs and microfinance options, especially for rural women, should be ensured. Women-focused business incubators offering mentorship, technical support, and networking opportunities will help grow their businesses. Providing training on export strategies and digital marketing will also enable women to expand their enterprises.

Improving access to affordable childcare and elder care will increase female labor participation. Partnerships to provide subsidized, high-quality childcare services will allow more women to work full-time, particularly in urban areas. As Vietnam's population ages, elder care facilities and caregiving support programs will reduce the burden on women, enabling them to remain active in the workforce.

Reducing the gender pay gap is critical. Strengthening equal pay legislation and enforcing it will ensure that women are paid the same as men for similar work. Pay equity audits in businesses will help identify and reduce gender-based wage disparities, improving women's overall economic contribution and financial security.

Expanding social protection for women, especially those in informal employment, is also necessary. Universal health coverage should be extended to all women, including those in the informal sector, ensuring access to reproductive and maternal healthcare. Pension schemes for women in agriculture and domestic work will provide retirement security, reducing poverty and inequality in later life.

Encouraging women's participation in rural development is crucial. Women in agriculture should have access to technology, training, and financial resources to increase productivity and move beyond subsistence farming. Forming women-led cooperatives will strengthen their bargaining power and improve market access.

Leveraging digital transformation for women's economic empowerment is essential for future growth. Digital literacy programs targeted at women will help them benefit from online work and e-commerce platforms. Expanding mobile banking and financial inclusion services will ensure rural women can participate in the digital economy.

Finally, tax and policy incentives for gender equality should be implemented. Businesses that promote gender diversity in leadership positions and adopt inclusive policies should receive tax incentives. Female-owned enterprises, especially in underrepresented sectors, should benefit from tax breaks and policy support. These measures will enhance women's economic participation and ensure a more equitable, prosperous future for Vietnam.

Enhancing working conditions and strengthening the protection of female workers are essential to improving their participation in the labor market and advancing gender equality. This requires the enforcement of labor laws that provide fundamental benefits such as minimum wage, social insurance, and maternity leave, particularly for those employed in the informal sector. Additionally, facilitating the transition of women from informal to formal employment through targeted training programs and financial support is crucial for enabling access to more sustainable and higher-paying job opportunities. Addressing the financial constraints that limit women's labor market engagement such as rising healthcare, education, and childcare costs through subsidies and affordable services is also critical. Furthermore, expanding digital infrastructure, skills development, and vocational training in high-growth sectors such as information technology, finance, and services can foster career advancement and entrepreneurship among women, contributing to broader economic development.

Conclusion

Promoting women's labor force participation necessitates a comprehensive approach to contribute to improve quantity and quality of labor force in order to get higher productivity as well as income per head for overcoming middle income trap by incorporating improved working conditions, financial support, and policies that reduce structural barriers. Key interventions such as flexible working arrangements, access to affordable childcare, and skill development opportunities will facilitate greater female inclusion in the workforce. Moreover, policies aimed at promoting gender equality in leadership roles, closing the gender pay gap, and extending social protections, particularly in rural areas, are vital for achieving sustainable economic growth and fostering gender parity in Vietnam's labor market.

Acknowledgements This chapter was funded by the University of Economics Ho Chi Minh City (UEH), Vietnam. Data collection was conducted by Nhan Thi Thanh Nguyen of the Vietnam–Netherlands Programme at the University of Economics Ho Chi Minh City (UEH).

Annex 1: Declining Fertility Rates and Current Policies in Ho Chi Minh City

Declining Fertility Rates

The crude birth rate in Ho Chi Minh City between 2015 and 2023 exhibited significant fluctuations. During the period from 2015 to 2019, the birth rate demonstrated a steady increase, rising from 12.6% in 2015 to a peak of 14.5% in 2020 (HSO, 2023). This upward trend may reflect favorable socio-economic conditions or the positive impact of pro-natalist policies implemented during this period. However, beginning in 2021, the birth rate experienced a marked decline, reaching 12.1% in 2023, a figure closely resembling the low levels recorded in 2015 (HSO, 2023). This decline can be attributed to several factors, including escalating living costs, modern societal norms that encourage young individuals to prioritize career development and delay childbearing, and the absence of effective family support policies.

The implications of this downward trend are profound. A shrinking future labor force and an increasingly aging population are expected to place substantial pressure on the social welfare system. To mitigate these challenges, it is imperative for Ho Chi Minh City to implement robust measures aimed at incentivizing childbirth. These measures should include financial assistance for families, the development of family-friendly infrastructure, and comprehensive public awareness campaigns to emphasize the importance of sustaining long-term population growth. Such interventions are critical to addressing the demographic challenges faced by the city and ensuring its socio-economic stability (Table 14.1).

To address declining fertility rates, Ho Chi Minh City has implemented a range of pro natalist measures designed to foster a more family-friendly environment. These policies tackle financial constraints, societal attitudes, workplace dynamics, and infrastructure challenges.

Financial incentives are a key element of the city's strategy. Women who have two children before the age of 35 are eligible for subsidies of at least VND 3 million (HSO, 2023). Additionally, low-income families are provided with comprehensive healthcare packages covering childbirth expenses, as well as prenatal and postnatal care. These measures aim to alleviate economic pressures on vulnerable households, making parenthood more accessible.

Public awareness campaigns seek to shift societal perceptions regarding family size and parenting. These initiatives emphasize the importance of sustainable population growth and aim to debunk the belief that raising children is prohibitively expensive. By promoting the benefits of having two children as part of a balanced family structure, these campaigns encourage a positive cultural shift toward parenthood.

Table 14.1 Causes and impacts

Causes	Impacts
High living costs	Families opt for fewer children due to economic burdens.
Changing lifestyles	Young people delay or limit childbirth.
Lack of supportive policies	Ineffective incentives for families to have children.

(*Source* GSO, 2022)

Table 14.2 Pro-Natalist policies

Pro-Natalist Measures	Intended Outcomes
Financial support	Increased fertility rates in the short term
Public awareness and education	Changes in social perceptions
Infrastructure development	Long-term sustainability

(*Source* authors)

Support for businesses focuses on incentivizing companies to adopt family-friendly policies. Measures such as flexible maternity leave, on-site childcare facilities, and tax breaks for businesses that support working mothers are designed to create a workplace culture that accommodates family responsibilities. These policies help parents balance professional aspirations with caregiving duties.

Infrastructure development forms another crucial component of the city's approach. Investments in free or subsidized healthcare and education for children under six years old are complemented by the development of recreational areas and daycare facilities. By addressing logistical challenges associated with raising children, these initiatives provide parents with greater confidence in their ability to create a nurturing environment for their families (Table 14.2).

Policy Recommendations for 2024–2025

To address the declining birth rate in Ho Chi Minh City, a range of targeted policies are proposed to create a family-friendly environment that encourages higher fertility rates.

Financial Incentives for Families

Providing financial support for families is a cornerstone of encouraging higher birth rates, as financial burdens are a primary concern for prospective parents. Direct subsidies, such as childbirth allowances, can offset costs associated with prenatal care, hospital deliveries, and postpartum recovery, making parenthood more financially accessible. Monthly childcare subsidies are instrumental in reducing the recurring costs of daycare, early education, and essential childcare supplies, which are particularly challenging for young families managing tight budgets. Tax benefits, including deductions for dependent children or credits for education expenses, provide a long-term mechanism to ease financial strain as children grow.

Additionally, addressing the significant cost of housing is essential. Affordable housing schemes can provide families with access to subsidized rents or government-supported housing developments that prioritize family needs, such as larger living spaces and proximity to schools and childcare facilities. Preferential loan programs for families with two or more children offer low-interest rates or relaxed repayment terms, making homeownership a realistic goal. By alleviating economic pressures through these incentives, families are more likely to consider having additional children, contributing to a sustainable population growth rate and strengthening social and economic stability.

Childcare and Education Support

Accessible and affordable childcare services are essential for reducing the financial and logistical challenges faced by families. Establishing subsidized daycare centers ensures that parents, especially working mothers, have reliable and cost-effective options for childcare. These centers should be strategically located near residential areas and workplaces to maximize convenience. Furthermore, enhancing the quality of early childhood education through standardized curriculums, well-trained staff, and modern facilities can contribute to better developmental outcomes for children, giving parents peace of mind.

To alleviate long-term educational costs, financial assistance programs such as grants, scholarships, or reduced tuition fees can significantly support parents. These measures are particularly beneficial for families with multiple children, helping to manage expenses associated with school supplies, extracurricular activities, and higher education. By combining accessible childcare services with financial support for education, these initiatives not only encourage family expansion but also contribute to the development of a well-educated, future-ready population.

Work-Life Balance Initiatives

Enhancing work-life balance is pivotal in supporting working parents and addressing barriers to parenthood. Paid maternity and paternity leave policies play a critical role by allowing parents time to bond with their newborns and recover from childbirth without the added stress of financial insecurity. Extending these leave periods ensures that parents can focus on their family's needs during critical early stages, fostering healthier outcomes for both parents and children.

Flexible work arrangements further enable parents to effectively manage their dual responsibilities of career and childcare. Options such as remote work, flexible working hours, and part-time opportunities allow parents to balance professional obligations with family life. Employers can also implement family-friendly policies, such as on-site childcare facilities or support for parental transition back into the workplace after leave. These initiatives not only reduce stress for working parents but also boost employee satisfaction and retention, benefiting both families and employers. By promoting a culture of flexibility and understanding, such policies make it easier for parents to thrive both at home and in their careers, encouraging higher birth rates and supporting overall family well-being.

Support for Young Families

Supporting young families is crucial for fostering a positive environment for marriage and parenthood. Reducing the financial burdens associated with weddings, housing, and childbirth can encourage couples to start families earlier. Subsidizing wedding expenses, offering affordable housing options, and providing financial aid for childbirth-related costs can make these significant life events more accessible and less stressful for young couples.

In addition, implementing youth-oriented programs can raise awareness about family planning options and promote informed decisions about balancing careers and family life. These programs can include workshops, counseling services, and campaigns that emphasize the importance of early planning and the benefits of parenthood. By addressing financial and informational barriers, these measures can create a supportive foundation for young families to thrive.

Public Awareness Campaigns

Public awareness campaigns play a crucial role in shifting societal attitudes and encouraging parenthood. Mass media campaigns should focus on celebrating family values and highlighting the joys and rewards of raising children. These campaigns can include testimonials from parents, success stories of family-friendly initiatives, and cultural messages that reinforce the importance of family life. Featuring relatable role models and influencers in these campaigns can further resonate with target audiences and inspire positive perceptions of parenthood.

Additionally, these efforts should clearly highlight government programs and resources designed to support families. Providing accessible information about financial incentives, childcare services, education grants, and work-life balance initiatives can reduce uncertainties about the costs and commitments associated with parenting. Digital platforms, community events, and public service announcements can serve as effective channels to disseminate this information widely. By fostering a supportive and informed environment, public awareness campaigns can help alleviate concerns, build confidence among prospective parents, and contribute to reversing the declining birth rate.

References

Albarico, G., & Galigao, R. P. (2024). Exploring education and labor market outcomes: Insights from diverse global contexts. *Pantao International Journal of Humanities and Social Sciences, 3*(4), 419–436. https://doi.org/10.69651/PIJHSS030419

Cameron, L., Suarez, D. C., & Rowell, W. (2019). Female labour force participation in Indonesia: Why has it stalled? *Bulletin of Indonesian Economic Studies, 55*(2), 157–192. https://doi.org/10.1080/00074918.2018.1530727

General Statistics Office of Vietnam (GSO). (2022). *Demographic trends and economic implications in Vietnam*. https://www.gso.gov.vn

General Statistics Office of Vietnam (GSO). (2024). *Statistical report on population and migration*. https://www.gso.gov.vn

Gupta, V. (2023). Determinants of female labour force participation in India: Evidence from supply side. *The Indian Journal of Labour Economics, 66*(1), 203–223. https://doi.org/10.1007/s41027-023-00431-y

Ho Chi Minh City Statistical Office (HSO) (2023). *Statistical yearbook 2023*. Ho Chi Minh City Department of Statistics.

İnce-Yenilmez, M., & Sevinç, H. (2020). The COVID-19 pandemic on women's employment: Impacts and consequences. *Iğdir University Journal of Social Sciences, 24*, 357–372.

Kapsos, S., Silberman, A., & Bourmpoula, E. (2014). *Why is female labour force participation declining so sharply in India?* International Labour Organization. https://www.ilo.org/sites/default/files/wcmsp5/groups/public/@dgreports/@inst/documents/publication/wcms_250977.pdf

Klasen, S., Le, T. T. N., Pieters, J., & Santos Silva, M. (2021). What drives female labour force participation? Comparable micro-level evidence from eight developing and emerging economies. *The Journal of Development Studies, 57*(3), 417–442. https://doi.org/10.1080/00220388.2020.1790533

Lim, K., & Zabek, M. (2023). Women's labor force exits during COVID-19: Differences by motherhood, race, and ethnicity. (Finance and Economics Discussion Series 2021-067r1). Board of Governors of the Federal Reserve System. https://doi.org/10.17016/FEDS.2021.067r1

Mitra, S., & Sinha, D. (2021). COVID-19 and women's labour crisis. *Economic and Political Weekly*, *56*(17), 49–51.

Nikore, M., Gupta, M., Prabhu, P., & Narang, V. (2021). India's missing working women: How Covid-19 pushed women out of formal labour markets. *International Journal of Social Science and Economic Research*, *6*(4), 1335–1355. https://doi.org/10.46609/IJSSER.2021.v06i04.015

Parida, J. K., & Bhagavatula, N. (2022). The labour market dilemma of young urban women in India: An outcome of family welfare optimization [Preprint]. Research Square. https://doi.org/10.21203/rs.3.rs-2107157/v1

UN Women. (2020). The impact of COVID-19 on women's and men's lives and livelihoods: Preliminary results from a rapid gender assessment. United Nations Entity for Gender Equality and the Empowerment of Women (UN Women). https://eca.unwomen.org/en/digital-library/publications/2020/07/the-impact-of-covid19-on-womens-andmens-lives-and-livelihoods

United Nations Population Fund Vietnam (UNFPA). (2021). Leave no one behind: Innovative interventions to reduce maternal mortality in ethnic minority regions of Vietnam. https://vietnam.unfpa.org/en/news/leave-no-one behind-innovative-interventions-reduce-maternal-mortality-ethnic-minority-region-0

World Bank. (2021). The labor market and the COVID-19 outbreak in Vietnam: Impacts and lessons learned for social protection. Washington, DC: World Bank. https://documents.worldbank.org/en/publication/documentsreports/documentdetail/858691625204880380

Index

H. T. Dinh, H. T. Nguyen, *Vietnam's Economic Leap*,
https://doi.org/10.1007/978-3-032-08904-5